McCARTHY TÉTRAULT

McCARTHY

BUILDING CANADA'S

CHRISTOPHER MOORE

TÉTRAULT

PREMIER LAW FIRM

1855–2005

DOUGLAS & McINTYRE
VANCOUVER/TORONTO

05 06 07 08 09 5 4 3 2 1

Douglas & McIntyre Ltd.
2323 Quebec Street, Suite 201
Vancouver, British Columbia
V5T 4S7
www.douglas-mcintyre.com

Library and Archives Canada Cataloguing in Publication

Moore, Christopher, 1950–
McCarthy Tétrault: building Canada's premier law firm, 1855–2005 / Christopher Moore.

Includes bibliographical references and index.
ISBN-13: 978-1-55365-101-7
ISBN-10: 1-55365-101-4

1. McCarthy Tétrault (Firm)—History. 2. Law firms—Canada—History. I. Title.

KE395.M66 2005 340′.06′071 C2004-906614-5
KF345.Z9A1 M66 2005

Jacket and text design by Ingrid Paulson
Illustration credits, see page 394.

Printed and bound in Canada by Friesens
Printed on acid-free paper

CONTENTS

INTRODUCTION

"THERE IS A KIND OF GENIUS to a firm this size," said a McCarthy Tétrault lawyer as we considered the forces that had built the firm into a large, strategically managed partnership that now operates across Canada and internationally as well. "The practice involves such teamwork that you need the infrastructure we have developed at McCarthy Tétrault."

The big law firm, in Canada as elsewhere, is a phenomenon of recent times. After the Second World War, Canadian statisticians categorized a law firm as "large" if it had more than four lawyers. As recently as 1972, only four Canadian firms had more than fifty lawyers (there were fifty-four lawyers at Toronto's McCarthy & McCarthy, the largest of the firms that would form McCarthy Tétrault). In 2004 several Canadian law firms had 500 lawyers; McCarthy Tétrault had more than 700.

Growth in the services that clients required drove the emergence of business law firms as large businesses in themselves. For mergers and acquisitions, corporate finance, capital projects and insolvency, Canadian corporations frequently need sophisticated legal advice that combines many legal specialties in complex and unpredictable ways. When boards and CEOs are betting the company, they need law firms that can assemble substantial teams of first-rate lawyers at short notice.

In 2004, Steel Company of Canada needed that kind of law firm. For twenty-five years, Canada's largest steel producer had seen declining steel prices erode its market position and create a liquidity crisis. (The company had 9,000 active employees and 15,000 pensioners.) McCarthy Tétrault had been advising Stelco on governance issues since the early 1990s. When the steelmaker's board decided to seek a court-supervised restructuring, McCarthy Tétrault was one of a handful of law firms considered for the assignment. "At the end of the day," said Blair Cowper-Smith, a key McCarthy Tétrault lawyer on the Stelco file, "they needed a big firm, and it was going to be one of four or five. What did McCarthy Tétrault have to offer?"

Stelco's difficulties made it almost a perfect client for the firm, the kind for which McCarthy Tétrault and its predecessor firms had spent twenty-five years preparing. "In the 1980s," Cowper-Smith reflected, "we could see more companies would become national and international in scope, and it made sense to us to provide the kinds of services they need. We had to be big, we had to have lawyers on staff who were specialists in a number of areas. We had to be one of what would be a relatively small number of firms capable of handling complex, multi-dimensional transactions. We said, 'That's the market we want to be in.'" By 2004 McCarthy Tétrault had concluded that the core of its business lay with about fifty large corporations and institutions across Canada that would frequently tap its substantial expertise in corporate finance, mergers and acquisitions, litigation, tax, insolvency, pensions, real property and the other legal services such clients required. "As we looked at Stelco's needs, McCarthy Tétrault could offer strengths equally in insolvency

McCarthy Tétrault's senior leadership team launched the firm's 150th anniversary in January 2005. From left, Owen Johnson, national practice group leader; Kenneth Morell, chief operating officer; Iain Scott, chief executive officer; and Trevor Bell, national professional resources leader.

and litigation. It's like having the cardiologists and the surgeons," said Cowper-Smith. By the end of 2004, with the restructuring hearings continuing and international banks and investors considering takeover bids or financing proposals for Stelco, more than fifty McCarthy Tétrault lawyers were working on the Stelco file.

These lawyers practised in several offices as well as in many legal specialties. "It makes no difference whether someone is two floors or a phone call or an e-mail away," said Cowper-Smith, citing a recent project for which one partner came from the Montreal office and another from Calgary to advise a client, "and the client probably never knew what offices they happened to work in." The firm's hard-won abilities to practise law in the courtrooms and boardrooms of all the principal business centres in Canada and beyond, in French or English, in common law or civil law, with Canadian, American or European stakeholders, had become essential aspects of the service a leading law firm provided to the large national and international corporations that were its key clients.

FOR ANYONE INTERESTED in the emergence of the very large law firm and what that phenomenon has meant to Canadian law and to the country's economy and society, there is no better case study than that of McCarthy Tétrault LLP.* In the 1980s, the predecessor firms of McCarthy Tétrault launched—against considerable opposition, only quelled in 1989 with a Charter of Rights decision in the Supreme Court of Canada—the era of the "national" law firm when they merged into a single firm operating in all the major business centres of Canada and internationally as well. The firms that would become McCarthy Tétrault had identified growth as not only a response to client pressures but also a strategy for competitive advantage. In 1983, one of them had predicted that "a firm with a limited local base will find it increasingly difficult to prosper in the face of the competition which the sophisticated and diversified national firms will offer." McCarthy Tétrault was formed to be that sophisticated and diversified national firm. As the first mover in Canada in regional expansion, it had positioned itself to exploit the competitive advantage that size and specialization could offer.

* "LLP" because, like most large law firms, McCarthy Tétrault has responded to recent legislation that permits professional partnerships in Canada to become "limited liability partnerships."

Since then, McCarthy Tétrault has been the largest law firm in Canada and a leader in developing new structures for law firm governance and administration. Having grown by the start of the twenty-first century into a $350-million-a-year organization applying sophisticated strategic planning in a highly competitive environment, McCarthy Tétrault has committed itself to finding and applying management methods to deploy the strengths of a single law firm that now comprises hundreds of lawyers with many specialties, located in many cities, working within two Canadian legal systems and a variety of domestic and foreign markets. From the 1980s to the early twenty-first century, McCarthy Tétrault has been a key participant in the most substantial transformation in the nature of Canadian law firms to occur since long-lived business law firms first came into being in the mid-nineteenth century.

In fact, McCarthy Tétrault's constituent firms had been present at that earlier historical moment, too. Its predecessor firms in Toronto and Montreal were established within a few years of each other in the period from about 1860 to about 1890 that saw the birth of large, long-lasting business law firms in most of Canada's leading cities. In the history of McCarthy Tétrault, we can follow how "downtown," or "elite" or corporate-law firms emerged in Canada in the mid-nineteenth century, how they grew and developed for more than a century, and how they were transformed into large, elaborately managed national and international law firms at the end of the twentieth century.

The growth and development of a Canadian law firm is the principal theme of this history of McCarthy Tétrault and its predecessors. The firms now known as McCarthy Tétrault have been sustained by the contributions of several of Canada's finest courtroom barristers, from D'Alton McCarthy Jr. and Eugène Lafleur, two great counsels active before and after 1900, through John J. Robinette, widely acknowledged to be the outstanding Canadian lawyer of the twentieth century, to Ian Binnie and

Charles Gonthier, two "alumni" of the firm who, from 1998 to 2003, constituted two of the nine justices of the Supreme Court of Canada, and Gérald Tremblay and Thomas Heintzman, who led the firm's litigation team in 2004. But for the most part this book is not a retelling of the great court battles and leading cases of these lawyers and their colleagues.*

The firms that formed McCarthy Tétrault have also represented the business law needs of great Canadian corporate enterprises. In Quebec, Ontario, Alberta and British Columbia, clients of McCarthy Tétrault's constituent firms have always included governments, banks and financial institutions, resource companies, industrial enterprises and development companies. In their days, Leighton McCarthy, Gordon MacDougall, Beverley Matthews, Robert Black, Yves Pratte and others acquired the same stature among corporate solicitors that their litigator colleagues held among courtroom barristers. They advised on deals, mergers, takeovers, financings and development projects that helped to create great corporate institutions, to harness Canada's natural resources through mines, pipelines and power dams, and to transform the fabric of Canadian cities through spectacular development projects. Still, this book provides relatively few detailed accounts of these transactions, partly because of client confidentiality restrictions but principally because McCarthy Tétrault lawyers have been involved in so many newsworthy transactions over the last century and a half that an attempt to cover even the most significant and dramatic ones would become little more than a summary.

This book is a history that is less about the legal work the lawyers have done for their clients than about the law firms they built, the factors that placed them among the dominant Canadian firms of their day, and the decisions that have placed McCarthy Tétrault in the front rank in the law firm environment of the twenty-first century.

*In recent years, biographies of some of the great Canadian lawyers have appeared, including, notably, *John J. Robinette: Peerless Mentor: An Appreciation*, by George Finlayson, himself a leader of the McCarthy & McCarthy litigation section for many years.

The Montreal law firm that evolved from the sole practice of Eugène Lafleur into Clarkson Tétrault before becoming one of the founding firms of McCarthy Tétrault in 1990 had a close relationship with the leading private hydroelectric resource company in Quebec for over fifty years. The Toronto firm, launched by D'Alton McCarthy Jr. and retaining his name throughout, was intimately associated for more than a century with one of Canada's principal life insurance companies. But in 2004 leading law firms had fewer secure, exclusive, long-term relations with particular clients, who can disappear in mergers (as Canada Life Assurance Company did in 2003), expropriations (as Shawinigan Power did in the 1960s) or insolvencies of the kind that threatened Stelco. Corporations now have most of their routine legal work done in-house by their own legal staff, and their in-house corporate counsel are much more inclined to put the specialized work out to tender, transaction by transaction. They negotiate rates and terms and may choose to spread their work around to more than one law firm.

In this more competitive "transactional" market for legal services, there are fewer secure lawyers and law firms. Even senior lawyers need to hone their business skills as well as their legal ones, while younger lawyers move among firms, go "in-house," or shift between large firms and specialized legal "boutiques." Competition among law firms has become intense, and corporate retainers that once supported many relatively small law firms in most Canadian cities are now likely to go to a handful of large law firms, most of which operate nationally or internationally. Law firm recruitment has become professionalized and competitive as law firms work more intensely than ever to identify, recruit, train and retain the talent on which their future prosperity will rest. Nowadays the recruitment pool, once largely restricted to well-connected young men, is much more diverse, and firms pursue equity and diversity policies as an integral part of their efforts to hire and retain the most promising lawyers.

In many ways, law firms have begun to look more like other businesses. It is almost a truism within large law firms that the "professional practice of law" has evolved into the "legal-services business." This is an international phenomenon that has become a Canadian one, and McCarthy Tétrault has been at the heart of the transformation.

THIS HISTORY OF McCarthy Tétrault and its predecessor firms began several years ago, when the partnership's leaders saw twin anniversaries approaching—the 150th anniversary of the Ontario branch of the firm and the 120th anniversary of its Quebec branch—and asked me to help them recapture the record of where they had come from. But perhaps there has been more than looming dates behind their interest in this history. Many senior lawyers and leaders within the firm, in Montreal, Toronto, Calgary or Vancouver, were vividly aware of having, during their professional lives, participated in a historic transformation in the nature of legal practice and the way lawyers work. Some were recently retired, others approaching retirement, others still in midcareer, but all had begun their practices in casually managed and informally led firms of ten or twenty or at most forty lawyers, in an era when a law firm was nothing like this large, branded, professionally managed legal-services enterprise that employs some 2,000 people across many cities and practises kinds of law and kinds of business that were unknown when they entered the profession of law.

Contemplating a history of their firm, these lawyers sensed that the culture of the firm, the legacy of stories and personalities and achievements that provide identity for it and reinforce a sense of pride in one's work and one's partners, could no longer be transmitted the way it used to be. In a firm with hundreds of lawyers in many cities, younger lawyers do not have the same kind of constant, informal contact with the seniors and leaders through which traditions were once passed on. The organization is simply too large to rely on casual transmission of firm lore and culture and a sense of where the firm has come from and what its values are. The origins of this book, therefore, may also express a wish to document in more formal fashion an institutional memory that can no longer flow so effectively through oral transmission.

McCarthy Tétrault is a fusion of four substantial law firms in four regions of Canada; indeed, how the constituent firms met the challenge of learning to operate as a single unit is one of the themes of this book. I have recorded McCarthy Tétrault's origins not in straightforward chronological fashion but as a series of individual firm histories. The first chapters follow McCarthy & McCarthy, which began in Barrie, Ontario, in 1855 as the law firm of the McCarthy family. McCarthy & McCarthy's first tentative steps into western Canada in the 1980s became the catalyst for the building of the national law firm, so sections about Alberta and British Columbia follow the Toronto chapters. Both Black & Company in Calgary and Shrum, Liddle & Hebenton in Vancouver were younger firms than their eastern counterparts, but both grew out of distinct regional legal cultures that I have sketched in the Alberta and British Columbia sections.

McCarthy & McCarthy's first mergers were in the west, but the firm could not be national without a strong base in Montreal, long the centre of the country's business and home to many of its leading law firms. The central chapters of the book turn to the unique legal culture of Quebec to follow the growth of the firm Eugène Lafleur founded in 1885 into Clarkson Tétrault and the key role the latter played in shaping the national partnership of McCarthy Tétrault that came about in 1990.

The formal mergers, however, were only one step in building McCarthy Tétrault. The final chapters follow the history of the merged firm through the 1990s, as the environment for law firms continued to change rapidly and the partnership explored new methods of managing legal practice on a grand scale.

ONCE MCCARTHY TÉTRAULT identified its need for a history of the firm, it commissioned me, on the advice of its publishing consultant, Ramsay Derry, to tell its story. The firm gave me unprecedented access to its archives and files, and its lawyers and staff were unfailingly cooperative and supportive through more than 100 formal interviews and many more informal appeals from a non-lawyer suddenly immersed in the world of a large law practice. I am grateful to W. Iain Scott, chief executive officer of McCarthy Tétrault, James C. McCartney, who was chair of the National Management Committee when I began my research in 2001 and took a particular interest in the project throughout, and to Jacques Tétrault* in Montreal, Sholto Hebenton in Vancouver, and Richard Shaw and Douglas Ewens in Calgary, as well as to all the individuals whose contributions are acknowledged in Appendix B.

*Of the two name partners of McCarthy Tétrault, Mr. McCarthy had been dead for more than a century when I started this book, but M. Tétrault still went to the office every day and I benefited from his thoughtful and courteous reflections.

McCARTHY & McCARTHY

A TORONTO LAW FIRM

D'ALTON McCARTHY BUILDS A FIRM | 1

IN 1877 D'ALTON MCCARTHY JR., a successful barrister in the town of Barrie, Ontario, began a new law firm in Toronto. By the end of the decade, McCarthy had made Toronto his home and his work there the centre of his practice. By 1882 the number of lawyers sharing the practice had grown to six, including Britton Osler, a lawyer whose stature matched McCarthy's. McCarthy, Osler, Hoskin & Creelman was suddenly among the largest law firms in Toronto, with a substantial litigation practice and significant corporate clients. McCarthy and his new firm had staked a place among the leading Canadian law firms.*

The new firm also reflected a shift in legal practice then taking place in Canada's leading business centres. In early nineteenth-century Canada, there had been few specifically "business" lawyers, because most businesses were still family enterprises. When the head of a family consulted the family's lawyer, there was no clear separation between personal and business matters. Most clients were individuals, and so were most law firms. Friends, or a father and son, might

*Traditionally, law firm names had commas: "McCarthy, Osler." In recent decades, names without commas have become standard in law firm branding: "McCarthy Tétrault." Rather than impose modern style upon the past or past style upon modern usage, I have included the commas in the historical chapters up to about 1980.

practise together, but partnerships were fluid, and there was rarely a "firm" that was much larger than the activity of its individual members or likely to endure much beyond them. D'Alton McCarthy's Barrie law firm, where he had practised alongside his father and later was joined by in-laws, broadly fitted this older model.

By the mid-1800s, however, new forms of business enterprise were emerging in the leading cities of Canada. Railroads, manufacturing enterprises, retail operations and insurance and finance companies were becoming large, permanent, incorporated entities. Increasingly, they had capital assets to manage, shares to issue, patents to protect, legislation to secure, organizations to plan and competitors to deal with or contend against. This newly substantial corporate community needed legal services more or less continuously. It began to need law firms that were similarly substantial and could deliver sophisticated advice on an ongoing basis for both the courtroom and the boardroom. A niche had been created, at least in the larger cities, for the kind of law firm that would outlive an individual lawyer. In the mid- to late nineteenth century, Canada saw the emergence of long-lived law firms whose practices were defined by the needs of corporate clients. These were the law firms that ever since have been called "the downtown firm," "the elite firm," "the Bay Street firm" or simply "the corporate law firm."

Such law practices had been emerging in Toronto for a number of years by the time D'Alton McCarthy came to town. Several Toronto law practices that grew to national and international scope in the late twentieth century can trace their origins to the mid-nineteenth century. Edward and Samuel Blake's partnership, launched in 1858, already served a mostly commercial clientele. Beatty, Blackstock and Howland & Arnoldi, both ancestors to the long-established Toronto firm called Faskens (now part of the national firm Fasken Martineau Walker), had begun in 1863 and 1875 respectively. The 1846 partnership of John W. Crawford and John Hagerty, which soon represented a cluster of banks and railroads, much later evolved into Fraser and Beatty and eventually merged into the national firm Fraser Milner Casgrain. For its part, the McCarthy and Osler partnership would eventually produce two pan-Canadian firms, McCarthy Tétrault and Osler Hoskin.

In opening his firm in Toronto, D'Alton McCarthy was linking its future to one of the fundamental transformations in Canadian law firm history: the emergence of corporate-law practice. Through its many transformations since then, the McCarthy law firm has served this corporate market for legal services. D'Alton McCarthy's new law firm in Toronto, however, also built on an already substantial legal tradition in the McCarthy family, one that went back to 1855 in Canada and at least 100 years further in Ireland.

THE McCARTHYS OF DUBLIN AND BARRIE

TWO THINGS STAND OUT about D'Alton McCarthy's male forebears. They were Irish, and they were lawyers.

In 1747 the King's Inn of Ireland, governing body of Irish lawyers, accepted one D'Alton McCarthy as a student-at-law. After completing his terms, including the mandatory two at the Inns of Court in London, this D'Alton McCarthy was called to the Irish bar in 1752. The careers of this lawyer's father (also D'Alton) and grandfather are unconfirmed, but there is a family tradition that the McCarthys had been lawyers back to 1705. Whatever the case, the McCarthys certainly were lawyers by the mid-eighteenth century. The D'Alton McCarthy who was called to the bar in 1752 married Martha Bucknell (who McCarthy family tradition says was an illegitimate child of Prince Frederick, son of King George II). Their son, Bucknell McCarthy, became a Dublin barrister like his father. He studied at Trinity College, Dublin, and at Gray's Inn in London and was called to the Irish bar in 1798. He married Anne Burgh, daughter of a distinguished Irish lawyer and baron (that is, judge) of the Irish Exchequer Court.

A son of Bucknell McCarthy and Anne Burgh, born in 1805 and named D'Alton after his grandfather, was articled at age sixteen and began practising as a solicitor in Dublin in the mid-1820s. He married Charlesina (or "Zina") Manners, the daughter of an Edinburgh lawyer, in Dublin in 1831 and they eventually had eleven children, including D'Alton McCarthy Jr., who was born in 1836.[1]

By the time D'Alton Jr. was born, D'Alton Sr. apparently had retired from his Dublin solicitor's practice, though he would have been only about thirty. The McCarthy family had moved to Oakley Park, a country estate at Blackrock near Dublin, where D'Alton Jr. was born. About a decade later, in the midst of the catastrophic Irish famine of the late 1840s, McCarthy Sr., his pregnant wife and eight of their children immigrated to Canada in 1847. Their eldest son, Bucknell, remained in Ireland.

These Dublin McCarthys were Protestants whose education, family ties and class made them part of the Protestant "ascendency" that ruled Ireland. So did their profession, because in eighteenth-century Ireland only Protestants could practise law. Yet the McCarthys' Protestantism would not have been taken entirely for granted, for the name "McCarthy" was Gaelic and therefore, in Irish terms, "Catholic." Family genealogy linked the McCarthys to ancient and lordly forebears such as Dermot McCarthy, lord of South Munster and builder of Blarney Castle, and all those ancestors were Catholics. There had been a conversion at some point, and Irish conversions were fraught with significance, particularly for lawyers.

One consequence of the eighteenth-century laws that had prevented Catholics from practising law in Ireland had been a small, steady flow of conversions to Protestantism among would-be lawyers who had close but discreetly covered ties to the old Catholic gentry, a group that urgently needed legal expertise to defend its estates and titles against the legislative assault the British and Irish-Protestant rulers of Ireland waged against Irish-Catholic interests all through the eighteenth century.[2]

By the mid-1700s, therefore, a notable minority of the Irish legal community consisted of former Catholics who devoted their legal careers to assisting Catholic clients in circumventing the web of laws and regulations intended to undermine surviving Catholic influences in Ireland.

The skills of these convert lawyers ("pervert" lawyers, in Irish-Protestant slang) were widely recognized, but for some generations their Protestant loyalties were much doubted. It is possible, though unconfirmed, that one of the McCarthy ancestors, perhaps the first lawyer in the McCarthy line somewhere early in the eighteenth century, may have launched the family into law by means of one of these judiciously planned conversions.

However, any McCarthy conversion must have taken place at least a century before the McCarthys immigrated to Canada. The D'Alton McCarthy who started his legal studies in 1747 was already a Protestant then, and by the 1790s Catholics had recovered the right to practise law in Ireland. If there was a conversion-by-convenience somewhere in the McCarthy ancestry, it was far back. The McCarthys were socially, devotionally and in all other ways thoroughly Protestant long before they immigrated to Canada West in 1847, and long before militant Protestantism became identified with D'Alton McCarthy's career in Canadian public life.

The McCarthys left for Canada during the Great Famine caused by the failure of the Irish potato crop, but what influence the famine had upon the McCarthy family's decisions is unknown. The family of a lawyer and landowner would not have faced starvation, as many poor Irish did across Ireland that year, but they would not have been immune to the economic chaos rippling out from the collapse of the agricultural economy, particularly if regular rent payments were vital to their income. Family tradition recalls that D'Alton McCarthy Sr. immigrated because a former law partner had entangled him in a business failure and debt, but the details are unknown.

More Irish fled Ireland and more arrived in Canada in 1847 than in any other year of the nineteenth century. It was a year of chaos and hardship for almost everyone leaving Ireland, and cholera and other lethal diseases accompanied their exodus, but it was the poor and weak above all who died during the migrations, and the McCarthys apparently came through their voyage unscathed. They brought with them an infant daughter who had been born at Oakley Park in 1846, and Zina McCarthy bore a son at their new home in November 1847. Mother and babies survived.[3]

Immigration to Upper Canada by qualified lawyers was uncommon, but Protestant gentry families were familiar among Irish immigrants to Canada in the 1840s. Protestants were then roughly twice as numerous as Catholics among Irish immigrants to British North America, and landowning and professional families were represented among them. Along with the "pull" of Canada, there was a "push" from Ireland. Early steps towards Catholic emancipation and ongoing economic troubles are credited with having encouraged Protestant gentry migrations to Canada from the 1830s on.

The McCarthys were following a path similar to that of several other families who would provide leading members of the Ontario bar. The Baldwin family from Cork, leaders among the early lawyers of Upper Canada, had at first settled in Durham County east of Toronto. The Blakes of Galway came to an agricultural settlement at Strathroy in 1832. Both families had come to Canada with the expectation that they could establish themselves as gentlemanly farming proprietors, and they turned to Toronto and the law only after discovering how difficult it was to recreate their old-world circumstances in Canada, where there was a woodland frontier to be tamed and no tenant workforce to do the hard labour.*

D'Alton McCarthy Sr. also aspired to become a landed proprietor, for he settled his family on farmland at Shanty Bay on Lake Simcoe, in the township of Oro in Simcoe County near Barrie. He could not have taken up legal practice upon arrival even had he wished. British (including Irish) barristers were freely admitted to practice in Canada West, but McCarthy was a solicitor. A technicality of the law required solicitors immigrating to Canada West to serve a full five-year apprenticeship (as more than one newly arrived solicitor had discovered to his fury). Nevertheless, McCarthy spent barely three years as a full-time farmer.

*The difficulty of Upper Canadian frontier life for immigrant gentry became a theme of Canadian literature through the writings of Susanna Moodie and Catharine Parr Traill, though their spouses were military officers rather than lawyers.

In 1851 a sister-in-law in Britain referred to his "farming projects" having "failed," and by then he was returning to the law. He signed articles about 1850, almost certainly with Barrie lawyer D'Arcy Boulton. In June 1855 he became a fully qualified common law attorney and chancery solicitor of Canada West (he never became a barrister) and began practising in partnership with Boulton. The McCarthy family had entered the rolls of Canadian lawyers.*[4]

D'Alton McCarthy Jr., who was about ten when his family immigrated to Simcoe County and in his teens when his father returned to legal practice, followed McCarthy Sr. into the family profession. He, too, articled with D'Arcy Boulton. He was called to the bar in 1859 and admitted as a solicitor in 1860. A younger brother, Thomas Maitland McCarthy, also took up the law, becoming a solicitor in 1861 and opening his own practice in Orangeville, where he eventually became a county court judge.[5]

*In mid-nineteenth-century Ontario most lawyers were barristers and solicitors, but the testing and qualification procedures were separate. Some lawyers, like D'Alton McCarthy Sr., qualified as one but not the other.

THE McCARTHYS' BARRIE PRACTICE

D'ALTON MCCARTHY SR., a midlife immigrant with a large family and striving to maintain a certain style of living, was said to have been "always a poor man." But in 1860 his son and namesake was well positioned for professional and financial success.

As a member of one of Barrie's handful of law firms before he was twenty-two, D'Alton McCarthy Jr. joined a small and favoured elite. He was one of barely 500 lawyers in a province with a population of about 1.5 million. Though his family was still new to Canada, he had impressive connections on which to build his career. D'Arcy Boulton, articling principal and partner to both McCarthys, was a third-generation Ontario lawyer whose family had been a pillar of the old Ontario "family compact." Boulton had Orange Lodge and Conservative political connections throughout the province (he became an MPP in 1867), and he and McCarthy Sr. briefly edited a political newspaper together. Many other notable families of Simcoe County, including the Gowans, Bernards, Ardaghs and Lallys, shared the McCarthys' Irish-Protestant origins and their commitment to the legal profession; they may well have helped draw the McCarthys to Canada and to Barrie. Father and son were soon integrated into extensive legal, political and social networks.[6]

Barrie, the county town of Simcoe County, was beginning a frontier boom when the McCarthys settled in the area in 1847. The county, established only in 1843, lies near the northern edge of southern Ontario farming country, and in the 1850s it still offered abundant land for new settlers. The 1850s and 1860s, just before the North American "wheat frontier" began to move towards the prairie west, were years of prosperity and expansion for Ontario agriculture. Simcoe County adjoined the timber country of the Muskoka and the Georgian Bay shore, and by the 1860s this region had supplanted the Ottawa and Trent Valleys as a prime timber source. Simcoe County lake ports such as Collingwood were becoming centres of lumber-milling, shipbuilding and lake commerce. Ontario's first railroad venture had been organized in the early 1850s to link Toronto via Barrie to the Collingwood docks.* As D'Alton McCarthy Jr. launched his practice in the 1860s, the region's economic expansion was intense. Barrie grew and prospered, and so did the McCarthys' law practice.[7]

By 1864 D'Alton Jr.'s law practice was doing well enough that he had an imposing house built near the centre of Barrie. In 1867 he married Emma Lally, daughter of Simcoe County treasurer Edmund Lally and sister to a local lawyer. She died in childbirth in 1870, and McCarthy then married her sister, Agnes, the widow of yet another local lawyer, Richard Bernard (through Bernard's sister, Agnes Bernard, Agnes Lally was a sister-in-law of Prime Minister John

*Not quite "via Barrie." Denied the concessions it wanted from the town, the railroad put its terminal in nearby Allandale and promised that grass would grow in Barrie's streets. But a spur line soon ran into Barrie and the county town benefited from the railroad.

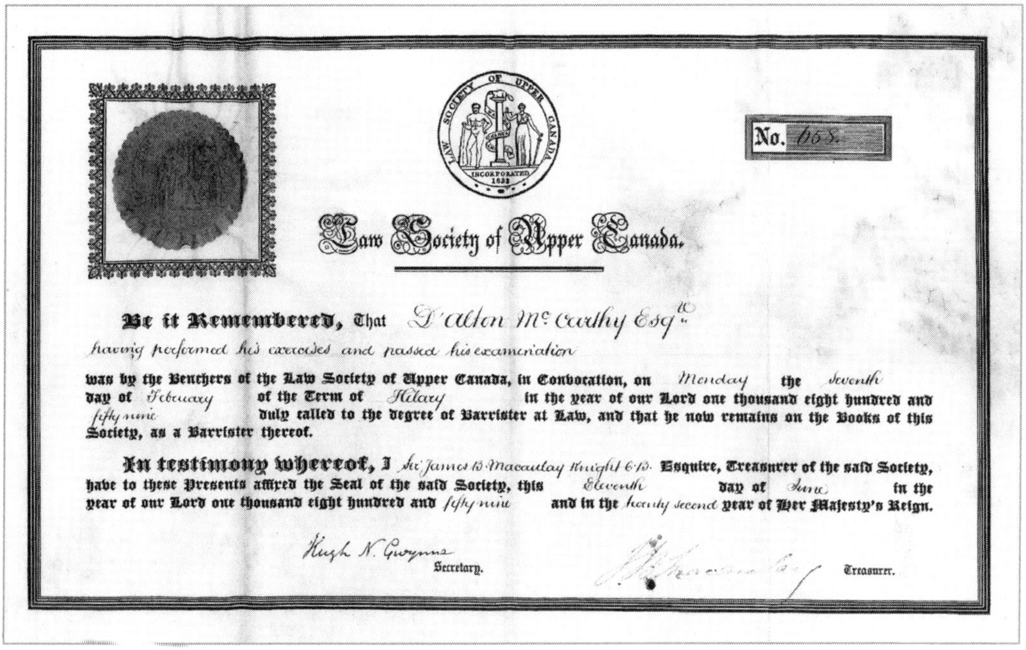

LAW SOCIETY OF UPPER CANADA INCORPORATED 1822

No. 658

Law Society of Upper Canada.

Be it Remembered, That D'Alton McCarthy Esq[re]
having performed his exercises and passed his examination
was by the Benchers of the Law Society of Upper Canada, in Convocation, on Monday the Seventh day of February of the Term of Hilary in the year of our Lord one thousand eight hundred and fifty nine duly called to the degree of Barrister at Law, and that he now remains on the Books of this Society, as a Barrister thereof.

In testimony whereof, I Sir James B. Macaulay Knight C.B. Esquire, Treasurer of the said Society, have to these Presents affixed the Seal of the said Society, this Eleventh day of June in the year of our Lord one thousand eight hundred and fifty nine and in the twenty second year of Her Majesty's Reign.

Hugh N. Gwynne
Secretary.

Treasurer.

The Law Society of Upper Canada called D'Alton McCarthy Jr. to the bar on February 7, 1859. McCarthy was admitted as a solicitor the following year.

A. Macdonald). McCarthy had a small daughter and son from his first marriage; his second marriage brought two Bernard stepdaughters into his household.

In about 1870 the two McCarthys separated from D'Arcy Boulton—who continued to practise in Barrie with other partners until his death in 1875*—and founded the first McCarthy & McCarthy law firm. Father and son, barrister and solicitors of Barrie, practised together until McCarthy Sr. died in 1873, at age 68. Land transfers, mortgages, wills and estates and related work would have been the firm's bread and butter, along with routine litigation, particularly at the quarterly assizes, and the general moneylending and brokerage work that law firms usually handled in that era. To accommodate its rural clients, the firm

* *Law Lists* show the handful of lawyers of Barrie splitting partnerships and recombining into different ones frequently, which seems to have been typical for the Ontario bar of the time.

had begun opening branch offices in smaller centres around the county as early as 1859. D'Alton McCarthy Jr.'s son, Lally, who articled with his father's old Barrie firm in the 1890s, described it then as "a large country practice," which probably would have described it in the 1860s and 1870s as well.[8]

It was not exclusively a "country" practice, however. McCarthy Jr. became solicitor to the local railroad and to Simcoe County. Several lumber companies became clients as his reputation grew and as he enjoyed courtroom successes in civil and criminal cases. Alfred Boultbee, a childhood friend and fellow lawyer, described the youthful D'Alton McCarthy as "smart, and keen, a witty conversationalist and a great favorite with the ladies," very fond of cricket and particularly of horses. By the time McCarthy was called to the bar, he was revealing more substantial talents. "He had a wonderful command of language and knowledge of men and was remarkable for the persistence with which he pursued his end and the dauntless courage he showed in maintaining his opinions," said Boultbee. "The Barrie lumbermen speedily availed themselves of his legal skill, and it not only brought him into notice in Toronto, it brought in the money."[9]

Another acquaintance described young D'Alton McCarthy in his legal dealings as "dignified almost to hauteur, abrupt to the verge of rudeness, and self-assertive, dictatorial, almost imperious." McCarthy's younger brother, John, venturing to offer some political advice, once sent him a letter saying, "I can express my ideas better in writing, when not exposed to your merciless logic.... Instead of giving you food for thought, I have only succeeded in fixing your opinions by the arguments you made use of to convince me." What McCarthy seems to have had above all was great intensity and absolute conviction in pressing his views, legal or political.[10]

D'Alton Jr. was soon deeply involved in Conservative politics. In 1867, in Canada's first federal election, he managed the Simcoe riding campaign for the Conservatives, and he himself ran in 1872 against a strong Liberal candidate. McCarthy lost, in an election marked by corruption on both sides, appealed the result, and still lost. As a consolation, Prime Minister Macdonald made him a Queen's Counsel, the only one at the Simcoe County bar. Finally, in 1873, McCarthy won a seat in another riding. In 1876 he was successful in his home riding of North Simcoe and from then to his death he was its MP, "the Simcoe boy." It was never a safe Conservative seat, but McCarthy was always effective in securing federal benefits for his county and constituents.[11]

By the 1870s D'Alton McCarthy Jr. was a power in Barrie. He had a growing legal reputation, a substantial practice and close ties to local business leaders, and he was the coming man in local and national politics. In 1871 he had been elected a bencher of the Law Society of Upper Canada. He could have remained a dominant figure in the law and public life of Simcoe County while expanding his stature throughout Ontario and in national politics. Nevertheless, just as he was securing his political future in Barrie and its hinterland, D'Alton Jr. transferred his legal ambitions to Toronto.*

*It is uncertain how early McCarthy developed a practice in Toronto. When leading Toronto counsel Robert Harrison became a judge in September 1875, he recommended that McCarthy be invited to fill his place in his firm. Though nothing came of it, McCarthy was evidently considered available.

At least two things drew McCarthy to Toronto. One was legal. His litigation skills and successes were beginning to be noted, and Toronto offered greater litigation opportunities than a county town. At the same time, his lumber-company clients had provided him with some valuable commercial connections, which may have alerted him to the potential for new-style corporate-law firms in the larger business centres. Barrie, an excellent base politically, may have become too small for his legal ambitions.

McCarthy's other incentive to move was pressing, personal, and financial. Barrie, and the McCarthys' legal business, had prospered in the Muskoka timber boom of the 1860s. But the depression of the 1870s brought a slump in demand and fierce price competition among Georgian Bay producers. That meant ruin for many entrepreneurs who had invested heavily in local mills and timber rights and who constantly needed legal counsel from the McCarthy firm. Worse for McCarthy, he had invested heavily in his lumber clients' enterprises and had lost a fortune. He held on to his substantial Barrie home—registered in the names of his wives and father-in-law—but he was left very heavily indebted. A friend estimated McCarthy's debts at more than $200,000, and they would weigh on him for a long time. In 1884, after several years of very successful practice in Toronto, McCarthy still cited his debts when he refused Prime Minister Macdonald's invitation to become minister of justice.[12] Whatever the positive attractions of Toronto legal practice, McCarthy also had an incentive to put some distance between himself and his creditors in Barrie and to go where the prospect of recouping his fortune was better.

He did not entirely abandon Barrie, either when he launched his Toronto firm in 1877 or when he moved to Toronto in 1879. He kept his name on the Barrie law firm for the rest of his life, though after 1879 its day-to-day affairs were led by his partner and future son-in-law, Frank Pepler.* McCarthy continued to take cases in the Barrie courts, and he sent his son to be trained in the Barrie firm. Barrie and its region, which he represented in the House of Commons, would remain the base of his political power and influence throughout his life. Eventually, McCarthy acquired a lavish country estate, "Tollendal," from his Lally in-laws and made it his Simcoe County base and his retreat from the practice in Toronto.† There on the shore of Lake Simcoe he supervised a farm and raised champion livestock amid surroundings that may have recalled the ideal of rural-gentry life that his father had left behind in Ireland.

*The Barrie firm became McCarthy and Boys in 1874, soon after McCarthy Sr. died. It was McCarthy, Boys & Pepler by 1876 and McCarthy, Pepler & McCarthy by 1880, when William Boys (later a prominent Simcoe County judge) had left and Jeffrey McCarthy (apparently no relation) had joined the firm. McCarthy, Pepler remained among the largest Barrie firms, with several branch offices around Simcoe County. Its long-time leader, Frank Pepler, was married to McCarthy's stepdaughter Emily Bernard, and lived in McCarthy's former home in Barrie.

†Tollendal (once Tullymullaly) in Ireland had been the estate of the Lally family, barons of Tollendal until the Catholic Jacobite holder of the title was exiled after the overthrow of Britain's Stuart dynasty in 1688.

McCARTHY'S TORONTO FIRM

THE PARTNERSHIP AGREEMENT that established D'Alton McCarthy Jr.'s first Toronto law firm on April 7, 1877, created something that a twenty-first-century counterpart might consider a "partnership of partnerships." The new firm, called McCarthy, Hoskin, Plumb and Creelman, was an association of three groups of lawyers. Adam Creelman, a recently called lawyer who took a one-third share in the new firm despite his very junior status, was the only partner who was not maintaining an independent practice. John Hoskin and Thomas S. Plumb, who were already practising together in Toronto, would continue their separate practice and retain its revenues, along with a one-third share in the new firm. McCarthy, who took the final third, specified that he would retain a separate interest in his Barrie practice and keep all his income from "suits and matters not arising out of the business of the firm."

This tentative beginning must have shown promise: in later agreements the partners demonstrated a growing commitment to the Toronto practice. By July 1, 1879, when the firm reorganized as McCarthy, Hoskin, and Creelman, McCarthy was much more involved. He would now receive two-thirds of the income, leaving Hoskin and Creelman with just one-sixth each, though they alone would pay Plumb and maintain two law students, Frederick Harcourt and William Clement.* McCarthy was still "of Barrie, Ontario," but he moved to Toronto during that year, and thereafter all the partners lived in Toronto. The next partnership agreement, in 1882, would establish a full partnership in which all the overheads (and the fast-rising income) of the Toronto practice were merged into the accounts of a single firm.[13]

Like nearly every leading law firm of the mid- to late nineteenth century, McCarthy's new firm in Toronto was headed by a barrister: in this

*Plumb, a partner in 1877, had been discovered in 1878 not yet to have been admitted as a solicitor, though he was a barrister. His name was dropped from the firm name and he gave up his partnership share. He was admitted as a solicitor in late 1879 but regained a share of the firm profits only in 1881. He left the firm before 1886.

case, himself. Already active at the Ontario Court of Appeal and the new Supreme Court of Canada, he soon brought in most of the firm's work and earned most of its income. Although corporate solicitors' work was growing in volume and importance as the business community began to look to lawyers to plan and administer and to help them avoid, rather than litigate, disputes, advocacy remained the most prominent part of business lawyers' work. Legal opinions and litigation services were still the key thing businesses expected from their lawyers, and many businesses still hired barristers first and let the ongoing solicitors' work follow.

D'Alton McCarthy Jr., lawyer, politician and founder of a great law firm.

A second top-flight barrister soon joined McCarthy in the leadership of his firm. Britton Bath Osler agreed to enter the firm in 1882 and on September 1, the firm became McCarthy, Osler, Hoskin & Creelman. McCarthy's son, Lally, who was twelve in 1882, much later recalled that his father returned from a case in Hamilton one Saturday night, "and on Sunday he told me what an extraordinarily brilliant counsel he thought Mr. Osler was and that he had asked him to join his Toronto firm, which he had consented to do." B.B. Osler was the second son in the remarkable Osler family founded by Featherstone Osler, an Anglican minister at Bond Head, Simcoe County. B.B. Osler had attended the same Barrie schools as D'Alton McCarthy, who was three years older. His brothers included Featherston Osler of the Ontario Court of Appeal, the financier Sir Edmund Osler, and the medical doctor and teacher Sir William Osler.[14]

B.B. Osler had begun his Ontario legal practice in Dundas and Hamilton, where he also had business interests, but McCarthy's invitation to move to the provincial capital evidently suited his rising ambitions: he, too, had been building a litigation practice that took him far beyond Hamilton. Osler also brought in new business clients, notably Canada North-West Land Company, a real estate arm of Canadian Pacific Railway, with which two of his brothers were associated. (For a time, indeed, McCarthy & Osler maintained a branch office in Regina for this client, though no lawyers worked there.) Other corporations that paid regular retainers to the firm in its first few years included Canada Life Assurance Company, Georgian Bay Lumber Company, Parry Sound Lumber Company, Canadian Manufacturers Association, Maritime Bank, and Steel Iron and Railway Works, though details of the legal services they required are largely unknown.

For almost two decades after 1882, D'Alton McCarthy and B.B. Osler were among the busiest and most effective counsel in the courts of Ontario and beyond. They did civil litigation, often representing railroads, lumber companies and insurance companies. One firm specialty seems to have been insurance litigation, then a rapidly evolving field. McCarthy argued many cases that addressed fundamental principles of the insurance industry as well as straightforward disputes over liability.[15] He also handled many contested-election cases for the Conservative Party (twenty-six in 1883 alone). In 1885 Osler went to Regina and Winnipeg as part of the team that prosecuted Louis Riel for treason. They each did prosecution and defence work in widely reported criminal cases around Ontario.* In the 1880s McCarthy led several dramatic murder trials in Barrie. In 1890 Osler went to Woodstock to prosecute the internationally reported case of Reginald Burchall, who had lured a well-to-do young Englishman to Ontario and then murdered him for his money.

*Full-time Crown prosecutors are a recent phenomenon. Long into the twentieth century, private lawyers were often retained to prosecute cases on behalf of the Crown.

While Osler became particularly renowned for his skill with witnesses and juries in the trial courts and was ranked among the country's leading criminal lawyers, particularly as a prosecutor, McCarthy became best known as an appeal-court specialist, particularly in civil and constitutional litigation.* Between 1878 and 1898 he argued at least 156 appeals at the Ontario Court of Appeal and 129 cases at the Supreme Court of Canada in Ottawa. He travelled frequently to Britain to plead before the Judicial Committee of the Privy Council. In his first reported Supreme Court appearance, in 1878, McCarthy sought unsuccessfully on behalf of the Conservative Party to overturn the election of Rodolphe Laflamme, a Montreal lawyer and Liberal politician (who had declined an appointment to the same Supreme Court when it was established in 1875). In the first case McCarthy took to the Privy Council, completed in 1882, he won a $100,000 verdict from Canada Central Railway. The company was held responsible for the sparks from a locomotive that had caused a fire in a lumberyard in Carleton Place, Ontario, belonging to McCarthy's client, Peter McLaren.[16]

Most of McCarthy's clients in his appeal cases were businesses, but sometimes the issues were constitutional as well as commercial. The Perth lumber baron Peter McLaren was a long-time McCarthy client who became his close friend. But when McLaren got into conflict with rival lumberer Boyd Caldwell over their competing uses of a local waterway, their battle became the test case for a key constitutional interpretation: did Ottawa have authority to regulate rivers and streams that prevailed over Ontario's regulations on the same matter? Issues beyond the usual commercial liabilities also arose in litigation between Citizens' Insurance Company, a frequent client of McCarthy, Osler, and a policyholder named William Parsons. Was their insurance policy a contract, under the authority of

*Osler also argued civil and appellate cases, and McCarthy hardly lacked skill in criminal work or with witnesses. Family lore preserves the story of his questioning of an accident victim in a civil case. McCarthy, representing the insurers, supposedly asked the claimant how high he could raise his injured arm. The witness laboriously lifted his arm to shoulder height. "And how high could you raise it before the accident?" asked McCarthy blandly. The witness shot the arm high over his head.

Ontario, or was insurance a branch of trade and commerce, subject to federal regulation?

These questions mattered to litigants struggling with duplicate (and conflicting) layers of regulation, but they also addressed the most explosive issue of federal-provincial relations in the still-new Dominion of Canada: what were the boundaries between Ottawa's authority and that of the provinces? Arguing such cases made D'Alton McCarthy one of Canada's key constitutional lawyers in the era when fundamental judicial interpretations of the British North America Act were being made.

Britton Bath Osler in 1885. He and D'Alton McCarthy Jr. gave the Toronto firm the tremendous litigation strength on which its reputation was founded in the 1880s and 1890s.

In the 1880s McCarthy fought a string of constitutional cases that eventually reached the Judicial Committee of the Privy Council in London. Even when the specified client was a lumberer or insurance company, McCarthy was also acting for the Government of Canada and Prime Minister John A. Macdonald's view of federalism. In most of these cases his real opponent was Ontario and Oliver Mowat, the province's premier and attorney general from 1872 to 1896. In these cases and others, McCarthy for Canada sought to establish that the British North America Act, and particularly the "trade and commerce" and "residual powers" language of section 91, gave the Government of Canada primacy over the provinces in economic and commercial policy and entitled Ottawa to broad latitude in circumscribing provincial actions in these areas.[17]

Mowat and the Government of Ontario sought to establish precisely the reverse. Ontario advocated a broad reading of the authority over "property and civil rights" and "local matters" that section 92 had conferred on the provinces. Mowat insisted each province was a sovereign power within Confederation, "not in any accurate sense subordinate to the parliament of Canada," but "independent and supreme within the limits of its own jurisdiction." He argued that in their own jurisdiction the provinces were entitled to wide authority, free from federal interference. Year after year he urged this interpretation on the Supreme Court in Ottawa, which rarely accepted it, and on the Judicial Committee in London, which often did.[18]

Mowat had been a very successful equity lawyer and judge before his return to politics in 1872, and even as premier he frequently made himself a member of Ontario's legal team in constitutional cases at the Privy Council.* McCarthy, one of many lawyers drawn into constitutional litigation defending federal primacy against Mowat's provincial-rights campaign, became one of the many who lost to Mowat and the jurisprudence of the Privy Council, which mostly supported Mowat's arguments for provincial autonomy. *Parsons v. Citizens' Insurance*, in which McCarthy unsuccessfully urged the federal case, would be cited for a century in judgements that sheltered provincial "property and civil rights" powers from federal "trade and commerce" initiatives. Similarly, in *St. Catharine's Milling* (1888), which also pitted McCarthy against Mowat, the Privy Council found that the northwestern Ontario timber and mineral rights in the area Canada acquired by Indian Treaty #3 belonged exclusively to Ontario, not to Canada, despite the federal government's responsibility for "Indians" and land treaties.

The Judicial Committee consistently ruled that the scope of the provinces' enumerated powers outweighed even the residual authority the

*Equity was a separate jurisdiction in Ontario law, with its own court, the Court of Chancery, until the courts of equity and common law were merged in 1881. Equity procedures offered a broader scope for considering "natural justice" principles than the precedent-bound common law courts. Equity practitioners handled a great deal of commercial and property work, particularly regarding trusts and mortgages. John Hoskin was McCarthy, Osler's leading equity practitioner.

federal government held in fields not specified in the division of powers. "What luck Mowat has had at the Privy Council!" Macdonald said in exasperation. McCarthy must have agreed, and he mused with Macdonald about abolishing appeals to the Privy Council, on the grounds that the British judges obviously did not understand Canada. Still, McCarthy continued to take appeal cases on many matters to London nearly every summer. His arguments for reinforcing Ottawa's authority within Confederation made little headway in London, but he had established a reputation as a top-flight counsel, capable of clear, powerful arguments put forward with absolute conviction and precise citations from case law.

Asserting central authority in court suited McCarthy's political convictions. He aspired to see strong national government promoting a strong Canadian nationality that would mirror and sustain "organic" local communities like his idealized Simcoe County. He hailed Canada's rapid expansion into the west as both an imperial and a national triumph, and he foresaw Canada being both a strong pillar of the British Empire and a great North American nation. His vision of the Canadian nation was unitary and British: there would be one culture, one language, one set of laws and one national government uniting all Canadians. These views, and his uncompromising expression of them, determined his political career.[19]

The defeat of Prime Minister Alexander Mackenzie's one-term Liberal government returned the Conservative Party to power in Ottawa in 1878, two years after McCarthy won the North Simcoe seat. McCarthy became a key adviser to Prime Minister Macdonald on legal affairs, elections and constitutional issues. When Macdonald needed a new temperance law to try to head off provincial claims in the field, McCarthy headed the parliamentary committee and is said to have drafted the legislation required in a single night. (His handiwork, the McCarthy Act, became the subject of yet more federal-provincial litigation before the Privy Council.) He was also a prominent figure in the Imperial Federation League, in those years an influential lobby for closer ties among countries of the British Empire.

In 1884 Macdonald repeated an offer to make D'Alton McCarthy his minister of justice. An appointment to the Ontario Supreme Court had previously been offered, though the prime minister did not want to lose North Simcoe, "which it would be *te absente*." But McCarthy declined both, citing the business debts he still had to shoulder. "The amount that I still owe the bank is very large," he wrote to Macdonald, "so large that it would be simply madness in me to give up my profession and attempt to float through. I must work away as I am doing for three or four years, when perhaps I may have relieved myself from the burden that has weighed down the best years of my life."[20]

To have joined Macdonald's cabinet would have required McCarthy to commit himself to politics over legal practice, but it would also have placed him among the old man's likely successors. Instead, by the end of the "three or four years" he mentioned to Macdonald, McCarthy had put aside such expectations. John Thompson from Nova Scotia, who took the federal Justice portfolio soon after McCarthy declined it, rapidly supplanted McCarthy as Macdonald's legal adviser, parliamentary partner and leadership heir. In any case, McCarthy was abandoning the consensus politics that Macdonald strove to practise. Macdonald continued to consult and court him, but McCarthy gradually became a lone-wolf advocate, passionately advocating his own rigorous views in politics as in law.

McCarthy's increasingly independent political path became evident after the Northwest Rebellion led by Louis Riel in 1885. McCarthy was at the Privy Council in London for most of that summer, but he urged Macdonald to take harsh measures, lest, he said, "a second Quebec" begin to rise in the west. In the aftermath of Riel's trial and execution, McCarthy expressed alarm at the strength and resilience of French-language culture in Canada. He was appalled by the success of Quebec's new premier, Honoré Mercier, whose Parti National took power in Quebec in 1887 on an ambitious platform of "French nationality." As evidence mounted that, far from developing the single English-speaking national culture McCarthy favoured, Canada was likely to retain its cultural and linguistic duality, McCarthy began to obsess over language policy. He told Macdonald the Conservative Party should "hold by the English provinces" and stop trying to "lean on" Quebec for support. Through the late 1880s, he became steadily less tolerant of Macdonald's efforts to retain support in both French Canada and English Canada.[21]

The Jesuit Estates controversy of 1889 committed McCarthy irrevocably to English-Canadian nationalism. Premier Mercier's Jesuit Estates Act, passed by the Quebec legislature in 1888, provided compensation to Catholic organizations for Jesuit properties that the British colonial authorities had expropriated a century before. Mercier's bill, the long preamble of which expressed official confidence in the future growth and strength of French Catholic Quebec, authorized the Roman Catholic Pope to arbitrate how the property compensation payment would be divided among various Catholic institutions. Both the bold preamble and the reference to the Pope horrified those English Canadians who saw little place in Canadian public life for the French language or Catholicism, and none at all for the Pope. McCarthy joined a bloc of Ontario Conservative MPs who sought to have Ottawa disallow Quebec's legislation. In the end, just thirteen MPs voted for disallowance. The "noble thirteen" then formed the Equal Rights Association (ERA) under McCarthy's leadership to campaign for a unilingual Canada.

McCarthy's speeches on the language issue became steadily more inflamed. Speaking in the Simcoe County town of Stayner in the summer of 1889, he told supporters, "Now is the time when the ballot box will decide the great question before the people, and if that does not supply the remedy in this generation, bayonets will supply it in the next."[22]

The English-language cause was popular in rural Ontario. For a time, McCarthy hoped the Equal Rights Association could unite anticlerical reformers and progressives with anti-French and anti-Catholic conservatives in a bloc that could topple Oliver Mowat's Liberals in provincial politics and reshape the Conservative Party in Ottawa. Mowat held his supporters together, however, partly by implementing some of the language restrictions the ERA advocated, and it was the ERA that was split by the divided ambitions of its own members. McCarthy emphasised language over religion and still sought influence in the Conservative Party, but rival ERA leaders from Liberal backgrounds were more concerned with church-state issues than with language, and they resisted linking the ERA to the Conservatives. The divided ERA failed utterly as an electoral force.[23]

As a prominent opponent of French-language rights, however, McCarthy became a valuable ally for the government of Manitoba when it sought to abolish the French-language rights and educational rights that had been established when the province joined Confederation in 1870. McCarthy spoke and lobbied vigorously in support of the suppression of French in Manitoba and across the west. In 1890, he introduced a private member's bill in the House of Commons to extend the attack on French-language rights from Manitoba into the North-West Territories. In the debate, McCarthy advocated the extinction of the French language throughout Canada, in the name of national unity.

What Canada needed, McCarthy argued, was "one language, one race, with one national life, and with a language common to us all...." His target was not religion, and though he used the term "race" he insisted, "There is no such thing as a Celtic skull, any more than a Saxon skull. It is only by language and by the community of language that men are formed into nations." He told the House, citing contemporary anthropological theory, that the issue was language, not ancestry, ethnicity or even religion. Amid all the efforts to build up a transcontinental Canadian nation, he said, it made no sense to be simultaneously "passing measures and promoting legislation which separates and divides the peoples into two separate races." He would rather have the whole country speak French, he said, than have half speak English and half French. "We ought to realize—most especially ought the French Canadians of this country to realize—that their true interest, as our true interest, is, at as early a day as possible, to have but the one language spoken in this country."[24]

McCarthy presented his views as dispassionate and scientific, but his vision of the extinction of the French language in Canada and his widely reported talk of eventually settling the issue with bayonets seem to have appalled the House. Macdonald said, "McCarthy has sown the dragons' teeth. I fear they will grow up to be armed men." McCarthy's language bill provoked members from all sides to review the nature of Canada, and it became the occasion for one of the great debates of the Canadian Parliament. The fiercest rebuttal came from the leader of the Opposition, Wilfrid Laurier: "I denounce this policy as anti-Canadian, I denounce it as anti-British; I denounce it as being at variance with all the traditions of British government in this country.... The honourable member... is opening the floodgates to passions which, once aroused, perhaps, no human power may be able to restrain." English-Canadian leaders from both sides of the House joined Quebecers and Acadians in expressing their outrage. McCarthy acknowledged at the end of the debate that he had been "abused by almost every honorable gentleman" in the House. Through the intervention of Justice Minister Thompson, McCarthy's bill was amended almost beyond recognition, and McCarthy himself voted against the final version.[25]

The rejection of his language proposals confirmed the extinction of D'Alton McCarthy's prospects for national leadership. Through the 1890s he remained influential with many Ontario Conservatives, but he was breaking with his party on more than language, and there was no chance of his being given the federal party leadership when Macdonald died in 1891. The Conservative "National Policy" of tariff protection for industry had never been popular among farmers, including McCarthy's North Simcoe constituents, who preferred cheap imports and open borders for their produce exports. By 1892 McCarthy was arguing that protection of urban manufacturers had continued long enough; he advocated more tariff-free trade with the United States. (Despite his presidency of the Imperial Federation League, McCarthy did not favour a sheltered trading zone within the empire.) McCarthy's economic policies were becoming similar to those advocated by Laurier's Liberal Party. In 1893 McCarthy formally left the Conservative Party over the tariff issue.

In 1896, however, language policy returned to national politics. After Manitoba had unilaterally abolished the legal standing of the French language and separate schools, the province's minority looked to the federal government to defend its constitutional guarantees. McCarthy was involved both as lawyer and politician. At the Privy Council he argued the province's case against the federal government in *Barrett v. City of Winnipeg*, for once asserting the authority of the provinces and denying the federal government's right to intervene. The Privy Council's ambiguous ruling threw the case back into the political arena on the eve of a federal election. The new Conservative prime minister, Mackenzie Bowell (himself an anti-Catholic Orangeman, but a loyal servant of his party), and his successor, Charles Tupper, both declared they would introduce federal remedial legislation to force the province into line. McCarthy, now wholly opposed to the Conservatives' Manitoba policy, became aligned with the opposition Liberals, whose leader, Wilfrid Laurier, offered "sunny ways" as an alternative to federal coercion. Laurier had concluded that anti-French sentiment in Ontario and the west, which McCarthy had done so much to legitimize, was too strong to resist. Confident that as a native son he could hold Quebec whatever he did, Laurier virtually abandoned French-language rights in Manitoba for the sake of power.

Laurier and the Liberals swept to victory in the 1896 election. McCarthy, re-elected in North Simcoe as an independent MP, savoured a kind of victory in the defeat of his old party. Soon, in fact, McCarthy was considering an offer to cross the floor and join the Liberal cabinet. It is unlikely that he could have had lasting influence in the Laurier government. Laurier might have recruited him, both to embarrass the Conservatives and to gain McCarthy's silence, but the two men's visions of culture and language in Canada were incompatible, as their exchanges in 1890 had confirmed. In any case, McCarthy never demonstrated any of Laurier's (or Macdonald's) willingness to make adroit compromises for the sake of power, and it seems unlikely that he could have served under Laurier for long. After 1890, despite the substantial sympathy for his views on language and culture that endured in English Canada, McCarthy found himself painted into a small corner of national politics. His opposition was feared and his talents respected by both parties, but he had been unable to sell his language policies to either or to build an independent political force.

McCarthy's legal career and law firm, meanwhile, continued to grow and prosper. He and B.B. Osler, both in their early fifties, remained dominant in the firm through the 1890s. Their steadily growing counsel fees (McCarthy charged $100 a day, one newspaper reported in awe; poor people would barely earn that in a year) were still half or more of all the firm's income. In 1891 the partners even agreed to dispense with the holdback from McCarthy's share of profits (made to reflect his absences on political business), citing the "comparatively small portion of time" he had recently devoted to parliamentary work. McCarthy continued to take important legal cases. During the 1890s he argued the Manitoba Schools case at the Privy Council, fought a large action by a group of contractors against Canadian Pacific Railway, engaged in litigation between the Soulanges Canal Company and the federal government and successfully defended Consumers' Gas in a major liability case. Osler, without a political career, may have been even busier. He travelled relentlessly on the Ontario trial-courts circuit, to London for Privy Council cases and around North America in pursuit of other business.[26]

As well as the two leaders' litigation work, McCarthy, Osler had a growing file of annual retainers from corporate clients and a substantial agency business from other law firms around the province. Among the corporations now retaining it were Hudson's Bay Company (starting in 1889), General Electric (1888), North-West Life Assurance (1894) and Dominion Bank (1898). In 1891 the firm began acting for Central

Canada Loan and Savings, the key business of rising financier George A. Cox. From 1893 it was also retained (probably for litigation matters) by Toronto Street Railway, owned by the railroad and electric-power entrepreneur William Mackenzie. In this era, George Cox and William Mackenzie were among the crucial business leaders whose efforts were building Toronto into a financial centre. The key legal counsel to both was Zebulon Lash of the law firm Blake, Lash, who was far and away Toronto's leading corporate counsel then, but the McCarthy, Osler foothold on the Cox and Mackenzie business would eventually blossom.[27]

The six principal McCarthy, Osler lawyers of 1882 became ten during the 1890s, keeping the firm among the largest in the city. No fewer than three of them, McCarthy, Osler and John Hoskin, were benchers of the Law Society.* By then they had as many as twenty-five employees, including the firm's long-time manager and accountant George Loveys, several male and female secretaries, a pool of law students, and other staff.

*As benchers, the partners did not always agree. In 1892, when Clara Brett Martin applied to become a student at the Law Society, McCarthy voted against the admission of women into legal studies. Osler and Hoskin voted in favour, and she was admitted.

The partnership's original offices had been in the Temple Chambers, 23 Toronto Street, at the corner of Toronto Street and Adelaide. In about 1893 McCarthy, Osler moved to the sixth floor of the Freehold Savings and Loan Building, just down the street at Adelaide and Victoria. The furnishings of nineteenth-century law offices were spartan by later standards, but the firm's early accounts for these premises include a few carpets and rugs amid the inventory of desks, cabinets, window blinds and letterpresses. A bill for telephone service was first included among the office overheads in 1883; typewriters are not mentioned until 1898. The firm had evidently maintained a small library from its foundation: In 1883 there were ninety volumes, including the *Revised Statutes of Ontario, Chitty on Pleading, Davidson's Conveyancing, Angle on Watercourses, Taylor on Titles, Smith's Mercantile Law* and Hubbell's *Legal Directory.*[28]

Firm income had risen spectacularly since 1877. Overheads remained relatively small, rarely amounting to 20 per cent of gross income. In 1888, 25 employees were paid a total of only $5,200, and rent payments for the firm's office were less than $2,000 in the 1890s. Meanwhile, the profits available for distribution to the partners rose from the $50,000-a-year range in the early 1880s to more than $70,000 for the late 1880s and to almost $90,000 in the early 1890s. Profits peaked at $102,000 in 1892, before levelling out at about $70,000 a year later in the decade. D'Alton McCarthy and B.B. Osler shared about 70 per cent of these profits. McCarthy's personal income from McCarthy & Osler alone averaged almost $24,000 a year during the 1880s and between $25,000 and $30,000 in the early 1890s.[29]

McCarthy was rich. The personal debts of the early 1880s could no longer have worried him much, though he always spent lavishly and poured his own money into political causes, and was thought by contemporaries to have amassed no great wealth. In any case, McCarthy always sought to live well. He "observed the niceties of life," a newspaper was soon to say, "...broad acres of land and bold horses and dogs and good friends." As well as developing his rural estate with its farm of pedigree livestock at Shanty Bay outside Barrie, he kept a large house in Ottawa for the parliamentary sessions. His Toronto home and principal residence was a substantial house on Beverley Street, where on many mornings he and his son, Lally, rode their horses out College Street to High Park and back.* Lally, who was sent for part of his schooling to Scotland, recalled that his father and other Canadian lawyers at the Privy Council "usually arranged to have their appeals set down for the July sittings of the Privy Council, so that they could combine business with pleasure," including the races at Ascot, the Buckingham Palace garden party, and "Canadian nights" at the Inns of Court.[30]

*McCarthy's household included his stepdaughter May Bernard, who had converted to Catholicism when she eloped with an Irish Catholic named Fitzgibbon. She later returned to the household with her daughter and became a Toronto society writer and columnist under the pen name "Lally Bernard."

Then, suddenly, the era of the founders ended.

On Sunday night, May 8, 1898, McCarthy left his home on Beverley Street, heading for Union Station and the night train to Ottawa for a meeting with Prime Minister Laurier, apparently to discuss joining the government. His coachman accompanied him, but McCarthy liked to drive, and he liked a horse with "life," in this case a high-stepping bay named Yukon. (Klondike, the second of a matched pair, had been left at the stable.) They were passing the Beverley Street Baptist Church at the corner of Beverley and Queen Streets when the church doors were suddenly flung open and Yukon was startled by the noise and light. The horse shied, and a wheel hit the curb. Taylor, the coachman, was thrown out, and the cart tipped over. McCarthy was caught in the wreck, his ribs smashed and one lung crushed. He was carried home, but he never regained consciousness, and he died on May 11. The death and funeral were national sensations. McCarthy was sixty-two.[31]

DALTON M'CARTHY SUCCUMBS TO HIS INJURIES

Dramatic Close of a Stirring Career Fraught With Big Events and Splendid Battles for the Welfare of Canada—An Eminent Canadian Struck Down in the Midst of a Busy Life.

Sketch of His Career and His Success in Politics and Law—Tributes to His Worth by Leaders in Parliament and by the Daily Papers in Toronto.

Dalton McCarthy died at 9 o'clock last night.

It was thought yesterday morning that his condition had considerably improved. But, during the thunderstorm in the afternoon, and the attendant rarefaction of the atmosphere, his breathing became troubled again. From that on, he was unconscious. The great Canadian statesman passed away, as if he had but fallen into a deeper slumber.

Death occurred so suddenly that there was hardly time to call the members of the family to the bedside. The cause of death was the pressure of fractured bone and cartilage upon the lungs. The heart beat for some moments after respiration had ceased.

The physicians were at the bedside continuously from the time of the relapse in the afternoon.

The members of the family have received many messages of condolence-

the loss which the House and country will sustain by his death."

The House adjourned and the members crowded down to the center of the floor and conversed in subdued tones upon the occurrence.

TRIBUTES TO THE DEAD.

What Local Newspapers Have to Say of the Late Mr. McCarthy and His Character and Career.

(The Globe.)

A National Loss—Canada's loss is great by the death of Dalton McCarthy. He died a private member of Parliament. If he had been a more docile party follower he could have passed out of the weariness and clamor of life the leader of a great party, perhaps Prime Minister. There can be hardly any doubt that after Sir John Macdonald, Sir John Thompson and Mr. McCarthy were the two ablest men that had place in the councils of the Conservative party during the last quarter of a century. How tragic the fate of both! Clear, frank, resolute,

The death of D'Alton McCarthy on May 11, 1898, was headline news in Toronto the following day.

After his partner died, B.B. Osler apparently shouldered even more of the burden of the firm, including some of McCarthy's big cases. His appointment books for the months after McCarthy's death show an unrelenting series of court dates and business trips, and his health collapsed under the strain. Osler suffered a nervous breakdown in the spring of 1900. While taking a rest cure in Atlantic City, he died of a heart attack in February 1901. He was sixty-one.[32]

Until the deaths of McCarthy and Osler, their law firm was a pre-eminent Canadian litigation practice with a substantial but quite secondary corporate practice. The stature of the firm had been tightly linked to the courtroom prowess, personal connections and national reputations of its two leaders. With their sudden deaths, a redirection became inevitable.

A SECOND GENERATION: McCARTHY & OSLER | 2

WITH THE DEATHS OF McCarthy and Osler, titular leadership in the firm passed to John Hoskin, a contemporary of theirs who had been a founding partner in 1877. Hoskin had a large chancery practice in wills and estates and advised many corporate clients. He maintained a separate practice as Ontario's first Official Guardian, representing children in cases where their legal interests might differ from those of their parents or other guardians. Hoskin was assisted and eventually succeeded as Official Guardian by Frederick Harcourt, who had been Hoskin's student when the firm began and became a solicitor in 1880 and a barrister in 1886. The firm became McCarthy, Osler, Hoskin & Harcourt in 1902 when another founder, Adam Creelman, left to become corporate counsel to Canadian Pacific Railway in Montreal. (Creelman had handled the Canada North-West Land Company file for McCarthy, Osler. Edward Beatty, who articled with him at McCarthy, Osler, later became president of the railroad.) In 1901 the firm recruited Christopher Robinson, a much-admired but elderly barrister, to take up some of its litigation files. When Robinson died in 1905, Wallace Nesbitt, recently resigned from a brief and discontented stint on the Supreme Court of Canada, replaced him as counsel.* But neither man had the potential to fill the shoes of McCarthy or Osler. No one in the firm had the stature or business-getting abilities of the two dead partners.[33]

In the first years of the 1900s it must have seemed that the firm of D'Alton McCarthy and B.B. Osler was rapidly shrinking away. As litigation clients turned to new stars of the bar, income slipped from $75,000 in 1900 to just $36,000 in 1906. Midcareer partners Charles McInnes and William B. Raymond left to join other firms in 1904 and 1906 respectively. Hoskin retired soon afterwards, after securing the departure of another partner, Andrew M. Stewart, known as "Deadman" because he never smiled. Stewart had briefly been D'Alton McCarthy's favourite junior and "devil," but he enjoyed a second profession as a gambler and often travelled to London for high-stakes card games at the St. James Club in Piccadilly. McCarthy had seen no problem in this, but Hoskin was old-fashioned.[34]

The deaths of the two founders soon forced a rapid transfer of leadership to the second generations of the Osler and McCarthy families. Although McCarthy's Toronto law firm had begun as an association of unrelated lawyers, in 1900 a successful Canadian law firm was still usually a family business to be shared with one's heirs. Lawyers had always practised with relatives and friends, and the emergence of larger corporate-law firms had not much changed the tradition of family enterprises. The largest Toronto law firm at the turn of the century, Beatty, Blackstock, was still essentially that of the Gooderham and Worts family business. The Blake firm employed several sons and nephews of the Blake brothers who had founded it, and it also included Zebulon Lash's sons, several Cassels and eventually several Oslers. As nephews and sons of D'Alton McCarthy and B.B. Osler took up legal careers, they, too, gravitated to their family firm.[35]

*As counsel, Nesbitt received office space and support from McCarthy, Osler. The firm gave him first refusal on all counsel work it did not do in-house and received all the solicitor's work on his cases. Otherwise, Nesbitt retained his own practice and income and received no share of firm income. Robinson's agreement would have been similar.

The leaders of this second generation were Henry Smith Osler, a nephew of B.B., and Leighton Goldie McCarthy, a nephew of D'Alton. They quickly became almost as dominant in the firm as their uncles had been. "H.S."—he continued the Osler tradition of relying on initials—was a son of Judge Featherston Osler. Born in 1862, he had joined his uncle's firm in 1889 and was not yet forty when B.B. Osler died. Leighton McCarthy was even younger. Born in 1869 and raised in Barrie, he had joined McCarthy, Osler in 1891, when D'Alton McCarthy invited him to switch his articles from the Barrie firm of McCarthy, Pepler in appreciation of Leighton's work in the North Simcoe election campaign. Leighton initially viewed his formidable uncle with some awe. He was both alarmed and honoured when D'Alton McCarthy considered running him against a Conservative cabinet minister in an 1895 by-election. In 1898, however, twenty-nine-year-old Leighton ran and was elected in the by-election held to fill his uncle's seat. Like his uncle, Leighton McCarthy sat as an independent member, working hard on local developments such as Collingwood harbour, promoting low tariffs and opposing French-language rights. He also did a good deal of political work for Toronto businesses, later recalling proudly his 1904 bill to incorporate the Grand Trunk Pacific, a new transcontinental railroad venture.

Leighton became closer to Laurier's Liberals than his uncle had been, but his support remained conditional. When Interior Minister Clifford Sifton quit the Laurier cabinet in 1905 in opposition to the French-language guarantees Laurier favoured for the new provinces of Alberta and Saskatchewan, Leighton McCarthy picked up his uncle's old cause and supported Sifton's successful efforts to block bilingual rights in the new provinces. Yet Laurier cultivated him. In 1908, when McCarthy chose not to run for re-election, citing pressure of work, Laurier expressed his regret and persuaded McCarthy to campaign for the Liberals in the Simcoe region. In 1911, when much of the Toronto business community rose up against Laurier's plan for free trade with the United States, Leighton McCarthy resisted the Bay Street consensus. He helped organize the Liberal campaign in Ontario and he stood for election again in North Simcoe, this time as a Liberal advocating his uncle's old free-trade policies. Amid a Liberal rout, particularly in Ontario, McCarthy was narrowly defeated, and he never returned to elective politics.* [36]

After Creelman left and Hoskin retired, the new Osler and the new McCarthy had become the firm's leaders and largest earners. Soon they were drawing 55 per cent of the profits of a six-partner business. More important, they had reversed the revenue decline. Profits rose to $60,000 in 1910 and as high as $100,000 before the start of the First World War. The decline in the number of lawyers at the firm also stopped. D'Alton Lally McCarthy, D'Alton Jr.'s only son, had joined the practice in 1895. H.S. Osler's brother Britton joined in 1897. Leighton McCarthy brought in his brother Frank in 1905, and Wellington Ault Cameron, a former secretary of the Law Society, joined in 1910. There were no further departures for several years. In 1913 McCarthy, Osler left its premises in the Freehold Savings and Loan Building and, after a brief stay at the Canadian Pacific Building at the southeast corner of King Street and Yonge Street, moved across Yonge to the eighth floor of the Dominion Bank Building.

In the first decade of the twentieth century Lally McCarthy began to revive the litigation tradition at McCarthy, Osler. He had begun "doing the agency work": handling business in Toronto's courts and court offices referred to the firm from lawyers around Ontario. Gradually the "general counsel work" that had been such a large part of the firm's business fell to Lally. With guidance from Wallace Nesbitt, he found courtroom practice gratifying and rapidly became a familiar figure on the legal circuit. He would "drive to his office in a high-wheeled dog cart, attend the City Hall, and handle eight examinations for discovery in two hours," said a contemporary, and his gift for putting any case before the judges in its most attractive light was soon noted.

*As late as 1916, Laurier was hoping to persuade Leighton to run again—or, if not him, Lally McCarthy. "If we cannot have a nephew of D'Alton McCarthy in the next Parliament, can we not have his son?" But Leighton broke with the Liberals in the conscription crisis of 1917, and Lally showed no interest in politics.

One early client, Toronto Street Railway, "proved of great advantage to me," Lally McCarthy recalled. William Mackenzie's TSR had acquired the transit monopoly from the city of Toronto in 1891 and ran all the streetcars (first horse-drawn, then electric) in the city. A McCarthy, Osler client since 1893, TSR was frequently in the courts defending against liability claims from traffic and pedestrian accidents, and Lally McCarthy took on an increasing volume of this work. Notice of his courtroom successes led to more opportunities. He began defending Grand Trunk Railway's liability cases and then those of the City of Toronto. After one unhappy experience prosecuting a murder, he stuck to civil actions and general litigation practice. He represented the Toronto *Star* in many libel actions. At some point he was retained by the Canadian Medical Protective Association.

The CMPA had been founded in 1901 to defend doctors against malpractice claims. When its Ottawa legal counsel, Francis Chrysler, first retained Lally McCarthy is unknown but it seems to have been early in the twentieth century, and Lally gradually became its principal defence counsel in Ontario. Because the CMPA was committed to defending its doctor members' reputations, it rarely sought out-of-court settlements of claims as a commercial insurer might. As a result, it was a valuable source of litigation work. Securing the CMPA as a client made medical-malpractice suits a staple of the McCarthy firm's litigation department for many decades.

Lally McCarthy seems not to have inherited his father's intense political commitments. At university he had studied divinity but his main interest seemed to be horses—prompting his father to ask whether he should send him into the church or set him up in a livery stable. He chose the law instead and articled in Barrie to get experience in general practice. Once established in Toronto, he was active in the militia, in the Toronto Hunt Club and in competitive cricket and polo. By the First World War he had married Lady Mary Robinson, a niece of the firm's former counsel Sir Christopher Robinson, and he was a gregarious figure in the clubbable circuits of Toronto business and society, with a well-known taste for the good life. By then he had a large and secure litigation practice and was a King's Counsel and a bencher of the Law Society.

Even as Lally McCarthy rebuilt the litigation practice, H.S. Osler and Leighton McCarthy were reorienting the firm's business decisively away from its previous emphasis on litigation. Leighton had done several fire insurance cases in the 1890s and briefly aspired to be "a leading counsel," but by the turn of the century both he and H.S. Osler were focussing their interests on their corporate clients. B.B. Osler and D'Alton McCarthy had also brought in corporate work, of course, but it was their nephews who underlined the primacy of corporate and commercial work as the fundamental business of the firm. It was an opportune time to do so: at the turn of the century, amid the long Laurier boom, the Toronto corporate world was undergoing a significant transition. Leighton McCarthy's career was intimately tied to these changes.

Toronto had had wealthy businessmen, industrialists and entrepreneurs for a long time. The Eatons, Masseys and Gooderhams ranked as established fortunes. Around the end of the nineteenth century, however, businessmen who had started in retail or industrial enterprises were moving into finance and investment. The city was developing financial sophistication as its business leaders founded or built up banks, trust companies, insurance companies, brokerage and investment houses, real estate firms and even international investment projects. The geographic range, economic scope and institutional complexity of their businesses expanded mightily. As this professionalization of Toronto business continued, their need for close involvement with their legal counsel also grew constantly.

"The old family lawyer... has become a thing of the past," declared Toronto lawyer and judge William Riddell in 1907. "His place has been taken by the business man, the acute pulse-feeler of the money market... more in the world and less in his chambers." Lawyers filled the role of management consultants, not just providing legal services but helping to design the structures and practices of business, helping to run them and often investing in them as well. Zebulon Lash, of the Blake Lash firm, was the leader in this kind of corporate practice in Toronto, counselling most of the city's leading financiers, including Joseph Flavelle, William Mackenzie and George Augustus Cox. "You told me it was not a bare legal opinion you wanted," he reminded Flavelle, "but it was my personal opinion of what it would be right for you to do." Lash eventually became an executive of Mackenzie's Canadian Northern Railway and grew immensely wealthy, less from his legal practice than from the business investments that grew out of it. Leighton McCarthy was about to enter into a similar practice, "more in the world and less in his chambers."[37]

Leighton McCarthy, lawyer, businessman and statesman, who led McCarthy & McCarthy from 1916 into the 1940s.

George Cox, who was soon to play a vital part in Leighton McCarthy's career, personified the evolution that was taking place in Toronto business. Initially a telegraph operator in Peterborough, Cox built a fortune as Canada Life's most successful insurance salesman and soon conceived the ambition to own the company himself. After founding the mortgage company Central Canada Loan and Savings, he moved to Toronto and invested heavily in its burgeoning finance and securities sector. He rapidly acquired the presidency not only of Canada Life but also of Canadian Bank of Commerce, National Trust, Dominion Securities, Imperial Life and

Manufacturers Life. All his companies did substantial amounts of business with each other.[38]

It has been argued that in the era when financial institutions like these were new and reliable investment information was scarce, entrepreneurs like Cox would inevitably do business with their own family and friends. Nevertheless, cronyism in companies that were entrusted with ever-growing amounts of other people's money generated a rising tide of criticism. Exposés in the press, prompted by insurance scandals in New York, led Prime Minister Laurier to establish the 1906 Royal Commission on Life Insurance. Cox (whom Laurier had appointed to the Canadian Senate in 1897) became its key target. The Commission noted how, in shifting Canada Life from mortgage lending into securities investments, Cox had made Canada Life the largest single purchaser of securities offered by his own Dominion Securities (which often put the funds raised into other Cox enterprises). Rather than investing for the benefit of the insurance policyholders, it was charged, Cox was using their money as a source of cheap financing for his family's enrichment.

Cox put up a bold front at the Royal Commission, insisting that it was natural, even inevitable, that companies like Canada Life and Dominion Securities (each the largest in its field) would do business with each other. Nevertheless, Manufacturers Life, which Cox controlled, admitted making improper investments in the enterprises of his partner, Henry Pellatt, and Cox-run companies were shown to have poured shareholders' and policyholders' money into the investment house run by Cox's son-in-law, A.E. Ames, even when Ames was close to insolvent and unable to raise funds on the open market. In 1907 the Commission declared, in words aimed directly at Cox: "Insurance companies tend to become powerful aggregations of money with financial rather than insurance aims," serving the interests of their owners over those of policyholders. "The conflict of Mr. Cox's interest with his duty is so apparent that the care of the insurance funds could not always have been the sole consideration."[39]

The Commission's findings encouraged the trend to "mutualize" insurance companies, making them owned by their policyholders. Canada Life's charter was revised, policyholders were guaranteed board representation and new restrictions were placed on insurance company investments. Many leaders of the Toronto financial community had been quicker than George Cox to accept the need for new business standards and more sensitive to conflicts of interest, fiduciary obligations and the rights of shareholders and policyholders. When Cox seemed inclined to continue to put his family interests first, business associates began to draw back from him. Joseph Flavelle, like Cox a Peterborough Methodist who had moved from industry into finance, concluded that "Cox does not possess the moral qualities which enable him to understand trustee relationships," and he resigned from the board of Cox's Canada Life. In 1911, lawyer Zebulon Lash did the same. By 1914, when both Cox and his eldest son died and control of Canada Life had passed to Herbert Cox, the insurance company sought to distance itself from Senator Cox's older style of doing business. It sought both new business methods and new legal counsel to re-establish the company's reputation. Leighton McCarthy was the new counsel to whom Canada Life turned, and he began to transform the relationship between McCarthy, Osler and Canada Life.[40]

D'Alton McCarthy had done legal work for Canada Life since 1876 and Leighton's father, Dr. John McCarthy, had been the insurance company's medical examiner in Barrie since 1878. At least since 1880, the Toronto firm had held a Canada Life retainer.* In the early 1900s, however, Leighton McCarthy, already both a well-regarded corporate counsel and an Ottawa insider, became much more important to the insurance company. At the time of the Royal Commission, it was McCarthy who helped the insurance company prepare its submissions, and he shepherded the revisions to its charter through Parliament in 1909. He later recalled that "Senator Cox, then

*B.B. Osler also had a Canada Life connection. Widowed in 1885, he married a daughter of firm president A.G. Ramsay in 1897. But that would not have helped the law firm much: Cox drove Ramsay out when he gained control of the insurance company in 1899.

in trouble with some members of his board, invited me to join the board of the Canada Life in 1909." McCarthy stayed on when Lash and others left and when Cox died. In 1916 he became the insurance company's corporate solicitor.* [41]

As McCarthy became more involved in Canada Life legal work, however, Canada Life began to vanish from the accounts of McCarthy, Osler. The partnership agreements of McCarthy, Osler had always permitted firm members to retain income derived from companies in which they were directors. Though this had probably been intended to cover director's fees and honoraria, Leighton McCarthy evidently interpreted it broadly, and he seems to have made Canada Life a personal client rather than a firm one. He may have been receiving Canada Life shares or options in lieu of actual payment, for he rapidly became an important shareholder in Cox companies such as Canada Life, Central Canada Loan and Savings and National Trust.[42]

Canada Life was not the only client Leighton McCarthy was cultivating in the decade 1906–16. "About the same time," he later recalled, "I had the good fortune to become associated with Mr. Arthur Vining Davis and other prominent Pittsburgh citizens in the introduction of the aluminum industry into Canada." Davis's Aluminum Company of America (Alcoa) had been drawn to Canada by its potential to provide abundant electrical power, and its Canadian subsidiary, Northern Aluminum, had been producing aluminum on the St-Maurice River in Quebec since 1900. Around 1908, McCarthy advised Davis on an ambitious plan to develop dams and aluminum smelters on the St. Lawrence River near Cornwall in eastern Ontario. That project fell through, though another McCarthy client, Cedar Rapids Power Company, did dam the river to supply Alcoa's Massena, New York, aluminum smelter. Davis eventually turned to Quebec's Saguenay River, where the American financier James Duke launched a massive hydroelectric development after the

*At first McCarthy was co-solicitor with Alexander Bruce, an elderly Hamilton lawyer who had advised the company when it was based in Hamilton. Bruce's son was a Canada Life manager.

In 1927 at Arvida, Quebec, Leighton McCarthy (right) joined his American industrialist client Arthur Vining Davis (left), Quebec premier Louis-Alexandre Taschereau (third from left) and local dignitaries for the opening of the Saguenay region's first aluminum smelter.

First World War. It was Davis's Alcoa that made the Saguenay power project successful by opening the world's largest aluminum smelter at Arvida, Quebec, in 1925. (Arvida, a new town, was named from the first letters of Arthur Vining Davis's three names.)

One of McCarthy's contributions to Alcoa was helping to ensure access to the bauxite resources of the Demerara River valley of British Guiana, then a British colony on the Caribbean coast of South America. The British government had stipulated that any exploitation of the resources of British Guiana must take place within British territory. McCarthy helped confirm (perhaps through his Ottawa connections) that Alcoa's smelter in Canada would fulfil this requirement—a crucial requirement for the development of the Canadian aluminum industry. In 1916 McCarthy became a director of the Demerara Bauxite Company, the Alcoa-controlled Guianese company that would supply bauxite to the Canadian smelters.

In 1928 Davis's Alcoa reorganized its international subsidiaries and incorporated Alcan, the Aluminum Company of Canada. Alcan's smelting operations were on the Saguenay and St-Maurice Rivers in Quebec, its global sales and marketing operations were handled from Montreal and final authority still rested with the parent company in Pittsburgh. But Alcan was incorporated in Leighton McCarthy's Toronto law office, and that office remained Alcan's official head office address until the 1940s. McCarthy and his office manager, J.F. Van Lane, were two of the three Canadian directors of Alcan. (The third was Montreal lawyer Aimé Geoffrion of Geoffrion, Prud'homme, a law firm with close links to Quebec premier Louis-Alexandre Taschereau, who had facilitated the Saguenay development.)

McCarthy's growing expertise in electrical power for industry attracted another American company, Union Carbide. Union Carbide, like Alcoa, was seeking sites with abundant hydroelectric power for the new calcium carbide process it had pioneered. In 1914 McCarthy incorporated Union Carbide Canada, which made him a director. It and other electrochemical companies built processing and manufacturing plants on the Niagara River and in Toronto, and they became long-time clients. Union Carbide, like the aluminum company, was also interested in Guianese sources of raw material, particularly manganese.

Nineteen sixteen seems to have been the crucial year for Leighton McCarthy's successful consolidation of a network of business interests and corporate legal clients. He had already secured the Canadian legal work of Alcoa and Union Carbide. That year he was elected to the board of Demerara Bauxite and appointed corporate solicitor to Canada Life. He still acted for lumber companies, insurance agencies and other old clients, as well as newer ones secured through his father-in-law, the banker and Muskoka Mills president Alexander H. Campbell.* These made a roster of clients large and secure enough to provide a

*Leighton McCarthy married Muriel Drummond Campbell in 1900. The Campbell family's cottage, Longuissa, on Muskoka Mills land on Georgian Bay, became a McCarthy summer place for generations. Leighton McCarthy died there in 1952.

lifetime's legal work. That year, the McCarthys and the Oslers went their separate ways. After almost forty years, McCarthy, Osler, Hoskin & Harcourt became McCarthy & McCarthy on one side and Osler, Hoskin & Harcourt on the other.

Law firms rarely split without acrimony, but almost nothing seems to have been recorded about personal relationships among the lawyers of McCarthy, Osler during the fifteen-year period when H.S. Osler and Leighton McCarthy shared the leadership of the firm. It seems completely unremembered whether friendship or rivalry prevailed among the McCarthys and the Oslers during their years in partnership or at the time of their parting. Lally McCarthy later described B.B. Osler as "a second father" and acknowledged no animosity between the families, but his memoir always slides over difficulties and rarely has an unkind word for anyone.

Curtis Cole, the historian of Osler, Hoskin, has pointed to the friction that would have been provoked by the small revenues the partnership was receiving from Canada Life when Leighton McCarthy was deeply involved in that business. An internal history of McCarthy & McCarthy written in 1976 (with the participation of partners who had known Leighton McCarthy) identified Canada Life as the client whose business persuaded McCarthy to launch his own firm, and Cole's suggestion that the other partners must have resented Leighton's hoarding of an increasingly valuable file seems entirely plausible.

It is clear, however, that even if the Canada Life account was the flashpoint, as many as three separate practice groups had been developing within McCarthy, Osler for several years: the Osler brothers', Leighton's, and Lally's.

By 1916, the brothers H.S. Osler and Britton Osler handled the needs of an impressive roster of commercial clients, ranging from Dominion Bank, headed by their uncle Sir Edmund Osler, to International Nickel, one of several American subsidiaries that had been directed to them through their relationships with two influential Wall Street law firms, Cravath,

Henderson and Sullivan, Cromwell. Leighton McCarthy's crucial clients, however, were now the Cox family businesses, particularly Canada Life, and the Canadian enterprises of Arthur Vining Davis and Union Carbide, and these interests drew McCarthy as much into corporate administration as legal practice. Lally McCarthy, meanwhile, had developed his own growing litigation practice in accident and medical liability cases, libel law and general corporate litigation. No stark conflicts are evident between these client groups, but not much linked them, either.

Each of these groups of clients apparently had a personal relationship with the Oslers or one of the McCarthys, as much as with "the firm." Even in this large "downtown" partnership, that is, clients' links to the firm remained personal; they expected to consult a particular lawyer as much as the law firm. In that context, partners could still walk away from a firm without much danger of imperilling their individual client relationships. Whatever the state of personal relations among the McCarthy, Osler partners, and whatever tensions had been provoked by Leighton McCarthy's relationship with Canada Life, it seems to have proven quite simple to split the partnership along family lines when the 1913 Articles of Partnership expired on May 31, 1916.

Any resentments that attended the split should have been eased by the fact that both new firms benefited financially. Osler, Hoskin & Harcourt retained most of the old firm's large corporate clients and saw a revenue drop of barely 10 per cent while shedding half its active partners (until the split, the three McCarthys had been entitled to 53 per cent of profits). The incomes of the remaining Osler partners jumped. Meanwhile, the reorganized McCarthy firm, with Leighton's new cluster of corporate clients and Lally's growing litigation accounts, soon had a larger income than the united firm had had. In 1918, net profits of the two firms together amounted to almost $150,000 ($84,000 at McCarthys, $65,000 at Oslers); McCarthy, Osler had never earned more than $104,000. The partners in the two firms were apparently more prosperous separately than they had been as one.

LEIGHTON'S FIRM | 3

AT THE END OF May 1916, the McCarthys moved out of the McCarthy, Osler offices in the Dominion Bank Building. (The bank was then the Osler brothers' client, and the Osler, Hoskin firm remained in the bank building until 1962.) On June 1, McCarthy & McCarthy opened for business just across the street, in the Canada Life Building at 46 King Street West. Three McCarthys, the brothers Leighton and Frank (then in the army and soon to leave for service in Europe) and their cousin Lally, owned the firm, but they chose, knowingly or not, to resume the name that D'Alton Sr. and D'Alton Jr. had briefly used in Barrie in the 1870s. "McCarthy & McCarthy" would endure long after the last McCarthy had left the firm.

The new McCarthy offices were a suite of rooms on the ground floor of the Canada Life Building, with three offices for the lawyers and a Dickensian chamber for the students, with tall, sloping desks and high stools. The McCarthys had left their library with Osler, Hoskin and for many years relied on the Canada Life library in the bowels of the building. Much later, this original McCarthy office suite was recalled as "dark and cramped" and "dirty and dingy" by lawyers who had begun there. Still, a female client who consulted Lally McCarthy recalled "the great mahogany doorway of McCarthy & McCarthy" and, inside, an atmosphere of "dignified quiet, almost gloom, with the women typists in their 'decent black,' offset by collars and cuffs of white."[43]

The old Canada Life Building on King Street in Toronto was McCarthy & McCarthy's home from 1916 to 1931.

There was one employed lawyer, Wilfrid Cox (a nephew of Senator Cox), and two students, William Beattie, who stayed on, and R.G. McFarlane, who did not. J.F. Van Lane, who was Leighton's personal assistant, became the firm's office manager. He would remain with McCarthys until 1947, keeping its financial records in his meticulous, tiny handwriting. The firm evidently began with three secretaries, Miss Finnerty, Miss Pierce and Miss Clarke, and one male employee, Jack Barlow. Other long-time staff would include Bert Laycock and May McLaren, who joined later in 1916 and was Frank McCarthy's secretary into the 1950s. Miss McLaren would later recall that on her twenty-fifth anniversary with the firm "Mr. Frank said, 'This is rather a special day, isn't it?' "—the longest personal conversation she ever had with him. When he had letters about a divorce to dictate, Frank McCarthy called in Laycock, the only man on the secretarial staff.

Several more lawyers soon joined. William Terry, hired as an office boy in 1917 at the age of twelve (he claimed to be fourteen), started studying law in 1923 and stayed with the firm when he was called to the bar in 1928. Terry eventually focussed on real estate work, particularly on mortgage transactions referred from Canada Life and from National Trust (of which Leighton McCarthy was also president). In 1919, the legal staff included H. Armour Harrison, Robert Laidlaw (later an appeal-court judge and the father of McCarthy litigation leader Douglas Laidlaw) and William Beattie, "Mr. McCarthy's right hand man," who worked on Canada Life matters and eventually moved over to join the insurance company.

Beattie was assisted for several years in his estates and real estate work for Canada Life by Edith Sheppard, a student of Leighton's who was one of the first female lawyers at any "downtown" Canadian law firm when she arrived as a student in 1921. Like most of the firm's young lawyers, Sheppard benefited from a family connection to the McCarthy firm: her wealthy family owned Georgian Bay Lumber Company, a McCarthy client since the Barrie days. Nevertheless, Leighton McCarthy described her as "the best student we ever had" to another woman who came seeking an articling position. Sheppard stayed with the firm from her call to the bar in 1925 until she gave up practice to marry in 1929. William Terry then took over the real estate work. A second female lawyer, Marion Darte, the daughter of a Union Carbide executive, practised at McCarthys from 1935 to 1947.[44]

Edith Sheppard, one of the first women to practise in a "downtown" law firm in Canada, worked at McCarthy & McCarthy from 1921 to 1929. She ceased to practise law in 1929 when she went to India to marry Captain A.J. Revell of the Indian Army at Bombay. Edith Sheppard Revell died at Bangalore, India, in 1934, leaving two small children.

William "Duke" West had joined in 1920, straight from law school after wartime service in Europe. His first task was to "junior" Lally McCarthy—to carry his bags, keep his schedule and help prepare his cases. West soon ceased going to court, but he continued to administer Canadian Medical Protective Association (CMPA) files for McCarthys for several decades and gradually took charge of work for other corporate clients. Succeeding West as Lally's junior was Salter A. Hayden. Hayden, a Catholic from Ottawa, had been practising in Toronto for a couple of years in a firm called Foy, Knox, Monahan, & Keogh, whose clients included Home Bank. In 1923, when Home Bank collapsed, Lally hired Hayden to assist him in the prosecution of senior officers of the bank. "Lally was bright, but despised preparation" (in the words of John Robinette, who admired him), and he liked juniors who could give him the gist of a case very rapidly at the last minute. Hayden excelled at that demanding task and learned a lot in the process.

Beyond Lally's practice, much of the firm's work flowed from Leighton McCarthy's executive role at Canada Life Assurance. In 1928 Leighton acquired majority control of Canada Life from the last of the Coxes and became its president. As Leighton was drawn even more into management of the insurance company, Frank McCarthy became the law firm's working head.* He focussed on Canada Life business and became an expert in insurance law and in the insurance company's mortgage business. (Salter Hayden recalled that McCarthy & McCarthy was sometimes referred to simply as Canada Life's legal department.) Though Alcoa and Union Carbide still paid substantial retainers and many small clients also used the firm, the book of business was not large enough to place McCarthys among Toronto's five largest law practices in 1932, when Oslers (with 14 lawyers and revenues of $200,000) was second only to Blakes in size and had double the revenues of McCarthys (nine lawyers, $93,000).[45] The firm's most significant revenue sources were Leighton's corporate clients and Lally's litigation practice. And McCarthys was about to lose Lally as well as Leighton.

Lally McCarthy was regarded as one of "the big three" among Toronto litigators of the 1920s and enjoyed a large and prominent practice. "He usually has quite important cases, which makes it interesting being in

*Frank McCarthy's 1917 marriage to a daughter of financier Sir William Mackenzie seemed likely to cement another valuable client relationship, but by then Mackenzie's commercial empire had collapsed and he was personally deep in debt. The main work McCarthys got was the winding up of his burdened estate after his death in 1923. Bertha Mackenzie was a Catholic, and the couple married in a Catholic service, but Frank McCarthy remained an Anglican and their son was raised as an Anglican.

the office, because you know everything that goes on behind the scenes," wrote Edith Sheppard in 1925. But the role of the litigation generalist was already a vexed one in corporate firms that were increasingly focussed on solicitors' practice. Not only at McCarthys, but at many of the big Toronto firms, it was the corporate specialists, not the litigators, who managed the large ongoing files. For his part, Lally had little trouble securing litigation briefs that had little to do with his cousins' corporate practice. Perhaps inevitably, these tensions were expressed in disputes over allocations. In 1916 Leighton and Lally had agreed they would take equal shares in the new firm (Frank's share was much smaller), but in 1926 Lally accepted nine shares to Leighton's twelve and Frank's four. This seems to have proved no more satisfactory. In 1928, a year before the 1926 agreement was to expire, the three tried a new arrangement.

Everyone admired Lally McCarthy's courtroom style. Legend has it that he once, after a quick briefing, began arguing the wrong side of a case. When warned, he continued unperturbed: "Your Honour, those will be my opponent's arguments, and these are the reasons to reject them."

Leighton McCarthy had just become president of Canada Life and was more than ever a business executive and investor rather than a practising lawyer, but "his" clients were still the firm's most valuable ones and he did not relinquish his very substantial income from the practice. That year the three partners agreed on a radical new financial agreement. For a year, each of them would keep all the revenues he brought into the practice. All they would share as partners were the overheads and salary expenses of the firm (of which Leighton accepted the largest share: five-eighths to Lally's two-eighths).

In the late twentieth century, lawyers nicknamed revenue divisions like this one "eat what you kill" policies. They were often symptomatic of firms where partners hoarded their own client files and might well go their separate ways. Indeed, in 1929, with McCarthy & McCarthy looking ahead to moving to the new Canada Life Building at Queen and University when it was completed, Lally McCarthy announced that he preferred to stay "downtown" and left the firm—even though it would be two more years before McCarthy & McCarthy actually moved. Out on his own, his litigation practice continued to bring him as many clients and cases as ever. He went on to be president of the Canadian Bar Association and wartime treasurer of the Law Society of Upper Canada.

The parting was superficially amicable, and Lally continued to take litigation files referred from McCarthy & McCarthy, particularly on the CMPA file. But Lally McCarthy did not work out a "counsel" relationship with his cousins, as prominent barristers often did with leading commercial firms. Salter Hayden, who in 1929 was unsure whether Lally expected to take him along, recalled being told fiercely by Leighton that McCarthy & McCarthy was not going to go under just because Lally was leaving. Hayden, who was already generating work of his own, stayed. As part of the reorganization that followed Lally's departure, Hayden, Armour Harrison and William Beattie became the first non-McCarthy partners in the firm in November 1929. A more traditional revenue-sharing allocation was restored.*

In 1931 the firm moved to a ground floor suite with its own entrance at Canada Life's landmark new building at University and Queen, just across from Osgoode Hall (the home of the superior courts, the law society and the law school) and the registry office. The Canada Life Building was the last

*Many years later, Beverley Matthews, a McCarthy loyalist to his fingertips, seemed to betray just a touch of satisfaction in recalling that Armstrong & Sinclair, the small firm Lally joined (with Kenneth Morden, the junior he took with him), "did not take very good care of him." Lally eventually became counsel to McMillan, Binch, where future chief justice of Ontario William Howland and others began their careers as his juniors.

large commercial building to be added to Toronto's skyline before the Depression took hold. Despite Lally McCarthy's show of disapproval, it was a very good address. In the 1930s the big insurance firms and their headquarters still had the kind of influence and visibility in the financial districts of Toronto and Montreal that later passed to the banks and the bank towers.

The Canada Life Building, a Toronto landmark on University Avenue and home to McCarthy & McCarthy from 1931 to 1968.

Corporate-law firms with substantial clients rode out the Depression better than most lawyers or, indeed, most businesses. Histories of Blakes and Oslers suggest those firms suffered relatively small and brief declines in income during the 1930s, balanced by reduced costs and wage cuts. McCarthys' net income did decline, from about $95,000 a year in the later 1920s to about $60,000 in the first half of the 1930s, but a substantial part of that reflected Lally's departure. Canada Life's retainer was unchanged, and the firm continued to hire lawyers and take on students at about the same rate (a 10-per-cent wage cut to staff was instituted in 1932). One boon for the firm's bottom line was Leighton McCarthy's decision in 1930 to take a much-reduced annual stipend instead of his partnership draw. With both Leighton and Lally out of the income pool, Frank McCarthy's income actually increased, from about $15,000 to about $20,000 a year. His new partners' earnings remained under $10,000 a year each, still a very handsome income in the 1930s.

During the Depression, McCarthy & McCarthy hired three lawyers who would have great influence over many decades. Beverley Matthews, who had had a summer job at the firm in 1926 and then articled there, was hired when he was called to the bar in 1930. James Walker joined two years later, and in 1936 John Blain came in as a student. It cannot be said that brilliant recruiting secured these three; hiring at McCarthys, indeed at all Canadian law firms, remained haphazard in this era, at least by comparison with leading American law firms.

Top Wall Street partnerships had long had their screening and training done for them by the handful of elite American law schools, but some American firms were already beginning to scrutinize transcripts as closely as social pedigrees. "Since law is an intellectual business, we want to find men of high quality," said a leader of the rising Houston firm Baker & Botts, describing how in the 1920s it began seeking out top students at law schools around the southwestern United States. In New York the "Cravath system," developed by Paul Cravath early in the century, had been taken up by several leading firms. By the end of the First World War, Cravath, Henderson not only sought out top graduates but also followed the "up-or-out" system, in which new partners were selected exclusively from among the associates and any associate who did not become a partner within about six years left the firm. At comparable Canadian firms, including McCarthys, lawyers often remained as employees for twenty years or more.[46]

Of the four men who would dominate McCarthy & McCarthy in the mid-twentieth century, Salter Hayden was non-establishment, a Catholic hired because he was good in court and shared Lally McCarthy's enthusiasm for horse racing. John Blain was a poor kid from east Toronto who was hired virtually off the street, straight from high school.* Beverley Matthews came from a well-to-do, private-school Toronto upbringing, but he had found his way to McCarthys

*Until the 1950s a high school graduate could enter the three-year program at Osgoode Hall, then Ontario's only law school, after two years of articling in a law firm and become a lawyer without any university experience. Blain followed that route and was called to the bar in 1941. A friend recalled that he barely owned a change of clothes in those years.

mostly because a friend played tennis with Armour Harrison. His job there was secure before he won the law school gold medal. James Walker had family money and an Oxford degree and had been called to the English bar, but he was introduced at McCarthys through a casual acquaintance and was hired after "minimal discussion," when he knew almost nothing of Canadian law.* All four became highly accomplished lawyers and made enormous contributions to the firm. Their arrivals, however, reflected luck more than planning on the part of their new employer.

"The practice was diverse: real estate, litigation, estates, some bank and commercial," was how Walker later recalled the firm in the 1930s. "Tax played a much less significant part, if only because there was much less tax, and the legislators still thought that tax law should be relatively intelligible. When Matthews and I took on a secured bond issue in the late thirties, we were unable to find any precedent in the firm and concluded the firm had never done one."

Beverley Matthews recalled the thirties as an era of "doing everything we could to keep alive," but at the end of the 1930s McCarthy & McCarthy still had the key ingredient of a leading law firm: a handful of big, steady corporate clients and some litigation strength. For most downtown firms, a bank was the best such client. For McCarthys it happened to be an insurance company. In 1939, when the law firm's gross income was $110,000, it billed Canada Life over $32,000, Union Carbide nearly $20,000 and Alcan $4,000. (Osler, Hoskin, however, had more than twice the gross income with only a few more lawyers.) Much of the new business that had come to McCarthys in the 1930s came by way of Salter Hayden, a vigorous and enterprising business-getter throughout his life.

*Walker later recalled that his Oxford marks were terrible ("an indifferent second class B.A." and a failed law course) and his legal knowledge minimal. But his manoeuvring was already astute. In 1931, the Law Society of Upper Canada would not recognize an English call to the bar without Ontario articles being served, but Manitoba's Law Society would—and Ontario recognized Manitoba credentials without restriction. On his return from Britain, Walker had himself called in Manitoba and then transferred to Ontario. "We'll soon close that rathole," rasped Law Society treasurer W.N. Tilley as he handed Walker his credentials, but McCarthys had hired him even before his Ontario call went through.

Hayden's early reputation was as a litigator, and he remained McCarthys' top courtroom lawyer until the late 1940s. He did substantial corporate tax and patent cases, took appeals to the Supreme Court and Privy Council and had even acted as special prosecutor at the Toronto assizes. Hayden, however, had the knack for turning his litigation business into ongoing retainers, and the solicitor side of his practice grew rapidly. "You are not in a vaccuum, you're out in the world. People talk...," was his description of how business flowed to him. "You become known, you develop a measure of success, and people start to say the person to see is Salter Hayden." Hayden was always open-minded about clients who wanted to see him. They long included raffish horse-racing cronies and dubious promoters as well as large corporations.

Hayden was also an active Liberal Party organizer who ran unsuccessfully in a Toronto riding in the federal election of 1935. In 1940 Prime Minister Mackenzie King rewarded him with appointment to the Senate. Hayden began a weekly commuting schedule between his McCarthy office and Parliament Hill, and in time he made himself a powerhouse of the Senate Banking Committee and a leading voice of business in Ottawa. He acknowledged that the Senate was also a wonderful source of clients, and he continued to gather corporate directorships, including Bank of Nova Scotia and Union Carbide, a file he inherited from Leighton McCarthy. In Hayden's view, Frank McCarthy always preferred "a few big comfortable clients" and looked askance at Hayden's energetic business development. But Hayden believed a firm either grew or shrank.

Hayden was not the only McCarthys member reviving its political traditions in the 1930s. Beverley Matthews sought a Conservative Party nomination in 1935, first making sure to secure the approval of Leighton McCarthy, who was still evidently the power in the firm. He did not get the nomination (and never ran again), but he helped manage Prime Minister R.B. Bennett's campaign in Ontario in 1935, and he became an important fundraiser for the Conservative Party. Leighton McCarthy, meanwhile, was also reconsidering active politics as he retired from the presidency of Canada Life.

Leighton McCarthy had broken with the Liberal Party over conscription in 1917 and had not been an early supporter of Mackenzie King, but he played a important role in reconciling the Toronto business community to King, and King remembered. ("McCarthy certainly could not have done more for the party at a stroke than he did in bringing together all these men," King wrote in his diary after a 1922 political dinner McCarthy arranged at Toronto's York Club.) In 1937 Leighton angled for a Senate appointment but King considered him too old at age sixty-eight, and Leighton refused King's offer to make him lieutenant governor of Ontario. In 1941, however, came a call neither could refuse: representing Canada to the American government and particularly to its president, Franklin Roosevelt.

"Leighton's hungry," said President Franklin D. Roosevelt, carving turkey for his friend, the Canadian ambassador to the United States.

Leighton McCarthy's son, John, had been stricken with polio in 1928, and when the McCarthys had sought treatment for him at the Warm Springs sanatorium in Georgia Leighton had met another patient, Franklin Roosevelt. The two men became friends and fellow trustees of the Warm Springs Foundation. When a new Canadian minister to Roosevelt's Washington was needed in 1941, King turned to McCarthy, not least because Roosevelt was rumoured to have said, "I don't care who gets the job, so long as it is Leighton McCarthy."

McCarthy, then 71 and semi-retired, originally intended to play a mostly ceremonial role in Washington. Both King and McCarthy intended the work to be done by the second-in-command there, the career diplomat (and McCarthy family friend) Hume Wrong. But McCarthy's political skills and ready access to Roosevelt apparently impressed the prime minister. As the United States entered the Second World War and contacts between the two countries intensified, King gave McCarthy more responsibility and more influence than either had foreseen.* In 1943, as Canada began upgrading its foreign legations to embassies, Leighton McCarthy became the first Canadian to hold the title of ambassador. He held the job until 1944 and continued to have unusual access to both King and Roosevelt. In 1943 Roosevelt even dropped in by military seaplane at the McCarthys' retreat on Georgian Bay for a little fishing. On the day Roosevelt died at Warm Springs in 1945, he was preparing for an evening with Leighton McCarthy.

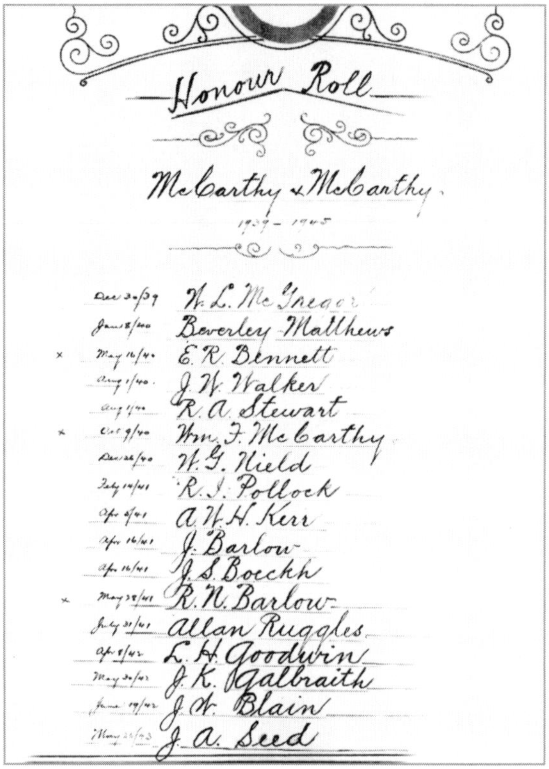
Honour Roll

McCarthy & McCarthy

1939 – 1945

W. L. McGregor
Beverley Matthews
E. R. Bennett
J. W. Walker
R. A. Stewart
Wm. F. McCarthy
W. G. Nield
R. J. Pollock
A. W. H. Kerr
J. Barlow
J. S. Boeckh
R. N. Barlow
Allan Ruggles
L. H. Goodwin
J. K. Galbraith
J. W. Blain
J. A. Seed

The Roll of Honour of McCarthy & McCarthy staff who went to the Second World War.

From 1939 to 1945 the war dominated life at the law firm, as elsewhere. Most of the younger

*Hume Wrong was evidently unaware of McCarthy's intentions for him and complained bitterly about being superseded by an elderly dilettante. Despite McCarthy's presidential access, Wrong is credited with key innovations in Canadian wartime diplomacy.

lawyers and staff went into the armed services, and three were killed in action. Frank McCarthy's only son, William, a law student turned bomber pilot, was killed on an operational mission in 1942. Staff member Reginald Barlow, also a Royal Canadian Air Force flyer, was lost in the Mediterranean theatre in 1943. Edwin Ronald Bennett, a McGill University law student articling in the firm in 1940 (and a nephew of former prime minister R.B. Bennett), was a major in Montreal's Black Watch Regiment by 1944; he was killed while leading infantry in Normandy.

A personal intervention by Leighton McCarthy secured Gretta Wong an articling position at McCarthy & McCarthy in 1943.

Jack Blain served in the motorized artillery in northwest Europe. Jim Walker worked at the Canadian Army Staff College in Kingston, Ontario, and then took up legal duties with the civil affairs branch of the Canadian Army. Beverley Matthews, who had been in the prewar militia, went overseas in the spring of 1940. He rose rapidly on the staff of the Canadian Army and served in Italy and northwest Europe. By the end of the war he was deputy adjutant-general of the Canadian Army overseas and a brigadier.

Some new lawyers had been hired during the war, and for a time McCarthy & McCarthy was remarkable among Toronto law firms for having four female lawyers: Marion Darte, June Ryan, Jean Oldrieve and Gretta Wong.[47] The presence of four women was partly due to the liberal attitude of Leighton McCarthy, who intervened directly in 1943 to secure an articling position for Gretta Wong, who became the first Chinese-Canadian female lawyer, but it also reflected the scarcity of male lawyers due to the war. Work increased greatly for the reduced complement of senior lawyers. Hayden, West and Terry later recalled working extraordinary hours and taking no holidays throughout the war, and West suffered a temporary health breakdown as the war ended. The other significant change in this era seems to have been the loss of the Alcan file when that company moved its Canadian head office and legal work to Montreal.* Several of Hayden's clients, notably Atlantic Sugar, the mining enterprises of Joe Hirshhorn and the investment business of Percy Gardiner (bequeathed from Lally McCarthy) took their place in the firm's revenue accounts.

There was no postwar boom immediately noticeable when lawyers and staff began returning from military service in 1945. "Prospects in the legal profession at the present time do not appear to us to be very encouraging.... The profession is already overcrowded and...there may not be enough work for all," a 1943 Law Society report on postwar prospects had predicted. Frank McCarthy had guaranteed all lawyers and staff in the services that their places would be waiting for them when they returned, but like many other leaders of the profession he feared a postwar depression and was cautious about taking on new staff.† At war's end only Frank McCarthy, Salter Hayden and "Duke" West remained as active partners. When the younger lawyers returned, the firm was ready for change, and the catalyst was Frank McCarthy's agreement in 1947 to turn leadership over to a new generation.

*Beverley Matthews much later recalled that the City of Toronto proposed a tax on head offices in the city and Alcan responded by threatening to move. McCarthys dispatched a young lawyer, R.M. Fowler, to City Hall and he returned with assurances that the tax would not be implemented. But it was implemented, Alcan moved to Montreal in 1942 and, as Matthews put it, "Mr. Fowler left our employ." Fowler did leave the firm, but not until 1945, and he had a successful legal career elsewhere. Alcan's move was probably inevitable, given the scale of its Quebec operations.

†Two McCarthy law students, Jack Seed and Walter McGregor, returned to the firm in 1945 after service as commissioned officers in the Canadian forces. Seed had done North Atlantic convoy duty and McGregor had been captured at Dieppe, but they learned when they returned to finish articling that Frank McCarthy expected them to accept a much reduced wage, because there were now five students, not two, to share the fixed allocation for students' wages. Seed and McGregor staged a brief "strike" in protest.

McCarthy, a small, loud, rather brusque man with deep solicitude for the firm, was close to sixty-five in 1947, but he continued to practise (and would do so for several more years). He had been devastated by the death of his son in the RCAF, but an unresolved debate about the future of the firm may also have influenced his decision to become a "counsel" on retainer, rather than remaining the leader and effective owner of McCarthy & McCarthy. McCarthy had always inclined to the view that the firm had enough clients and enough lawyers and was comfortable as it was. He continued to express those views into the 1950s. But Salter Hayden, Beverley Matthews and James Walker, the leaders of the new generation, advocated growth. George Finlayson, who joined the firm in 1951, recalled Matthews lamenting that whenever he recommended taking on new clients Frank McCarthy would say, "We have no one to do the work." When Matthews proposed hiring lawyers, Frank invariably responded, "What would they do?" West and Terry tended to share McCarthy's caution, but after 1947 such wary attitudes about the firm's future ceased to dominate at McCarthy & McCarthy.

Frank McCarthy, who inherited leadership of McCarthy & McCarthy from his brother Leighton.

4 HAYDEN, MATTHEWS AND WALKER

On December 1, 1947, a new agreement wound up the old partnership and instituted a new McCarthy & McCarthy. Frank McCarthy received the title of "counsel," with a retainer and office space. Active ownership passed to a new partnership of six: Salter Hayden, Duke West, William Terry, Beverley Matthews, James Walker and Archibald Kerr. Terry, Matthews, Walker and Kerr were becoming partners for the first time, though they had been in the firm for between fourteen years (Kerr) and nineteen years (Terry).

Had the new leaders aspired to put their names on it, McCarthy & McCarthy might have become Hayden, Matthews & Walker in 1947. But the partners evidently appreciated the tradition in the McCarthy name, and perhaps they also wanted to avoid issues of rank among themselves. To forestall any likelihood of such rivalries arising, they specified in their new partnership agreement that the McCarthy & McCarthy name could be changed only by unanimous consent. In the allocation of revenues, however, Salter Hayden came first. The new partners agreed to divide net revenues into eighty shares: Hayden held thirty-two, West, Terry, Matthews and Walker had eleven each and Kerr got four.

Salter Hayden, still involved in litigation but always an instinctive business-getter (and from 1951 the influential chair of the Senate Banking Committee), delegated much work to his juniors. Union Carbide, for instance, which he had inherited from Leighton McCarthy, passed down to his protege Jack Blain, and Blain rapidly became an expert on corporate finance issues. Clients whom Hayden had nurtured in the 1930s also continued to be an important part of the firm's growing revenues, but he was always something of a sole practitioner within the partnership, full of energy and spontaneity, his practice defined largely by whatever came in the door.

The Senator: Salter Hayden in the 1950s.

Beverley Matthews was equally committed to growth, but not the kind that came haphazardly as clients happened to take note of the firm and its lawyers. More than Hayden, Matthews began to see McCarthy & McCarthy as an entity whose growth could be planned and managed. "Being biggest does not necessarily make a law firm best, but it gives it the opportunity to be the best" was his aphorism. He wanted to give his firm that opportunity by planning and managing its growth.

Despite their shared commitment to growth and McCarthys, Hayden and Matthews were not friends. Their personalities were very different. Matthews was conservative in style as well as politics and he sought to associate his firm with the best clients, clubs and circles. He and Walker, his closest friend and confidant, were always concerned with the image and dignity of the business. They disapproved of some of Hayden's clients and connections, such as Samuel Ciglen, a lawyer and investor who was eventually jailed for income tax evasion. Yet the coolness between Hayden and Matthews was never a public issue. Going their separate ways, as predecessors in the firm had done in 1916 and again in 1929, never seems to have been likely.

Matthews, a brand new partner, had once been Hayden's courtroom junior ("I treated him the way Lally treated me," said Hayden, a partner since 1929), and in the new firm his allocation was at first far smaller than Hayden's. But in 1947 Matthews was no one's junior. He was not only a retired army brigadier but also a valued organizer and fundraiser for the federal and provincial Conservative parties. He was past counsel to an Ontario Royal Commission, soon to be president of the Toronto Board of Trade and a governor of the University of Toronto. All these, along with his social connections and his forceful personality, were making him a significant figure in Toronto business circles. It was by focussing on the organization of the firm as managing partner, however, that Matthews really put his stamp on McCarthy & McCarthy, whereas Hayden, the senior partner, continued to go his own way, almost as if there were two firms within one. "Matthews showed you could work with someone without liking them," observed one of his associates. "He simply defined problems and dealt with them."

Active management remained somewhat unusual in Toronto law firms in the 1950s. Bay Street law was still dominated by a handful of old firms with up to twenty lawyers and large, long-standing clients. Around them clustered many smaller firms, often with just two to five lawyers who did not have a large bank or leading insurance company among their clients but preserved their own roster of corporate clients as part of a diversified practice. Some new firms, including the one founded by J.S.D. Tory in 1941 and Borden and Elliott (founded 1930), were making inroads into the Bay Street legal community. Others, like the long-established Smith, Rae, Greer, were slipping out of the first rank. Law firm partners could still spend most of their time simply practising law and doing business with the clients they had and those that approached them. If they did not have an "owner" in the style of Leighton McCarthy, the dominant partners could consult as needed without spending much time on firm administration. "Rainmaking," bringing in clients, remained the only significant obligation of law firm leadership and most of that was done by personal connections or reputation, rather than by intense planning. In many firms, the managing partner was little more than the one designated to supervise the support staff and pay the bills. But new conditions in postwar Canada were creating new opportunities for law firm management.

In the 1950s, when many firms were content to remain small, Beverley Matthews began to plan for the constant growth of McCarthy & McCarthy.

The first was economic growth. By the time the new partners took charge at McCarthy & McCarthy, a quarter-century-long period of almost uninterrupted economic growth was taking hold. The wartime industrialization of Canada had been transformed into peacetime industrial expansion in manufacturing, resource development, transportation and many other fields. Unprecedented amounts of investment capital flowed into the economy. The scale and complexity of corporate enterprise in Canada was increasing rapidly, and all of it generated new fields of work for lawyers.

At the same time, new layers of regulation and public-sector administration were beginning to transform state involvement in Canadian business and Canadian society. One notable example was the new labour codes worked out during the war, which suddenly made collective bargaining a vital concern for Canadian industries and their lawyers. Another was the new Income Tax Act of 1947, which for the first time obliged corporations and their lawyers to begin considering the tax implications of nearly every transaction. Labour and tax became two of the first fields in which "full-service" law firms would soon need to offer particular expertise to their corporate clients: an era of legal specialization was beginning.

The number of lawyers in Canadian business centres would grow at an unprecedented rate for decades, but the amount of legal work available for them would grow even faster. Corporations operating on a new scale needed much more legal work, and they needed firms that could do larger, more complicated transactions across a broader range of legal specialties. Downtown law firms were not precisely obliged to become larger, but Beverley Matthews was among the new leaders who identified the opportunity for growth and began to plan for it. Matthews soon ceased going to court and substantially reduced his active practice of law. He began focussing instead on two objectives, client relations and firm management.

One of the first indications of the new regime at McCarthys was its recruitment of legal talent. The first articling student taken on was John Lawson in 1948. In time Lawson became an associate and a partner. In 2005, as a retired counsel still active about the firm, he was the longest-serving member of the McCarthy Tétrault organization. Other students soon followed, but McCarthy & McCarthy was also recruiting some prominent lawyers.

In 1949 John J. Robinette had been in practice for twenty years. A law school prizewinner, an admired teacher and editor of the *Law Reports* and a Law Society bencher since 1946, Robinette had a high reputation among litigation lawyers as well as recent public fame as counsel to the notorious accused murderer Evelyn Dick. He was practising with a small firm that was disintegrating when Matthews, a friend since their school days, recruited him to McCarthys. Unlike Hayden and Lally McCarthy, who both liked to be attended in court by juniors, Robinette was something of a loner; all his life he did much of his own research. Matthews offered him a counsel relationship with no partnership obligations. Robinette would be provided with office space and his choice of support staff and juniors, and he could bill McCarthys or his own clients himself.

McCarthy & McCarthy's counsel John J. Robinette in the 1950s.

Robinette's arrival instantly revived McCarthys' reputation as a litigation firm, particularly since Salter Hayden was moving out of litigation practice as the Senate and the boardroom took up more of his time. Robinette quickly took up major cases for the firm and began writing bold, vigorous opinions for its clients. Meanwhile, his own high-profile victories drew attention to McCarthys as the home of top counsel. The firm quickly discovered his presence there drew clients—and students who wanted to do litigation with the master.

In 1949 McCarthys also recruited Harold Fox, an experienced patent attorney and author of standard texts in patents and copyright. Apart from his patent practice, Fox was also the proprietor of Lightning Zipper Company of St. Catharines, which had held the exclusive North American patent on the zipper until the 1940s. The zipper had made

Fox very wealthy—with some help from Salter Hayden, who had acted for the company in a drawn-out set of patent-infringement cases. After the zipper patent expired, Fox turned to legal scholarship, earned a Ph.D. and began writing patent-law texts. Learning he wanted to renew his specialist practice in Toronto, McCarthys recruited him. Fox became counsel to the firm and the nucleus of a substantial practice in patent law and intellectual property, which after twenty years employed half a dozen lawyers and patent agents.

Tax was another field in which McCarthys needed expertise. Demand for lawyers who understood the corporate-tax implications of the new Income Tax Act was high. Given the complications of the new tax regime, commercial firms found it was no longer sufficient to leave tax questions in the hands of corporate-law generalists; they needed tax-law specialists. Heward Stikeman and Stuart Thom, who were among the lawyers who had participated in the drafting of the act while working for the government in Ottawa, soon built significant practices advising corporate clients on the intricacies of the new tax regime, Stikeman with his own firm in Montreal and Thom with Osler, Hoskin in Toronto.

At McCarthys, Salter Hayden had been giving tax-law advice to many of his corporate clients, and he had delegated some of that task to John Blain. Blain, however, was increasingly focussed on large corporate financings. It was not until 1956 that McCarthys recruited John B. Macdonald, known as the author of a tax textbook, to develop a specialized tax department for the firm. Macdonald recruited a young lawyer named David Ward to work with him, at a time when two tax lawyers represented a substantial amount of expertise. In 1961, however, Macdonald and Ward decided they could do better in their own specialized firm, and they joined a third lawyer from another firm to found what became Davies, Ward & Beck, which soon became a competitor in tax law and related fields of corporate practice. With its tax department gone, McCarthys urgently needed a replacement. Salter Hayden, by his connections in Ottawa, identified William

Latimer, senior tax counsel at the Department of National Revenue, and Latimer joined McCarthys in 1961. He rebuilt the firm's tax practice and hired new tax specialists, including Ron Robertson and Arthur Scace, before he died, still in his early fifties, in 1973.

The "old" McCarthys had long had a real estate practice, partly in mortgages for Canada Life and National Trust and otherwise for individual clients who were buying and selling small properties. That began to change in 1948 when Matthews was asked to lobby the Ontario government on behalf of the Brewers' Retail chain, which feared it was threatened with privatization. That threat soon evaporated even without Matthews' intervention, but the relationship between McCarthys and Brewers' Retail continued. Brewers' Retail was developing properties all over Ontario, but the firm it relied on had only three lawyers and was already consulting Jim Walker of McCarthys about financings for the beer retailer. One of the three, Douglas Milne, decided that his firm was both too small for the work and unlikely to grow; in 1956 Milne moved over to McCarthys, taking Brewers' Retail with him. William Terry remained the leader of McCarthys' real estate lawyers, but the firm was shifting its emphasis from private real estate and insurance company mortgages. It rapidly increased its expertise in the new commercial-property financing and development projects that were beginning to transform Canadian cities and industrial parks.

Harold Fox, the patent-law scholar recruited to McCarthy & McCarthy in 1949.

Recruiting lawyers from other firms was still disapproved of in the traditionally uncompetitive Toronto legal community of the 1950s. But a gap was opening between practices intent on expansion and those inclined to stay small, and many lawyers could see it. When the senior partner in his small corporate-law firm died in the early 1960s, Ian Douglas recalls, Douglas told his partners they should seize the moment and hire several bright young associates: "Our incomes will go down for a couple of years, and then we will make money like we have never done before." But his partners liked the firm as it was, so Douglas began looking around. Jack Blain, with whom he had been involved in some mining deals, took him to lunch with Matthews, who made him an offer at the table, and Douglas began a long career at McCarthys. Mergers of whole law firms, common in the 1980s, were rare in the 1950s, but in the late 1940s Matthews discussed a merger with J.S.D. Tory ("I came back and said, 'That won't work, we'd be in a fight in two weeks' time,'" Matthews later recalled).* In the 1950s, when Matthews was working closely with Collamer Calvin on banking projects, Fasken & Calvin considered but declined Matthews' proposal to merge the two firms.

Despite its growth, McCarthys in the 1950s was not yet entirely secure in the top ranks of Toronto law firms. Blakes and Oslers maintained their lead as the largest, and other downtown firms were growing, too. Basil Cheeseman, who practised in Calgary in the 1950s and later joined McCarthys in Toronto, remembers that when he considered a move to Toronto in the early 1950s he hardly thought of McCarthys as one of the leading firms. Still, McCarthys was moving up. In the 1950s the Ontario legal-profession population grew at an annual rate of 3.5 per cent, the biggest firms at about 7 per cent and McCarthys at 8.5 per cent. It would not much longer be mistaken for "Canada Life's legal department."

Canada Life remained a significant client, with Jim Walker doing financing projects on a new scale for it, but Matthews was repositioning

*Peter Beattie recalled that Matthews viewed with disfavour the way that Tory's roster of clients had grown rapidly during World War II while rival lawyers like Matthews were away at the war.

the firm from "a high-quality small firm with a certain level of top-drawer clients [into] a firm that dealt with a whole range of specialties." With its new lawyers and its growing sophistication in several fields of law, there were many opportunities beyond the traditional clients. The "new" McCarthys and its lawyers could claim to be strong in civil litigation, corporate finance, banking, commercial real property and in patent law, as well as more general practice.

James Walker, corporate lawyer and conscience of the Toronto office in the 1950s, 1960s and 1970s.

Perhaps the most important new commercial-law link for McCarthys was in banking. In each Canadian city, dominant law firms were almost always those that had a bank client. In the postwar boom, the leading banks were rapidly outstripping competitors (like insurance companies) in total capitalization, in financial importance, and in the volumes of sophisticated legal work they commissioned. McCarthy & McCarthy had done routine mortgage work for National Trust for decades, but it had never had a relationship with a bank until Matthews joined the board of Dominion Bank (a long-time Oslers client) in the late 1940s. In 1954 he and Collamer Calvin, a director of Bank of Toronto, helped spearhead a merger of Dominion Bank and Bank of Toronto. McCarthys acted for Dominion Bank and Fasken Calvin represented Bank of Toronto. For the newly merged Toronto-Dominion Bank, now one of the largest in the country, Fasken Calvin did litigation and McCarthys its other legal work. Jim Walker started the banking practice, but he soon brought in John Clarry, who rapidly became an expert in banking law.

According to McCarthys lore, Salter Hayden, still senior partner and proud of it, was rather piqued by Matthews' successful role as a bank director. In 1955 he was recruited to a bank board of his own, with Bank of Nova Scotia. McCarthys never did all of Bank of Nova Scotia's legal work, but the relationship did establish it as the only major Toronto law firm with two bank clients. Indeed, in 1959 and again in 1961 McCarthys was drawn into secret merger negotiations between Toronto-Dominion Bank and Bank of Nova Scotia and consultations with the minister of finance. Banking practice became a mainstay of the commercial department and the firm later became counsel to the Canadian Bankers Association and eventually to many foreign banks setting up operations in Canada.

The partnership's ability to do work for two banks simultaneously became an inspiration for another Matthews strategy. "We were a firehouse law firm," Peter Beattie, who joined the firm in 1956, said of his early years there. "People came to McCarthys when Oslers or Blakes could not act for them, or when their usual counsel had a conflict." At the beginning this may have been a strategy born of necessity, but Matthews concluded there could be advantages to being available to many clients rather than depending on steady work from just a few. Later, as legal work became more competitive and major clients began to shop around, McCarthys discovered it had been preparing for the age of the "transactional" law firm, when work was secured "deal by deal" rather than by permanent retainers from faithful clients.*

Matthews was less successful in his quest to secure a railroad's legal business. (Years later, when lawyers from the Canadian Pacific Railway's Toronto law firm, Tilley, Carson, joined McCarthy & McCarthy, friends would joke that Matthews had finally got the railroad's lawyers, instead.)

*A Law Society committee, considering the problem of conflicts, once asked Matthews how his firm could serve two banks. "I act for the Toronto-Dominion, and my partner acts for the Nova Scotia," said Matthews loftily. "And we do not speak."

But in the mid-1950s pipelines seemed to be the new railroads. When the federal government built the first natural gas pipeline across northern Ontario to deliver Alberta gas to eastern consumers, long-time client Percy Gardiner brought the firm the work of Lakeland Gas, which was seeking franchises for gas distribution in southern Ontario. Soon after, British Columbia promoter Ralph Farris retained McCarthy & McCarthy to set up and advise Northern Ontario Natural Gas, later Norcen, in the building of spur lines that would deliver gas to the towns of northern Ontario. McCarthy lawyers became the incorporating directors and officers of the new company and the law firm sought regulatory approvals and negotiated franchise agreements with two levels of government. It advised on bond financing for the project and undertook the elaborate real-property law interpretations that underpinned the easements and expropriations needed for the construction of the pipeline.*

*Lawyers who appreciate the sheer intellectual challenge of legal work point to Philip Walker's opinion as a virtuoso thinking-through of the new legal technicalities of pipelines as real estate.

Several years later, in 1962, when TransCanada PipeLines undertook to acquire the northern Ontario section of the main cross-country pipeline from the federal government (which had built that section in the 1950s), McCarthys secured TransCanada's legal work. The pipeline company's purchase of the northern Ontario line hinged on a massive bond issue in which the company's legal advisers, Borden & Elliott, also represented the underwriting firm, Nesbitt Thomson. Beverley Matthews was already a director of TransCanada; its board, after considering Borden & Elliott's divided loyalties, decided to make McCarthys its counsel on the deal. The new business immediately plunged the law firm into a huge financing project and an intricate title registration process for TransCanada. In effect, the federal government could not transfer title to the pipeline until it received payment from TransCanada, while the bondholders could not advance the money to TransCanada without guarantees of clear title. Since the property in question was over 1,000 kilometres long and crossed scores of townships, the transaction required an intricate scheme in which telephone connections were opened to every registry office across northern Ontario, so that all the transfers could be registered simultaneously. In the end, successful transfers of title for the whole pipeline were completed in less than two hours. TransCanada PipeLines continued to use McCarthy & McCarthy as its legal counsel and became one of its largest clients.

The 1950s had transformed the scale of the McCarthys legal business. In 1948 the gross income of the "new" firm had been $336,000; the figure rose to $741,400 in 1955, $1,225,000 in 1960 and $2,175,000 in 1965. Since the partnership hardly grew in those years, the per-partner income at McCarthy & McCarthy was rocketing upwards. The firm's accounts, however, also suggest something about Matthew's management. Contrary to the unwritten axiom of law firm economics—the aim of partner-owners is always to turn firm equity into personal income—the McCarthys partners began taking out far less in income than profits might have permitted.

The 1947 partnership agreement had fixed the partners' share of allocations for two years. Soon thereafter a more flexible annual disbursement, negotiated among the partners but managed by Matthews, became the norm. Salter Hayden remained the best-paid partner for several years (peaking at $130,000 in 1956), but Matthews and Walker soon pulled away from the others. They each drew $100,000 in 1956, and in 1959 so did Hayden. And there their remuneration essentially stopped rising. These three, the top partners, continued to earn $100,000 a year for another decade, and the other senior partners received from $50,000 to $75,000. In other words, the partners had achieved the difficult feat of agreeing to defer income for the sake of the firm. Where they had received 59 per cent of gross firm income in 1950, their share fell to 54 per cent in 1955 and 43 per cent in 1960. With their allocations more or less capped and few new partners being admitted, more of the fast-rising income of the firm was available for investment in expansion.

Even capped, what the top partners paid themselves were very substantial incomes for the 1950s, and partnership allocations were scarcely their only source of revenue. Corporate lawyers of the 1950s faced few of the conflicts and insider-trading issues that prevailed later, and they frequently invested in client firms. When a scandal erupted over Ontario cabinet ministers and a judge, Leo Landreville, who had received gifts of Northern Ontario Natural Gas stock while the company was seeking provincial regulatory approval in the late 1950s, the subsequent investigations identified Beverley Matthews among the many directors and other insiders who had also invested heavily in NONG. No wrongdoing by Matthews was implied; it remained common for lawyers to take advantage of their knowledge of impending deals to make nearly risk-free investments. Business lawyers like Matthews found it possible not only to be very well rewarded from their law practices but also to generate much more substantial wealth from related business activities.*

In those years, Matthews was said to spend half his time "thinking about the firm, the clients it needed and the lawyers who could handle their work," and that meant McCarthys was much more seriously managed than many of its competitors. Matthews did not have the full-time business commitment that Leighton McCarthy developed with Canada Life, but he, too, was a businessman in the law almost as much as a practitioner of law. As vice-president of Toronto-Dominion and a director of such market leaders as TransCanada PipeLines, British-American Oil and later its successor, Gulf Canada (and also of its American parent, Gulf Oil), he had business networks that were as vital to the firm in the 1950s and 1960s as Leighton's had been in the 1920s and 1930s. Despite its growing revenues, new clients and activist management, McCarthys in the early 1960s remained a conservative law firm in many ways. Its

*It is said that in the early 1960s a young McCarthys lawyer cited his growing family and his mortgage payments in asking Matthews for a raise in salary. Matthews asked him what his income was. When the lawyer said what his salary was, Matthews stared at him and then called to Jim Walker in the next office, "Jim, Ron here is trying to live on what we pay him!"

client recruitment was a very traditional kind of "rainmaking," depending largely on Matthews' (and Hayden's, and to a lesser extent other lawyers') social and professional networks.

The partnership was just as traditional with regard to recruitment and promotion. In the 1950s there was not yet much competitive pressure on law firms to find and recruit the most promising young lawyers. John Godfrey, a rising young partner with an interest in management at Campbell, Godfrey, Lewtas (much later part of the megafirm Fasken Martineau), had started to systematize his firm's recruitment by going after top law graduates from Osgoode Hall and the University of Toronto law schools. Borrowing from processes already long established in New York, his firm started paying new associates significant salaries and other benefits, and it began to promise partnerships within seven years to those who made the grade. For much of the 1950s Campbell, Godfrey had little competition in these endeavours.

McCarthys was not immediately stirring itself to seek out promising students. It had grown as much by key lateral hires as by recruiting students; indeed, McCarthys in the early years of Matthews' leadership hired students as much for their social connections as for demonstrated ability. John Clarry, who eventually succeeded Matthews as head of the practice and whose lawyerly skills are hugely admired by his colleagues, had a stellar career as a law student in the late 1940s but, even though both Matthews and Walker had known him in the army, they made no efforts to recruit him until after he had completed a series of articling positions at minor law firms. George Finlayson, who joined McCarthys a year later in 1951 (and went on to a very successful career in litigation and on the bench), recalled that he was hired because his father worked with Matthews in the Conservative Party. In fact, he understood that all the students hired that year got in on social rather than academic credentials. In the same era, several otherwise unpromising students were hired in hopes that their business-executive fathers might send work to the firm.

McCarthys did hire many young lawyers who proved to be extremely talented, but the attraction must have been the firm's reputation or the chance to work with leading lawyers on big files, rather than McCarthys' active pursuit of them or the prospects for good pay and prompt partnership. For McCarthys did not innovate in partnership selection, either. Beverley Matthews had been an associate for seventeen years before becoming a partner, and the new partnership team of 1947 did not quickly move to speed partnership admissions for the lawyers they employed. For a time, long-serving lawyers were called "junior partners," a title that seems to have been largely honorific and was finally phased out in 1976, after the modern "partner-track" system had developed.

During the 1950s only John Blain (who was called to the bar in 1941 and became a partner in 1953) and John Clarry (called 1950, partner 1959) became full partners. That their initially small partnership shares were an improvement upon an associate's wages only shows how little employed lawyers were paid. Blain, who was already handling sophisticated international financing deals of great value to the firm, received an income of $2,500 in 1953, his first full year as a partner. (By 1957 his share was $40,000.) In the 1960s it took serious agitation by the "juniors," several of whom had solid reputations and up to eighteen years' experience, before the first substantial block of new partners was admitted to full partnership in 1968. By then the firm was adapting to the modern associate-to-partner system that all the Toronto corporate-law firms were adopting.

In comparison with the rather liberal attitude of Leighton McCarthy, a wealthy businessman and establishment Torontonian who nevertheless had hired Catholics, women and bright young poor kids practically off the street to work at his law firm, the McCarthy & McCarthy of the 1950s and 1960s was selective in its hirings. As it strove to secure for itself a place in the top rank of corporate legal business in Toronto, it became more specific about the religion, upbringing and family background of the lawyers it preferred to hire. In particular,

Salter Hayden, William Terry, Beverley Matthews and Duke West, stalwarts of the Toronto office in the 1950s and 1960s.

there were no Jews in the firm. The number of Jews entering the legal profession in Ontario had been rising gradually since the 1920s, but there were very few in "non-Jewish" Toronto firms until the 1960s. Campbell, Godfrey was apparently the first downtown firm to hire a Jewish lawyer, in 1955, and other leading firms did not soon follow suit. John Clarry recalls with pain a recruitment effort from the 1960s. McCarthys, finally beginning to take student recruitment seriously, sent letters to the top students graduating from the law schools—but not to the Jewish ones. "It was just assumed Jewish lawyers had their own law firms...and perhaps, wouldn't be accepted in the firm."

Daniel G. Cooper, hired in 1971, was the first Jewish associate hired for general corporate practice on the partner-track system. Eric Gertner, who joined McCarthys in 1984 and built its research department, recalls that as a top graduate in 1974 he received no offers from McCarthys or any of the major firms, and he assumed that was because he was Jewish. The experience of women was similar: There were fewer female lawyers in Hayden's and Matthews' firm in the 1950s and 1960s than there had been under Leighton McCarthy in the 1940s. Into the 1970s McCarthys hired very few women, even then usually under special circumstances, and they were mostly channelled into fields of law often regarded as minor or secondary. There would be no female partners at McCarthys until the late 1970s.

Matthews, who said he had seen too many law firms ruined by hiring the sons of partners, had always opposed the hiring of family members, and he refused to bring his own lawyer son into McCarthy & McCarthy.* But this was still an unorthodox opinion among Canadian law firm leaders, and Matthews' viewpoint did not soon become McCarthys' policy. Senator Hayden had brought his son Gerald into the firm in 1950, and W.C. Terry's daughter Helen practised with McCarthys from 1963 to 1974. Dale Robinette, the daughter of J.J. Robinette, also practised at the firm (though her father, not being a partner, was not in fact her employer). This kind of family hiring had built the original McCarthy firm, as well as Oslers, Blakes and many other leaders, and it ceased to be common practice in Toronto only in the 1970s. Here, too, Canadian practice ran well behind American experience, where anti-nepotism agreements had come in much earlier as part of the general professionalization of law firm management.†

*In 1985, after Beverley Matthews had retired, John Clarry hired his son, R.B. "Biff" Matthews, who moved to McCarthys from a firm he found too small to serve his growing clients.

†Vancouver lawyer Sholto Hebenton, who in 1990 became the first national chair of McCarthy Tétrault, worked briefly at the Wall Street firm Dewey, Ballantine in 1965. He recalls lawyers there needing a Toronto law firm but dismissing McCarthy & McCarthy as soon as they saw the name in the legal directory: "We're not going to hire a brother act!"

5 | PROFESSIONAL PRACTICE

In the mid-1960s McCarthy & McCarthy remained a rather traditional firm, proud of its origins, restricted in its clients and its lawyers and old-fashioned in its ownership structure. Yet it was becoming a new-look law firm with an expanding range of legal services, enlarged revenues and, particularly, a leadership committed to competition and growth. Nothing symbolized the new look more than the partners' new offices in the Toronto-Dominion Centre.

Well into the 1960s, Toronto was a city of older buildings. The new City Hall, harbinger of architectural change, did not open until 1965, and the skyline remained dominated by the Royal York Hotel and other long-established buildings from before the Second World War. Law firm accommodation was of the same vintage as the predominant architecture of the downtown core. Many prestigious practices still occupied plain and crowded quarters with few amenities, where students and staff shared vast, noisy secretarial pools and technology hardly went beyond a Gestetner machine. Air conditioning was a luxury and a curiosity; green linoleum floors were more typical than marble or mahogany panelling. McCarthys' offices in the Canada Life

Building (the firm had moved from ground floor premises with a separate entrance to the seventh floor) were more comfortable than many, but they remained plain and unostentatious. Their move to the Toronto-Dominion Centre would end all that.

When Toronto-Dominion Bank concluded early in 1962 that its 1913 headquarters at King and Bay Streets had become too small, Allen Lambert, its president, decided the bank must create a landmark that would transform the Toronto skyline and revive the downtown business core by spurring demolition of scores of existing buildings, including the beautiful former Bank of Toronto Building. The T-D Bank decided to acquire almost the entire block of prime real estate south of King Street and west of Bay Street. It would build not simply a main branch and headquarters but a complex on a scale never before seen in Toronto, with a set of spectacular modern office towers, broad plazas and a large underground commercial centre.

McCarthys was part of the project from the start, not least because Beverley Matthews, a vice-president of the bank, was a confidant of Lambert's. The first task for the development was land assembly. In association with the real estate firm A.E. Lepage, a shell company officered by McCarthy lawyers quietly began purchasing properties on the target block. "You couldn't tip your hand" by having the bank buy the properties, recalled John Clarry. "So a couple of law clerks in the firm—one of them was Al Stewart, who was a great member of the firm for many years—became very large property owners in downtown Toronto!" One of the buildings on the site, however, was the Seagram Building, owned by the Bronfmans of Montreal. They were not inclined to sell and were themselves deeply involved in commercial-property development. As a result their company, Cemp Investments, became a partner in the deal instead of selling its building. Clarry recalled how he and Cemp's lawyer, Phillip Vineberg of the Montreal firm Phillips & Vineberg, sat down "with two blank pads of paper...and wrote up the original agreement between Cemp and the bank." The bank intended to own the property underlying the buildings and, since it did not wish to give anyone a mortgage on its own headquarters, elaborate legal steps were required to give investors in the project the security they needed without compromising the bank's title.

In its early years the Toronto-Dominion Centre, the modernist landmark designed by architect Mies van der Rohe, dominated the Toronto skyline. No bank had launched a commercial development on the scale of the Toronto-Dominion Centre.

The Bank Act of 1962 closely regulated what properties a bank could own, declaring, "The bank may acquire and hold real and immoveable property for its actual use and occupation and the management of its business." But J.J. Robinette gave his opinion that this stern phrase provided sufficient authority for a bank to build a 56-storey tower, several adjacent buildings and a huge commercial concourse, most of which the bank would not itself use or occupy at all. In November 1962 Allen Lambert publicly announced the launching of the Toronto-Dominion Centre. At about the same time the projects' leaders, having rejected the original architect's workaday design for the main tower, recruited Mies van der Rohe, whose design for the Seagram Building in New York had already been hailed as a modernist masterpiece. The first two towers of the Toronto-Dominion Centre, designed by van der Rohe and his Toronto associate John Parkin, were completed in 1967 and 1969. Eventually the complex would include a cluster of five tall, black monoliths, together with a matching low-rise bank pavilion, broad stretches of courtyard, a vast underground shopping centre and several levels of underground parking.

The Toronto-Dominion Centre transformed downtown Toronto and, indeed, all the cities of Canada. Imposing new towers with bank logos at the top began rising in the downtowns of all the country's major business centres. In a few years the Toronto-Dominion Centre, at first almost alone in the sky above King and Bay, was joined by the Royal Bank towers (1975), First Canadian Place

(1975) and Commerce Court (1973), as well as many non-bank towers, and the Toronto-Dominion underground concourses became linked into a network that gradually spread beneath much of the downtown core from Front to Queen Street. The project also gave impetus to the 1960s demolition trend, which stripped city cores of most of their architectural heritage and left them for many years with broad expanses of parking lots around a few soaring towers.

McCarthys was among the original tenants of the Toronto-Dominion Tower and moved in on January 1, 1968. Beverley Matthews himself chose the forty-seventh and forty-eighth floors for the firm's offices (claiming it was because he had been in the 48th Highlanders and would be able to remember which button to press in the elevator). It was a large commitment for the partnership (rental expenses jumped from $132,000 to $490,000 in a single year), but the impact on the firm's visibility in the Toronto business and legal scene was just as great. Post-1968, there was no longer any of the doubt that might have lingered a decade earlier about McCarthy & McCarthy's place in the big leagues of Toronto law firms. Its move from an insurance building to a bank tower symbolized its shifting allegiance, just as the major banks consolidated their status as the financial and commercial heavyweights of the Canadian economy. And the firm's new premises in the Toronto-Dominion Tower set a new standard of elegance in law office accommodation.

The firm now had two floors in an imposing tower, with spacious offices, spectacular views and elegant design (soon to include an expansive corporate art collection). Shortly after the move, McCarthys became the first Toronto law firm to hire a full-time professional law librarian, Christina Wright, to put its new library in order. This all set a higher standard for elite law firms, but it was new also for clients. McCarthys was declaring that legal clients, at least McCarthys' kind of legal clients, no longer expected their lawyers to behave as ink-stained scriveners in Dickensian warrens. They would be willing to support their legal counsellors in surroundings such as the T-D Centre provided. If that was a gamble, it paid off almost at once. Soon it was firms that did not have quarters in prestige high-rises that looked out of step. McCarthys' move set off a rapid shifting of downtown law firms into newer and much more expensive premises. Fasken Calvin and one or two other prominent firms also moved into the Toronto-Dominion Centre, but McCarthys had the feature that came to epitomize the new standard in legal offices. The circular staircase, custom-built while the building was being framed, which linked McCarthys' two floors, quickly became a legendary symbol of the new style in law-office design.*

The change was more than architectural. In 1966 a rare meeting of partners and junior partners had been held to approve the move and also the decision to take more expensive premises on an upper floor. The increased overheads demanded increased revenues; they were in effect a commitment to further growth. As office manager George Colvin acknowledged in a memo to the partners in January 1967, "costs related to the move are substantially higher than originally anticipated... [but] this move has been approached with a view to expansion." The increased costs, he said, could "be provided for by looking to an increased income from an expanded staff." Nor need the handful of partners alone bear the burden, Colvin went on. There had been, he said perceptively, "insufficient regard placed on the potential contained in the lower echelons."

The lower echelons were about to step forward. In 1968 McCarthys, which had admitted one new partner since 1959, admitted seven lawyers into full partnership: Peter Beattie, Ian Douglas, George Finlayson, Gerald Hayden, Douglas Laidlaw, Donald Sim and Patrick Vernon. It was joked that the firm needed "more names on the lease" (actually, Colvin had created Cartan Office Services as the partnership's management company in 1965, precisely so that individual partners would no longer be directly responsible for the rent), but in fact the "silver seven" had begun demanding admission to the partnership, and very narrow

*McCarthy Tétrault in Toronto now has circular staircases linking several levels of the T-D Centre and still awards pins based on the original staircase design to long-service employees.

ownership of the growing firm could not long be sustained. In the next six years, nineteen more partners would be admitted. Many of the new partners of 1968 had worked for the firm for fifteen years or more, but by 1974 the associate-to-partner schedule conformed to the modern standard of five to seven years of associate status preceding a decision on partnership. No longer would lawyers remain as employees for a decade or more. The oligarchy of a handful of partners was ending.

In one way, the partnership-promotion system in leading Toronto law firms continued to differ from the American pattern. From the early twentieth century, elite American firms had often employed up to four associates per partner. Collusion over pay scales had kept associate salaries low, and New York firms benefited from the labour of relatively low-paid associates who competed among themselves in aspiring for scarce partnership positions. In Canada, however, as the modern partner-track system took hold in the 1960s, the partner-associate ratio soon became close to one-to-one. A high proportion of associates could look forward to making partner within a few years.

By the time Canadian firms adopted a partner-track associate system, evidently, competition for graduating students had become more keen and the salary expectations of the best students were much greater. As a result there was much less profit for law firms in an associate's labour. In 1977 an internal study at McCarthys indicated that the net revenue generated by associates was about $400,000, or barely 5 per cent of firm revenues that year. Nevertheless, a firm that attempted to lower the wages and raise the numbers of its associates would have had difficulty getting the recruits it wanted. The roughly one-to-one partner-associate ratio remained common in most Canadian law firms, including McCarthys.

McCarthy & McCarthy's recruitment of law students took a step forward at about the time of its move to the Toronto-Dominion Centre. The instigator of the change was a future leader of the firm, Arthur Scace. A Toronto lawyer's son, Scace had earned degrees from the University of Toronto and Harvard University before heading to

Oxford University as a Rhodes Scholar in 1962. While in Britain he wrote to McCarthys about summer student work. The firm responded enthusiastically, and Scace launched into tax practice with McCarthy & McCarthy after his call to the bar in 1967.*

Scace soon began teaching at Osgoode Hall Law School, then still downtown and just across University Avenue from McCarthys' offices in the Canada Life Building ("I may even have been teaching before I got called," he recalled). When a greatly revised Canadian Income Tax Act became law in 1971, Scace consolidated his growing reputation in tax practice by publishing one of the first texts on it, and he quickly became a leader in McCarthy's growing tax department. While teaching at the law school, Scace concluded that McCarthy & McCarthy was failing to spot and hire the best possible graduates. Other firms were beginning to plan their recruiting strategies, and McCarthys needed to respond.

"I was tied into Osgoode Hall and knew the academics as well as the practice people...and in those days you could call the dean and say, 'What good people do you have?'" Scace recalled. Student recruitment had been the responsibility of John Clarry and Patrick Vernon for some years, but Scace quickly convinced Clarry that his own student contacts were better, and within a year of his hiring he was running the firm's recruitment program, first on his own, later with David Gordon. The casual circumstances of his own hiring gradually gave way to more sophisticated recruiting programs and to more intense competition among law firms for the best students and among law students for the most coveted jobs.[48]

*On his return from Oxford Scace still had to obtain a Canadian law degree, but while he was an Osgoode Hall student the firm paid him summer wages at the same $50 a month that LL.B. graduates articling at McCarthys received. For a time Scace became famous among the staff as the only student in firm history to have an office of his own.

"BIG FIRMS MAKE LAW"

McCARTHY & McCARTHY of the Toronto-Dominion Centre era was a big firm and growing fast. The 31 lawyers of 1962 (all but eight were salaried associates) had become 57 lawyers, 30 of them partners, by 1972. They would double their numbers, to 112 lawyers, by 1982. Fear of being burdened by the leasing costs of the T-D offices soon faded as revenues grew at a spectacular pace. McCarthy & McCarthy billed over $1 million for the first time in 1958. The figure was $1.2 million in 1960, $2.9 million in 1968 and $4 million by 1972. Revenues would surpass $10 million in 1979 and jump to $22 million in 1982.

One aspect of McCarthys' expanding stature was what its veterans now recall as a golden age of the litigation department. By the 1960s, John Robinette was at his professional peak and the clients and students he attracted, as well as the sheer strength of his example, had rebuilt McCarthys' litigation tradition at a time when many corporate-law firms were turning away from litigation. In the 1950s Robinette had continued to take some sensational criminal trials, including the defence of Steve Suchan, who was hanged in 1952 for killing a police officer earlier that year—Robinette's only executed client.* Robinette never lost his interest in criminal law, and as part of his legacy McCarthy & McCarthy's litigation section remained slightly unusual among large corporate firms in maintaining a criminal defence practice.

Gradually, however, Robinette shifted his emphasis from criminal law to civil litigation cases. He found them more interesting, he said, and McCarthys and its clients appreciated the change, too. For several decades Robinette engaged in many high-profile civil litigations on behalf of McCarthy clients. He continued the medical malpractice cases the firm had long done for the Canadian Medical Protective Association. He fought the case of the Herbert Cox will, which attempted to bequeath the Cox family's Canada Life fortune as a charitable trust for Canada Life's employees, all the way to the Privy Council in London (and lost, much to the chagrin of Frank McCarthy, who had drawn the will in the first place). But many clients with no connection to McCarthy

*Suchan's mother, a cleaner in the Canada Life Building, approached Robinette to defend her son one night when he was working late at his McCarthy & McCarthy office.

also came to retain Robinette, perhaps most famously in the Texas Gulf Sulphur mineral-exploration litigation, which lasted from October 1966 to April 1968 and was at the time the longest civil trial in Canadian history. Robinette acted for Leitch Gold Mines, which lost its $500-million claim against Texas Gulf but won just enough to pay its legal bills.

Robinette's first associate, John Brooke, accepted a judicial appointment in 1963, but by then the young lawyers attracted to McCarthys by Robinette's presence were giving the firm "bench strength" in litigation that was unmatched by any of the other big firms. Robinette liked to do his own research and it was not his style to go into court with a line of juniors carrying bags and papers for him, but his example—and the endless courtesy and respect that was the other side of his solitude—inspired many of the young lawyers who had joined McCarthys because of Robinette.

In court, Robinette operated with Olympian calm. He was not averse to letting the sheer strength of his reputation draw judges into agreement with his arguments, but his courtroom style was unfailingly polite and thoughtful. In contrast George Finlayson, who joined the firm in 1951, and Douglas Laidlaw (1954) boasted of being called "street fighters" or "junkyard dogs." They earned reputations for brawling verbally with opposing counsel and even judges, and they were often turbulent around the office as well. But they developed great technical skills in the courtroom and in the preparation of cases, and they brought in many big wins for grateful clients.

Laidlaw pleaded fifty cases before the Supreme Court of Canada in a relatively brief career. His constant client was the Canadian Medical Protective Association and its medical malpractice cases. The CMPA, always ready to fight a case rather than compromise a doctor's reputation in a settlement, gave its litigators abundant opportunities to go into court, and Laidlaw used the unending sequence of malpractice cases to hone his own skills and those of many juniors. Still, like most of the litigators, he was a generalist. Early in his career he won a settlement for the laid-off engineers of the Avro Arrow project that set new standards in employment law, and a decade later he led the defence in the enormous Hamilton harbour dredging bid-rigging case. Robinette remained a giant, but Laidlaw became the team leader of litigators as well as "a work magnet" who kept the department growing in size and reputation.

Beverley Matthews, Lois Robinette, and John Robinette.

With the CMPA retainer and lots of corporate clients coming to McCarthys with their civil litigation problems, the litigation department was able to recruit and train more promising juniors, building strength upon strength. John Francis joined the firm in 1960, Burton Tait in 1964, Colin Campbell in 1965, Alan Lenczner and Tom Heintzman in 1967, and Ron Slaght in 1970. Marvyn Koenigsberg, the first female litigator to crack the all-male barrier—and confront the macho ethos—of litigation, joined in 1974, left briefly and returned in 1976. At the time, McCarthys was almost the only one of the elite Bay Street firms to maintain a large litigation practice, particularly one where the litigators did not necessarily shy away from criminal trials, divorce and family work and other projects remote from the concerns of most corporate lawyers and their clients.

Other departments were blossoming as well. McCarthys now had a steady stream of bank work for the Toronto-Dominion Bank and the Bank of Nova Scotia, much of it directed by John Clarry. In 1970, when the general counsel to the Canadian Bankers Association retired, Clarry's great reputation in banking law—and a vigorous lobby by Allen Lambert and Beverley Matthews—secured his appointment as the new counsel to the association. His fifteen-year tenure there gave McCarthys a window on bank policy and banking legislation that no other firm could match, enhancing its ability to advise banks on the evolution of banking law and legislation. When foreign-owned banks were authorized to operate in Canada as "Schedule B" banks, McCarthys secured several of them as clients.

In the 1960s and 1970s the banks and their law firms had become increasingly frustrated with the Bank Act, which they found inadequate to meet the needs of Canadian banking and corporate finance. Pending change in the act, McCarthys' banking lawyers began building what one of them, Bradley Crawford, later described as "the crystal staircase." Much as Robinette had reinterpreted the language of the Bank Act to authorize the Toronto-Dominion Centre, McCarthys' lawyers began pushing bold interpretations of other sections of the act, always construing them to permit the new activities and programs the banks and their clients needed. Wherever judges and colleagues proved sympathetic to the enlarged interpretations, McCarthys made that victory a stepping stone to another extension of what banks could do.

In effect they were revising the Bank Act by case law and legal opinion. As a result, many of the crucial innovations banks sought had already been established in practice well before they were formally incorporated in revisions to the Bank Act. For Brad Crawford, this represented the essence of what big law firms did. "Small firms practise law, big firms make law," Crawford liked to say. A big law firm, he argued, had the skills and the reputation, as well as the clients with substantial legal issues, to shape and revise the law, not simply to see it applied. It was not exclusively a matter of size, though size helped a firm to assemble the resources and attract the clients who made such work possible. A firm like McCarthys still did lots of more routine legal work, Crawford acknowledged, but he was convinced that what

The litigation department of McCarthy & McCarthy in 1979 celebrates John J. Robinette's fifty years of legal practice: front row, Burton Tait, Roy Stevenson, Colin Campbell, Marvyn Koenigsberg, Robinette, Elizabeth Stewart, Douglas Laidlaw, Alan Lenczner and Ronald Slaght; back row, George Finlayson, Gerald Sadvari, Ken Peel, Thomas Heintzman, Michael Royce, William Cornwall, John Finlay, Joseph Colangelo and Paul Morrison.

really distinguished elite practices and justified to commercial clients the costs of employing them was the "transformative" work they did in reshaping and reinterpreting law. Crawford himself had begun as a law professor. He first came to McCarthys only briefly, to observe real practice. He soon concluded there was more intellectual challenge in the law firm than the law school and he stayed. But he retained the nickname "Prof," and much of his practice involved research into legal issues at the leading edges of banking practice, including seminal work in new banking law as direct deposits, interbank transfers and eventually on-line banking replaced traditional paper cheques and bank drafts. Crawford eventually succeeded Clarry as counsel to the Canadian Bankers Association.

Not every specialization proved successful. Since the appointment of Harold Fox as counsel to the firm in 1949, McCarthys had built up a substantial practice in patent law with several lawyers and patent agents who had been attracted by Fox's expertise. But the patent specialists remained somewhat apart from the rest of the firm, and in 1970 the whole department abruptly walked out to form a firm devoted to patent law and patent agency. Fox, then 75, died soon after, but the others built a successful patent agency and intellectual-property law firm called Sim, Hughes.* McCarthys struggled for several years to regain a foothold in patent law. Like the departure of the tax specialists in 1961, it was an early warning of the risk of specialization: the specialists, once their reputation was established, might conclude they could do better in their own "boutique" practice.

In the 1970s McCarthy lawyers had opportunities to "make law" in a number of specialist fields that few had noticed or predicted. Daniel G. Cooper, who had joined the corporate department in 1971, began doing increasing work in the leasing and operating of computer systems. Cooper noted the special legal problems that were emerging out of leases for computer hardware and software. He began to follow new problems in patent and copyright, in the licensing of software and in the unique aspects of sourcing and supply agreements for computing services. In the 1970s hardly anyone used or understood computers to any great extent, but Cooper took time out to learn more about the new technology. For a short time he seemed the only lawyer around who knew the leading edges of law as it related to the computer business. Out of that expertise he developed the beginnings of an information technology practice at McCarthy & McCarthy. With the launching of the personal computer era in the 1980s and the dot-com explosion of the 1990s, this field would become a great strength for the firm.

Communications law became another example of one lawyer's interest coinciding with a sudden expansion of legal opportunities. Peter

*One Fox legacy was a scholarship in his name that assists British and Canadian law students to work or study in each other's countries. Over the years, McCarthy Tétrault has hosted many Fox Scholarship students.

Grant, an accomplished musician before going into law, had an interest in cultural issues, and a law school legal-history paper he wrote on the evolution of Canadian-content regulations for television was published just as the Canadian Radio-Television Commission (later the Canadian Radio-television and Telecommunications Commission) was being established. Grant, still an articling student at McCarthys, found himself being consulted by Pierre Juneau, the powerful Ottawa bureaucrat who headed the CRTC. Grant took a sabbatical from McCarthys to write a text on communications law and then went "on loan" to the CRTC itself, which began using McCarthys as its outside counsel. J.J. Robinette and Tom Heintzman established fundamental precedents in the communications field while acting on behalf of the CRTC. When Grant returned to McCarthys, however, the firm switched from acting for the commission to representing companies appearing before it. As Canadian telecommunications monopolies were broken up in favour of regulated competition, McCarthys developed a large and profitable telecommunications practice.

Specialties like Cooper's and Grant's had initially provoked some controversy within the firm. John Clarry, leader of the corporate department and by the 1970s Beverley Matthews' strong right arm and likely successor, saw potential in the specialized fields they were entering. Clarry judged that McCarthy & McCarthy could gain an advantage by investing in emerging fields of law that might grow and become valuable; he encouraged members to take courses and sabbaticals and to undertake research in time spent away from the firm. Not all partners agreed. Many thought a lawyer was a lawyer, and they did not want to support lawyers who were not billing clients regularly. "There was not much support for it, except from me, and I guess Matthews and then Hayden, too," recalls Clarry. "Other lawyers in the firm thought these people were off on a side track, indulging in something that entertained them, but they weren't in the mainstream of law.... There were expenses in this, and by this time people were looking at billings."

A few years later a similar controversy erupted over the creation of a research department. Osler, Hoskin had created a research capability, almost inadvertently, in the 1950s when it hired Bertha Wilson, who became a kind of expert counsel to everyone else in that firm before she went on to a judicial career that led to the Supreme Court of Canada. Clarry thought McCarthy & McCarthy could also benefit from expertise in legal research, but the suggestion was vetoed several times by partners who believed that lawyers who did not do their own research were hardly lawyers at all. The litigation department in particular was skeptical of the need for research capability.

Clarry got his way in 1984 but Eric Gertner, who left the Ontario Law Reform Commission to launch the new research section, soon discovered his position remained controversial. "When I came, I was told I would mostly work on the corporate section, and I had an office on the corporate floor. And that surprised me, because I had absorbed the idea that law was really litigation, was courtroom stuff, and I could see the need for research there. I came to see that there was still the view that litigators were renaissance men, that they could do anything and could do it well. So I took the view that that was fine with me.

"In six months, I was down on the litigation floor." One reason was that specialist legal research began to demonstrate its utility in what proved to be among the litigation department's big wins, the Lac-Corona litigation over control of a hugely valuable northern Ontario gold mine. The case had been initiated by Doug Laidlaw and was eventually won by Alan Lenczner and Ron Slaght. "There were crucial questions of law to be sorted out—the law of confidence was crucial.... It was a big win, and we were the underdogs, and we won a reputation, and some of it affected the research department." As civil litigations became larger, more complex and more based on masses of documents, legal research gradually became an essential aspect of litigation departments. In 2002 Gertner estimated that his research team advised 250 McCarthy lawyers a year, besides training the firm's students in legal-research processes.

Clarry's advocacy for a research capacity within the firm came to be seen as brilliant planning.

As specialized departments developed, there remained the ongoing work of the corporate section, always the backbone of a large downtown law firm. McCarthys continued to attract the work of many of Canada's largest corporations and its client list in the late 1970s demonstrated the depth and breadth of the practice's corporate client base. In 1977 McCarthys' top ten clients provided 20 per cent of its income, and the top 25 per cent were a third of billings. In the 1970s the view of McCarthys partners was that the firm should strive to reduce this dependence and expand its network of smaller clients. In reality the firm was typical of most law firms, in that a small cluster of clients usually provided a large share of all income.*

*By the end of the century, 80 per cent of McCarthy Tétrault income came from just 7.5 per cent of the firm's roster of clients.

Canada Life, by then a century-old client, was regularly McCarthy & McCarthy's single largest source of billings in the 1970s. Union Carbide, recruited by Leighton McCarthy before World War I, remained a top-ten client. Atlantic Sugar, a Hayden client from the 1930s, remained in the top twenty in most years of the 1970s and the Canadian Medical Protective Association, which had relied on McCarthys since Lally McCarthy's day, was usually in the top five. The cluster of banking firms in the top twenty-five clients included not only Toronto-Dominion Bank, Bank of Nova Scotia and the Canadian Bankers Association, but smaller financial institutions. Wood Gundy, Nesbitt Thomson, Goldman Sachs, Thorne Riddell and other blue-chip names from the financial and accounting sector occasionally cracked the list of leading clients.

TransCanada PipeLines, secured as a client by Beverley Matthews in 1962, led an energy-client sector that included Gulf Oil, Polysar and others. The real estate section, transformed by the Toronto-Dominion Centre project of the mid-sixties, often atttracted similar development projects that became important clients, at least temporarily. Pacific

Centre in Vancouver, Edmonton Centre in Edmonton, Eaton Centre in Toronto and various development corporations associated with them all were high-value clients during the late 1970s.

New clients appeared as well, some only briefly. The abortive Canadian Arctic Gas consortium was a big client for a few years and so was Ontario Transportation Development Corporation, set up to develop a magnetic-levitation rail system that was soon abandoned. The CRTC, drawn to McCarthys by Peter Grant's expertise in communications law, was the twelfth-largest client by 1977, but it soon vanished as the firm began acting for broadcasting and "telecom" clients appearing before the commission.

Two new clients that would last longer were Noranda Mines and Canada Packers, both top-ten clients by the late 1970s. They had recently been brought to McCarthys by Daniel Harvey, previously a senior partner at another firm, Holden, Murdoch. Harvey had left that firm due to internal conflicts over competing mining-firm clients, but after a few years he concluded his own small firm was too small to serve such clients effectively. When he joined McCarthys in 1973 Harvey brought not only Noranda and Canada Packers but also his associates Jim McCartney, later a leader in the firm, and Daryl McLean, one of the first women to become a force within McCarthys' commercial section.

One force driving the evolution of corporate-law departments in the 1960s and 1970s stemmed in part from the 1964 securities scandal known as "Windfall." The outcry over stock-market manipulations led to a new Ontario Securities Act in 1967, and it was soon followed by the Ontario Business Corporations Act, the Canada Business Corporations Act and similar legislation in other provinces. These new statutes substantially increased the obligations upon corporations, their directors and their officers in organizing and financing corporate activity.

Corporate lawyers quickly felt the consequences. Securities law now required "full, true, and plain disclosure" in corporate-finance prospectuses and made corporations liable for the claims made in them. The drafting of prospectuses, once considered largely a marketing task, suddenly generated substantial demand for lawyers who could master the details of a corporate client's business and speedily produce a full and accurate prospectus.*

Into the 1970s, lawyers drafting prospectuses worked closely with printers; each change to the text required new typesetting, which in turn required fresh proofreading. Shouldering the bulk of these tedious but vital chores, younger lawyers and students learned the business in detail (and also revealed who had the patience, the meticulousness and the commitment required to ensure accuracy). These processes required teams of lawyers and helped fuel the rapid expansion of corporate departments—and of the average size of law firms—from the 1960s to the 1980s. Gradually, word processors reduced the proofreading burden and fax machines and electronic delivery sped the delivery schedules, but the growth in complexity, in demands from clients and in firm size all encouraged specialization.

Into the 1970s most corporate lawyers considered themselves generalists and expected to cover most aspects of corporate law, other than tax, themselves. Over time, several subsets emerged within the business-law field; corporate finance and mergers and acquisitions each became a substantial and complex field. Young lawyers began to specialize in one or another, and increasingly they would work together on large-scale recapitalizations, takeovers or corporate reorganizations as teams of specialists. Continued growth in firm size went hand in hand with ongoing specialization and compartmentalization.

Developments in securities regulation naturally had a significant impact upon the process of mergers and acquisitions. Peter Beattie, who

*In 1978, advising the Government of Canada on the prospectus for a $250-million issue of bonds, McCarthys had to include in the text an analysis of the potential for the separation of Quebec and the possible impact upon the bonds. Given the sensitivity of the text, McCarthys lawyers had the wording reviewed personally by Prime Minister Pierre Trudeau.

joined McCarthy & McCarthy in 1956, recalled that there were virtually no rules for takeovers when the Levy family business consulted the firm about its plans to acquire Russell Industries in 1960. The shares were acquired before anyone else had a chance to bid, but Beattie pointed to the ease and speed of that takeover as one factor leading to securities-law reform. The securities rule book continued to expand; Beattie remembered it as 25 pages in 1960, about 100 in the late 1970s and 400 pages by the 1980s. As late as 1979, however, when Beattie acted for the Hudson's Bay Company in its battle to acquire Simpsons department stores, it was still unusual for commercial takeovers to provoke extensive legal skirmishes in the courts or before the regulatory agencies.

"At that time, there had been very little drama in this. There might have been a maximum of a dozen lawyers in Toronto who really knew anything about that type of transaction." In the HBC-Simpsons battle, Simpsons attempted to divest itself of much of its value by initiating a large dividend payout after "the Bay" made a fixed cash offer based on the pre-dividend value. Yet only a litigator and two or three corporate lawyers took part in McCarthys' successful efforts to overcome that strategy on behalf of the Bay. With each successful attack or defence, however, the complexity of takeover offers and the legal strategies used for them grew. "Once you became involved in huge amounts of due diligence work, then it required teams and teams of people to read every page and examine every issue," recalled Beattie. By the late 1980s, when McCarthys advised the Hiram Walker company as it resisted a takeover bid from the Reichmann family, large numbers of lawyers were involved on each side.* [49]

One consequence of specialization was a steady retreat from small-scale legal work for individual clients. McCarthy & McCarthy lawyers had once done wills and estates, personal real estate transfers,

*The Reichmann interests eventually acquired Hiram Walker, but only after raising their offer by over a billion dollars. Given the value McCarthys had earned for the shareholders, Beattie felt entitled to bill Hiram Walker $2 million. Just before the takeover was completed, he hand-delivered the invoice and collected the cheque from the outgoing management shortly before they were all dismissed. Managers installed by the new owners tried but failed to stop the payment.

motor-vehicle litigation and divorce work as part of their general practice. While the firm continued into the 1990s to do such work for friends and clients, routine legal work for individual clients gradually gave way to concentration on more substantial retainers, generally from corporations rather than individuals. The firm also put more emphasis on its traditional disinclination to act against corporate interests. In 1979, when the rising litigator Alan Lenczner was offered an interesting case by a labour union, Beverley Matthews reiterated the "previously unwritten policy of the firm that McCarthys will not provide services for trade unions under any circumstances." As they specialized, corporate-law firms like McCarthy & McCarthy became more than ever inclined to leave the representation of such clients to other lawyers.*[50]

*In 2004 most large firms had ceased to practise family law, but McCarthy Tétrault continued a very successful family law practice led by Toronto partners Steven Grant and Gerald Sadvari.

LOOKING TO THE FUTURE

BEVERLEY MATTHEWS was seventy in 1975, still near the peak of his powers and still a vital force in the firm. In some ways he was a reincarnation of D'Alton McCarthy, even to the love of outdoor activities with dogs and horses. In 1976 Matthews would mark the sixtieth anniversary of McCarthy & McCarthy (and the 100th anniversary of its move to Toronto) by inviting the whole firm to his country estate at Shanty Bay, just down the shore from D'Alton McCarthy Jr.'s Tollendal estate. Matthews had the same energy and personal magnetism as the firm's founder. Everyone noted his commanding presence and his great personal charm; it was said he was the kind of man who sat at the head of a round table. He had a personal and political network at least as broad as D'Alton McCarthy's and, unlike McCarthy, he remained a consummate political insider. He was for many years chief fundraiser of the Conservative Party and Prime Minister John Diefenbaker offered to make him a senator or Canadian ambassador to the United States.

Matthews had also developed a sense of his firm's history. After the historian William Kilbourn wrote *Pipeline* in 1970, Matthews suggested he consider a history of McCarthy & McCarthy next. When that fell through—Kilbourn concluded the firm's records were not adequate for a substantial history—Matthews organized an internal typescript history, largely based on the memories of the senior partners.[51]

In the early 1970s Matthews began preparing for his eventual retirement by creating McCarthy & McCarthy's first management committee.[52] Matthews, whom one of his partners admiringly described as "a direct descendant of Louis XIV through Lorenzo de Medici," had not been converted to rule-by-committee as the governing principle at McCarthy & McCarthy.* Appointment to the new management committee was by invitation, and for many years committee members dragged chairs into his office for the committee's monthly meeting. The partners still had tremendous deference to his views, his plans, even his allocations. Some of his responsibilities were gradually being transferred to John Clarry, who had emerged as both Matthews' and everyone else's preference as the successor, but Matthews still dominated the firm as much as he chose. One meeting concerned the annual financial report and the minutes of the discussion say, in their entirety, "The annual financial statements were discussed and after a few brief comments BM said, 'Let us close the discussion and be joyful.'"†

Matthews also relied on his office manager, Edward King, who succeeded George Colvin in about 1970. The rising size and income of the

*One proposal for a lunch meeting, with food to be brought in, provoked a brief reply: "Mr. Matthews believes sandwiches are hazardous to health." Instead the committee should conclude its business, then retire to his club for lunch.

†A new partner in the mid-1970s recalls Matthews coming to him with a card on which all the partners' names had been listed in order of seniority. Beside each partner's name a share of the year's profits (then expressed as points out of 100) had been written in pencil. Only the last numbers, beside the three newest partners' names, were unchanged. Every other number had obviously been erased and rewritten many times as Matthews made the rounds of the partners. The newest partner thought it best not to propose further revision.

firm were leading to managerial innovations. McCarthys first had its books done by an accounting company (Clarkson Gordon), rather than by its staff bookkeeper, in 1968, and King was eager to apply management methods to the operations.* He pursued news of innovations American firms were making in law firm management, such as reducing the one-secretary-per-lawyer ratio by extending the use of pool secretaries—a change much resented by many of the lawyers. The firm's first computer went "online" (the word was already in vogue) in 1974, and King began compiling annual billing statistics in 1975.

Beverley Matthews, managing partner of McCarthy & McCarthy, in his prime in the 1970s.

In January 1977 King reported that the introduction of computerized billing had reduced the amount of work-in-progress, or WIP (that is, work done but not yet billed to the client), from 42 per cent to 30 per cent of billables. Other Toronto law firms, he noted, were following McCarthys' lead into computerization, but most still had work-in-progress rates of over 35 per cent. WIP would gradually become a critical tool of business-like management of the practice and a subject constantly monitored by administrative staff; King's 1977 memo seems to have marked its first recorded use at McCarthy & McCarthy.

Administrative changes continued to be reflected in the work experience of staff. For many years "staff" meant secretaries almost exclusively,

*King had once worked in management at a dairy company. Matthews claimed his partners were sometimes irritated by King's habit of saying, "Well, that is not how we did things at Pet Milk."

one per lawyer, taking dictation and typing drafts, first on manual typewriters, later on electric typewriters and gradually on dedicated word processors and then personal computers. Wills required letter-perfect typing, without a single strikeover. (The invention of "correction fluid" provoked serious debate: could it be used in will drafting?) Many senior support staff recall the frustration of making a single error at the foot of a long page with six carbons underneath it and having to tear it up and start again.

Long-time staff members of McCarthy Tétrault in Toronto, all of whom began work at the Canada Life Building before 1968, at a 1997 reception: front row, Diane Papadopoulos (1964), Margerie Koren (1956) and Doreen Duncan (1956); back row, Angie Crawley (1967), Gloria May (1965), Mary Coulter (1964), Margarette Livie (1962), Joan McLarney (1962) and Beverly Mortley (1966).

In 1964 the litigation department hired Jim Bristow, an English-trained law clerk, to build a law clerks department within McCarthy & McCarthy. Clerks, who did a wide range of case management and administrative support tasks, were still almost unknown in Canada, but they quickly caught on in several of the larger firms and Bristow became one of the founders of the Institute of Law Clerks, which in 1968 began to train and certify clerks, many of whom began as secretaries.

In the old Canada Life Building the secretarial staff had a lunchroom, and a good deal of socializing went on. That declined with the move to the multiple floors of the T-D Centre. There was, however, one factor working in the other direction: the baseball team. In the 1970s and 1980s McCarthys' team was active in a law firm baseball league every summer. It was always an all-female sport but lawyer Ross Butters coached, senior lawyers attended regularly and the partners paid for uniforms and expenses.

The 1970s also began the breakdown of the great social distance that once separated lawyers and staff, the days when everyone was "Mr." or "Miss," small talk was discouraged and senior partners were Olympian figures to whom no one dared to speak. In the Canada Life Building, white-gloved elevator operators moved everyone aside when Senator Hayden arrived in the lobby so that he could ride up to his office in solitary dignity. There were no elevator operators in the Toronto-Dominion Centre, and while other passengers might not presume to speak to Mr. Matthews in the elevator, he did not ride alone.

In 1976, at Beverley Matthews' country estate near Barrie, McCarthy & McCarthy celebrated its own sixtieth anniversary and the hundredth anniversary of D'Alton McCarthy's Toronto firm: from left, Joy Clarry, Beverley Matthews, Salter Hayden and John Clarry.

Because of his stature among his partners, perhaps also because he had begun to plan a transition of power as meticulously as he had planned so much else since the 1950s, Beverley Matthews never faced the rebellion some aging leaders faced at other once autocratically run law firms. In the 1970s the most evident discontent came from a handful of female lawyers who began to challenge the male ethos of the firm.

Matthews was a man's man, most comfortable in boardrooms, fishing camps and all-male retreats such as the Toronto Club and the York Club. Doing business at the club, holding firm dinners at the club, socializing at the club; these were pillars of the legal and business community in which he had earned his many successes. None of them made any place for women, and by the mid-1970s McCarthys had a few women who were unwilling to tolerate that situation.

Daryl McLean, who had come to McCarthys with Daniel Harvey in 1973, discovered the unwritten rules when she became pregnant in 1975. Consideration of her admission to the partnership ceased. If she was still an associate next year, the management committee agreed, then she could be considered. Meanwhile, McLean was told she would qualify for unemployment insurance like any other female staff member going on maternity leave. McLean, a Maritimer with strong views about "pogey," indignantly refused even to apply for UI. She took a month's leave of absence when the baby was born, returned to work and got her partnership in 1976.

At about that time, some of the women in the firm began meeting occasionally to support one another and work for changes there. Dinners and partnership meetings at the Toronto Club became one of their targets. The clubs were all-male, and the women understood that exclusion from the clubs meant exclusion from an important element of the work of the firm. They were particularly offended when Matthews continued to schedule partnership meetings and dinners in places where women were admitted only on special occasions and then only by the side door. "Those fights were good times," remembers Marvyn Koenigsberg, "because there was an end in sight, and we achieved what we had to do. Beverley Matthews said: 'But the women's door at the Toronto Club is a much nicer door.' 'That's all we want,' I said, 'the power to choose.'" Eventually, as part of the general decline of club culture in law firm operations, firm meetings and dinners moved to hotel ballrooms, and fitness clubs began to replace men's clubs in the priorities of the partners.

Not all the confrontations that took place left such positive memories. A series of dinners the female lawyers organized in the late 1970s spawned the legend that they had formed a branch of SCUM, the "Society for Cutting up Men." Koenigsberg swears that was a joke, as was another organization called WITCH (no one seems to remember the basis of the acronym, but it began with "Women" and ended "from Hell"). A more substantial product of the women's complaints about their marginalization was the Gender Committee, which undertook research into numbers of women, working conditions and recruitment parameters. Eventually the Gender Committee became the firm's Diversity Committee, which continued to work on issues of minority access and diversity.

One issue given focus by the women was leaves and sabbaticals. Female lawyers, they pointed out, needed maternity leaves and opportunities for part-time work while they had young families. They began to suggest that such breaks in their career path should not undermine their rights to promotion and partnership. With such claims, they introduced the long-lived debate that set quality of life against billable hours, a discussion with particular resonance for female lawyers but one that resonated for some male lawyers, too. The women's campaign for increased opportunities for leaves and part-time practice meshed with some requests by male lawyers seeking study leaves or opportunities to write or teach law. A request by Alan Lenczner, a rising litigator, for a sabbatical in 1975 was turned down, but a system of sabbatical leaves and maternity leaves was gradually worked out.

In 1975, office manager King circulated to the management committee a memo about the long-range future of the firm. King's printouts from the computer were providing new data about the firm's income, where it came from and who earned it. King pulled together for the committee some provocative statistics about the firm's revenues, its lawyers and their clients. He suggested that the time was right to start doing some serious planning for McCarthys' future direction. Startled, the firm struck its first "Long Range Planning Committee."

The committee report, received in 1977, traced how far McCarthy & McCarthy had come: from 15 lawyers in 1957 to 77 in 1977. The authors estimated that 1977's annual growth rate in number of lawyers (about 10 per cent) was unlikely to continue, but they pointed out that a modest 5-per-cent rate would produce 135 lawyers by 1987 and urged the partners not to consider such a figure "preposterous." (It was, of course, a substantial underestimation.) They concluded that "there is a deep consensus in the firm that we must be prepared to grow over the next decade."

Most of the conclusions of the Long Range Planning Committee were safe, comfortable and traditional. Indeed, not much of the new statistical data spilling out of King's computers made it into the planning report. The authors dryly noted that in this modern age any report must have some statistics, but all they provided was some sketchy data on the pace of increases in the number of lawyers. They noted that most businesses would measure growth in profitability rather than number of staff but made no attempt to do so themselves.

As far as the committee on long-range planning could tell, the future looked much like the past. No substantial reorientation in the shape of the firm or the nature of legal practice was seen on the horizon. The committee advised that all the lawyers would have to become business-getters if the firm were to continue to prosper, but that kind of advice had been standard for most of the century. Overall, the authors found a strong consensus among the partners that "it is essential that the working atmosphere be preserved, even at the cost of increased profitability or money incomes." McCarthy & McCarthy was as big, as rich and as elaborately managed as any law firm in Canadian history, but concepts such as marketing and profitability-per-partner were still far from the thinking of the lawyers asked by their partners to do the firm's forward thinking.

Shortly after the delivery of the planning report, some of the firm's clients began asking McCarthys more and more frequently if they could send some lawyers to undertake some piece of work that had arisen in Alberta. By the late 1970s Calgary was rapidly becoming the hottest place in the country to do business, and McCarthys was being drawn into it. The Calgary market for legal services suddenly became the catalyst for fundamental changes at McCarthy & McCarthy, indeed for the largest redefinition of how law firms practised that had been seen since the era in which D'Alton McCarthy had founded the firm.

BLACK & COMPANY

LAW AND BUSINESS IN CALGARY

CALGARY LAW AND CALGARY LAW FIRMS | 6

When a few lawyers at McCarthy & McCarthy began to consider practising law in Calgary as well as in Toronto in the 1970s, they were entering a city and province with its own legal traditions and strong views about just who should practise law there. In a decade when tensions between east and west within Canada were reaching fever pitch, law firm expansions would provide a new front for east-west rivalries, one that would eventually lead to precedents in constitutional law as well as a revolution in law firm organization in Canada.

Just about a century before McCarthy & McCarthy began looking west, one H.Y. Bleeker, from Belleville, Ontario, became the first lawyer to practise in what is now Alberta. Bleeker opened an office in Edmonton in 1881 (when Alberta was still part of the North-West Territories) and then moved south to Calgary in 1882 to become Calgary's first lawyer. He would soon incorporate the town of Calgary and become town solicitor.

The transcontinental line of the Canadian Pacific Railway reached southern Alberta in 1883, and a small police outpost named Fort Calgary was swiftly reborn as the centre of business and transportation for the region. Soon cattle barons, encouraged by the railroad and by federal land policy, developed vast ranches on the southern Alberta grasslands recently acquired by treaty from the Blackfoot Nation. Calgary at once became the cattlemen's headquarters and the transit point for the beef they shipped, and they created many enduring Calgary institutions, including The Ranchmen's Club and the Calgary Exhibition (which grew to include the Stampede in 1912).

James Lougheed, a Toronto lawyer who arrived in Calgary a few months after Bleeker, was among the first to seize upon the opportunities in the new town. Having secured the position of local counsel for the railroad and Hudson's Bay Company, Lougheed immediately began investing in Calgary real estate and ranching properties. In the midst of the region's first economic boom, he had launched its first great legal career and law firm. Eventually Lougheed would be a federal cabinet minister and senator. He would receive a knighthood and serve as lieutenant governor of his province.

Well before Alberta became a province in 1905, Calgary had developed its own legal institutions, leading lawyers and bar traditions. When the region was still part of the North-West Territories, officers of the North-West (later Royal Canadian) Mounted Police were empowered to act as stipendiary magistrates for the region. Police Superintendent James MacLeod had not only founded Fort Calgary but was its first magistrate and justice of the peace. Formal courts were established for the North-West Territories in 1887. Arthur Sifton, a Manitoba lawyer who moved to Calgary in 1889, became territorial chief justice in 1902. He sat at Calgary, as did Charles Rouleau, originally from Quebec. In 1890 an Irish immigrant named P.J. "Paddy" Nolan, the most colourful member of the early Calgary bar, persuaded his dozen fellow lawyers to found the Calgary Bar Association, principally to express their concern about competition from unlicensed real estate conveyancers. Calgary became a city in 1893, and in 1898 the Calgary Bar Association helped form a territorial law society. When the Province of Alberta was established in 1905, Alexander Rutherford, an Edmonton lawyer recently arrived from Kemptville, Ontario, became the first premier and Sifton became the first chief justice of Alberta. The territorial law society then became the Law Society of Alberta and received statutory powers to govern the profession in the new province.

Patrick "Paddy" Nolan, raconteur, bon vivant and pillar of the Calgary bar in its early years.

In the first decade after the railroad arrived, the southern Alberta region centred on Calgary had far more cattle than people and Calgary remained small. Only after a great wave of immigration to the Prairies began after 1896 was most of southern Alberta opened up for farm settlement. Thereafter, Calgary and the province grew rapidly. Between 1901 and 1911 Alberta grew from 75,000 to 375,000 people. Calgary's population increased tenfold to 44,000, though the *Law List* identified only 38 lawyers in town in 1910.[53]

Thereafter Calgary, its economy and its lawyers experienced a long cycle of booms and busts. The ranching boom of the 1880s had established the town as the regional economic capital. The settlement boom of the first years of the twentieth century confirmed that, and by 1920 Calgary had some 120 lawyers, the largest number anywhere in the province. Calgary's next boom began with the discovery of oil at Turner Valley, just outside Calgary, and oil fever resurged at the end of the First World War. In the early 1920s, it was said, "there was no one who was anyone at the Calgary bar who was not director of at least one oil company and counsel to several more."[54] The later 1920s, however, were difficult years for most of southern Alberta. The Great Depression and the retreat of farming from southern Alberta during the drought of the 1930s sapped Calgary along with the rest of the region. Oil exploration surged again at Turner Valley in the late 1930s, with new discoveries and new royalty financing systems to rebuild investor confidence, but the Calgary bar remained not much larger than it had been in the twenties.*

The next great Alberta oil boom began in 1947, launched by discoveries at Leduc and Redwater, near Edmonton. Since Calgary had already made itself the centre of oil industry finance, the Leduc boom generated huge amounts of work for Calgary lawyers, as did natural gas finds and the launching of a national gas pipeline system during the 1950s. In the 1950s and early 1960s the growth rate of the city rivalled what it had been at the beginning of the century, even though the availability of cheap offshore oil in eastern Canada and the eastern United States kept Alberta's oil out of those large markets. Then in the mid-1970s the global energy crisis associated with the rise of the Middle Eastern oil cartel produced Calgary's greatest economic boom ever, confirming Calgary's primacy in the Canadian oil and gas business. The sudden fourfold increase in world oil prices launched Calgary into a new energy boom on a scale the city had never witnessed. Investments in energy and related sectors built Calgary into a Canadian business centre of the first rank. For Calgary lawyers the pace and the scope of the work available, not only in oil and gas but in nearly all corporate law fields, expanded enormously.

The sudden surges of demand for legal services that these economic booms had created in Calgary had usually been answered by the arrival of

*The uncertainties of Depression law practice are described in Professor Louis Knafla's study of the Calgary law practice of Adam Goodall and James Cairns. During the 1930s Goodall developed a significant oil and gas practice, but Cairns spent most of his time doing little but attempting to collect debts and execute seizures.

The founding benchers of the Law Society of Alberta in 1907, including Senator James Lougheed, third from right.

migrant lawyers. From 1885 into the 1970s, eastern lawyers were drawn to the opportunities provided by each successive economic boom in southern Alberta. Lawyers from Ontario and the Maritime provinces very largely built the early bar of Alberta. In Calgary's early days, nearly every prominent lawyer was a newly arrived easterner. Richard B. Bennett described prospects to an Ontario lawyer in 1903: "The fact is a young man with push and enterprise...will make more money in a year by speculating in real estate and going in for life and fire insurance and a little law than he would make in five years in Ontario." Bennett was himself an eastern lawyer. He had come west from New Brunswick in 1897 to join James Lougheed, by then a senator and a large property owner too busy to handle his growing law practice. They became partners as Lougheed, Bennett.

R.B. Bennett quickly became a leading litigator and an influential corporate solicitor, and a businessman as well. Like Lougheed, he amassed substantial wealth from commercial investments in Alberta. Other pre-1905 immigrants from the east who rose to prominence at the Calgary bench and bar included Nicholas Beck, Charles McCaul, David Lynch Scott, William Walsh and Horace Harvey. Maitland McCarthy, a nephew of D'Alton McCarthy Jr. from Orangeville, Ontario, moved west in 1903 to establish a law practice in Calgary. McCarthy was the Conservative Member of Parliament for Calgary from 1904 to 1911, when his Ontario cousin Leighton was also an MP. Maitland McCarthy later became an Alberta judge.[55]

Young Albertans became the majority of the local bar in the 1930s and 1940s, but Alberta remained hospitable to migrant lawyers from the east. One Ontario law student turned Calgary lawyer, Eric Harvie, was drawn into the oil business almost from its start. In the depressed 1930s Harvie accumulated mineral rights from landowners and developers all over Alberta. By the end of the Second World War, Harvie controlled subsurface rights to 200,000 hectares in the province. The Leduc discovery of 1947 instantly made him one of the wealthiest men in Canada.* [56]

The oil boom of the late 1940s and early 1950s produced a surge of Calgary legal business that happened to coincide with a struggle over legal education in Ontario, during which the Law Society of Upper Canada refused to call graduates of the University of Toronto's new law school to the bar until they completed further studies at the Law Society's own law school, Osgoode Hall. Many of the university graduates headed for the booming legal market in Calgary, where they could get an immediate call and excellent prospects of work.† The next great energy boom, the one that transformed

*Another family attracted by the brief surge just after the First World War was the Clarry family from Ontario. John Clarry, managing partner of McCarthy & McCarthy during its move west, had been born in Calgary, and though his own family moved back to Toronto, his uncle eventually became Alberta's deputy attorney general.

†One 1950 University of Toronto law graduate who moved west, Basil Cheeseman, later recalled that "most" of his graduating class headed to Alberta and British Columbia. Cheeseman returned to Toronto in 1966 and joined McCarthy & McCarthy.

Calgary in the mid-1970s, produced yet another migration of lawyers from eastern Canada to Alberta. Close to half of those admitted to the Alberta bar in those years were law students and lawyers moving in from outside the province.[57]

FROM LOUGHEED, BENNETT TO BLACK & COMPANY

THROUGHOUT THE TWENTIETH century, law firms descended from the one James Lougheed founded in 1882 remained among the largest in Calgary. The Lougheed, Bennett firm split in 1922, in an acrimonious parting between R.B. Bennett and his former partner that produced the most famous feud of the Calgary bar. Bennett had expected Lougheed to yield the firm to him. Lougheed saw things differently, and Bennett discovered while on business in Britain that the practice had reorganized itself without him. Bennett struck back, and the result was years of litigation and the formation of two rival firms. For a couple of decades senior members of Bennett's new firm and the reorganized Lougheed, McLaws firm would cross the street to avoid each other. In 1945, when a new lawyer named Robert Black joined the Bennett firm, he was instructed that speaking to members of the Lougheed firm was still frowned on,

Richard B. Bennett, Calgary lawyer and prime minister of Canada 1930–35. (Glenbow Alberta Archives)

though the feud had begun the year he was born. In the end, Bennett secured most of the major clients of the old Lougheed, Bennett firm, including the Canadian Pacific Railway, and added the Alberta litigation work of the Canadian Medical Protective Association and many more clients. The Bennett firm became the largest in Calgary.

R.B. Bennett succeeded Maitland McCarthy as Conservative MP for Calgary in 1911; he went on to be the first westerner to be prime minister of Canada. After he retired to Britain, he died in 1947, having long since left his law firm in the hands of the Scottish lawyer Alexander Hannah, New Brunswicker Everett Chambers and litigator Henry Nolan, the Calgary-born son of Paddy Nolan and a future justice of the Supreme Court of Canada.* In the decades after the Second World War, leadership in what had been Bennett's firm gradually passed to two Albertans, Maclean E. Jones and Robert Black, and the partnership took the name Jones, Black in 1974. "Mac" Jones specialized in oil industry matters and became dominant in Calgary's energy bar as the originator of many new techniques in oil and gas law. From the 1950s to the 1970s Jones brought in work that helped sustain Jones, Black as the dominant energy law practice and the largest law firm in Calgary.

*Robert Black recalls that Alexander Hannah periodically made long train trips to the east to consult clients. He did not like having his office mail opened while he was away—unless it was important. Hannah's formidable secretary taught Black an odd legal skill: how to roll a letter out of its envelope using a pencil and then, if the subject was judged "unimportant," replace the letter in the envelope without breaking the seal, to await Hannah's return.

Robert Black had a large and diverse practice as a legal and business counsel. He aspired to be a traditional generalist lawyer, with personal as well as business clients, but two of his clients in particular, Calgary Power Limited and the investment dealers for Nova Corporation (formerly Alberta Gas Trunk Lines), drew him deeply into large-scale corporate-finance projects. Calgary Power, a company founded in 1911 by Bennett and fellow New Brunswicker Max Aitken (later Lord Beaverbrook), dominated electrical power generation and supply throughout southern Alberta. It was a long-time client of the Bennett firm; Black had succeeded Everett Chambers as its general counsel and as a director. Calgary Power's substantial investment needs frequently took Black to Toronto, Montreal and New York. Working with eastern investment dealers and large Wall Street law firms like Davis, Polk, Black encountered a scale of practice still largely unfamiliar to Calgary lawyers.

Then, in 1980, Robert Black discovered that Calgary Power was the target of a hostile takeover bid from a fast-growing, Calgary-based gas and electric utilities company then called Canadian Utilities, now Atco Utilities. Atco's legal counsel was Jones, Black—his own firm.

For decades the relatively small community of Calgary entrepreneurs had been forming, merging and closing down a great many energy enterprises. As former rival companies became allies and former allies became rivals, conflicts had long been a fact of life for the handful of favoured law firms that served the Calgary oil patch. In Calgary's 1970s boom, with too many urgent deals being brought to too few law firms, that situation had intensified. It remained common throughout the Canadian bar in the 1970s for lawyers within a single firm to maintain largely separate practices, and standards regarding intrafirm conflicts were evolving. The consensus at Jones, Black in 1980 was that it should be possible for its lawyers to continue representing both Atco and Calgary Power, despite the half-billion-dollar fight between them. Black, however, insisted that a client the size of Calgary Power was entitled to the full resources of its law firm, which instead were mostly being marshalled on the other side.

Jones, Black brought in outside counsel for the fight between the contending clients, but Black concluded the conflict was irreconcilable and could not be papered over. On June 30, 1980, he left the firm he had joined in 1945. Jones, Black reverted to its roots and became Bennett Jones. Black formed his own firm. He took with him the

Calgary Power file and all his principal clients, but only his secretary, Nancy Hendricks, and a single associate lawyer, Brad McManus, left Jones, Black with him. From that isolated position Black helped Calgary Power, which became TransAlta Corporation in 1981, defeat the Atco takeover bid. But for Black the breach with his old partners was permanent. "There was a coolness," Black said with deep understatement. "I'm not quite at the point of crossing the street," he added, alluding to the Bennett-Lougheed feud he observed in the 1940s, "but...."

McCARTHYS LOOKS WEST

JUST AS ROBERT BLACK was finding himself out on his own, with his long-established clients pressing more work on him than he could handle, some of the lawyers at McCarthy & McCarthy in Toronto were developing a consuming interest in Calgary's legal opportunities.

For decades, Toronto-based Imperial Oil and a handful of other energy giants, mostly foreign-owned, had dominated large-scale capital investment in the Calgary oil patch. Traditionally, other Calgary entrepreneurs looking for financing had gone east to the investment dealers and lawyers of Bay Street and Wall Street. By the mid-1970s, however, Calgary's growth was changing that relationship. Many more Calgary energy businesses were now big enough to expect that even the largest players would come to them, or lose out. In any case, the sheer volume of corporate-finance work going on in the mid-seventies' Calgary boom was taxing the capacity of the Calgary bar and attracting the interest of out-of-province lawyers.

"I was doing public financing work, and the investment dealers in particular, but also the banks, were setting up offices or expanding their offices in Calgary in order to be able to compete," recalled Jim McCartney, then a midcareer corporate lawyer at McCarthys in Toronto. "People like me were living on airplanes, flying to Calgary early in the week and flying home at the end of the week." It was mostly corporate lawyers whose clients were sending them west, but Doug Ewens, a McCarthys tax law specialist, was also going regularly to Alberta to advise clients such as Dome Petroleum on the tax aspects of drilling funds and other ventures. Litigator Colin Campbell also found himself commuting west: "The firm did a lot of work for TransCanada PipeLines, and because they were in conflict with all the oil and gas producers, no major firm in Alberta could represent TransCanada." Several McCarthy litigators frequently found themselves in Calgary for regulatory hearings.

Robert Black in his Calgary office soon after he founded Black & Company in association with McCarthy & McCarthy of Toronto.

In the summer of 1979, Jim McCartney discussed the Calgary situation with John Clarry, who was the leader of McCarthys' corporate section and about to succeed Beverley Matthews as head of the firm. An important element of McCarthys' business was shifting west, they agreed, and there were too few lawyers in Calgary to handle all the work to be done there. Why should McCarthys confine itself to a single city when the work was leading elsewhere? Clarry asked for a memorandum, and in October McCartney delivered six pages entitled "Business Opportunities in Calgary" to McCarthys' management committee.

> We should investigate the possibility of setting up an office in Calgary. It appears that our long term prospects may be enhanced if we do and may be diminished if we do not....
>
> The dramatic growth in the oil and gas industry in Alberta has led to a commensurate growth in the demand for legal services, particularly in Calgary....At present the Calgary law firms are severely strained in their efforts to meet the demands. While they may be able to attract able young lawyers, they must be experiencing difficulties in attracting older, more experienced ones. This situation should remain the same for the next five years or so....[58]

On the strength of McCartney's memo, the McCarthy management committee formed a "Calgary Committee." It reported back in January 1980, and it repeated McCartney's emphasis on the unique business opportunity in the west: "Massive financings will be required for exploration programs and for construction of transportation and processing facilities...a large part of the financing activity will take place in Calgary. Without a Calgary connection McCarthy & McCarthy could lose part of its market share of these financings and with a connection might well increase its share."[59]

Jim McCartney's memo had suggested moving Toronto lawyers to Alberta and seeking a merger with a Calgary firm. The Calgary Committee, however, focussed more on the temporary "overhang" of legal work the Calgary boom was creating and advised against an early merger with a Calgary firm. It proposed instead a more cautious first stage: to have a dozen or so McCarthy lawyers take the exams that would allow them to become fully qualified members of the Alberta bar.* Some of these lawyers might move to Calgary, and some Alberta lawyers might even be recruited, but the committee's proposal was

*Lawyers practising briefly in another jurisdiction could receive temporary practice privileges from the local law society. When they practised only the law of their own jurisdiction or were advising clients from their own province, no permission was required. The uncertain boundaries of how much practice required a lawyer to seek admittance to the local bar was one of the concerns of McCarthy lawyers in the late 1970s as the volume of work they did in Alberta grew.

Toronto-centric: "In major projects, it is expected that the Toronto firm would be the principal counsel and that the Calgary firm would be Alberta counsel."[60]

The proposal to move into the Alberta legal market generated vigorous discussion in the management committee and the full partnership, but it was approved by both, and in the spring of 1980 a dozen McCarthy partners in Toronto began preparing to take Alberta's entrance exams. They organized regular Monday morning seminars in which they took turns tutoring the others in aspects of Alberta law. "We did it very seriously," recalled Doug Ewens, the Toronto tax practitioner who was in the first group. "You are out of practice in the writing of exams, and also everyone thinks the bar exams are a no-brainer, so you better not fail." Jim McCartney, who had been out of law school since 1964, remembers budgeting fifty hours of study shortly before the exam.

Another concern was the resistance that was expected to come from the Law Society of Alberta. "You assume that the Alberta bar, when they see applications from a single firm coming in, a dozen at once, they're going to figure out what you are up to—and maybe adjust the examinations accordingly!" said Ewens. Ewens acknowledged Alberta's testing process remained objective and fair, but concern about the Law Society's reaction to McCarthys' plans was well grounded. Basil Cheeseman, a McCarthy lawyer who had practised in Calgary from 1951 to 1966 and remained a qualified Alberta lawyer, briefed Law Society of Alberta officials about McCarthys' ambitions in March 1980. He found them distinctly unwelcoming. Bernard Kelly, the secretary of the Alberta Law Society, phoned Cheeseman in Toronto in the fall of 1980. Cheeseman's notes of the conversation are noncommittal, but the Law Society understood that McCarthys had been firmly "warned off" from expanding into Alberta.[61]

By the fall of 1980, despite these rumblings, McCarthy & McCarthy had a group of Toronto lawyers ready to be called to the Alberta bar the following spring. Also that fall, Ian Douglas, another Toronto partner, returned from a meeting of the board of the British-American Banknote Company to report that his fellow director, the top-flight Calgary lawyer Robert Black, was now out on his own and was urgently in need of senior business lawyers to help serve his clients. Beverley Matthews and John Clarry quickly made contact with Black, and Black travelled to Toronto in November 1980 to discuss an alliance. He had never had significant dealings with McCarthy & McCarthy, but his rapport with the Torontonians was immediate, and their interests were remarkably well aligned. Black could give the Torontonians local credentials and a significant client base in Calgary; McCarthys could provide the sophisticated legal support Black and his clients urgently needed.

The fortuitous encounter with Robert Black shifted McCarthy & McCarthy's plans for Calgary into a higher gear. When Black left Jones, Black in June 1980, McCarthys' only firm commitment regarding Calgary had been to help some of its Toronto lawyers qualify for Alberta practice. Securing Black's participation, however, would commit McCarthys to sharing in a great deal of ongoing legal work for Black's Alberta clients. That would make a substantial office in Calgary inevitable. Some Toronto partners would have to move west as soon as possible, and more lawyers would have to be found in Alberta.

"Moving to Calgary, that was the first time in the firm that we prepared a financial feasibility projection. We had to sit down and guess how much income we might make, how many lawyers we could support, what the rent would be, what the costs would be, and so on," recalled John Clarry. He became the one who wrote most of the detailed proposal, with office manager Edward King providing technical and logistical advice on office space, computing and accounting systems and other aspects of administering one firm in two provinces.

As the Calgary project grew more important in 1980 and 1981, McCarthys' management was itself in transition. In January 1980, just as the original Calgary proposal came to the management committee, Beverley Matthews formally relinquished the chairmanship to

John Clarry, though committee meetings and even partnership meetings continued to be held in Matthews' office for several more years. Matthews had excelled at taking the pulse of his colleagues. A handful of influential senior partners had determined most issues, and most decisions were foregone conclusions by the time he took them to the management committee. The management committee continued to nominate both its own members and the members of a growing network of other committees; partnership approval of nominations remained largely a formality. Votes by the full partnership were unknown.

John Clarry in 1984, as managing partner of McCarthy & McCarthy.

Officially, Matthews' withdrawal produced no formal change in the firm's governance structure. But Matthews had wielded personal authority and influence of a kind that could not have continued as the firm grew. "As the firm grew bigger [and] people were hired that didn't have a chance to get to know him personally, a number of frustrated younger lawyers would get very upset with him," recalled John Clarry. For his part, Clarry would manage by involving many partners in a growing range of committees and, even more, by unending informal consultations with his much-expanded network of partners. As the size of the firm grew relentlessly through the 1980s, the demands of that kind of consultation would tax even Clarry's patience and diplomacy. At the same time, projects like Calgary and the ever-expanding administrative systems of the firm were demanding more managing by the managing partner, even though Clarry retained important client responsibilities. "I realized," Clarry said, "what I guess everyone else was realizing, that the management of a large law firm is a job in itself."

In January 1981 and more formally in April, Clarry put his Calgary feasibility study and cost estimates to the partnership in Toronto and asked for authority to open an office there in partnership with Robert Black. It was the first formal vote the partners of the firm had held. The vote was not unanimous, but the partnership ratified the proposal. In anticipation of approval, McCarthy & McCarthy had already submitted to the Law Society of Alberta a lengthy memorandum, signed by Clarry, which set out in detail the firm's intentions. McCarthy & McCarthy, it declared, would open an office in Calgary, staffed by lawyers who would be qualified to practise in Alberta but would all be partners or associates of McCarthy & McCarthy.[62]

It was quickly settled that three Toronto partners would move to Alberta to launch the new venture. Patrick Vernon, a senior corporate lawyer with connections in Calgary and a wide acquaintanceship among corporate decision makers from his role as national finance chairman for the federal Progressive Conservative Party, would move to Calgary to manage the new office. Also prepared to move were Doug Ewens and Richard Shaw, two promising younger partners from the tax and corporate practices. With the firm covering their relocation expenses, these three agreed to spend at least three years building the new practice in Calgary along with Robert Black and his Alberta associates. They could then return to the Toronto office if they chose. Several more McCarthy partners who were also becoming members of the Alberta bar would remain in Toronto but be available to support them.

McCarthys had boldly told the Law Society of Alberta in March that it proposed to use its own name for the Calgary office, but the Law Society's rules were uncompromising on that point: only the names of lawyers in actual or past practice in Alberta were acceptable. It was quickly accepted that the new firm in Calgary would be called "Black & Company" instead. All the Alberta-qualified partners in McCarthys would be partners in the new Black & Company, and all Black & Company partners would be partners in McCarthy & McCarthy. This dual partnership was a crucial link between the firms. To satisfy Law Society requirements, the firms would keep separate accounts and bill each other for services rendered, but since McCarthys could pay its partners however it chose, it would be able, if need be, to support either office with partnership income from the other.

By late summer Calgary accommodations and staff (led by new office manager Alice Lee) had been secured. The Vernon, Ewens and Shaw families left Toronto and settled in Calgary. Key clients were briefed about McCarthys' new western venture. On September 1, 1981, Black & Company opened for business in the Esso Plaza. The founding partners were Robert Black, Patrick Vernon, Douglas Ewens and Richard Shaw, with associates Bradley McManus and Robert Nowack, in Calgary, along with all the Torontonians qualified to practise in Alberta: Basil Cheeseman, Tom Forbes, Edward Kerwin, Jim McCartney, Murray Paton, Peter Quinn and Blair Cowper-Smith.

THE MOTIVES FOR LAW FIRM EXPANSION

MCCARTHY & MCCARTHY's move into Calgary began with the unique opportunity of the Calgary oil boom and then adapted to the happenstance of Robert Black's sudden availability. But the causes of law firm expansion ran deeper. The multi-office law firm was becoming an international phenomenon by the late 1970s. A few American law firms had maintained offices in Britain and Europe since soon after the Second World War, and a few British firms were operating in New York. Baker & McKenzie, founded in Chicago in 1949, had offices in 20 countries by 1979 and already called itself an international rather than an American firm, though its offices mostly advised their business clients on American rather than local law. In expanding their operations to follow their clients, corporate-law firms were beginning to follow the lead of accounting firms, which had long since developed national and international networks to serve international business.[63]

The first group of McCarthy & McCarthy lawyers called to the Alberta bar celebrate with Robert Black before the Calgary court house in 1981: from left, Jim McCartney, Murray Paton, Black, Peter Quinn, Douglas Ewens, Thomas Forbes, Blair Cowper-Smith and Calgary associate Brad McManus.

After 1971, American bar associations began relaxing their prohibitions on interstate law firms, and many American law firms broadly similar to McCarthy & McCarthy opened branch offices in other American cities. Leading firms in major American cities wanted their own offices in New York, while New York firms had begun following their clients to other business centres such as Chicago and Los Angeles. Many New York and regional firms already had offices in Washington, where lawyers and law firms had long dominated the political lobbying process.[64]

The trend to move beyond single-city law practices was also evident in Canada. The Montreal firm Phillips & Vineberg had opened a small office in Paris and another in Hong Kong. Courtois, Clarkson had gone into Brussels in 1975. Stikeman Elliott, also of Montreal, had opened a London, U.K., office in 1969 and another in Toronto in 1971. Stikeman Elliott's move into Ontario was prompted by the drift of corporate headquarters from Montreal to Toronto and the volume of legal work Stikemans was referring to Toronto firms. It proved uncomplicated: Heward Stikeman and Fraser Elliott, both members of the Ontario bar, simply set up a separate Ontario firm in their own names and began hiring Ontario lawyers.[65] These were still isolated cases, but in early 1980 the Calgary Committee of McCarthy & McCarthy had noted rumours that other Toronto and Montreal law firms were looking at expansion to Calgary. Indeed, Courtois, Clarkson, which in 1981 was forming an Ontario-Quebec liaison arrangement with McCarthys, had begun negotiations with a Calgary law firm in 1977 and had encountered the disapproval of the Law Society of Alberta.

The ideas expressed in McCartney's "Business Opportunities in Calgary" memo, in other words, reflected trends already established in corporate-law practice outside Canada and beginning to take hold in Canada. However, the project was not simply an imitation of American models; the Calgary proposal also reflected slow transitions taking place deep within the Canadian legal profession.

For centuries, spokesmen for the profession had defined lawyers as members of a learned and honourable profession, one that rejected fee competition, advertising, marketing and anything else that might blur the distinction between their profession and a mere trade or business. "The principled rejection of the profit motive" was the hallmark of the legal professional, said Sir James Aikins, the wealthy Winnipeg lawyer who founded and led the Canadian Bar Association in the early twentieth century.[66]

This belief that lawyers served a public purpose rather than private profit may have been self-serving but it remained strong. Litigation lawyers in particular retained a court-centred, lawmaking view of their profession, and the legal community as a whole had long accepted the credo that its privileges of self-government and its monopoly of legal practice were balanced by obligations to service and the public good, which were not compatible with the ethos of the competitive marketplace. In 1980 this was not merely an antique holdover. Lawyers in every province were still governed by powerful law societies whose rules and protocols against competition, advertising and other forms of businesslike practice had been proliferating, not shrinking, during the 1960s and 1970s. In the traditional ideology, clients came and went; a lawyer's essential engagement was with other lawyers and the law itself. Legal careers were based not on economic growth or maximization of profit but on making and upholding the law as counsellors and advocates, and perhaps eventually as judges.

The shift to a different ethos of legal practice was a long time in the making. McCarthy & McCarthy's 1977 long-range planning report still assumed the primary goal of the firm was to provide a congenial atmosphere for the practice of law, "even at the cost of increased profitability." In 1979, when law societies and the Canadian Bar Association, under pressure from courts and competition tribunals, were beginning to revise their attitudes on advertising by lawyers, Beverley Matthews reiterated, "The policy of this firm at this time is that there will be nil advertising." Within barely a decade McCarthys would employ a full-time director of marketing, but in 1979 such things remained unthinkable to most lawyers. Business development at even the largest firms mostly meant ensuring that lawyers joined the right clubs, were active in their community, and kept in touch with the business and professional milieu.

Nevertheless, Beverley Matthews, for all his traditionalism, had been a business executive as much as a lawyer, as had his predecessor, Leighton McCarthy. They had both devoted their careers to the growth of McCarthy & McCarthy as a firm committed to supplying the legal requirements of large corporate clients, many of whom had national or international operations. By 1980 the firm had 90 lawyers and annual revenues well over $10 million; it was already investing in computing and managerial systems and expanding its use of law clerks and other support staff. Despite the noncommercial credo of the profession, all these innovations were intended to generate service efficiencies and profits, much the way other businesses did.

Lawyers at large corporate-law firms like McCarthys were increasingly moving away from the idea that their law practice could or should exist outside the marketplace. Securing and retaining the legal work of corporate clients was increasingly competitive and service-driven; lawyers who responded to the pressure of legal competition were becoming as likely to say that they worked in "the legal-services business" as to speak the older language of "the professional practice of law." They were much more ready to presume that the rules of the market, rather than dictates of law societies or the traditions of the bar, should govern their law practices and their legal careers.

The shifting from one ethos to another, from the learned and honorable profession to the legal-services business, was a long, slow process. It remained—and remains—normal for lawyers to subscribe to aspects of both. But the Calgary proposal was imbued with the latter concept of legal practice. The original memo about Calgary was entitled "Business Opportunities" and all the firm's subsequent statements on the subject emphasised competitive advantage, the benefits of growth, the opportunities for profit and, above all, the need for McCarthys to adapt itself to the changing market defined by the needs of large corporate clients and competition from rival law firms.

This viewpoint was not exclusive to Toronto or to McCarthys' Calgary Committee. In 1980, when Robert Black left Jones, Black, other Calgary lawyers assumed he would soon link up with one of the existing firms there. But Black saw little advantage in taking his client files to another overburdened and probably conflicted Calgary firm. His experience in corporate financings had turned his thoughts further afield. As Clarry reported to his partners in December 1980, after their early discussions: "Black has emphasised the fact that the

Calgary law firms are incapable of handling the load of sophisticated work which they are called on to perform because of the shortage of experienced people. He... holds the view that more, not larger, firms which are capable of handling major projects are needed in Calgary.... The needs of business today are for firms which are not confined to provincial boundaries alone."[67]

"I had always thought," Black said in 2001, "that with the trade barriers that we had, we just weren't doing things right, that we needed a national firm. I was always very sensitive to the fact that when you were filing a prospectus, you were filing it in five or six jurisdictions and you were getting comments from each one, and it just didn't seem right." Black's view, like the one taking hold at McCarthys, was that effective service to corporate clients demanded new forms of law firm organization adequate to the national and international operations of the business world.

However, opposition to interprovincial expansion was strongly entrenched and sure to be heard from. Black found his clients were supportive of his new association with the Toronto lawyers, but his lawyer friends in Calgary were very dubious about his plan to work with McCarthys. "The advice always was that those lawyers in Toronto will take advantage of you. And I kept saying, 'But you know, I'm a big boy,' and I had great experience with Toronto lawyers, and I had learned a great deal. I had no qualms whatsoever." The more serious challenge would come not from the doubts of colleagues but from the institutional response of the Law Society of Alberta.

7 BLACK ET AL. V. LAW SOCIETY OF ALBERTA

THROUGHOUT THE 1970S the Law Society of Alberta had been admitting floods of out-of-province lawyers and law students, but it admitted them as individuals becoming part of the thriving Alberta legal community, to be governed by its rules and standards. The Alberta bar, for all its welcoming of immigrant lawyers, maintained a strong sense of its independence and of its particular institutions and traditions. Neither the bar nor the governing body were going to extend the same welcome to the branch office of a big corporate law firm from the east.

The attitude of the Law Society of Alberta mattered a good deal. Throughout Canada, the fundamental requirement for the practice of law was that one become and remain a member in good standing in one's provincial law society. This was no mere formality. The law society in Alberta, like that in each province, maintained close supervision of its members. By the 1970s law societies set standards for admission to the bar and standards of practice, and they ran programs to compensate victims of unscrupulous lawyers and to provide lawyers with errors-and-omissions insurance. These alone gave the governing bodies a strong interest in maintaining authority over their members, but their governing mandate ran far more widely. Law societies controlled advertising and marketing, right down to the names law firms used and the size of the signs they hung out or the ads they put in the telephone companies' Yellow Pages. Law societies had authority to audit the accounts of their members and to enforce standards for the management of clients' money. They forbade "fee-splitting" and similar arrangements with non-lawyers and non-members. They exercised broad supervision of the ethics and practice standards of lawyers within their jurisdiction. Law societies held legislative authority to enforce these rules, and they could exercise an ultimate sanction: for serious misbehaviour or refusal to cooperate, they could remove a lawyer's membership and prevent him or her from practising law.

In 1980, most Canadian law societies had become concerned about interprovincial law firms. At a technical level the arrival of non-resident firms raised issues of how law societies would maintain authority, scrutinize accounts, investigate malpractice and generally uphold their particular rules and standards. More broadly, several law societies expressed concern that "branch plant" law firms would undermine local bars and lead to the erosion of vigorous, independent local bars that could serve local needs for legal services. Still, law society opposition to interprovincial expansions was not entirely foreordained. In 1971 the Law Society of Upper Canada had welcomed the arrival in Toronto of the Montreal firm Stikeman Elliott.* [68]

Alberta was not Upper Canada, however. During the 1970s traditional western resistance to eastern neglect and eastern exploitation had been transformed into a determination that this oil boom would change Alberta's relations with the rest of Canada and permanently put an end to western dependency. Since 1971 the Conservative provincial government led by Peter Lougheed, a grand-

*As a new firm whose namesake principals were still practising, Stikeman Elliott could use the same name anywhere its two leaders were admitted to practice. McCarthy & McCarthy complained that law society rules on firm names disadvantaged a long-established firm named for lawyers who were no longer living.

son of Senator Sir James Lougheed, had been making great strides in building the province's oil and gas revenues, as well as supporting diversification of the local economy and working to ensure that Calgary would became a national centre for business and finance. The spectre of eastern lawyers swooping in to create branch plant law offices to cream off the best legal work and ship it back to head offices in Toronto or Montreal ran contrary to everything Albertans were striving for in the 1970s and 1980s. Calgarians, in particular, were at once proud of the rapid strides their city was making yet defensive about any new threat of humiliation from the east.

The benchers of the Law Society of Alberta had opposed out-of-province firms before McCarthys came on the scene. When the Calgary energy firm Ballem, McDill negotiated an agreement to exchange work with the Montreal firm Courtois, Clarkson in 1977, the Alberta benchers had mounted informal pressure that persuaded the two to abandon their plans without ever making them public. At first the Law Society expected the same tactics would put an end to the McCarthy venture. Bernard Kelly, the Law Society secretary, told Basil Cheeseman in November 1980 that McCarthys' proposal was "unacceptable." When McCarthy & McCarthy formally presented its plans in March 1981, bencher Robert Fraser called Robert Black in Calgary and declared the proposal was "improper," and that McCarthys knew it was "unacceptable" and could expect a strong Law Society response "putting them straight."

The McCarthys team, however, had researched the Alberta rules and concluded they had the right to proceed and should not be deterred by what they viewed as protectionist bluster. In December 1980 Clarry had quoted to his partners Robert Black's view "that the Alberta Law Society, in common with others, is backward in not recognizing what the chartered accountants have long since accepted." Clarry argued that "the resentment of some practitioners should not deter us and would be dissipated once we had been operating there a short time."

When the Calgary office of Black & Company in association with McCarthy & McCarthy opened in September 1981, there was no public response from the Law Society of Alberta. In the same month, the Federation of Law Societies (representing all the provincial and territorial governing bodies, and responding to debate at its summertime meetings) established a committee led by Winnipeg lawyer Marvin Freedman to investigate the issue of interprovincial law firms. John Clarry sent the committee a long statement of McCarthys' position. The firm guessed that the Law Society of Alberta might not act on the McCarthy-Black situation before the committee reported to the federation in mid-1982.

The Law Society of Alberta was still considering rule changes in January 1982 when William Code, a Calgary litigator and the Law Society's outgoing president, sent discipline chair E.A. Hutchinson a formal complaint "with respect to Mr. Black's actions." Code based his complaint on one of Robert Black's business cards, which a friend had received from Black at a Christmas party. The card gave two addresses: one at Black & Company in Calgary, one at McCarthys in Toronto. "I am aware that there is a proposed change in the rules covering the situation of Black and McCarthy specifically, but I think that an investigation should be made," wrote Code, declaring that earlier rulings of the Law Society prohibited a Law Society member from being a member of two firms or associating with an out-of-province firm.

Black was informed of Code's complaint against him in late February 1982. He replied in March, asking to be shown the rulings that Code alleged to be in force. This exchange of letters effectively ended the discipline process. In December 1982 Code's complaint was formally dismissed; the Discipline Committee declared, "There is no ruling in force... in regard to which Mr. Black is in breach."

From the time Black & Company began operating, however, the Law Society was quietly engaged in a more substantial response. Even though a Law Society special committee established in April 1981 cast doubt on the grounds for action against McCarthys and Black & Company, discussions of draft rules against interprovincial firms continued at the Law Society through the fall. The proposed change in the rules to which Code had referred was finally made public in February 1982. All members of the Law Society of Alberta were notified of a new rule, rule 154: "An active member who ordinarily resides in and carries on the practice of law within Alberta shall not enter into or continue any partnership, association or other arrangement for the joint practice of law in Alberta with anyone who is not an active member ordinarily resident in Alberta."

Early Black & Company lawyers Len Bannicke, Douglas Ewens, Edward Kerwin, Robert Black, Richard Shaw, Brian Malone and Stephen Clark.

The rule was to come into force on May 1, 1982. Once it did, all the Alberta partners of Black & Company would evidently be in breach of it and liable to suspension or other discipline unless they severed their association with McCarthy & McCarthy. Law Society officials acknowledged in the press that as far as they knew Black & Company was the only firm the new rule would affect.

By early March, Black & Company and McCarthys had retained legal counsel, the Edmonton firm Milner, Steer, and the new rule provoked a flurry of meetings and memoranda among the partners of Black & Company and McCarthys. Could the Alberta benchers be deterred? Could a compromise be found to appease them? Was the ruling beyond the powers of the Law Society of Alberta? And, if so, should a legal challenge to the ruling be attempted?

Patrick Vernon, managing partner in Calgary, set out a case for moderation, writing on April 9, 1982 that litigation would alienate "many senior people in Calgary.... I believe it [contesting the rule] would detract from our ability to develop and broaden the base of our Calgary practice." Vernon saw a possibility that if all the Toronto-based partners resigned from Black & Company before May 1, the Alberta partners might technically be in compliance with the rule, even if they remained partners in McCarthys. That, he suggested, might prevent the inevitable hardening of positions that a lawsuit would cause and allow time to change the Law Society's position or even to elect some more sympathetic benchers. Vernon acknowledged that his Calgary partners were not much taken with this argument. Richard Shaw and Doug Ewens believed that "technical compliance" would weaken the firm's position without deterring the benchers from their ultimate purpose of shutting down the interprovincial association.[69]

In March and April 1982, McCarthys' Alberta legal counsel and several of its own litigators began delivering opinion letters about the legality of the new rule. By April 13, Milner, Steer of Edmonton delivered its opinion: "Rule 154 is *ultra vires* the benchers" because it constituted an amendment to Alberta's Law Society Act, an action only the Alberta legislature was entitled to undertake. Several of McCarthys' own litigators also provided opinions. From Newfoundland, where he was part of the team litigating a major case pitting the Government of Quebec against the Government of Newfoundland over Churchill Falls power, George Finlayson (assisted by Barry Ryan, then a law student) delivered a memorandum advising that rule 154 could be attacked as *ultra vires* and an unreasonable restraint of trade. Douglas Laidlaw declared the benchers' "whole concept is erroneous and approaches the ridiculous." Burton Tait wrote that "the conduct of the Law Society of Alberta is improper" and in restraint of trade. Tait acknowledged the reticence of lawyers to fight a governing body, but suggested, "If Black & Company were our client as distinct from our *alter ego*, I do not believe we would hesitate to act."

Most of these opinions were available when McCarthys' management committee met on April 13, 1982, to review strategy. Clearly

Black & Company leaders Patrick Vernon, Douglas Ewens, Richard Shaw and Robert Black.

there were grounds for litigating against the Law Society's new rule, but first an effort at accommodation would be made, even it meant consideration of changes such as those Patrick Vernon had mentioned. The Alberta benchers were to meet in Red Deer on April 24. Black & Company secured permission to have J.W. Beames, an Edmonton lawyer with Milner, Steer, make a submission to them in person, with the leading partners in Black & Company in attendance.

Beames, himself a past president of the Law Society of Alberta, told the benchers: "Our purpose in seeking an audience with you is to urge you to withdraw Rule 154. I submit to you that the Rule, even if it is valid and enforceable (and I will submit to you that it is not), is retrogressive and cannot be said to serve the public interest, or even that of the profession." Beames laid out in detail the steps Black &

Company had taken to conform to the society's rules and argued that the links between Black & Company and the Toronto firm in no way undermined the Law Society's powers to protect professional standards or the public interest. "The real reason for the rule is protectionism, which is not a proper basis for making it."[70]

The lively discussion that followed revealed both hawks and doves among the Alberta benchers. Asked if dropping the last four words of the rule, "ordinarily resident in Alberta," would ease Black & Company's problems, Beames suggested it might, and some benchers appeared willing to support such an amendment. The Black & Company lawyers who had attended went away from Red Deer with some optimism.* Indeed, the Law Society soon informed them that implementation of rule 154 would be delayed from May 1 to September 1. In the event, the benchers did not meet all summer, and so the date was soon set further back, to January 1, 1983. It appeared that Black & Company might have swayed the Law Society with its arguments that proper supervision of the profession was not threatened and that protectionist measures would not stand. The problem might yet go away.

*Doug Ewens recalled that cigars were brought out on the drive back to Calgary, with the result that lingering fumes pervaded his family's new station wagon for months afterwards.

During the discussion in Red Deer, one bencher asked ruefully, "Who had gotten to the editorial writers?" The Law Society did appear to be losing in the court of public opinion, although Black & Company declared it had done no public relations work to promote its plan. Even in Alberta, newspapers found the argument that the Law Society's new rule was simply economic protectionism more persuasive than the Law Society's claim to be defending Alberta against eastern carpetbaggers. Bencher E.A. Hutchinson declared, "This business of the Ontario lawyers trying to serve their clients better is balderdash. The whole issue comes down to a power struggle between Toronto and the hinterland."[71] But editorialists mostly concluded that competition, even from Toronto, was likely to benefit consumers of legal services in Alberta and that Alberta lawyers had no good reason to inhibit competition. Traditional notions of law as a profession with responsibilities and privileges that exempted it from the rules of the marketplace still had some influence with lawyers, but they meant little to the public.

By the late summer of 1982 the Law Society of Alberta learned it had also lost the debate within the Federation of Law Societies. After consulting the federation's member organizations, the Freedman Committee on Inter-provincial Law Firms had found only the Law Society of Alberta firmly opposed to interprovincial law firms. The committee itself concluded: "We believe the arguments in favour of permitting inter-provincial law firms are persuasive and that it is likely that such organizations will make a positive contribution." It proposed that the federation's member societies should change any rules that stood in the way of interprovincial law firms. The lone dissenter among the six members of the Freedman committee was Robert Fraser, the Calgary bencher who had told Robert Black that McCarthys' Calgary project was improper and unacceptable. In a minority report, Fraser argued that effective control of the profession could not survive the emergence of law firms "which would be controlled and would operate in the main from outside the province." The majority report, however, declared, "We are satisfied that law societies will still be able properly to regulate lawyers' conduct and protect the public interest." Due to opposition from the Law Society of Alberta, the federation did not adopt the Freedman recommendations, but the other Canadian law societies expressed general agreement.*[72]

In October 1982 Jim McCartney, who had initiated the Calgary process in 1979 and was now one of the Black & Company partners qualified to practise in Alberta (though still based in Toronto), sent another memorandum to McCarthys' management committee. Noting there was some hope of "compromise" on rule 154, which still had not been implemented in

*By no means all Alberta lawyers supported rule 154. Neil Bowker, long-time dean of law at the University of Alberta, head of Alberta's law reform commission and an honorary bencher, denounced the rule and the philosophy behind it in a letter to the Law Society in November 1982.

Alberta, McCartney suggested it was time to begin moving to a larger goal: making McCarthy & McCarthy truly a "national law firm," one that would serve its clients from offices in all the major business centres of Canada.[73]

But the Calgary problem was not over. The benchers of the Law Society of Alberta returned to their consideration of rule 154 on November 26, 1982, and the advocates of compromise were outnumbered and outvoted. Rule 154 would be implemented in its original form on January 1, 1983. The benchers also killed any chance of the Black & Company lawyers achieving "technical compliance" by passing another rule, 75B: "No member shall be a partner in or associated for the practice of law with more than one law firm."

In May, Black & Company's counsel had told the benchers in Red Deer that rule 154 was neither valid nor enforceable, but Black & Company and McCarthys had held back from a legal challenge as long as discussions continued. They had concluded, however, that if the Law Society decided to put its rule into effect, they should take pre-emptive action, rather than have to defend themselves after the rule came into force. On December 16, 1982, the partners of Black & Company went to the Alberta Court of Queen's Bench in Edmonton, asking that rules 154 and 75B be declared *ultra vires* the Law Society, in restraint of trade, and in contravention of the guarantee of mobility rights in the new Canadian Charter of Rights and Freedoms. They also sought an injunction to prevent the Law Society from enforcing its new rules against Black & Company pending a verdict in the case. The injunction was granted, and both sides prepared for trial.[74]

The Canadian Charter of Rights and Freedoms, which now became one aspect of the court battle, had come into force on April 17, 1982. The Charter's mobility rights clause, section 6-2b ("Every citizen...has the right...to pursue the gaining of a livelihood in any province.") was new and untested law. In the spring of 1982, several of the opinion letters McCarthys had received about rule 154 had noted the potential applicability of section 6-2b. Although the Law Society's rule did not prevent lawyers from moving to Alberta, it might be found that it impinged on the new Charter right by restraining their freedom to gain their livelihood depending on the provinces in which they chose to live, to work, and to form partnerships.

Richard Shaw represented the Alberta region of McCarthy Tétrault at its merger with Clarkson Tétrault in 1990.

Senior counsel had mostly been cautious about relying on Charter issues. McCarthy litigator George Finlayson noted that if the Charter were invoked at all, "each of the provinces...would wish to have a say in the matter and we would not finish until we had been in the Supreme Court of Canada." J.E. Redmond, the Milner, Steer litigator who would lead the case for Black & Company (and another past president of the Law Society of Alberta), said of the Charter in his advice to McCarthys in April 1982: "This is such new and untested legislation that one can really do no more than speculate." In late November 1982, as Redmond prepared the statement of claim against rules 154 and 75B, Robert Black noted, "Our current instructions to Redmond are not to plead the Charter because so many additional parties would become involved."[75]

On his copy of Black's memo, his partner Richard Shaw scribbled opposite this passage: "Disagree—go with everything." Shaw was a corporate lawyer, not a litigator or a constitutional specialist but, as one of those who had reorganized his whole career by moving to Calgary for the sake of the interprovincial firm, he had a substantial interest in the case. By the time Black & Company's statement of claim was filed in December, Shaw was not the only one who was inclined to "go with everything." At almost the last minute, infringement upon mobility rights was added to the causes of action against rule 154. It was just as well, for the case would indeed not finish until it had been to the Supreme Court of Canada and the mobility rights clause that was new and untested in 1982 would prove vital.[76]

Going to trial meant abandoning lingering hopes for compromise and a quick resolution. The action was launched in December 1982, but Black & Company's final statement of claim ("the amended amended amended statement of claim") was not filed until December 1983, the final defence statement not until May 1984. The Alberta Queen's Bench gave its judgement in August 1984, and that verdict would lead to almost five more years of appeals. During all those years, Black & Company would operate under the protection of the injunction it had applied for in December 1982. Meanwhile, even under the shadow of rule 154, Black & Company had a law firm to run.

BUILDING BLACK & COMPANY

SEPTEMBER 1, 1981, the day Black & Company opened for business in Calgary, also was the implementation date of the energy pricing agreements that flowed from the federal government's National Energy Policy of October 1980. With the National Energy Policy, the federal government of Prime Minister Pierre Elliott Trudeau sought to keep Canadian energy prices below world levels and to capture more energy revenues for the federal government, rather than for the producing provinces alone. The pricing agreements that followed had required long and bitter negotiations between the Canadian and Alberta governments, and they provoked deep resentment in Alberta against the eastern "grab" at the province's wealth and resources. As a result,

McCarthys' move into Calgary came at a time when relations between Alberta and the rest of Canada were under particular strain.

In retrospect, the pricing agreement was also seen as the end of the great Alberta oil boom of the 1970s. The federal restrictions—and also the global decline in the price of oil as the Organization of Petroleum Exporting Countries' hold upon energy pricing eroded—put a cap on profits from Alberta's energy exports, and the flood of investment that had drawn McCarthys' lawyers to Calgary began to slow. At the same time, increased global production and new energy conservation measures in consuming nations was putting an end to the sellers' market in oil. Steep and steady increases in world energy prices, upon which both the Alberta oil boom and the federal government's new energy policies had been predicated, peaked near $40 a barrel and then reversed themselves. By 1985 Calgary would see the return of $10-a-barrel oil and Alberta's greatest oil boom had turned to bust.*

*The Calgary market in private housing went bust, too. Doug Ewens and Richard Shaw, having bought at the top of the market when they arrived in 1981, would not recover the purchase value in their homes for a dozen years.

To the extent that McCarthy & McCarthy had ever hoped that it could ship the "overhang" of legal work the oil boom had caused in Calgary back to Toronto to keep Ontario lawyers busy—something widely alleged by the Law Society of Alberta and vigorously denied by McCarthys' spokespeople—the end of the oil boom definitively killed that possibility. As activity in the Calgary oil patch slowed, so did business for investment dealers, real estate developers and all the other beneficiaries of the oil boom, including lawyers. Once more the Calgary boomtime phenomenon of too much work chasing too few lawyers reversed itself. Lawyers would again have to compete for work, in Calgary as elsewhere.

"The Toronto office could provide incredible assistance," recalled Richard Shaw of Black & Company's early years. Much of the fledgling firm's administrative work, for instance, was being supported by staff and systems in Toronto. "But McCarthy & McCarthy was not well known in the Calgary business community. We learned very quickly that there were very long established ties to the older firms, and they were very difficult to penetrate. So McCarthy & McCarthy was not God's gift to the business community in Calgary." Doug Ewens added, "At McCarthy & McCarthy in Toronto, there [was] this pipeline load full of work that keeps spilling onto your desk." It was not the same in Calgary. "We very quickly learned that the clients didn't want to be dealing with people in Toronto. They wanted you at the meetings. They wanted your judgement and advice." The market, in effect, was demanding delivery on exactly the promise that the partners had made to the Law Society of Alberta: that even as an integral part of the Toronto-based McCarthy & McCarthy law firm, the Calgary office would be made up of Alberta lawyers practising Alberta law in the Alberta legal-services market.

In that postboom context, Robert Black's Alberta clients provided crucial support to the building of a locally rooted firm. TransAlta Corporation's need for legal work was large, not only in corporate and finance work but also in real property, litigation and tribunal work. In addition, Black was soon requested to advise the board of Hudson's Bay Oil and Gas throughout its takeover negotiations with Dome Petroleum. The firm was also retained as counsel to the underwriters providing financing for the Alberta gas pipeline company Nova Corporation. "National" clients of McCarthy & McCarthy also became Black & Company clients. When TransCanada PipeLines, a long-time McCarthy client in Toronto, acknowledged the western shift of the energy business by moving its head office to Calgary, having an office in Calgary enabled McCarthys to retain the work by shifting responsibility for it to Black & Company. By late 1982, even before the suit against the Law Society had been launched, one-year-old Black & Company was identifying a need for more lawyers and more space. In 1983 the firm moved to larger premises in the TransCanada PipeLines Building (later called the Western Gas Tower).*

*Black & Company remained in that building until 1990, when it needed additional space and moved to the Canada Trust Tower (later the Alberta Energy Tower), where it occupied three floors. It remained there in 2004.

Most of the new Black & Company lawyers were Albertans. Len Bannicke, a senior energy lawyer formerly with Hudson's Bay Oil and Gas, joined as counsel to the firm, and Barbara Romaine, a securities lawyer, became the first lawyer to move to Black & Company from a rival Calgary law practice. Brian Malone, an established Calgary litigator, joined Black & Company in October 1983 and was the first Albertan (other than Black) to become a partner. Malone, a New Brunswicker who had moved to Calgary in 1979, had few fears about joining a firm the Law Society was trying to put out of business. "I figured, look, this is going to happen... national firms were the way of the future," he recalled. Even if the Law Society triumphed in the short term, he concluded, Black & Company clients like TransAlta would still need representation. Malone quickly took on a great deal of regulatory work for TransAlta and other clients.

Barbara Romaine of Black & Company went on to be president of the Law Society of Alberta and then a judge.

More Toronto lawyers eventually followed Vernon, Ewens and Shaw from Toronto to Calgary. "The people that McCarthys sent were always top-drawer people," recalled Malone. "They didn't solve a local problem in Toronto by shipping it west.... they sent excellent people." In 1984, when Patrick Vernon returned to Toronto after three years managing the Calgary office, Edward Kerwin moved west to take over the managing partner's role in the Calgary office. (Robert Black, already sixty in 1982 and deeply involved in his clients' affairs, had no intention of managing the firm, even when it bore his name.) A young member of the Toronto banking law practice, Stephen Clark, spent a year in Calgary as McCarthys tried to extend its strong links to Toronto banks into the west. When TransCanada PipeLines moved to Calgary, Gary Girvan, a rising young lawyer in the corporate section, moved west for a year to smooth the transfer. Michael McIntosh also moved west, and some lawyers hired in Calgary moved to the Toronto office, including Glenn Friesen, then a young associate in litigation who eventually returned to Black & Company in Calgary, and William Hopkins.

Nevertheless, the idea that having offices in two provinces would mean a constant circulation of lawyers between the offices soon fell victim to the reality of lawyers' commitments to home and family and to the need for local knowledge and connections. By 1986 Black & Company had grown to 26 lawyers, and a large majority of them were Albertans hired as students and associates or as lateral transfers from other firms.

The Calgary project had been driven by corporate lawyers and their perception of their clients' needs. No litigation specialists were among the lawyers who transferred west. Senior litigators might be retained to fight cases almost anywhere, and over the years John Robinette, Doug Laidlaw, George Finlayson and other senior McCarthy litigators had become qualified to argue cases in many Canadian provinces. They assumed that they could fly to another province whenever necessary, without taking on any permanent involvement there. At the same time, the Toronto litigation team had a very strong esprit de corps, based on their conviction that they were part of a litigation tradition unsurpassed by any firm in Toronto, if not Canada. While some litigators were willing to shed the growing burden of Alberta regulatory hearings that had kept them commuting to Calgary, as a group the litigation department had been spectators in the westward expansion driven by the corporate department.

While the corporate lawyers soon showed themselves willing to see Alberta matters being handled by Albertans whom they hardly knew, the litigators expressed more concern about the standards they knew in

McCarthys' cowboys celebrate their entry into Alberta: from left, Jim McCartney, Richard Shaw, Patrick Vernon, Thomas Forbes, Edward Kerwin, Douglas Ewens and Peter Quinn, with their spouses.

Toronto. Brian Malone, the first Alberta litigator to join Robert Black at Black & Company, was also the first to become aware of the close scrutiny litigation partners in Toronto intended to give any potential recruit from outside Toronto. As late as 1990, when Thomas Ferguson, another senior Calgary litigator, was negotiating a move to McCarthys' Calgary office, he found his obligatory visit to Toronto "almost like I was running the gauntlet to see whether I would pass muster."

Throughout the 1980s, as Black & Company became steadily more integrated into the Calgary legal community, it was still also an offshoot of the Toronto firm. There was a Calgary managing partner, but Black & Company relied on accounting and administrative systems based in Toronto. Fundamental decisions about the two firms were still largely the responsibility of the Toronto management committee.

There was also constant financial support from the larger office. The Calgary office made money every year. Revenues grew steadily, even in the difficult years of the mid-1980s, and approached $8 million by the end of the decade (when McCarthys' gross revenues in Toronto were just reaching $50 million). But costs rose steadily, too. In the 1980s overheads and staff salaries frequently exceeded 80 per cent of gross revenues at Black & Company. (In Toronto in the 1980s such costs were about 55 per cent of revenues.) As a result, the partners in Black & Company drew much of their income as McCarthy partners rather than as Black & Company partners. There was, in effect, a steady subsidy for the Calgary venture by the Toronto-based partners. "In the long run, I think it is an excellent decision," said Toronto partner Arthur Scace in a 1989 interview, "but we in Toronto have subsidized them every year since they started."[77]

There were benefits flowing back to Toronto, as well. Early in 1984, Jim McCartney itemized some of the work Toronto lawyers received from being part of a firm that was on the ground in Calgary. The oil giant Amoco, originally a Black & Company client, was consulting McCarthys' mining law group on a mining venture. Other Black & Company clients in Calgary were retaining McCarthys' Toronto lawyers on Toronto Stock Exchange matters, on international licensing issues and on many finance and tax aspects. Through Black & Company's efforts, corporations based in Calgary were channelling work to specialist lawyers in the Toronto office that would have gone to other Toronto law firms.[78]

By the end of the 1980s Black & Company had almost forty lawyers. It was not the biggest law firm in Calgary, or in the top four, but it had become a substantial practice with a blue-chip client base, prominent lawyers, and rising revenues. Shaw and Ewens had settled into Calgary and become a permanent part of the Calgary firm. Shaw had succeeded Edward Kerwin as Calgary managing partner in the depths of the energy bust—and had to lay off several lawyers in 1989. Barbara

Romaine, by then a partner, had been elected a bencher of the Law Society of Alberta.

As the lawsuit against the Law Society of Alberta continued, tensions continued between Black & Company and the rest of the Alberta bar. Rival firms liked to tell promising students at interviews that Black & Company would not last, and when the Queen's Counsel appointment that Brian Malone had been told to expect did not materialize, he wondered if the Law Society had wielded its influence against him. But most Black & Company lawyers said the dispute was just business, with both sides pursuing their own interests. Black & Company lawyers worked and socialized with lawyers who supported the Law Society against them without sensing any personal hostility. "It was an institutional fight rather than a personal one," said Patrick Vernon. He recalled how the Calgary energy law firm Burnet, Duckworth & Palmer, neighbours in the Esso Plaza building, gave the fledgling Black & Company unstinting access to its law library. When Jim McCartney was admitted to the Alberta bar in 1981, he was presented for his call to the bar by an old friend who was one of the benchers opposing McCarthys' entry into Alberta. "I personally was never confronted by any animosity," recalled Doug Ewens. "Never once did we find that animosity from other lawyers got in the way of doing deals."

The only lawyer who recalled feeling the struggle personally was Robert Black. Coming so closely after his conflict with his old partners in Jones, Black, the confrontation with his own Law Society affected him most acutely. He did sense personal hostility to his eastern alliance from lawyers he had known most of his career. At one point in the trial in Edmonton Black became ill, and he grew alarmed that he was finding a mere piece of litigation stressful enough to affect his health and well-being. He visited a doctor and was relieved to discover that his illness was purely physical: he had picked up a parasite from contaminated water in the hotel.

In August 1984, Mr. Justice Dea of the Alberta Court of Queen's Bench delivered his verdict. It was an unqualified win for the Law

Society. Dea accepted that interprovincial law firms threatened the Law Society's ability to govern its members. He therefore concluded, "The rules are not an abuse of the defendant's legislative authority nor an improper use thereof." Instead, he ruled, they constituted a reasonable limitation upon the plaintiffs' Charter rights. Dea found both Law Society rules "reasonably necessary for the protection of the public interest and the ability of the defendant to perform its statutory duties to the public and the profession."[79]

Doreen Pickles, one of first staff members hired at Black & Company (as a receptionist) and later a law clerk there, recalled the staff being gathered together in the aftermath of Justice Dea's verdict. They heard that Black & Company had immediately launched an appeal and, pending the outcome of the appeal, it was seeking to prevent the Law Society from applying its rules at once. But the injunction might be denied. "We don't know what's going to happen this weekend," she recalled being told. "There's a possibility they're going to close the doors, they're going to close us down. But don't worry, we'll take care of you all."

In the event, the injunction was allowed. The doors stayed open at Black & Company, the staff was reassured, and the case proceeded to the Alberta Court of Appeal. There, on March 4, 1986, the appellate judges overturned the trial judge's verdict on constitutional grounds. They concluded that both of the Law Society's new rules unreasonably violated the Charter of Rights and Freedoms and could not stand. The Law Society immediately appealed this judgement, and so the struggle between Black & Company and the Law Society of Alberta set the stage for the Supreme Court of Canada to issue its first substantial ruling on mobility rights and freedom of association under the Charter. That verdict, however, would have to wait until 1989.* [80]

*The Law Society's opposition to interprovincial firms had not deterred every Calgary firm from looking into the possibility. In 1985–86, while the lawsuit continued, McCarthys and Black & Company had long and very secret merger talks with two prominent Alberta firms. No agreement was reached with either, partly because McCarthys was preoccupied with its Vancouver plans. In 1988 Bennett Jones of Calgary opened an office in Saskatchewan.

FROM A CALGARY OFFICE TO A NATIONAL FIRM

MOST OF THE ARGUMENTS for expanding to Calgary could always have applied well beyond Calgary. If McCarthys was going to provide services to clients across provincial and national borders, as accounting firms did, there were many cities apart from Calgary it might consider as sites for future offices. In the early 1980s the firm already had a link with Clarkson Tétrault in Montreal. It was taking an interest in opportunities in Hong Kong, and it was closely following the expansion moves of American and Canadian law firms. Still, its move into Alberta really had been driven by the unique business circumstances prevailing there in the late 1970s. McCarthys went to Calgary without any master plan to continue elsewhere—even though it cloaked its proposal to the Law Society of Alberta in March 1980 in a larger purpose, declaring, "The immediate proposal to establish the firm in Alberta is part of a broader objective of becoming a national firm with offices in a number of major cities across Canada."[81]

In October 1982, with Black & Company a year old (and still officially unchallenged by the Law Society of Alberta), Jim McCartney suggested to McCarthys' management committee that it was time to look beyond Calgary, to begin fleshing out the national firm idea. McCarthys formed a National Law Firm Committee, led by McCartney, early in 1983. By fall the committee presented a set of proposals, rooting its case for national expansion in the partners' shared interest in the growth and prosperity of McCarthy & McCarthy. "If national law firms develop, then a firm with a limited local base will find it increasingly difficult to prosper in the face of competition which the sophisticated and diversified national firms will offer. The common business phrase, 'They have the horses,' will be applied."

The committee also made the case for speed. It noted that the lawsuit in Calgary had deterred other firms from moving in, giving McCarthys an advantage in that market. That advantage would vanish from Calgary if the legal challenge ended, and similar advantages might not remain available elsewhere. "If there are advantages to being national, then the first firm to become national will gain prominence while the others are trying to catch up." Beyond making the case for committing McCarthy & McCarthy firmly to the principle of national expansion, the National Law Firm committee had two further proposals.[82]

First, it recommended that McCarthys seek to build a single national partnership, not a loose association of independent law firms. "While benefits have been derived from association with Clarkson Tétrault, we have clearly not promoted their interests to the same extent that we have promoted the interests of Black & Company, and vice versa.... A loose association is unlikely to be perceived to have significant advantages so far as clients are concerned."

Second, the committee recommended an immediate search for a merger partner in Vancouver. McCarthy & McCarthy already had an associated law firm in Montreal, the other great centre of business and law in eastern Canada, and was as strongly entrenched as the law would permit in Calgary, rapidly growing into one of the key business centres of Canada. That left only Vancouver. Winnipeg, Halifax, Ottawa and other Canadian cities all had substantial corporate-law firms, but they did not match the number of head offices in Montreal, Toronto, Calgary and Vancouver and the volume of high-level business law they generated. Vancouver, on the other hand, despite struggling with a serious recession and labour strife in the early 1980s, was Canada's third-largest city, its gateway to the increasingly significant Pacific Rim, and about to be the host of a world exposition, Expo 86. With a presence in Vancouver, McCarthys would secure for itself a place in all the principal business centres of Canada. Its status as a national firm would be beyond dispute.

In November 1983 a McCarthy & McCarthy partnership meeting endorsed all three proposals: to build a national firm, to favour mergers over associations, and to seek a merger with a Vancouver law firm. Jim McCartney and Harry Macdonell were already in preliminary discussions with several west coast law firms. By January 1984 they were on their way to Vancouver to survey potential partners.[83]

SHRUM, LIDDLE & HEBENTON

WEST COAST INNOVATIONS

A NEW LAW FIRM IN VANCOUVER | 8

IN VANCOUVER AS ELSEWHERE, law firms and legal careers had always been made locally. In 1984 the leading firms were mostly ones that had come to prominence soon after the city was founded almost 100 years earlier. They were powerfully linked to the dominant sectors of the local economy and accustomed to receiving, almost as their due, the best clients and the best young lawyers. McCarthy & McCarthy's eventual Vancouver partner, however, was not one of these. A much younger law firm, founded specifically to challenge the old established firms, became the west coast partner in the emerging national firm.

British Columbia, settled from the sea, had at first looked to Britain, not eastern Canada, for its judges and lawyers. The colony's first trained judge, Matthew Baillie Begbie, and its first lawyer, Henry Pering Pellew Crease, were British barristers who came directly from Britain to the Pacific coast colony. Yet as early as 1859 an Ontario lawyer named George Barnston was admitted to the colonial bar. George Walkem, a future premier of British Columbia, arrived from Quebec in 1863 to open a law practice in the gold rush Cariboo country. After British Columbia became a province of Canada in 1871, the

British Columbia bar gradually drew closer to its eastern Canadian counterparts, particularly in the years following the completion of the transcontinental railroad in 1885 and the founding of Vancouver in 1886. In 1884 the Province of British Columbia gave the provincial Law Society, founded in 1869, authority to govern the legal profession, much as its counterparts in Ontario and other parts of Canada did.

As on the Prairies, the railroad's arrival on the west coast stimulated a surge in local and national business enterprises. The railroad also brought in many eastern lawyers eager to serve them. Notable immigrant lawyers included the future judge Lyman Poore Duff from Ontario and Vancouver law firm builders J. Wallace Farris and Joseph Russell from New Brunswick. British and eastern Canadian immigrant lawyers and the students whom they trained (there was no university law school in British Columbia until 1945) gradually built a flourishing provincial bar, with respected litigators, influential corporate counsel, and specialists in local issues such as mining law and admiralty practice. Its luminaries included Duff, who went on to be chief justice of Canada, and J.W. Farris who, apart from being provincial attorney general and a Canadian senator, became one of the country's leading courtroom advocates. His brother, Wendell Farris, rose to be chief justice of British Columbia.

As elsewhere in Canada, British Columbia had a distinctly Anglo-Protestant bar for most of the twentieth century, although British Columbia's small minority communities produced some notable lawyers, including Samuel Schwartz, who in 1914 became the first Jewish judge in Canada, the flamboyant Vancouver defence lawyer Angelo Branca, and others. In 1912 Mabel French, a lawyer from New Brunswick, became the first woman admitted to the British Columbia bar. Lyman Duff's brother-in-law, J. Edward Bird, was an early example of an anti-Establishment streak within the British Columbia bar; he defended miners after labour disturbances at the Nanaimo coal mines and later went to Winnipeg to defend workers charged with sedition after the 1919 Winnipeg General Strike.[84]

In British Columbia, as in the Prairie provinces, lawyers who got in at the beginning and secured the legal work of the banks, the railroad, and the early shipping and resource companies had the chance to build law firms that would retain their pre-eminence for most of the twentieth century. At the middle of the twentieth century the Vancouver firm Russell & DuMoulin was British Columbia's largest law firm. It also claimed to be the oldest; it had been founded in 1889 by Joseph Russell, who arrived from New Brunswick and quickly secured the legal work of the Canadian Pacific Railway's local land agency.[85]

Davis & Company, another leading Vancouver firm in the 1950s, was also almost as old as the city itself. Edward P. Davis, from Ontario, had been a very early member of the Edmonton and Calgary bars before moving on to Vancouver in 1892 with retainers from both the CPR and the Hudson's Bay Company. Davis quickly added the Bank of Commerce and Crow's Nest Coal Company to his list of clients. He was both a powerful corporate counsel and a dominating litigator. By 1910, when he was fifty, Davis was described as "so admittedly at the head of his profession that he is not regarded as having a rival."[86]

Another leading Vancouver firm in the 1950s was Bull, Housser & Tupper, formed by the 1927 merger of two firms founded before the turn of the century, one of which had been headed by Sir Charles Hibbert Tupper, son of the Nova Scotian Confederation-maker and early prime minister Sir Charles Tupper. In the 1950s Farris, Vaughan, launched in 1903 by Senator J.W. Farris and continued by his son John L. Farris (a future chief justice of British Columbia), remained a leader in both litigation and corporate work.[87]

These firms, and one or two others that had begun almost as early, secured most of British Columbia's corporate legal practice, and they kept it. In much the way that a handful of firms launched in the mid- to late nineteenth century had remained dominant in the legal markets of Montreal and Toronto, the partnerships that took control of the corporate-law market in Vancouver before or soon after 1900 had remained almost impervious to challenge by new contenders far into the twentieth century.

Gordon Shrum, who articled in the late 1950s at a slightly younger establishment firm, Campney, Owen & Murphy, recalled how the head of the firm, Ralph Campney (who had recently been minister of national defence in the Louis St. Laurent government), would return from an annual visit to Toronto and Montreal having secured for another year the west coast legal work of Eaton's and Bank of Montreal, no matter what the local managers might have preferred. As Shrum put it, "The conventional wisdom was that if you had the client, that was what you needed for a firm. You could hire any kind of person to do the work." With all the important clients locked into permanent relationships with a handful of leading corporate-law firms, it was difficult for a new firm to break in. Although the old firms, and their profits, tended to be tightly controlled by a handful of partners, they seemed almost immune to challenge from other lawyers, and ambitious young lawyers seemed to have few alternatives.[88]

In 1960, Gordon Shrum joined two other young Vancouver lawyers who had decided to try breaking the closed circle of the city's leading law firms.

THE SHRUM, LIDDLE & HEBENTON FIRM

KEITH LIDDLE, doing conveyancing work at Campney, Owen & Murphy, began looking for broader horizons in 1959, and he approached Alec Robertson, a lawyer's son from Victoria who had been a top student at the University of British Columbia Law School and had done graduate work at Harvard Law. Both men were interested in business and in practising corporate law, and they shared a sense that the established firms were not so good as to be beyond challenge. They agreed to launch a new firm together. Their plan, recalled Robertson, "was to build something. We would start at the top." With just two lawyers and few clients, the new firm of Robertson & Liddle took up offices in the Burrard Building on West Georgia Street, then the newest and most prestigious corporate address in downtown Vancouver. They opened on January 1, 1960, and soon recruited Shrum, who had recently been UBC Law School's gold medallist, as their third partner in Robertson, Liddle & Shrum.

In its early years the firm's bread and butter came from the mortgage and real estate financing practice that Keith Liddle built up. Alec Robertson, though his ambitions lay mostly in corporate law, also did some prosecution work and found himself becoming the firm's litigator. Provincial megaprojects rapidly became another source of work. Gordon Shrum's father was a key adviser on the economic development plans of Premier W.A.C. Bennett and one of the province's most influential people. When Gordon Shrum Sr. headed B.C.'s Hydro-Electric Power Authority, his son's new law firm did a good deal of work on hydroelectric planning issues. When Shrum Sr. moved on to build Simon Fraser University, an instant university in the forests of Burnaby Mountain in Greater Vancouver, the firm did land assembly work for the university's mountaintop campus and advised the administration on governance, labour relations and other issues.

The business that Gordon Shrum Sr. provided was crucial in the practice's early years, but the three founders had intended theirs to be the antithesis of the kind of law firm that relied on patronage and friendships. They had begun on the theory that if they built a really good firm, clients would come to them. In pursuit of that goal the partners borrowed heavily and poured in their own money. They had the best-designed premises in Vancouver (Gordon Shrum, who had worked in graphic design before turning to law, maintained a lifelong interest in the subject) and their growing library and staff consumed most of the firm's revenues. Above all, the partners were on the lookout for talent. "We held the contrarian view that...we were going to hire really good people and maybe something good would come of it," said Shrum.

Notable among the "really good people" they went after was Sholto Hebenton, a banker's son from the Okanagan Valley who had won

British Columbia's Rhodes Scholarship and done legal studies at Oxford, followed by a Master of Law degree at Harvard. Keith Liddle convinced his partners that Hebenton was the kind of talent their firm needed, whatever the cost. Shrum put up some money and Liddle flew to New York to persuade Hebenton, who was then working at the prestigious New York firm Dewey Ballantine.* As soon as he began his pitch, however, Hebenton interrupted him. He and his wife had already decided to return to Vancouver. He would accept the offer; indeed, he could have accepted it by telephone.

"Heb" would prove to be the kind of talent the firm wanted, but two problems ensued. First, his Oxford and Harvard studies had not qualified him to practise law in British Columbia. Law Society of British Columbia rules required that he article with a lawyer of ten years' experience, and none of the principals of Robertson, Liddle & Shrum had been practising for ten years; Hebenton had to article at Russell & DuMoulin.† The second problem was money. The firm had guaranteed its new lawyer a minimum income, which meant that once he started working for them he regularly took home more than the partners did. The strain of building a firm, rather than deriving income from it, was beginning to tell on Alec Robertson, who unlike his partners had a family to support and no other income. Early in 1965, a few months after Hebenton arrived, Robertson departed to become in-house counsel to the British Columbia forest products giant MacMillan Bloedel, which could provide him with both an income and the high-level corporate law practice he wanted.‡

Hebenton therefore became a partner almost as soon as he was called to the bar. Robertson, Liddle & Shrum became Shrum, Liddle & Hebenton, with Keith Liddle yielding his seniority to the value of the Shrum name. Soon Hebenton was not just a partner but a driving force. Working closely

*Liddle claimed that for years, whenever the firm did anything expensive, "Gordon's paying for it" was the refrain. Indeed, Shrum did have a negative income from his partnership in several of the early years.

†Hebenton recalled that his articling position was expedited by the fact that Leonard DuMoulin, the head of the firm, had known his family in Kelowna. "We don't hire people that way any more."

‡After several years at MacMillan Bloedel, Robertson practised for many years at the law firm Davis & Company in Vancouver.

with him was another newly hired young lawyer, Paul Beckmann, whose talents Gordon Shrum had spotted while teaching a bar admission course. Beckmann had a commerce background and a head for figures, and he immersed himself in the firm's accounts and management: "I became really quite knowledgeable about the business and economics of the practice of law. Most law firms... were stuck in their routine or they had a head of the firm who wasn't about to make any significant changes. Whereas we would make all kinds of changes." Hebenton and Beckmann promoted ideas about service to clients, time management practices, allocation systems and delegating to non-lawyer administrators, all of which advanced the founding partners' ambitions to build a modern, even avant-garde, law firm.

Gordon Shrum and Sholto "Heb" Hebenton led Shrum, Liddle & Hebenton into its merger with McCarthy & McCarthy in 1989.

Gordon Shrum became a kind of lawyer's lawyer to the partnership, respected for his intelligence, judgement and meticulous research but a little detached from routine practice. Hebenton gradually became the practice leader and particularly the firm's recruiter. Any British Columbia law student who won a scholarship to a prestigious law school in eastern Canada, the United States or Britain could expect a letter or call from Hebenton, inviting him or her to visit the firm at Shrum, Liddle & Hebenton's expense. Since most Vancouver law firms still expected students to go to them, "we got ahead of the curve in terms of recruiting," said Hebenton. Not all the "eastern stars" caught on, but even those who left could prove useful. Peter Leask and Lynn Smith, two early recruits who soon left to teach law at UBC, became talent spotters there for the firm. Going in the other direction, UBC law professor Byran Gibson joined for a brief secondment in 1974, decided the law firm was more stimulating than the law school, and stayed.

Shrum, Liddle & Hebenton's recruiting philosophy was expensive. It paid its associates above Vancouver's going rates and Hebenton, Beckmann and others became drawn into the firm's habit, pioneered by Robertson and Liddle, of deferring their own incomes for the sake of growth.

Winton Derby, from Alberta, joined soon after Beckmann and became the litigation leader. The firm's next notable hire was Mitchell Gropper, a Saskatchewan-born lawyer who had articled in Vancouver, done graduate legal studies in Britain, and taught law at the University of Western Ontario. When Gropper joined Shrum, Liddle & Hebenton in 1969, Keith Liddle had already built a substantial real estate practice. The continuous expansion of British Columbia's resource industries in the 1960s and 1970s had been reflected in a sustained building boom in head office properties in downtown Vancouver, including many financed by Liddle's key client, Coronation Credit Corporation.* Other clients included McDonald's Restaurants, just beginning to venture into Canada, and later another venture by the McDonald's western franchisee, a restaurant chain called Keg Restaurants. McDonald's was at first looked at skeptically by many of the Shrum, Liddle & Hebenton lawyers, who were glad of the work but couldn't imagine anyone making money on nineteen-cent hamburgers.

Soon after joining Shrum, Liddle & Hebenton, Mitch Gropper gave a useful bit of legal advice to his brother-in-law's employer, a rising property development firm that was changing its name to Daon Developments. He was soon rewarded with the Daon account. Under the leadership of Jack Poole, Daon in the early 1970s began expanding its property development empire far beyond Vancouver and, within a decade, it had made itself one of the three largest property development corporations in North America. Gropper's practice rose with it. "Mitch

*Liddle: "They were providing financing for a lot of the buildings that were under construction in Vancouver at that time in the downtown core. Every building I walk by, [I say to myself] 'I remember doing that.'" Coronation Credit eventually merged into Versatile Corporation, a truck builder and later a west coast shipbuilding company.

and his secretary, who is now his wife, went fast into the first word processors," recalled Keith Liddle. "Mitch would fly off to a development deal somewhere and take his secretary and their big word processing machine, and Mitch would be facing a whole team of lawyers on the other side and he would out-produce them all."

By the late 1970s commercial real estate provided 40 per cent of Shrum, Liddle & Hebenton's gross revenue and the Daon work quarterbacked by Gropper provided the largest part of that. In 1980 Shrum, Liddle & Hebenton, having already relocated from the Burrard Building to the newer Bentall Centre farther down Burrard Street, moved its twenty-five lawyers and their staff again: into the gold-tinted Daon Building at 999 West Pender Street. Meanwhile they had attracted another property developer, Joe Houssian, who in the mid-1970s had launched a development company named IntraWest and initially came to the firm for tax advice from its rising young tax specialist, Rosemarie Wertschek. In 1981 a Shrum, Liddle & Hebenton survey of its clients still listed IntraWest as a small client with growth potential, but in the 1990s IntraWest became one of the world's leading ski resort operators and a significant client for what by then was McCarthy Tétrault.[89]

Mitchell Gropper (left) helped Shrum, Liddle & Hebenton build its business law practice; Winton Derby was a leader of the litigation department.

The scope and complexity of Daon's investments raised cutting-edge issues in corporate finance, securities and international taxation. Shrum, Liddle & Hebenton's long and expensive commitment to hiring the best was beginning to pay off, as the firm's young medallists and scholarship winners came up against work that was challenging, profitable and constant.

In 1973 Shrum, Liddle & Hebenton had hired two top students from UBC Law School, Rosemarie Wertschek and Trevor Bell, both future leaders of the firm who began by working closely with Gropper. Wertschek came from a Vancouver working class immigrant family; she had given up a Cambridge fellowship in mediaeval history largely for economic reasons. She at first avoided Shrum, Liddle & Hebenton for its "egghead" reputation. She wanted to go "where the money was," she said, but she was converted partly by Shrum, Liddle & Hebenton's enthusiasm for her and also by the entrenched sexism of other firms she interviewed. (Gropper, a Jew, had also felt more welcome at Shrum, Liddle & Hebenton in 1969 than at some other Vancouver firms.) In Vancouver as elsewhere, barriers to minorities in the legal profession fell wherever legal skills replaced social standing as the key to recruiting. Shrum, Liddle & Hebenton had placed itself at the cutting edge in both trends.

Soon after Wertschek joined, Gropper decided she had the makings of a tax lawyer and arranged for her to study with the accounting firm Coopers & Lybrand for a year. Wertschek, initially fearing she was being sidelined while the other young lawyers were working on deals, put in full days at Coopers & Lybrand, then went to the law office to put in nearly as many hours there. The accounting experience (and the extra hours) soon became the basis of a stellar career in tax law.*

Early in 1976, with both a recession and inflation battering the economy, Gropper assigned Wertschek to look into a problem Daon had brought to the firm. The Canadian government's 1971 tax reforms had cut back on tax exemptions available for rental property investments; Daon (still fairly small) was having trouble finding investors for an apartment project near the Burrard Street Bridge. Wertschek sat down with the Income Tax Act ("I was unencumbered by the past at the time. What did I know?") and began taking notes.

*Some clients were slow to grasp the role a female lawyer could play. Keith Liddle recalls an incident from the 1970s: "Mitch had a client that had an involved tax problem, so he took the client down to Rosemarie's office and introduced them. And Rosemarie has got the tax acts from every jurisdiction in the world, and she's going from this one to that, and she's moving the money all over the place, and it finally ended up back where the client wanted it and no tax payable. The client went back to Mitch and said, 'Mitch, where did you find a secretary like that?'"

By the time she was finished, the firm had cobbled together a string of potential minor deductions and incentives that could be combined into a substantial tax saving for investors. "We put it together that summer and fall, got a tax ruling on it, and in November they hired some real estate agents to market the thing.... The thing was an enormous success in no time at all, it was like wildfire. Every developer who had product that wasn't moving was phoning: 'Who knows how to do this?'" Shrum, Liddle & Hebenton had invented the MURB, the Multiple-Unit Residential Building tax credit, which became a centrepiece of real estate investment strategies across Canada until the tax laws changed again some years later.

In the recession of the early 1980s, skyrocketing interest rates and a downturn in office leasing produced a financial crisis at Daon. Leveraged to the hilt, the property developer suddenly lacked the cash flow to cover its interest payments. It was so large, however, that creditors held back from petitioning it into bankruptcy. Shrum, Liddle & Hebenton's lawyers used that delay to search for alternatives to a forced liquidation. "That was Mitch," recalled Wertschek. "Really, that was his brainchild. There was a team of people going to the library, burning the midnight oil, sweat pouring from your brow, because any moment there could be a tap on the door and the bankruptcy petition would be served."*

What the team came up with to shelter Daon from liquidation was the Companies' Creditors Arrangement Act, or CCAA. This was a federal law, introduced in the 1930s and little used thereafter, which provided a framework within which courts could protect a company from being forced into liquidation and supervise a restructuring effort that addressed the interests of all parties. During North America's inflation-plagued recession of the early 1980s, emergency bailouts like that of the Chrysler Corporation had begun emphasising "rehabilitation," rather than liquidation, as the preferred alternative for insolvencies among very large corporations that were "too big to fail." In Canada there was a shared

*At the time, Gropper had left Shrum, Liddle & Hebenton to work in-house for Daon. As Daon's financial difficulties increased, he returned to Shrum, Liddle & Hebenton.

interest among judges, creditors and struggling companies in finding some equivalent to the "chapter 11" processes that were being relied upon in the United States. CCAA became the germ of that bankruptcy protection and rehabilitation process.

"Other people used it more than we did, but we built it," Wertschek said of the way the CCAA became part of the standard tool kit of Canadian law and business. Daon eventually emerged from CCAA protection. It reorganized as BCE Developments and was eventually folded into the property development giant Brookfield Limited. (Daon's head, Jack Poole, later re-emerged as chair of the 2010 Vancouver-Whistler Winter Olympic Games Committee.) For Shrum, Liddle & Hebenton the legal work generated by the CCAA restructuring of Daon and other corporations was some consolation for the loss of Daon's ongoing property development work. If the maxim "small firms practise law, big firms make law" is accurate, innovations like MURBs and the CCAA process suggest that Shrum, Liddle & Hebenton was at least starting to play in the big leagues.

Within a few years of joining Shrum, Liddle & Hebenton, Rosemarie Wertschek was developing a leading-edge tax law practice.

By 1984 the practice employed forty lawyers and was growing rapidly. It was still well behind the four or five largest Vancouver firms (with seventy to eighty lawyers each), but it was securely placed in the second tier. It had expanded from a general corporate and real estate practice into corporate finance, securities, taxation, labour and other specialties, and its reputation among British Columbia lawyers was high, at least in certain ways. Kevin Wright, returning from Cambridge University in England in 1985, found other Vancouver law firms telling him in interviews that his academic record and credentials in legal scholarship would make him a good fit at Shrum, Liddle & Hebenton.* [90]

Shrum, Liddle & Hebenton still retained the idea with which Alec Robertson and Keith Liddle had started it: that it was possible for a law firm to succeed by raising the standards maintained by Vancouver's established firms. As late as 1979 Earl Phillips, a future managing partner in Vancouver, found that Shrum, Liddle & Hebenton's recruitment set it apart from other British Columbia firms, which still implied they were "doing you a big favour giving you an articling interview." Ideas about firm management and client service that were rote by the end of the century were still innovative twenty years earlier when Shrum, Liddle & Hebenton was applying them. "One of the knocks on lawyers in those days was that they took a long time and had a reputation for saying no," recalled Hebenton. Shrum, Liddle & Hebenton was already instilling client service practices as straightforward as answering phone calls without secretarial screening and replying to mail the same day. "Helping the client to find a way, rather than saying 'No, you can't do that': those ideas are now universal. But we had a bit of a jump."

*In 1988, shortly before its merger with McCarthy & McCarthy, a Shrum, Liddle & Hebenton brochure noted the firm of seventy-one lawyers included five Rhodes Scholars and three Commonwealth Scholars.

The firm was equally proud of its ideas about governance. Though Hebenton was the acknowledged leader (Gordon Shrum was not practising actively and Keith Liddle left the firm in 1981 to make a career change), Shrum, Liddle & Hebenton had no designated managing partner until continued growth required the appointment of one in 1987, and it long maintained a very flat hierarchy. Associates tended to be drawn into the partnership rapidly (the assessment period was raised to just four years in 1984). Most issues were handled by biweekly Friday morning meetings and an array of committees. Earl Phillips recalled joining a meeting on his second day as a lawyer at the firm in 1981 and being handed the latest monthly financial statements. ("I said, 'Are you sure I'm supposed to have this?'")

Compared with other Vancouver firms, where closely held leadership and payment by seniority had remained fundamental, Shrum, Liddle & Hebenton's allocations process rewarded productivity and was otherwise relatively egalitarian. The allocation criteria were largely developed by Paul Beckmann, who joked that his system was working when all partners were equally dissatisfied. In fact, a 1984 management review commissioned from Clarkson Gordon suggested that the associates, far from being the cash cows of law firm legend, were still actually costing Shrum, Liddle & Hebenton partners slightly more money than they brought in.* [91]

Shrum, Liddle & Hebenton was not without problems or detractors; there were departures and threats of departures over the years, particularly when several of the real estate partners considered going out on their own. Some partners also felt Shrum, Liddle & Hebenton's habit of recruiting for brains had begun to make it a firm of "relatively introverted, book-studious people." Consensus decision making demanded more and more unbillable time as the firm grew. But on the whole it was a firm where even the leaders were relatively young. Hebenton, in effect the senior partner, was still in his forties in 1984. The firm enjoyed an esprit de corps, based on youth, energy and success, that extended even to its newsletter. The *Shrumbleton News* had been launched with the usual motive—to distribute administrative memoranda—but it rapidly grew into a lively, competitive exchange of caricatures, photocopy collages and inside jokes. Its humour was mostly impenetrable by outsiders but cherished by the many Shrum, Liddle & Hebenton lawyers who contributed material frequently.[92]

One thing Shrum, Liddle & Hebenton was not doing in January 1984 was thinking about becoming a national law firm. The call from McCarthy & McCarthy came pretty much out of the blue.

*McCarthy & McCarthy's 1984 Long-Range Planning Report also suggested associates were barely profitable there. Associates in Canada had probably ceased to be the exploited cheap labour celebrated in law firm mythology. Compared with their counterparts in large American law firms, they seem to have been fewer in number and more likely to become partners.

"LAND WARS IN ASIA" | 9

LATE IN 1983, the partners of McCarthy & McCarthy in Toronto had approved the management committee's plan to seek a merger partner in Vancouver. Even before then, members had started preliminary conversations with a handful of Vancouver law firms, and individual McCarthy lawyers with contacts in Vancouver made suggestions. Before Harry Macdonell and Jim McCartney, the leaders of the National Law Firm Committee that had spearheaded the proposal, visited Vancouver in January 1984, McCarthys had assembled a list of likely merger candidates and made contact with several of them. Still, beyond what the published *Law Lists* offered, the Toronto office did not have a great deal of knowledge about Vancouver firms. Having concluded that the largest partnerships in Vancouver were unlikely to be interested in any merger discussion, they focussed their attention on half a dozen mid-size firms.[93]

Shrum, Liddle & Hebenton had not been on McCarthys' original list. But Sholto Hebenton and Arthur Scace, the Toronto tax partner and emerging leader at McCarthys, were both members of the Canadian Rhodes Scholarship organization. When Scace spoke to Hebenton of

McCarthys' interest in Vancouver, Hebenton immediately suggested his own firm should be a candidate. In the event, some of McCarthys' target firms expressed little interest in merging with a Toronto firm. Others, on closer inspection, seemed less attractive as potential partners. Shrum, Liddle & Hebenton, on the other hand, jumped quickly to the top of the short list for McCartney and Macdonell.

In 1983, Gordon Shrum organized twenty-fifth anniversary celebrations for his University of British Columbia law class. A highlight was the conferring of an honorary degree on John Robinette. Shrum's firm and Robinette's soon began discussing merger possibilities.

What sparked their interest was the ethos of the Vancouver firm, the fact that it had already gone a long way towards becoming the kind of client-driven, business-oriented, quality-maximizing law firm that proponents of the national firm within McCarthys aspired to build. In effect, Shrum, Liddle & Hebenton had always had more brains than clients. Despite its success in recruiting and retaining legal talent, it rarely secured the retainers of large national clients or established regional clients whose large, sophisticated and reliably profitable legal work generally underpinned leadership in the legal marketplace. (A notable exception was a local branch of a national bank, which in the 1970s went to Shrum, Liddle & Hebenton for its reputation for "getting it done" rather than saying no.) National clients, of course, were exactly the kind McCarthy & McCarthy already served and was hoping to serve right across the country through its national firm platform.

The invitation to consider a merger met some resistance at Shrum, Liddle & Hebenton. Most unusually, the partners went to great lengths to keep the prospect secret from associates and staff. For some time the merger proposal had the code name "Project 1812" (based on McCarthys' Toronto phone number 362-1812). Among the Shrum, Liddle & Hebenton partners there was some instinctive west coast resistance to the powerful east, particularly among "refugees" from eastern law schools and articling experiences. Someone went through the Martindale Hubbell law lists and circulated the observation that McCarthys had more lawyers older than the oldest Shrum, Liddle & Hebenton lawyer than Shrum, Liddle & Hebenton had lawyers.* Rosemarie Wertschek recalled that her initial reaction was "the old guys are selling us out to the suits," just as she was acquiring some seniority in the firm. (It says something about both Vancouver and Shrum, Liddle & Hebenton that a leading tax lawyer at an eminent corporate-law firm considered someone else "the suits.")

Wertschek soon quieted her alarm and became a supporter of the merger. Indeed, a consensus in support developed among the Shrum, Liddle & Hebenton partners. "We had no thoughts" about national firm mergers before the approach from McCarthys, recalled Mitch Gropper, but he found that as he and his partners discussed "not bricks and mortar, but philosophy of practice" with the lawyers from McCarthys and Black & Company, "we came away feeling this was just a good fit." To one partner who asked, "Are these the best guys to join?" Gropper retorted, "Well, of the people who are out here wanting to do this, they are!"

Some concerns about being swallowed by the easterners and losing what was distinctive about Shrum, Liddle & Hebenton remained. On the other hand, the merger appealed to the partners' sense that Shrum, Liddle & Hebenton was the kind of firm that did smart, cutting-edge things before others did. Byran Gibson recalled, "We were meeting at the golf club at a great big table, and virtually everybody said, 'You know, there's good and bad. An awful lot of my practice is local. But the 10 or 15 per cent that isn't is what gives me the kick. Having the

*In 1984 Shrum, Liddle & Hebenton had about forty lawyers and McCarthys about 140.

firm in Toronto or Montreal will help keep me at the cutting edge the way I wanted.' "

Another motive, mostly in the background but spurring each side towards a merger, was Vancouver's potential role as Canada's gateway to the Pacific Rim. McCarthy & McCarthy had already begun talking about the prospect of an office in Hong Kong (where Phillips & Vineberg and Stikeman Elliott of Montreal both had opened offices, though at substantial expense). McCarthy & McCarthy saw a presence in Vancouver as the appropriate stepping stone towards Asia. At the same time, some at Shrum, Liddle & Hebenton were already aware of the "flyover effect"—the potential for business to pass directly between Asia and eastern Canada—and saw the alliance with a large Toronto firm as giving Shrum, Liddle & Hebenton more, not less, opportunity to gain a foothold in the costly competition for opportunities in Asia.

In the spring of 1984, contacts and discussions between McCarthys and Shrum, Liddle & Hebenton intensified. Tom Heintzman of the litigation department visited from Toronto. So did Robert Black, from Calgary, who was able "to provide them with some comfort from the point of view of one who has had the experience of having merged with the McCarthy & McCarthy monolith." Black found the Shrum, Liddle & Hebenton lawyers "friendly and enthusiastic... committed to making an out-of-province link." The discussions about allocations, pension plans, computer systems and other technicalities seem to have reassured the Vancouver lawyers who had had concerns about the merger. In November 1984 the two firms signed an agreement in principle for a merger to be completed on February 1, 1985.[94]

The proposal was for a full merger of the two firms under the name McCarthy & McCarthy. "In the long run," the agreement declared, "to maintain separate accounts in each region, deal separately with financial responsibilities in each region and allocate profits solely according to the profitability of each region, would create stresses and require systems and procedures which would tend to keep the regions apart rather than draw the national operation together." Nevertheless, only after some transitional years would the firm have unified leadership and a single set of committees deciding the allocation of profits, the admission of new partners, and other fundamental partnership matters on behalf of Vancouver, Calgary and Toronto. The Toronto firm had stressed from the beginning it expected its name to continue and the much smaller Vancouver firm agreed, though the merged firm continued to exploit the brand equity in the name "Shrum, Liddle & Hebenton" in British Columbia, and letterhead and other documents noted that McCarthy & McCarthy was "the merged firm of McCarthy & McCarthy and Shrum, Liddle & Hebenton."[95]

McCarthys was more profitable than Shrum, Liddle & Hebenton, both in the share of gross revenue that was retained by the partners and in the average profit per partner, and the merger would not automatically raise the remuneration of Vancouver partners to the Toronto level.* But the opportunity to share in the prosperity of the larger unit was clearly there, while the Vancouver office still retained a fair amount of autonomy in local matters. In effect, having spent years investing in itself, Shrum, Liddle & Hebenton might be about to reap the dividends.[96]

The merger, of course, was conditional on the approval of the law societies in both provinces, but there was reason for optimism. The law societies of both British Columbia and Ontario had expressed general approval of the Federation of Law Societies' Freedman Report, which had recommended the acceptance of interprovincial mergers. The Law Society of Upper Canada had voted its approval of interprovincial firms in 1982 and had introduced new rules covering them early in 1985. The Law Society of British Columbia had taken no specific action, but it had not expressed opposition to the concept of interprovincial law practices during the 1982 discussions.

*The merger negotiators estimated that revenue per lawyer was 5 per cent lower at Shrum, Liddle & Hebenton, though their average billable hours were greater. More significantly, McCarthys retained 45 per cent of gross earnings as partnership profit, whereas the comparable figure at Shrum, Liddle & Hebenton was 34 per cent.

In November 1984 Shrum, Liddle & Hebenton informed the Law Society of British Columbia of its intention to merge with McCarthy & McCarthy. Its submission included a survey of developments regarding national law firms, and it concluded: "We would appreciate receiving assurance from The Law Society of British Columbia that the Society will not object to the proposed merger of Shrum, Liddle & Hebenton and McCarthy & McCarthy."[97]

THE SECOND LAWSUIT OVER INTERPROVINCIAL LAW FIRMS

ASSURANCE FROM THE Law Society of British Columbia was not forthcoming. The society referred the question of interprovincial firms to a committee, and Shrum, Liddle & Hebenton's hopes of having quick approval for a 1985 merger had to be abandoned. Meanwhile, the attorney general of British Columbia, Brian Smith, expressed reservations of his own about Toronto lawyers moving in on British Columbia legal work. "I would be most concerned if the contemplated mergers did result in the major re-direction of decision making on legal and business matters from Vancouver to Toronto," Smith wrote to the treasurer of the Law Society in December 1984. "Will it serve the public interest of this Province?" Smith believed it would not.[98]

Bencher Ronald J. McKinnon, who led the Law Society of B.C.'s investigation, presented a report in April 1985 that mostly set out the pros and cons of interprovincial mergers. McKinnon himself (at the time a small-firm, small-town practitioner) eventually concluded that the lawyers who opposed mergers were making "medieval guild house objections," but representatives of several large firms in Vancouver shared the attorney general's doubts and were disappointed with the McKinnon committee's refusal to come out strongly against mergers. Jack Giles of Farris Vaughan Wills & Murphy, a confidant of the Attorney General, contended, "If national firms are not stopped, our profession will become a branch office profession. There will be only two classes of firms: national firms and small firms. All the major work will be done by the national firms." The Law Society put off a decision again while the report was circulated more widely.[99]

The merger question finally came up for decision at a Law Society meeting in Trail, B.C., in May 1985. Paul Beckmann of Shrum, Liddle & Hebenton, an elected bencher since 1980, put the motion: that the Law Society had no objection to interprovincial mergers. The debate was vigorous. Beckmann's right to vote on his own motion was challenged, there was reference to the Black & Company lawsuit that was currently before the Alberta Court of Appeal and hostility to eastern interlopers was strongly expressed. "It was typical McCarthys," said one bencher. "They marched in here and said their name would survive, that they were going to do this and that...." Though some large-firm benchers and several from small firms did support the motion, one bencher concluded, "There was an orchestrated move on the part of the big firms to make sure it didn't go through." Beckmann's motion was defeated: fourteen against, seven in favour.[100]

The rejection of the motion meant only that the Law Society remained without a policy on interprovincial partnerships. In June 1985, however, Attorney General Smith intervened more directly. He introduced (and the legislature quickly passed) an amendment to the Barristers and Solicitors Act, the law that set out the Law Society's powers. Once proclaimed into law late in 1985, the new clauses prohibited British Columbia lawyers from entering into partnerships with out-of-province lawyers or law firms, unless all the out-of-province lawyers were themselves members of the British Columbia Law Society.

Smith argued that the decision to permit or restrict interprovincial mergers should not be the responsibility of the Law Society. In his view, the regulation of national law firms raised questions of the public interest that should be addressed in the Barristers and Solicitors Act, not by a vote of the lawyers themselves. He was not, he said, opposed to interprovincial mergers in all circumstances. But in 1985 he feared that, with

British Columbia still at the low ebb of a deep recession, its law firms would be scooped up "at the bottom of the market." There were political considerations as well. The litigation bar strongly shared the concerns of the large firms about the threat to the independence of the local bar posed by national firms, and since Smith had recently presided over deep and unpopular cuts to litigators' legal aid incomes, the intervention was a useful fence-mending initiative for the attorney general.* [101]

McCarthys and Shrum, Liddle & Hebenton had previously agreed that they would not move ahead without clear official approval from the British Columbia authorities, certainly not while the Calgary litigation dragged on. As Sholto Hebenton put it repeatedly in correspondence with his partners and the McCarthy team, "We should not get into *two* land wars in Asia at the same time." Had the attorney general not intervened, he felt, it might have been possible to bring the Law Society around from its hotly debated and less than conclusive decision to withhold its approval of interprovincial mergers. But a challenge to provincial legislation would be expensive and slow and probably bad public relations as well. By 1985 it was widely expected that Black & Company's suit against the Law Society of Alberta would eventually establish the law regarding interprovincial firms throughout Canada; a second lawsuit was unnecessary. As a result, Shrum, Liddle & Hebenton and McCarthy & McCarthy agreed they would not fight the B.C. legislation directly.

*Many lawyers also saw interprovincial mergers as a trend they disliked but would be forced to follow, once it was permitted to start. Brian Smith (who served as chairman of B.C. Hydro after leaving the B.C. legislature) noted in 2002 that, as a consultant on energy privatization projects, he was himself counsel to one of the national firms whose creation he had tried to prevent in 1985.

THE INTERVAL: 1984–88

AFTER THE ATTORNEY GENERAL'S intervention, McCarthy & McCarthy and Shrum, Liddle & Hebenton agreed to continue an informal association with a view to a future partnership when the legislative situation was more favourable. Hebenton urged that if a full merger was impossible the firms should sign an agreement on some other kind of link. "We want to have an agreement with you which states that we have created an association. What that association consists of is less important than that it exists." On the whole, McCarthy & McCarthy was reluctant to be drawn into a situation that provided none of the benefits of partnership yet might cause lawyers in both firms to be "conflicted out" of cases in which the other was involved. But in Hebenton's view, "If we cease adding fuel, the fire may burn down." The affiliation agreement Hebenton sought was finally signed in September 1986.[102]

By that time, the attorney general's amendment that banned interprovincial firms *was* being litigated in British Columbia. Despite McCarthys' and Shrum, Liddle & Hebenton's decision that they would not be drawn into legal action in British Columbia as well as Alberta, someone else had gone ahead. Two Ontario lawyers, David Porter and David Martin, had formed a small firm in Toronto to do criminal defence work, including drug conspiracy trials. When David Martin moved to Vancouver and was called to the B.C. bar, it occurred to him that since drug traffickers often operated nationally rather than locally, there might be a place for an interprovincial criminal defence firm. As a result Martin and Porter continued their partnership from separate cities. Although they had actually shared no work after Martin moved west, their two-person interprovincial firm now fell afoul of the attorney general's amendment to the Barristers and Solicitors Act. Martin promptly launched a Charter challenge against it and retained Thomas R. Berger, a former British Columbia politician and judge nationally renowned for his northern-pipeline inquiry, to act for him.*

Instead of a conflict that British Columbians might have characterized as the "Toronto monolith" attacking the autonomy of the west, the lawsuit commenced by David Martin could

*Martin & Porter never did any interprovincial work and the principals went their separate ways. Martin continued to practise in Vancouver, but before *Martin v. Attorney General* was concluded David Porter joined McCarthys in Toronto and became a long-time member of the litigation department of McCarthy Tétrault.

be seen as the effort of a small practitioner asserting his rights against interference from an overbearing law society and the government itself. Shrum, Liddle & Hebenton immediately supported the Martin lawsuit, and the firm and several of its partners soon formally joined as parties to *Martin v. Attorney General of British Columbia.* Shrum, Liddle & Hebenton contributed to the costs of the action and provided one of its litigators, Martha O'Brien, who worked closely with Berger during the case. The constitutional right of lawyers to form interprovincial firms was now before the courts in both Alberta and British Columbia, and the partnerships seeking to form the McCarthy-Shrum-Black national firm were involved in both actions.

Several lawyers at Shrum, Liddle & Hebenton eventually concluded that the delay in their merger plans caused by the litigation proved beneficial. Hebenton in particular later thought that in 1984 the partners at the two firms knew too little about each other and had only a vague idea of what the merger would do for their practices, their incomes or their control over their own workplaces. During the four-year delay caused by the litigation, he worked to keep his own partners well informed about their future partners across the country. He maintained a constant communication with McCarthys, with Black & Company in Calgary and also with Clarkson Tétrault of Montreal, who were not directly party to the McCarthy-Shrum-Black alliance but increasingly were included in the national-firm discussions.* "We continue to feel very comfortable with 'the family' and look forward to developing stronger and more formal ties as time goes on," Hebenton wrote to John Clarry in 1986 as the still separate firms began developing teleconferences on tax issues and other fields of specialization.[103]

In Hebenton's view, the firms and their people came to know each other during the enforced delay.

*As detailed elsewhere in this book, in 1984 Black & Company was in its third year as McCarthy & McCarthy's Calgary office, but that relationship remained threatened by the Alberta Law Society rules against such associations. In 1984 Clarkson Tétrault had had a "best friends" association with McCarthy for a few years but remained much less formally linked than Black & Company or Shrum, Liddle & Hebenton intended to be.

They consulted often, began adopting the best of each other's practices and emerged at the end of the process much better prepared for a single partnership. The delay the litigation in B.C. had imposed also allowed time for an important internal debate to be worked out within McCarthy & McCarthy.

Despite McCarthys' November 1983 partnership vote in favour of the "national law firm," not all members of the Toronto firm shared the National Law Firm Committee's vision of national expansion. The progress towards a merger in Vancouver soon provoked a debate within McCarthy & McCarthy, in which litigation partners took the lead on one side against corporate lawyers on the other.

It is a truism of law firm expansion that courtroom lawyers, less closely tied to large clients and more closely tied to local courts and local procedural specialties, are often less committed to geographical expansion than the solicitor partners. The litigation department of McCarthy & McCarthy had not been strongly committed to the Calgary project, but in Calgary there had at least been the expectation that the partnership as a whole would soon profit from the "overhang" of legal work available there. With the economic downturn in Alberta and the start of the costly litigation against the Law Society, those prospects faded. Some partners—not only litigators, but litigators most forcefully—began questioning the benefits of that venture. The national-firm plan and the expansion into Vancouver provoked more vigorous questions, even before the intervention of the B.C. attorney general.

Litigators had actually helped launch the Vancouver initiative. In mid-1983, a mid-size Vancouver firm with a very strong litigation team had approached McCarthys through Doug Laidlaw and Alan Lenczner of the litigation department to suggest they become allied in some form, and for a time it was a candidate in McCarthys' west coast merger plans. However, as corporate firms rose past it in McCarthys' rankings, some of the McCarthy litigators' doubts returned.[104]

"It has not been suggested that the merger will be of any net benefit to the litigation department," Michael Royce wrote in August 1984. "I, along with many other members of the litigation department, was in effect prepared to indulge the commercial department in its Vancouver venture in the interests of firm harmony." But, he noted, even some of the corporate partners now seemed to "doubt that there will be any financial benefit, now or in the future, from merging with a firm which, while young and aggressive, is located in a centre of relatively insignificant legal or financial importance by world standards, and has traditionally been less profitable than McCarthy and McCarthy."[105]

Despite such doubts, there were elements of the merger even the skeptics liked. In the economic downturn of the early 1980s, work in the business sections at McCarthy & McCarthy had slowed while the litigation department remained very busy. The imbalance in billable hours that situation provoked led to debates about relative allocations of firm profits. Royce pointed to Shrum, Liddle & Hebenton's allocations system, which seemed to give more weight to billable hours, as a model McCarthys might learn from. In an internal memo he called Shrum, Liddle & Hebenton "substantially more aggressive and business-like than McCarthy & McCarthy in its organization, dedication to office technology, and determination of compensation." Even merger skeptics, that is, admired elements of the Vancouver practice's approaches to law firm management.[106]

Yet questions about going into Vancouver continued. Ronald Slaght wanted more information about how the merger would affect allocations. Douglas Laidlaw, a leader among the Toronto litigators, told his partners in August 1984, "I have come to the conclusion that [the merger] would not be right for us at this time." This seems to have been a temporary position; at other times Laidlaw was more positive about expansion and his influence helped bring fellow litigators back into support of the national-firm venture.[107]

In the midst of these discussions, the litigation department suffered two great losses. The first was the tragic death of Laidlaw, who had become the latest keeper of the torch passed on from D'Alton McCarthy, Lally McCarthy, John Robinette and the other great courtroom lawyers. Laidlaw was killed in a traffic accident on a Toronto freeway on August 15, 1984, at the age of just 56. At the time of his death he was deeply engaged in the long and immensely complicated litigation over the Hamilton harbour bid-rigging case. His sudden, shocking death, followed a few months later by George Finlayson's departure to become a judge of the Ontario Court of Appeal, left the litigation department without two of its strongest members and abruptly thrust responsibility down to more junior litigators.[108]

Advocates of the national firm continued to argue not just about the Vancouver merger proposal but also whether the national firm was essential to McCarthys' prospects for a competitive, successful future. Before a vote to approve in principle the merger with Shrum, Liddle & Hebenton, John Clarry spoke vigorously in favour of the expansion program to which the firm had been committed for five years. "Multi-branch law firms are one of the phenomena of the decade—in the United States, Great Britain, Australia as well as Canada," he argued. He urged the skeptical partners to see this as more than a short-term financial speculation. "This is not an accounting exercise, but a matter of confidence that this is the right way to direct our growth." The merger proposal was carried.[109]

The debates provoked by the decision to move into Vancouver were among John Clarry's last challenges as managing partner of McCarthy & McCarthy. He retired from the position in mid-1985, at the age of sixty-five, though he remained an active presence in the firm. Clarry had been a consensus leader who had devoted much time to walking the corridors to consult his partners, ensuring there was sufficient understanding and support that decisions could be taken with a minimum of formal voting. Clarry's long experience at the firm had made him well placed to play that role, but he was aware of the growing difficulty of that style of governance. The size of the partnership and the administrative responsibilities of the managing partner had been growing steadily, and so had the will of the partners to influence the decision-making process. Like other growing law firms, McCarthys had to find new models of leadership for its new scale of operation.

Clarry's successor as managing partner, chosen by the management committee after broad consultation but no formal vote, was Harry Macdonell. Macdonell, a McCarthy & McCarthy lawyer for just ten years, had begun his career in corporate law at the rival firm of Fasken Calvin in Toronto. In 1970 he had been recruited to Montreal to work for one of his clients, British Newfoundland Company, or Brinco, then building the massive hydroelectric power development on the Churchill River in Labrador. Macdonell eventually became chief executive officer of Brinco. After the government of Newfoundland purchased the Churchill Falls operations, he returned to the practice of law. He had worked frequently with Jack Blain and other McCarthy lawyers and admired the firm, and Blain and Beverley Matthews recruited him to McCarthys. Though Macdonell anticipated resuming legal practice, Matthews and Clarry always saw Macdonell as a future leader of McCarthys. Even before becoming managing partner, Macdonell had been active in the national-firm project. In the early 1980s he helped initiate the liaison between McCarthys and the Clarkson Tétrault firm in Montreal, and he was deeply involved in McCarthys' search for a west coast merger partner and its negotiations with Shrum, Liddle & Hebenton.

Vancouver was McCarthy & McCarthy's first experience in negotiating a merger with an independent firm. The Toronto negotiators had begun with the objective of making McCarthy & McCarthy into a national firm, not simply part of a loose affiliation of independent firms. Initially, they may have assumed that Toronto's technological systems, accounting methods and management structures would remain the norm and that Shrum, Liddle & Hebenton would largely be absorbed into the Toronto practice.

Their discussions in Vancouver soon revealed, however, that no matter how attractive the national-firm concept was, Shrum, Liddle & Hebenton would be no more willing than any other firm simply to become a branch office answering to managers in Ontario. Macdonell quickly concluded that if the Vancouver lawyers believed they had been reduced to second-tier status they were likely simply to walk away sooner or later. A merger of unequals, dominated by Toronto's much larger revenues and numbers of lawyers, was certain to fail. Since the scale of business being done in the Toronto office ensured that its interests were unlikely to be neglected, Toronto had little to gain and much to lose if it tried to assert too much control over the terms of the merger.

Harry Macdonell, managing partner of McCarthy & McCarthy 1985–89.

As a result, the November 1984 Agreement in Principle between McCarthys and Shrum, Liddle & Hebenton made strong statements about the benefits of full integration of the two into a single partnership, but it also provided for at least an interim period in which a significant degree of regional autonomy would remain. The merged firm would be governed by a National Management Committee, to which Toronto, Vancouver and Calgary would name three, two and one members respectively, despite Toronto's preponderance in actual numbers of lawyers. It was agreed that a single set of committees would eventually determine allocations, partnership admissions and other crucial matters for the whole firm, but only after a three-year transitional period during which such decisions would continue to be made in each office. Each region would retain (or, in Calgary's case, acquire) responsibility for policy implementation and day-to-day operations.[110]

Jim McCartney, an early convert to Macdonell's ideas on the necessity not to insist on too tight a merger, recalled his discussion with a Toronto administrator who emphasised the efficiencies and cost savings that could be made by expanding various administrative systems used in Toronto. Instead, the Toronto office seemed to be accommodating Shrum, Liddle & Hebenton's wish to retain its own procedures. "He came to me and said, 'Why are we doing this?'" said McCartney. "And I said, 'Because we want to make a deal.' A light bulb went on, and then he dedicated himself to making it happen."

Although the British Columbia Law Society and attorney general had blocked the merger anticipated by the 1984 agreement, its terms survived to become the basis of the merger that did take place in 1989. And when Clarkson Tétrault began considering a merger with McCarthys, the Vancouver agreement played a role in convincing the Montreal firm that regional autonomy could survive within a merged firm. Macdonell looked on the terms worked out between McCarthys and Shrum, Liddle & Hebenton as among his key contributions to the building of the national firm.

THE END OF THE COURT CASES

DAVID MARTIN'S CASE against the attorney general of British Columbia, to which Shrum, Liddle & Hebenton had formally become a party in 1987, moved slowly. Mr. Justice Callaghan of the British Columbia Supreme Court finally heard the arguments of the parties in June 1988, when the Black & Company case was already before the Supreme Court of Canada. The Martin case was rooted almost entirely in the mobility rights and freedom of association clauses of the Canadian Charter of Rights and Freedoms, but much of the legal skirmishing addressed the question of whether there was a public interest argument that might entitle a government or a law society to restrict lawyers' freedom of association. Shrum, Liddle & Hebenton's counsel, Tom Berger, presented evidence from B.C. business leaders who supported Shrum, Liddle & Hebenton and testified in court to their desire to be free to retain national firms when they saw fit. In reply, the attorney general's counsel presented written statements from seven prominent B.C. lawyers who argued that if national firms were permitted, legal work, legal talent and legal power would all flow to the centre, causing a loss of Law Society control over professional practice and ultimately a loss of local autonomy and a strong, effective local bar.[111]

Sholto Hebenton wrote sardonically to Jim McCartney that "we in this firm are of mixed views, whether the seven letters constitute comedy or tragedy." Justice Callaghan seems to have been no more impressed. His judgement, issued on September 6, 1988, firmly dismissed all the arguments that the public interest or the needs of the Law Society authorized limitations on law firm partnerships. "There is no doubt that the maintenance of a strong indigenous bar is essential to the administration of justice in any area, but the formation of inter-provincial law firms would not weaken such a bar. In the long term such arrangements would strengthen it," he wrote. He found the attorney general's 1985 amendments of the Barristers and Solicitors Act violated the Charter and were in no way a reasonable limitation that could justify overriding its provisions. Shrum, Liddle & Hebenton and McCarthy & McCarthy were free to merge.[112]

The decision had been widely expected. By 1988 the government of British Columbia had become strongly committed to free trade with the United States and had urged the professions to purge their regulations of any protectionist barriers to trade. The government was also being lobbied by the Hong Kong financier Li Ka-shing, who was investing heavily in British Columbia, and by Li's Canadian lawyers, Stikeman Elliott of Montreal and Toronto.[113] When Justice Callaghan's decision was announced, Brian Smith had already left politics. His successor as attorney general immediately announced there would be no appeal. The Law Society of B.C., which had been reconsidering the merger issue since 1987, declared the judgement was "not unexpected," and within a month of the judgement the benchers had passed a set of previously prepared rule changes to govern interprovincial law firms. With that, Shrum, Liddle & Hebenton and McCarthy & McCarthy went ahead with a merger almost exactly as planned in 1984: a full merger, but with attention to regional interests.*[114]

Karen Sharlow, the most junior partner of Shrum, Liddle & Hebenton in 1989, signs the McCarthy & McCarthy merger document with Trevor Bell, the managing partner, and Gordon Shrum, the most senior partner.

In Vancouver, Sholto Hebenton worked desperately to get the merger details settled and the papers signed, to prevent rival law firms from stealing the glory of founding the first national firm. In a letter to Jim McCartney shortly before the *Martin v. Attorney General of British Columbia* decision came down, he noted that in 1983 McCarthys had been at the head of the parade in national and international expansion. But in 1988 Stikeman Elliott lawyers were already operating informally in Vancouver, and the American multinational law firm Baker & McKenzie and the newly affiliated Fasken Campbell (of Toronto) and Martineau Walker (of Montreal) were showing interest.

*The partnership agreement provided no formal interim period of regional autonomy, but stated that regional profitability would be "a factor" in allocations and that regional views would be "of primary importance" in decisions on partnership admissions.

"We have an overwhelming desire, which I trust you share, not to be the fourth national firm to open in Vancouver."[115]

While Vancouver was eager to move forward, Clarkson Tétrault of Montreal, not yet ready for a full merger but wishing, if it did merge, to help found rather than merely to join a national firm, was promoting a "partnership of partnerships" and recommending postponement of a full merger between the Toronto and Vancouver partnerships. Hebenton reported to his Shrum, Liddle & Hebenton partners with some admiration how "the accomplished diplomats of McCarthy & McCarthy gave substantial support for our position but, like all good diplomats, left themselves an escape route." However, McCarthy & McCarthy's September 1988 decision not to enter any new association with the Montreal firm short of a merger cleared the way for the McCarthy-Shrum merger.[116]

Harry Macdonell signs the Shrum, Liddle & Hebenton merger agreement in the Toronto boardroom, watched by Jim McCartney and Dale Robinette.

In a flurry of signings at the end of January 1989 (the end of the fiscal year for both firms), the partnership of Shrum, Liddle & Hebenton ceased to exist. All its former partners simultaneously became partners in McCarthy & McCarthy, which accepted all the obligations of the vanished firm, along with the right to use the Shrum, Liddle & Hebenton name locally during a transitional period. At the time of the merger, McCarthys and Black & Company had over 200 lawyers and Shrum, Liddle & Hebenton had grown to more than seventy. The merger made McCarthy & McCarthy for the first time the largest law firm in Canada.[117]

With the B.C. merger completed, everything now hung on the Supreme Court of Canada's judgement in the case *Black et al. v. Law Society of Alberta*. A loss there would force Black & Company, now a forty-lawyer operation in Calgary, to separate itself from McCarthy & McCarthy. The British Columbia government had evidently lost the inclination to fight, but a victory for the Law Society of Alberta would reaffirm the authority of law societies and provincial governments to restrict the out-of-province associations of lawyers, if they chose.

Instead, the Supreme Court decision on April 20, 1989, less than three months after the merger of McCarthy & McCarthy with Shrum, Liddle & Hebenton, was another victory for the Charter rights of interprovincial law firms. In the end, the Charter issues that had seemed so implausible in 1982 had been the only ones put to the Supreme Court judges by J.E. Redmond (the Alberta lawyer who had represented Black & Company at the trial court and both appeals) or by the Law Society of Alberta's counsel. Three of the five participating judges agreed that both of the Law Society of Alberta's new rules against law firm mergers—rule 154 prohibiting extraprovincial partners, rule 75b prohibiting partnership in more than one firm—offended the mobility rights clause (section 6-2b) of the Charter of Rights and could not be justified under section 1 as reasonable limits upon the rights of citizens. And although two judges dissented from that conclusion about mobility rights, they declared that both rules violated the freedom of association clause (section 2) and that rule 154 was not saved by section 1. All five judges found one reason or another to uphold McCarthy & McCarthy's right to practise law in Calgary as well as Toronto. "It was a sweet day," said Arthur Scace, by then the new managing partner in Toronto. It was even sweeter in the Black & Company offices in Calgary.[118]

Since Black & Company's partners were already partners in McCarthy & McCarthy, there was little to be done to wind up the separate existence of the Calgary firm and to merge Black & Company and McCarthys into a single entity. On May 2, 1989, an advertisement in the

Calgary *Herald* triumphantly announced that the previous day "Black & Company and McCarthy & McCarthy (the merged firm of McCarthy & McCarthy and Shrum, Liddle & Hebenton)" had merged under the name McCarthy & McCarthy, "Canada's first national law firm and the largest firm in Canada."

Black et al. v. Law Society of Alberta, as one of the first Supreme Court rulings to interpret freedom of association and mobility rights in the new era of the Canadian Charter of Rights and Freedoms, became a significant case in post-Charter legal studies. McCarthys partner Richard Shaw was pleased to find that his daughter, having lived with the case for most of her formative years, found herself studying it in law school at the University of Calgary.

The victory party: Richard Shaw, Robert Black and Douglas Ewens celebrate the Supreme Court of Canada ruling at Black's home in 1989.

It also transformed the circumstances of major Canadian law firms. What McCarthy & McCarthy had initiated in 1979 became the law of the land in 1989. Despite the view of a lawyer in one Calgary law firm who declared defiantly in 2001 that when it was necessary to call his partner a son of a bitch he didn't want to have to make a long distance call, large law firms had to consider whether to use their new freedom to branch out. Leading firms in most Canadian cities began investigating national associations, branch offices and merger possibilities. Nevertheless, the trend towards national mergers did not develop nearly as rapidly as McCarthy & McCarthy and Shrum, Liddle & Hebenton lawyers had feared. Many leading firms in the largest Canadian cities remained proudly independent until the late 1990s.

The Law Society of Alberta's fight against interprovincial mergers soon seemed a quixotic quest from the distant past. In 1997, on the fiftieth anniversary of the call to the bar of Robert Black, the Law Society of Alberta presented him with the Law Society Medal. At the presentation ceremony the president of the society apologized for the fact that the society had challenged the propriety of his association with McCarthy & McCarthy. The long battle, he said, had been "an exercise which the Law Society of Alberta had to go through in order to grow up."[119]

Meanwhile, the expanding firm of McCarthy & McCarthy still had one large piece of its national firm yet to complete: Montreal. Montreal remained Canada's second-largest business centre and home to a significant number of corporate head offices; clients whom McCarthy & McCarthy planned to attract with its "national firm" platform would expect it to be strongly present in Montreal. In a country where "national" increasingly meant "bilingual," an institution without a significant presence in Quebec and a significant capacity to operate in the French language was going to be severely handicapped in any effort to claim national influence.

The law firm that McCarthy & McCarthy, now securely established in Calgary and Vancouver as well as in Toronto, hoped would become the vital Montreal anchor of the national law firm was no stranger to its potential partners. Clarkson Tétrault had maintained an association with McCarthy & McCarthy since 1981. Though less than half the size of the Toronto firm (even before McCarthys' western mergers in 1989), Clarkson Tétrault was among the four largest law firms in Montreal. Like McCarthys, it was strong both in corporate practice and in litigation. Through the 1980s the two firms had organized business and social contacts among their partners. They had discussed shared ventures in Ottawa and overseas. They had occasionally exchanged expertise in particular fields of law, and they had occasionally referred clients to each other. Strengthening this relationship was implicit in McCarthys' "national law firm" agenda.

CLARKSON TÉTRAULT

THE LEGACY OF EUGÈNE LAFLEUR

EUGÈNE LAFLEUR'S LAW FIRM | 10

THE QUESTION OF expanding beyond its home city and province had been preoccupying the leaders of Clarkson Tétrault as long as those of McCarthy & McCarthy. But in the practice of law, as in much else, Montreal and the Province of Quebec were very much a distinct society. The Montrealers' response to opportunities beyond their own province was shaped by the ways their local legal community had evolved over many years.

The firm that in 1990 was called Clarkson Tétrault had always identified itself with one of the great Canadian barristers of the early twentieth century. Eugène Lafleur had begun the firm in 1885. He built its reputation and led it until his death in 1930. Thereafter, the firm's name had changed every time a partner retired, but it had often called itself "Fleural," from an ancient cable address based on the names of Lafleur and his partner and heir as leader, Gordon MacDougall. Clarkson Tétrault, as the law firm became known in 1982, called its principal boardroom the Salle Lafleur and continued in other ways to emphasise its inheritance from its founder.*

*Lafleur's name was dropped in 1933, when new Quebec bar regulations required the use of active partners' names only. The bar abolished that regulation in 1979. Three years later the firm "fixed" its name as Clarkson Tétrault.

Like D'Alton McCarthy, Eugène Lafleur was a successful litigator who founded a long-lived firm with great strengths in both corporate practice and litigation. Oddly enough, Lafleur, like McCarthy, was a Protestant with a Catholic pedigree.

Eugène Lafleur, eminent litigator, founder and inspiration of the Montreal firm.

The Lafleurs, despite their Protestantism, were an old Quebec family. Like many founding families of French Quebec, they traced their ancestry in the male line to a soldier who had come to New France with its garrison. Pierre Coussi *dit* Lafleur arrived at Montreal in the 1690s, married twice and left sons who carried on his name. But soldiers in New France's colonial troops all bore nicknames, literally *noms de guerre,* and the nickname often supplanted the surname entirely. Most descendants in the Coussi *dit* Lafleur family eventually adopted the Lafleur name.

In the 1830s Eugène Lafleur's father, Théodore, became one of the early converts of a group of Swiss evangelical missionaries working in Montreal and nearby rural areas south of it. The leaders of this Protestant mission sent Théodore Lafleur and another young *Canadien* to study in Geneva. While there, Lafleur married a Swiss woman, Adèle Voruz. On their return to Quebec he became a Baptist minister and teacher, eventually settling in Longueuil. Eugène Lafleur was born there in 1856, and he and his brothers went to

English schools and to McGill University, where he received a B.A. and entered the law school in 1877. In adult life Eugène left the Baptist Church and became an Anglican. Like his father he married a Swiss woman, Marie-Alice Voruz, to whom he was related on his mother's side.[120]

In 1881 Eugène Lafleur graduated with McGill Law School's gold medal and was called to the bar. (His brothers became a McGill professor of literature and a Montreal cardiologist). While at McGill, Lafleur articled with John S. Archibald, who taught criminal and constitutional law and was later a prominent Montreal judge. Lafleur began his active practice, however, with a business lawyer, Ivan Wotherspoon, formerly of the venerable Montreal business law partnership Badgley & Abbott. In 1885 Lafleur launched his own firm, one that would bear his name until 1933 and evolve into Clarkson Tétrault.

The Montreal legal world that Eugène Lafleur entered as a student in the late 1870s had been transformed in the generation before he joined it. Between the 1840s and the 1870s, as Montreal became Canada's most important centre of business and industry, the Montreal bar shaped itself into the country's most sophisticated legal community, particularly in the field of commercial law.

THE ORIGINS OF THE MONTREAL BAR

NEW FRANCE HAD LARGELY done without lawyers. Notaries handled the colonists' routine transactions, but there was not much scope for lawyers when the royal courts were dominated by judges with many of the broad powers of European investigating magistrates.* As a result, Quebec's legal profession essentially developed after the inauguration of the British regime in 1763, and the province's distinctive legal system really began to take shape in 1774. In that year Britain, having accepted the impossibility of overthrowing the property systems,

*The profession of notary has continued in Quebec into the twenty-first century. Notaries deal primarily in real estate transactions but also draft wills and marriage contracts and have exclusive jurisdiction to execute deeds of hypothec (mortgages) concerning real estate.

inheritance practices and commercial codes that underpinned Quebec society, acknowledged that the legal system must remain rooted in those realities. The 1774 Quebec Act confirmed that while criminal law in Quebec would follow English practices, civil law would be based on the legal code inherited from the French regime.

The Quebec Act guaranteed that in the British colony of Quebec, legal codes that had come from France's *ancien régime* would continue to regulate property transactions, commercial dealings, family and marriage laws, wills and estates, and other fundamental matters. The Constitutional Act of 1791 preserved this distinction when it divided Upper Canada (the future Ontario, which inherited the English common law) from Lower Canada, where civil law would continue.

In 1765 two francophones, Pierre Panet and Pierre Mézière, and two anglophones, Henry Kneller and William Conyngham, were the first lawyers admitted to practice in Quebec. While the Quebec bar continued to have a substantial anglophone contingent, francophone membership grew rapidly, and the law quickly became a favoured career for young graduates from Quebec's classical colleges. These lawyers rapidly became leading members of Quebec's new francophone professional class and made themselves prominent in journalism, intellectual life and particularly politics, as well as law. They dominated the elected Assembly of Lower Canada from the time it was founded in 1792.

Until at least the 1830s many anglophone leaders, including lawyers, continued to press for the abolition of the French Civil Code as part of a general campaign to anglicize Quebec's institutions. As late as 1838, William Badgley, then pre-eminent among Montreal's commercial lawyers, complained that the survival of the Civil Code from the *ancien régime* meant that British citizens in Lower Canada were subjected to an "antiquated system of French jurisprudence, detrimental to their interests and foreign to their habits."[121]

With equal vigour, francophone lawyers and political leaders defended the legal code along with the seigneurial landholding system and the French language itself. The legal system had become a cultural talisman. Lawyer-politician Étienne Parent's phrase "Notre langue, nos institutions, et nos lois" put the legal system among the three fundamental attributes in which French Canada's political leaders saw the safeguards for Quebec society. Disputes over the preservation or restructuring of the legal system were a continuing theme in the political agitation in the years before the rebellions of 1837–38, at least for lawyers, who were prominent in the conflict on both sides.

The late 1840s, however, saw a rapid and remarkable breaking of this log-jam over the legal system. Over a couple of generations, more anglophone lawyers had grown used to Civil Code practice and had begun to appreciate its subtleties and virtues. Perhaps more important was the achievement of representative democracy in 1848, which gave elected francophone leaders (with lawyers like Louis-Hyppolite LaFontaine and George-Étienne Cartier prominent among them) a solid share of control over the levers of power. Lawyers and politicians in the francophone community grew less hostile to considering changes in the legal system once it was clear they would wield substantial influence over the process.

As anglophones accepted the civil law tradition and francophones accepted that reform need not mean empowering unsympathetic outsiders to abolish all their customs, lawyers and legislators from both communities began work on a fundamental reorganizing of Lower Canada's legal code. In 1854 the legislature, aided and advised by commissions of judges and lawyers, abolished the traditional land tenure system based on seigneurial title. It then moved on to a fundamental overhaul of the civil law itself, a task delegated in 1857 to judges René-Edouard Caron, Charles Dewey Day and Augustin-Norbert Morin. Developing the new code would take nine years, culminating in the Civil Code of Lower Canada in 1866.

The Civil Code highlighted the accommodation francophone and anglophone lawyers had built since the 1840s. During the decade that the reform commission worked, the revision process required the active support of francophone lawyers and politicians, such as Morin and Cartier, to secure passage of the legislation. It also needed the support of the anglophone business community and of leading commercial lawyers and jurists, many of whom, like Charles Day and William Badgley, were anglophones. The new Civil Code of Lower Canada, a substantial intellectual achievement, was also a political and social one.[122]

Drafted in both languages by francophone and anglophone contributors, with each version having legal force, the code recognized and entrenched the emergence of new social and economic realities in Quebec. The codifiers had purged the old civil law of antiquated sections based on the *ancien régime's* traditional notions of society, where each rank and order had been given prescribed legal privileges and duties. They wrote out of it the traditional materials related to feudal land tenure and the special laws affecting artisans, merchants, aristocrats and other social groups. They downplayed traditional ideas that gave primacy to landed property, customary law and reciprocal obligations among social classes.

In the Civil Code of Lower Canada, the section entitled "Obligations" gained pride of place. Though it drew on an intellectual heritage that went back to Roman roots, Obligations was essentially the law of contract. Its primacy in the revised code indicated how, in Quebec as in much of the western world, freedom of contract was succeeding rank, title and the rights of landed property as the guiding principle of jurisprudence. Unlike in France, Quebec's codifiers did not establish a separate Commercial Code. Instead they included all aspects of the law within the Civil Code (and associated Code of Procedure). They sought to define such matters as property and labour not as special fields of law but as commodities subject to contract like everything else.

Reformist in its attack on old concepts of law and society, the new code remained deeply traditional in other ways. Its sections on marriage and family law were carefully respectful of the prerogatives of the Catholic Church. In this, Quebec's new code diverged from the Code Napoléon, France's earlier revisions of the pre-revolutionary legal system (which, among other things, required civil as well as religious marriage ceremonies). The new Quebec code also became in some ways more restrictive of women than the old laws. The *ancien régime* had permitted some exercise of legal authority by women who ran businesses or became household heads; the new code reflected the stricter patriarchy favoured in the mid-nineteenth century by both Victorian British society and Roman Catholic social thought.

These reforms in the legal code were accompanied by institutional changes to modernize the bar itself. Since 1763 Quebec's lawyers had been supervised by the chief justice and licensed by the governor. In 1849, however, the legal profession took control of its own governance. That year, the Barreau du Bas-Canada and local bar associations in Quebec City, Montreal and Trois-Rivières were incorporated and given authority for discipline and education and generally for the governance of the legal profession. Toussaint Peltier became the first *bâtonnier*, or president, of the Barreau de Montréal, which soon assumed responsibility for Montreal's law library, maintained until 1853 by a private group of lawyers. These changes went hand in hand with rapid expansion in the number of lawyers. Almost as many lawyers (608) were admitted between 1849 and 1867 as had been before 1849 (645).[123]

The mid-nineteenth century also saw rapid changes in law teaching in Quebec. Early lawyers' training had been based exclusively on articling in the office of practising lawyers. In 1853–54, however, faculties of law opened at McGill University in Montreal, which had been teaching some law courses earlier, and at Université Laval in Quebec City. The Montreal branch of Laval's Faculté de Droit opened in 1878 (and was transferred to the Université de Montréal in 1920). After the law schools opened, it remained possible to study law exclusively by apprenticeship rather than in a law school, and practising lawyers, rather than academic law professors, continued to dominate the personnel of the law schools until the 1930s. Nevertheless, the movement towards scholarly training in the law went hand in hand with the ambitious new Civil Code to lay fresh intellectual foundations for law and for legal education in Quebec.

At the same time, the courts were reorganized. Many new courthouses and registry offices were built around the province during the 1850s and 1860s, including the Palais de Justice in Montreal, which opened in 1856. During the 1870s lawyers pushed for reform of the Quebec judiciary. In 1873 they went so far as to refuse to plead before the Court of Appeal, whose judges they denounced as incompetent. A prominent commercial lawyer and *rouge** politician, Antoine-Aimé Dorion, first as *bâtonnier* and then as federal minister of justice, spearheaded this drive to improve the judiciary, which culminated with his own appointment as a reform-minded chief justice of Quebec in 1874.

*The *rouges* were a progressive faction in Quebec politics and eventually merged into the Liberal Party.

All this work of modernizing legal institutions and marshalling the law's intellectual resources reflected one underlying condition: Montreal's mid-nineteenth century rise as the centre of commercial and industrial capitalism in British North America and the new Dominion of Canada. As business conditions produced new challenges and opportunities for lawyers, Montreal, better than any other Canadian city, provides evidence of the emergence of the commercial law firm in the early nineteenth century.[124]

Montreal commercial law of the nineteenth-century business boom may be said to have begun with figures like William Badgley, who entered practice in 1823 just as commercial and industrial capitalism was replacing the private family enterprise as the dominant form of business in and around Montreal. Badgley was later joined by John Abbott, another successful commercial lawyer and future prime minister of Canada, and their firm evolved into McMaster, Meighen, which became part of the national law firm Borden Ladner Gervais in 2000. The firm Carter, Church & Chapleau, formed in 1879 by a group of commercial and political lawyers, would eventually become the eminent Montreal firm Ogilvy Renault.[125]

There were francophone corporate lawyers, as well. George-Étienne Cartier represented the Grand Trunk Railway and was counsel to the Seminaire de Saint-Sulpice as it launched into commercial development of its extensive property holdings around Montreal Island. His political rival, Antoine-Aimé Dorion, also had a large commercial practice. But English-speakers led most of Montreal's larger business corporations, and a growing proportion of the lawyers advising them came from English Montreal. Anglophone lawyers outnumbered francophone lawyers in Montreal until about 1850, and they continued to dominate commercial practice for much longer. Nearly all these commercial lawyers practised in the banking and financial district centred on Place d'Armes and St. James Street in Old Montreal.[126]

In the first half of the nineteenth century, as commercial and industrial corporations came into being in British North America, lawyers created the means by which new clients would carry on business. Montreal, as the most advanced business centre in British North America, was the source of most of the innovations. The commercial lawyers advised newly emerging business corporations on their bylaws, financing procedures and governance structures. They became corporate secretaries, board members and often investors in the firms they advised, and they worked out many of the procedures by which companies would run themselves. Many of them doubled as politicians and drafted much of the legislative infrastructure that the new commercial sector required: limited liability for companies (established 1849), simplified incorporation procedures (1850) and bankruptcy regulations (1850). Later, as Montreal's stock exchange and its great financial institutions developed, their lawyers would have similar influence on banking and securities legislation. Gradually Montreal's business law firms became larger, more specialized and more formally organized. Before the end of the nineteenth century they had formal partnership agreements, clusters of corporate clients and offices in the financial district.[*] [127]

THE LAW PRACTICE OF EUGÈNE LAFLEUR

EUGÈNE LAFLEUR, fresh from McGill Law School and with its gold medal, was admitted at least to the outer circles of Montreal's legal elite in 1881 when he joined the practice of Ivan Wotherspoon, a commercial lawyer who had practised with Carter, Church & Chapleau. Lafleur, however, seems never to have aspired to become a commercial solicitor. He sought out a classical advocacy practice, gradually focussing (somewhat like D'Alton McCarthy Jr. in Toronto) on appellate cases in the higher courts.

By 1885 Lafleur had left Wotherspoon for a firm under his own name.[128] He had a partner named Normand Rielle until 1890 and then was a sole practitioner for some years.[†] In 1886 he earned professional and public notice by winning a $10,000 libel action for lawyer and politician Rodolphe Laflamme, a federal minister of justice of the 1870s who in 1875 had declined an appointment to the new Supreme Court of Canada.[‡] In 1889, Eugène Lafleur took a dispute over the interpretation of a will to the

*Halifax's legal community had been deeply involved in marine and mercantile business law since the mid-eighteenth century. Still, Montreal's commercial and industrial expansion generated many new challenges in corporate law.

†Normand-T. Rielle was called to the bar in 1884. His practice may have been focussed on real estate, for Montreal street directories show that his brother, a land surveyor, kept an office adjacent to Lafleur & Rielle. After 1890, Rielle practised on his own without any great prominence.

‡Laflamme had Louis Riel and Wilfrid Laurier among his law students, and he was prominent in *rouge* and Liberal circles for decades. He would have known Lafleur's father through the Institut Canadien, the radical political and literary society in which both had been members.

Supreme Court. He won, establishing a key point in the interpretation of the Civil Code's sections on wills and confirming his reputation as one of the rising appellate counsel in the country. Much later in his life, Lafleur still took pleasure in that early case.

Eugène Lafleur in a late photo that suggests the gentle personality spoken of by his admirers.

Lafleur, who had been born with a slight malformation of the spine, was small and stooped, and his personal and courtroom style was generally reserved, quiet and intellectual. "He was a quiet and exquisitely modest human being," said a lawyer who admired him. "His cases were won largely by study." Lafleur had nearly become a classics professor instead of a law student, and all his life he maintained his interests in Shakespeare, drama, scientific advances and even in Sanskrit. He approached law with the same scholarly spirit. The part-time teaching position he accepted at McGill Law School in 1891, when his courtroom eminence was not yet fully established, reflected and sustained his intellectual interests. He continued teaching until 1921, when he was sixty-five.[129]

The fields Lafleur taught at McGill, international law and the "private conflicts of laws," were not abstract academic subjects. Montreal business law was based on the Quebec Civil Code, but financing for Montreal's commercial enterprises came from Britain and the United States, and Montreal's businesses invested across Canada, in the United States and (by the turn of the century) in Latin America. As a result the city's commercial transactions had to be informed by British, American and even Latin American law as well as Canadian law. Even within Canada, provincial laws differed widely and frequently conflicted with federal laws, so commercial lawyers headquartered in Montreal faced constant questions of which laws would apply to their commercial agreements and to disputes that crossed provincial or national boundaries.

In that context of overlapping and conflicting laws, Montreal business had a vital and growing need for authoritative advice on what laws should govern private transactions across jurisdictional boundaries. Lafleur, by making himself the most trusted legal interpreter of these issues, developed a specialty that attracted many commercial and private clients. Partly because the marital and family networks of Montrealers also ranged far beyond the boundaries of the Civil Code, Lafleur was consulted frequently on marriage and property laws and other personal and family matters.

Lafleur's most famous international law case involved a border dispute he was asked to arbitrate between Mexico and the United States. At issue was the location of the border in a region where the boundary river had shifted course. Lafleur presented his conclusion in 1911, but the United States refused to accept the decision until 1963. Within Canada, however, abundant cases arose in the field of public law, particularly from the conflicting statutes of overlapping political jurisdictions. Federalism and the intricacies of the British North America Act continued to generate conflicts among the provinces and between the provinces and Ottawa. The Supreme Court of Canada was still a new institution, a majority of whose judges came from the common law tradition, though they ruled on appeals concerning Civil Code cases from Quebec as well as common law ones from the rest of

Canada. As an advocate able to plead in either language about both traditions and the conflicts between them, Lafleur became a familiar figure at the Supreme Court of Canada in Ottawa well before the First World War. Between 1889 and 1930 he would argue 294 reported cases before the Supreme Court.

Along with two or three other lawyers, Eugène Lafleur became perhaps the most trusted and relied-upon Canadian counsel in high court cases involving disputes between the provinces and Ottawa, and between corporations and regulatory agencies. His stature at the Supreme Court was immense: once, when rebuked by the chief justice of Canada, Lafleur bowed, folded his papers and walked out of court. The hearing resumed only after the chief justice had withdrawn his remark.[130]

The Judicial Committee of the Privy Council, based in London, England, remained Canada's final court of appeal (in criminal cases until 1930, in civil cases until 1950), and Lafleur also had an extensive practice there. The British law lord Lord Dunedin said that on purely legal questions Lafleur shared the stature of the greatest English and Scottish pleaders. He is said to have averaged two cases a session at the Privy Council throughout his career, though only thirty-six of his cases there were reported. Over the years Lafleur represented the governments of Canada, Ontario, Quebec, all the western provinces and most of the Maritime ones, at either the Supreme Court or the Privy Council.* [131]

"It seemed to be a matter of which one hired him first," according to his biographer, David Williams, except that Lafleur regularly represented Quebec in litigation with Canada and never represented Canada against his home province. He maintained a large practice in constitutional and regulatory matters—particularly regulatory challenges

*Another forum where Lafleur pleaded at least once was the Senate. In 1916, when every divorce in Canada required an act of Parliament, he and Gordon MacDougall represented Montreal industrialist Hamilton Gault in an acrimonious petition for divorce in which Gault and his wife each accused the other of adultery. Prominent Toronto lawyer Hartley Dewart represented Mrs. Gault. The petitions were eventually withdrawn.

before the Board of Railway Commissioners—but his cases ranged very widely, from issues of Native title to women's rights and many commercial disputes. He was retained for appeals not only by clients of his own firm but also by virtually all the leading law firms of Montreal and the other business centres of Canada.* [132]

In 1908 Quebec passed legislation decreeing that mixed Protestant-Catholic marriages could only be performed by Roman Catholic priests. Lafleur informed a group of Quebec Protestants that he believed the law was valid, though he personally disapproved of it, but when the law was referred to the Supreme Court of Canada in 1912 he argued the case on behalf of the Protestant committee (and lost). A decade later, when Quebec gave Jews a share of control of Protestant school boards Lafleur advised the Protestants that the legislation was invalid, and he won that case for them at the Privy Council.

*Lafleur was beginning his prime courtroom years at about the time D'Alton McCarthy Jr. died in 1898. I have found no cases where they met each other in court.

In September 1929, when Quebec remained the only jurisdiction in Canada to prohibit women from practising law, Lafleur advocated for women's admission at the Council of the Quebec Bar. His motion that the Barreau du Québec should not object to legislation that would permit women to practise law passed (with the support of *bâtonnier* Louis St. Laurent's tie-breaking vote), but the bill in question failed to pass the Quebec legislature. While Lafleur personally believed women's rights should be recognized, he also believed that only legislatures had the authority to do so. In 1921, he had advised Emily Murphy of Edmonton that the courts would reject her claim that women were entitled to be appointed senators. When Murphy and four other women appealed to the Privy Council against a Supreme Court of Canada verdict that did deny women's eligibility to be senators, Lafleur represented the Government of Canada against the "famous five." The "Persons Case" in July 1929 proved to be his last Privy Council appearance, and he lost. Lafleur based his case upon the long, unbroken line of judicial interpretations against women's rights, but the Privy Councillors dismissed such thinking as "a relic of times more barbarous than these." Women, however, did not gain the right to practise law in Quebec until 1941. No women practised in Lafleur's firm before 1966.[133]

Lafleur was appointed King's Counsel in 1899. He was elected *bâtonnier* of the Barreau de Montréal in 1905–6, when he was fifty, and then as *bâtonnier* of the provincial bar. A Liberal but not politically active, Lafleur consistently refused all judicial appointments. "I like the smell of powder," he told an associate. In 1907, despite Prime Minister Wilfrid Laurier's personal intervention, he had declined an appointment to Quebec's Court of King's Bench. In 1918 his name was among those proposed for a Supreme Court appointment, but there was opposition to a Protestant receiving one of the seats "reserved" for francophones, and the appointment went to Pierre-Basile Mignault.[134] Nevertheless, in 1924 Prime Minister Mackenzie King, with the support of Governor General Lord Byng and many of the leading Canadian lawyers, put strong and persistent pressure upon Lafleur to accept appointment as the chief justice of Canada. Despite a series of meetings with Byng and King, Lafleur would not budge, arguing that young men were needed to rejuvenate the court. If fear of political controversy over his religion influenced him at all this time, he did not say so.*

While refusing any judicial appointment, Lafleur did play a quasi-judicial role during much of his career. He was constantly consulted for opinions on a vast range of legal questions and a substantial part of his practice lay in counselling other lawyers on points of law. Apart from his growing experience and an extraordinary memory for details, his resources included his extensive case notes (in an era when many cases went unreported) and his own extensively annotated copy of the Civil Code. Many of the opinions he wrote read like judgements and

*Lafleur was sixty-eight in 1924. Justice Frank Anglin, who was appointed chief justice, was ten years younger.

would have been accepted by his clients as carrying much the same authority.* [135]

From an early stage in his career, Lafleur practised almost entirely as a barrister. He believed law was an intellectual pursuit and he liked to take cases for their intellectual challenge; his limited interest in fees became legendary among his partners. Not that he flinched from billing large fees: in 1911 he charged the United States and Mexico $50,000 for his arbitration and indignantly refused to lower his fee when the American government offered less. But for small clients and small cases he was often inclined to charge $100 when his partners thought $1,000 might have been appropriate.

Lafleur could afford this casual attitude to fees. Accepted rates of reward for lawyers were such that anyone who worked as much as he did was guaranteed a fortune. Lafleur could disdain to negotiate with important clients or to worry about his fees from small clients because his practice made him rich in any case. In the 1920s his income was $50,000 to $85,000 a year. Long before that he had maintained a large house on Peel Street staffed by a team of servants, as well as a farm at Hudson, Quebec, and a cottage on the shore in Maine. While he lived simply, pursuing cultural and intellectual interests with the same quiet intensity that typified his professional work, he had a nearly limitless income to spend on what drew him. He and his wife, whom he had married in Geneva in 1896 when he was forty and she twenty-seven, raised two daughters and two sons. Marie-Alice Lafleur died in 1920. One of their sons, Maurice-Théodore Lafleur, and Raymond "Benny" Parsons, a son of their daughter Madeleine, would eventually join his law firm.[136]

*In 2002, Alan B. Gold, retired Chief Justice of Quebec, described how, as a young lawyer in the 1940s, he listened to his principal, Marcus Sperber, KC, tell of going to consult Eugène Lafleur on difficult cases in the years before the First World War. Lafleur would lead Sperber to a room where every shelf and table was heaped with files. "Young man," Lafleur would say, "I have a case here which I think will be of interest to you." He would pull a file from one of the heaps, blow off dust, and say, "Yes, your issue arose here when. . . ."

Lafleur's reputation ensured that his firm would attract ambitious young litigation lawyers. Charles A. Pope, who joined the firm in 1908, assisted Lafleur in several appellate cases. (Pope, like several other members of the firm, went overseas with English Montreal's own regiment, the Princess Patricia's Canadian Light Infantry, and he was killed in action in Belgium in 1916.) Gregor Barclay, who joined in 1910 and became a partner in 1917, and William B. Scott, who joined in 1913, would maintain the partnership's litigation strength. By the beginning of the twentieth century, however, the firm was beginning to create a corporate practice that would balance its eminence in litigation.

William B. Scott joined Lafleur & MacDougall in 1913 and, after a distinguished litigation career, was named associate chief justice of the Quebec Superior Court in 1952. His brother Frank Scott, the renowned poet, professor and civil libertarian, served briefly with the firm in the 1920s.

Lafleur never retired. Well into his seventies he kept up a steady round of Supreme Court and Privy Council appearances and maintained his relentless production of legal opinions on many issues. In 1930 he was in Ottawa, preparing for one more Supreme Court appearance, when he suddenly became ill. He took to his bed in the Château Laurier but developed pneumonia and died unexpectedly on April 29, 1930.[137]

11 THE DEVELOPMENT OF CORPORATE PRACTICE

BY THE LATE NINETEENTH CENTURY, corporate solicitors were beginning to rival courtroom advocates for prestige and leadership in the law firms of Montreal, as elsewhere in the western world. At the same time, Montreal's economic growth and industrialization of that era was increasingly becoming the preserve of anglophone corporate, industrial and financial institutions. While the francophone bar continued to grow and thrive in commercial law as in other fields, the largest anglophone business and financial enterprises in the city increasingly concentrated their legal affairs in the hands of anglophone lawyers. Lafleur's law firm exemplified both the rising influence of corporate practice and the increasing presence of anglophone lawyers. His most important partner and successor was a corporate lawyer rather than a courtroom advocate, and an anglophone.

Lafleur declined almost every corporate directorship offered him; he believed an advocate should remain dispassionate about the cases and clients he might be offered. Gordon MacDougall, however, was almost exclusively a corporate lawyer, with clients and directorships that made him a power in the boardrooms of Montreal for decades.

MacDougall, a product of Montreal High School, a star of McGill sports teams and valedictorian of his class at McGill Law School in 1894, joined Eugène Lafleur upon graduation and immediately became his partner in Lafleur & MacDougall.* Like Lafleur, MacDougall also taught at McGill Law School, starting just four years after his graduation and lecturing on Civil Procedure and other subjects until the 1930s. MacDougall did litigation and general practice at first, but in 1898 he secured his entry to the ranks of Montreal's elite corporate practitioners when he drafted the trust deed and other incorporation documents for Shawinigan Water and Power Company.

In the first half of the twentieth century, Shawinigan Water and Power Company was a key participant in the development of Quebec's hydroelectric power. Long-distance transmission of electric power had proven itself feasible in 1895, when power from Niagara Falls began supplying the city of Buffalo, New York. North of the border, engineers and financiers almost immediately turned to the hydroelectric-power potential of Ontario and Quebec.[138]

Local entrepreneurs began to exploit the hydro power of Shawinigan Falls, north of Trois-Rivières on Quebec's St-Maurice River, in 1895, and they were soon joined by the Boston financier John Edward Aldred. Aldred was a native of Lawrence, Massachusetts, one of the mill towns where abundant water power had made possible New England's nineteenth-century industrial development. He quickly recognized the potential of Shawinigan Falls. Abandoning his career in Boston finance, he moved to Montreal and committed himself to the hydroelectric industry, becoming treasurer of Shawinigan Water and Power upon its incorporation in 1898, then serving as its president from 1909 to 1933. Aldred's new company laid out the town of Shawinigan Falls and invested heavily in dam building, power plant construction and industrial development on the St-Maurice River. With the support of successive provincial governments that were consistently pro-development, anti-union and generous with grants of public resources to private investors, Shawinigan Water

*The partnership agreement, if there was one, apparently does not survive.

and Power would continue to expand power production on the St-Maurice River for the next three decades. It would eventually control the hydro potential of the entire river system and sustain most of the industrial development in and around Shawinigan and Trois-Rivières.

Gordon MacDougall, whose association with John Aldred and Shawinigan Water and Power laid the basis for the corporate practice of Lafleur & MacDougall in the early twentieth century.

Shawinigan's newly abundant electrical power soon attracted Alcoa Aluminum, which opened Canada's first aluminum plant at Shawinigan Falls in 1900. Aldred also attracted the pulp and paper mill of Belgo Paper Company (later Consolidated Paper) and the calcium carbide plant of Shawinigan Carbide. In 1903 Shawinigan Water and Power Company completed what was then the longest electric-power transmission line in the world, from the falls to Montreal, and made itself a supplier of electricity to the city of Montreal. Its other power lines soon reached Quebec City and the Eastern Townships as well, and the company was Quebec's largest power-generation company throughout the first half of the twentieth century. Gordon MacDougall, a mill owner himself for a time, became an expert in the legal aspects of power generation and transmission. He was Shawinigan Water and Power's key corporate counsel throughout this expansion and a member of its board of directors until his death in 1947.[139]

In 1910 Aldred's company began supplying electricity to Montreal Light, Heat and Power Company, controlled by Sir Herbert Holt, and in the 1920s Shawinigan Water and Power aggressively expanded its hydro-electric production. Unlike the Montreal company, however, which held a very profitable monopoly on electrical distribution in the city of Montreal (until it was nationalized in 1944, in a first step towards the creation of Hydro-Québec), Shawinigan Water and Power had to continue to promote new industries as markets for its electricity, and it built one of the most sophisticated engineering departments in Canada. During the First World War, the research and development facilities of Shawinigan Carbide helped make Shawinigan Falls into the centre of the nascent Canadian chemical industry.[140]

Lawrence Macfarlane, a partner in Lafleur & MacDougall from 1903 and name partner in its successor, MacDougall & Macfarlane, until his death in 1944.

In 1931 Shawinigan Falls became the site of a petrochemical project launched by Canadian Industries Limited, or CIL, a newly founded company that was jointly owned by the American chemical giant DuPont and its British counterpart Imperial Chemical Industries, or ICI. CIL began as a manufacturer of explosives but soon moved into chemicals and built the Shawinigan Falls facility to manufacture Cellophane and other innovative petrochemical products. CIL became another long-time Lafleur & MacDougall client. Eventually the law firm would be housed in CIL's Montreal office tower.[141]

For several decades, lawyers at Lafleur & MacDougall handled large financings for the many companies involved in the Shawinigan industrial complex led by J.E. Aldred, as well as diverse issues involving power line development, patents, corporate law, real estate, labour law and various pieces of litigation.* Lawrence Macfarlane, a recent McGill graduate, joined the firm as a partner in 1903 and soon extended its expertise in the development and financing of hydroelectric systems. In 1913 Macfarlane was a crucial adviser to and then vice-president of Alabama Traction, Light and Power Company, a Montreal holding company that raised funds in Britain to develop hydro resources in the southern United States much as Aldred's companies had done in Quebec.[142]

Throughout this era, Lafleur & MacDougall had close and comfortable relations with governments in Quebec City. Through most of the early twentieth century, Quebec's Liberal and Union Nationale provincial governments encouraged English-Canadian and American corporate interests to pursue economic development projects on very favourable terms, so long as they accepted the conservative social and educational policies favoured by the Roman Catholic hierarchy of Quebec. The only Quebec government to buck these trends was the 1939–44 Liberal government of Adélard Godbout, whose social policies included educational reform and votes for women and whose economic policies included support for labour unions and the creation of Hydro-Québec through the nationalization of private power companies. After Maurice Duplessis' Union Nationale took power in 1944, these policies were reversed and Shawinigan Water and Power remained in private hands.

Through his close association with the Aldred interests, Gordon MacDougall had ensured the prosperity of Lafleur & MacDougall for a generation. Law firms need good lawyers in order to grow, but they also need big clients. In Shawinigan Water and Power and the companies associated with it, Lafleur & MacDougall had found clients who would continue to generate the work and the pursuit of excellence in corporate law that kept the firm at the leading edge of Montreal's commercial-law community for several decades.

*Once a year, MacDougall travelled to Shawinigan Falls to negotiate the firm's fees for that year.

AN ESTABLISHED FIRM

EUGÈNE LAFLEUR ALWAYS had his offices in the heart of Montreal's financial district around Place d'Armes and St. James Street. He and Normand Rielle moved to the sixth floor of the New York Life Building, Montreal's first high-rise office tower (at eight storeys) when the building opened in 1888. Later Lafleur moved his office to the new Royal Trust Building that opened in 1913. In 1929, however, J.E. Aldred began building a new landmark nearby on Place d'Armes and the law firm prepared to move. The Aldred Building, Montreal's tallest when it was completed in 1931, housed the headquarters of Shawinigan Water and Power, Gillette Razor Company and other Aldred interests. It was also one of the first Montreal corporate headquarters designed with abundant leasing space for legal and financial firms and other tenants. As soon as the Aldred Building opened, Lafleur & MacDougall moved into the Aldred Building's twelfth and thirteenth floors.

The Aldred Building on the Place d'Armes, home to the Montreal firm from 1931 to 1962.

A handsome and innovative showpiece at the centre of Montreal's business district, the Aldred Building was luxurious for its time, with bronze and marble detailing and art-deco reliefs on every floor. Lafleur & MacDougall lawyers' offices occupied the perimeter by the windows, with a large secretarial pool in the centre. Eventually each lawyer's office was equipped with a buzzer attached to a numbered sign in the secretarial pool; when a buzzer sounded, the secretaries looked up to see whose number had lit up and whose lawyer was calling her in.[143]

Few memories survive of the ambiance of the firm in the Lafleur & MacDougall years. Eugène Lafleur, despite his wealth and eminence, is remembered as being modest and polite to everyone, but in his era it was very much the fashion for senior lawyers to cultivate a cold, austere demeanour, and the early twentieth century was typified by stiff formality in most Canadian law offices. Great social distance was maintained between lawyers and staff, even between senior and junior lawyers.*

Among the staff who joined at about the time of the firm's move to the Aldred Building was Ida Strachan, who began as a receptionist in 1929. When she retired in 1982, at the age of eighty, Mrs. Strachan was officially bookkeeper and petty-cash dispenser but generally functioned as a "mother" to all: no lawyer's wife could have a baby without receiving a crocheted layette from Ida Strachan. Other long-time staff members included office manager W.F. Henderson, who joined as handyman in 1897 and retired as office manager in 1946; Frank Wright, who joined in 1928 and succeeded Henderson, and secretary Florence Rogers, a legendarily fast typist and a chain smoker, who sat all day with a towel on her lap to catch cigarette ashes so that her smoking did not slow her typing.[144]

*Office lore recounts how MacDougall once called his office manager to his office and then kept him waiting at the door. Just what MacDougall had been doing is now lost, but when he finally called his employee in, he said, "I've probably made more money while you were standing there than you'll make in a whole year."

When the firm's younger lawyers returned from military service at the end of the First World War, the character of Lafleur & MacDougall was already well established. It had a strong litigation department, on one hand, and a substantial corporate practice on the other. Litigation was headed by Eugène Lafleur, of course, who continued to argue a seemingly endless stream of leading cases in the highest courts. Other litigation lawyers, attracted to the firm by Lafleur, also came into prominence in the 1920s and 1930s. Both Gregor Barclay and William Scott had joined the practice before the war and returned to it after military service overseas. After Lafleur died, Barclay became the senior litigator, and when he was appointed to the Quebec Court of Appeal in 1934 Scott succeeded him. Eventually the litigation team included John Chisholm, who joined in 1927, and George Miller Hyde, hired in 1929.

In the 1920s and 1930s Gordon MacDougall and Lawrence Macfarlane led the commercial side of the firm and, not long after Lafleur's death, the name of the partnership became MacDougall & Macfarlane. By then MacDougall was a director not only of Shawinigan Water and Power and its associated companies but also of Royal Bank of Canada, Royal Trust, Canadian Marconi and several electric-power and transportation companies. At his death in 1947 he was described as "one of the leading corporation counsels in Montreal." Macfarlane had died three years before that and before his death seems to have been overshadowed somewhat by a younger lawyer, William Macklaier, who joined the firm in 1924 and became MacDougall's heir as a business generator and the leader of the commercial practice.[145]

James Taylor, manager of the Montreal office 1927–37.

The practice's first "political" member was Adrian Knatchbull Hugessen. He was an English blueblood, a younger son of Lord Brabourne and a graduate of Eton, but he studied law at McGill, settled in Montreal and joined Lafleur's firm in 1914. Hugessen eventually handled the growing CIL account. In the early 1950s, antitrust rulings in the United States forced the breakup of CIL, which until then had been jointly owned by DuPont Chemicals and the British chemical giant ICI. Hugessen was deeply involved in the reorganization of CIL. The Canadian company became two separate entities, DuPont Canada and CIL, and the latter remained a substantial client.

Hugessen became counsel to and a governor of McGill University, maintaining the link that Eugène Lafleur and Gordon MacDougall had built by their teaching there. Hugessen also became a key Montreal organizer and fundraiser for the Liberal Party of Canada, and in 1937 Prime Minister Mackenzie King appointed him to the Senate.* Other lawyers on the commercial side at MacDougall & Macfarlane in these years included corporate finance specialist Henry Weir Davis, Larrett Smith, whose field was real estate, and James Anglin.

Eugène Lafleur had given opinions in both languages, but the rise of great industrial and financial corporations in Montreal had strengthened English Montreal's relative control of business and law in the city, and by the 1930s Lafleur's law firm was completely English-speaking. The only other francophone in the practice before 1945 was Lafleur's son, Maurice, who joined in 1922 but died in 1930, just a few months after his father. Into the 1960s the partnership drew almost all its lawyers from McGill Law School and from the social and commercial world of English Montreal.

MacDougall had become Lafleur's partner as soon as he joined the firm, and Macfarlane's admittance to partnership had been nearly as fast. Thereafter, leadership became much more closely held, as was customary among major law firms in Montreal and elsewhere in Canada at the time. Gregor Barclay, who joined in 1910, became a partner in 1917, but William Scott and Adrian Hugessen, both prewar hires, had to wait until the 1930s to have their names included in the firm name, and no other names were added until 1944. The system by which successful associates were admitted into the partnership after a fixed number of years did not develop in Canadian law firms for some decades.†

*Hugessen's Senate appointment resembled that of Salter Hayden of McCarthy & McCarthy in 1940. Both men suited Mackenzie King's intention to fill the Senate with young Liberal organizers who would remain active senators for years.

†A two-level partnership seems to have emerged in the 1920s. Macklaier, who joined in 1923, reported in *Who's Who in Canada* that he became a partner in 1930, but his name was not added to the firm name until Macfarlane's death in 1944. In the early 1960s, the partnership agreement temporarily established an explicit difference between "A" and "B" partners, with "B" partners' remuneration being decided by the "A" partners, who alone had their names included in the firm name.

The Lafleur firm (MacDougall & Macfarlane from 1933) was one of Montreal's larger law practices in most of this period. It came closest to being the largest local firm in the early 1930s, when Lafleur's team of litigators and MacDougall's corporate solicitors totalled twelve lawyers. In all of Canada, only Brown, Montgomery, McMichael (the future Ogilvy Renault) in Montreal and the Blake, Cassels and Osler, Hoskin firms of Toronto were larger. After Lafleur's death, none of his litigators matched his unrivalled pre-eminence at the bar, and by the 1950s no single commercial client seems to have yielded the volume of work Shawinigan Water and Power Company had provided earlier. Still, the firm remained among the leading English Montreal law practices. Appointments as King's Counsel were standard for leading members, and the partners' standing is suggested by a more exclusive honour: their frequent election as *bâtonnier* of the Barreau de Montréal. Lafleur had been *bâtonnier* in 1905, and although the Montreal bar elected an anglophone as *bâtonnier* only one year in three, between 1921 and 1960 Gordon MacDougall, Lawrence Macfarlane, William Scott and Adrian Hugessen each served a term.*

Adrian K. Hugessen, son of a British lord, became a Montreal lawyer and member of the Canadian Senate.

*Until 1974, the *bâtonnier* of the provincial bar was chosen from among the regional *bâtonniers*. Lafleur, Macfarlane and Hugessen each served as both Montreal and provincial *bâtonniers*.

The litigators who came after Eugène Lafleur never shared his disinclination towards judicial appointments. Gregor Barclay, who was appointed to the Quebec Court of Appeal in 1934, began a very long series of appointments of the firm's members to senior judicial positions. George Miller Hyde followed Barclay to the Court of Appeal in 1950, and in 1952 William Scott became associate chief justice of the Superior Court in Montreal, leaving the leadership of the litigation practice to John Chisholm and later to Peter Laing and Charles Gonthier. On the commercial-law side, William Macklaier succeeded MacDougall and Macfarlane very successfully after their deaths, and he rapidly developed a very large commercial practice. He joined the boards of leading Canadian and American companies, including Bank of Nova Scotia, Sheraton Hotels and Canada Life Assurance Company. The staff remembered Macklaier as the only lawyer in the firm who consistently kept two secretaries busy in the 1950s, and he generated a great deal of work for its younger commercial lawyers. Macklaier's contemporaries Larrett Smith, H. Weir Davis and James Anglin had less dynamic but still significant commercial practices. In 1952, when William Scott went to the bench, the firm became Hugessen, Macklaier. The partnership agreement of the time was informal, with an emphasis on seniority.[146]

William Macklaier was a prominent figure in the business community and leader of the Montreal firm's commercial practice until his sudden death in 1963.

In the 1950s Shawinigan Water and Power Company remained a steady client, but it was no longer the industrial and financial leader it once had been. Then, with the death of Premier Duplessis in 1959, the future of private power utilities became one of the leading issues of Quebec politics.

12 A CHANGING FIRM IN A CHANGING PROVINCE

THE ELECTION OF the new Liberal administration of Jean Lesage in 1960 marked the beginning of what became known as Quebec's "Quiet Revolution." Quebec in 1960 was in many ways already a modern society, heavily urban and industrial, with a standard of living not so far behind Ontario's. Yet for decades Quebec had preserved an image of itself as a fundamentally traditional, rural society. Social services, education and health had long been administered by the Roman Catholic Church, which retained great influence on the province's cultural and intellectual life. Until the 1960s, high school education remained optional (and fee-paying), and barely 4 per cent of university-age Quebecers received any higher education.

The Quiet Revolution converted the Quebec provincial government to state activism. The state rapidly began to replace clerical leadership and entrenched tradition as the bulwark for language, culture and society in the province. The Lesage government established Quebec's first Ministry of Education and moved rapidly to institute universal, free public education and to encourage much higher rates of participation in post-secondary schooling. At the same time as it took control of education, hospitals and social services, Lesage's government renewed traditional struggles between Quebec City and Ottawa to ensure that the vital tools of social and economic policy were in the hands of Quebecers.

"Maîtres chez nous," the slogan of the Lesage government, meant overturning the old accommodation that had tacitly left much of the economic leadership of the province in the hands of Anglo-Quebecers. No longer would businesses owned and run by non-francophones have unchallenged control of the Quebec economy, and no longer would they draw their professional, technological and managerial talent so predominantly from the small circles of English Montreal.

After 1960, Quebec governments began to assert greater influence in the economy, and particularly in the control of Quebec's natural resources, notably hydroelectric power. The rise of Hydro-Québec to monopoly control of Quebec's hydroelectric resources through the expropriation of private utilities was one of the crucial steps in the Quiet Revolution. That policy was pursued eagerly by the Union Nationale government of Daniel Johnson that replaced Jean Lesage's Liberals in 1965, and the mighty dams on the Manicouagan River in northeastern Quebec became symbols of the achievements of the new Quebec.

Quebec expropriated Shawinigan Water and Power's hydroelectric businesses in 1963. William Macklaier represented the company in the expropriation proceedings, but the business that had underpinned the corporate practice of his law firm for half a century was lost. Just as the process was being completed, Macklaier died suddenly of a heart attack, aged just sixty-two. Jacques Tétrault, who had recently joined the firm and who worked with Macklaier on the Shawinigan expropriation file, remembered the tremour that ran through the practice at Macklaier's sudden death: "We thought it was the end of the world for the firm."[147]

The end of Shawinigan Water and Power and the death of William Macklaier proved not to be the end of the firm at all. Despite the loss of its business leader and the expropriation of its largest client, Hugessen, Macklaier still had a roster of first-rate lawyers with blue-chip clients.

The secretarial pool of the Montreal firm in the Aldred Building before 1962, with long-time staff member Margaret Donovan in the foreground.

The general prosperity of Montreal in the pre-Expo years of the mid-1960s also provided new corporate clients, notably in commercial real estate, and the firm continued to prosper. As fundamental changes worked their way through the politics and society of Quebec in the 1960s and 1970s, the law firm also began to reinvent itself.

One sign of Montreal's continuing vitality in these years was the general movement of business "up the hill," away from St. James Street (gradually becoming known as Rue Saint-Jacques) and Old Montreal towards Boulevard René-Lévesque (then Dorchester Street). Place Ville-Marie, the new Central Station, and the Queen Elizabeth Hotel, all of which opened in the early 1960s, led the movement, and in 1962 Hugessen, Macklaier joined the migration. It left the Aldred Building for the twenty-second and twenty-third floors of CIL House (later known as Maison Royal-Trust and still later as Telus Tower), a new high-rise adjacent to Place Ville-Marie at 630 Dorchester Street West. There, a gradual transformation of the firm that began in the 1960s set the stage for a rapid redefinition in the 1970s.

The Lafleur firm—it became Chisholm, Smith, Davis & Anglin after Macklaier's death in 1963—remained one of Montreal's leading law practices. Among its competitors, Ogilvy Renault was by far the largest firm in Montreal and was justifying its long-established nickname as "the factory" by its continuous growth (twenty-four lawyers in 1952, thirty-five in 1962, sixty-one in 1972).[148] Martineau Walker, founded in 1907, had established itself as Montreal's second-largest law firm, jumping from twelve lawyers in 1962 to thirty-six by 1972. McMaster, Meighen, descended from the law practice that William Badgley launched in the 1820s, also remained among the leaders, with twenty-three lawyers in 1972. There were several rapidly growing francophone firms in the 1960s, of which Deschênes, deGrandpré (twenty-three lawyers in 1972) was the largest. Phillips & Vineberg, founded by Jewish lawyers long denied access to the city's leading law firms (and their clients), was also growing along with clients such as the Bronfman enterprises. Notable among younger firms was Stikeman Elliott, founded in 1952 on the tax law expertise of Heward Stikeman, which gradually focussed on a specialized range of tax planning and business law services for commercial clients.

Chisholm, Smith, Davis & Anglin (twelve lawyers in 1952, fifteen in 1962, nineteen in 1972) grew less rapidly than some of these competitors in the 1950s and 1960s. Still, it remained a substantial and well-respected firm in the Montreal legal marketplace, with some significant corporate clients and unusual strengths in litigation. By the 1960s, the litigation side was led by Peter Laing, Charles Gonthier and James Knatchbull Hugessen, the son of Senator Adrian Hugessen. Laing, a Montrealer schooled at an English private school and the Inns of Court, had lost both legs while serving with British forces in North Africa. He joined the firm in 1944 and soon became a colourful presence in Montreal courts and around the office, legendary for his command of conversational Latin and for surging down the corridors with his wooden legs creaking "like a ship in full sail." In addition to his substantial court practice, Laing succeeded Senator Hugessen as a governor of and counsel to McGill University, where he wielded particular influence as the son-in-law of Montreal press magnate John W. McConnell, a leading donor.

Charles Gonthier, whose quiet brilliance carried him to the Supreme Court of Canada, returned as counsel to McCarthy Tétrault upon his retirement from the court in 2003.

Charles-Doherty Gonthier, a much quieter presence, built a substantial litigation practice. Gonthier, a bilingual lawyer who grew up in Ottawa as the son of the federal auditor general, came to Hugessen, Macklaier in 1957 to replace Jacques-Yvan Morin, a young Quebecer with degrees from Cambridge and Harvard. Morin, whom Senator Hugessen had recruited, was leaving to teach at the Université de Montréal law school, and Gonthier took over his litigation duties. In the 1970s and 1980s, Morin would be a prominent member of René Lévesque's Parti Québécois government and an architect of its constitutional proposals for an independent Quebec. For his part, Gonthier, first in association with Senator Hugessen and later on his own, developed a very extensive practice in civil litigation and regulatory practice until he was appointed to the Quebec Superior Court in 1974. In 1989 Charles Gonthier became the first member of the firm to be named to the Supreme Court of Canada. Senator Hugessen's son James, a graduate of Oxford, McGill and the

Université de Montréal, joined the firm in 1958 and specialized in civil litigation and regulatory practice (and also taught civil procedure at the McGill Faculty of Law) until his appointment to the bench, first to the Superior Court of Quebec in 1972, then to the Federal Court of Canada in 1983.

By the late 1960s, the firm had several rising lawyers on the commercial side. Richard Weldon's banking practice (which included much of Bank of Nova Scotia's work in Quebec), his drafting skills, and his concern for accuracy were remarked on by all the young lawyers for whom he was a patient teacher and dedicated mentor. Ross Clarkson, a McGill gold medallist of 1948, had built up a practice in real estate, wills and trusts and general corporate work, and he too became a mentor to many of the younger lawyers. R.E. "Benny" Parsons, a grandson of Eugène Lafleur and an English-trained barrister who had joined the firm in 1955, had a blue-chip "old Westmount" clientele that included the Molson family. Jacques Tétrault, a future leader and name partner, came to the firm in 1963 with an expertise in tax law developed at another Montreal law firm, Duquet McKay, and he gradually broadened his practice into general corporate law. Weldon and Clarkson came from prominent business and legal families of English Montreal. Tétrault's father, a businessman, intended his sons to have business careers and had them educated at English-language schools and at McGill University, whereas their sisters attended French-language convent schools.[149]

An imposing francophone figure who emerged on the corporate side of the firm during the 1960s was Edmond-Jacques Courtois. When he joined in 1945, Courtois became the partnership's first francophone lawyer since the Lafleurs and also its first graduate of the Université de Montréal law school. Courtois came from a Montreal business and professional family and joined the firm after sea duty with the Canadian Navy in World War II.* He began in

*Courtois' Université de Montréal law school classmates, many of whom (notably Pierre Trudeau) were anti-conscription if not anti-war in the early 1940s, recalled how Courtois stood out: he sometimes attended classes wearing his uniform as a naval reserve officer.

general practice and did a good deal of litigation at first, but he soon became William Macklaier's protege and eventually his heir as the firm's business-getter and board representative.

When Macklaier died suddenly in 1963, Courtois, still in his early forties, succeeded him as a director of Bank of Nova Scotia and smoothly stepped into the job of "relationship lawyer" with leading clients. As the natural gas pipeline business expanded in Quebec in the 1960s, as in other provinces, Courtois became a director (and eventually chairman) of Gaz Métropolitain, which soon became a significant client. His Quebec and national directorships would include Rolland Paper, Carena Bancorp, CAE Industries and Canada Life. He became a prominent figure in Montreal business circles, though as a lifelong Progressive Conservative Party supporter he was mostly a political outsider until the emergence of Quebec Conservatives under Brian Mulroney in the 1980s. One of Courtois' outside boards helped make him a celebrity in Montreal: he was president of the Montreal Canadiens hockey club and the Montreal Forum during the Canadiens' glory days.

Richard Weldon, a banking-law specialist, led Laing, Weldon towards becoming a bilingual, francophone-majority law firm before his sudden death in 1976.

The 1960s brought a changing of the guard from an aging leadership to these younger partners. Jacques Tétrault recalls that "it was when youngsters like me started pressing" that the old rules of payment by seniority began to give way to an allocation system more closely linked to productivity. In 1963, half the firm's revenue was still allocated by seniority. The 1965 partnership agreement, however, divided the income by a negotiated agreement on each partner's value to the firm.[150]

John Chisholm, Larrett Smith, H. Weir Davis and James Anglin, the elderly "name partners" in 1966 (and the last members to have known Eugène Lafleur), were all gone by 1970, and the firm became known as "Laing, Weldon." The retirements marked a generational shift, and the new attitude that was coming to the fore went further than youth and allocations. The new leaders were preparing to abandon the clubbable Westmount ambiance that had prevailed for a more modern, businesslike style, and they also rejected the ethnic exclusiveness long typical of leading law firms in Montreal as elsewhere.

Michael Levinson discovered one aspect of this changing perspective in 1969, when Benny Parsons and Terry Dingle, two rising partners in what was then called Smith, Anglin, were eager to recruit him. Levinson, a successful Montreal notary who had just qualified as a lawyer, had worked frequently with Smith, Anglin but he had doubts about joining the firm. "How," Levinson wanted to know, "is Jewish Mike Levinson going to work out at Smith, Anglin?" He remembers the reply: "Mike, we are in the process of rejuvenating ourselves. Very shortly we are going to be the youngest, most dynamic firm in the city, and you are going to be an integral part of it." Levinson chose Smith, Anglin with its new attitudes (and its substantial real estate practice) over a rival offer with a larger starting salary.[151]

Like other minority lawyers across North America, Levinson was encountering the transformation that occurred when some law firms began to recognize that those that emphasised legal skills were more likely to prosper than those that still relied on social connections. When they did, walls against minorities usually fell, and in the 1970s Laing, Weldon's hiring practices put it near the leading edge. After 1969 it hired several more Jewish lawyers. Elizabeth Duquet, the firm's first female lawyer, had been hired in 1966. She married and left Montreal a year later (which rather strengthened some male partners' traditional doubts about hiring female lawyers), but several more women were hired early in the 1970s.*

As the transformation of French Quebec continued apace in the 1960s and 1970s, Laing, Weldon quite suddenly became a thoroughly bilingual workplace. The firm's will and ability to break down the isolation that had long typified an English-language Montreal business law practice demonstrated that a new attitude and a new dynamism would prevail at Laing, Weldon. The young francophone lawyers beginning to flood out of the Université de Montréal and other French-language law schools in the first wave of the Quiet Revolution suddenly found that working at the law firm of Eugène Lafleur was not impossible at all.

Labour law happened to become one early point of entry. The firm had always assisted corporations with labour matters as part of its general corporate practice, but in 1965, with law firms beginning to explore the benefits of specialization, Laing, Weldon recruited Raymond Caron, then a senior practitioner in the labour field, who built up a dedicated practice advising corporate clients on labour relations issues. In the late 1960s and early 1970s, union membership and union militancy were both rising rapidly in Quebec. Labour conflict was endemic in Quebec's aging heavy industrial sector, often pitting traditional anglophone managers against radical francophone unions. The marathon bargaining sessions, disputes, injunctions and litigation that accompanied industrial relations at the time kept the Laing, Weldon labour lawyers busy. The practice required bilingual skills, and the young lawyers drawn into labour practice at the firm over the next decade were almost all francophones—Richard Beaulieu, Hélène Leroux, Louis Lacoursière and others. Other experienced lawyers recruited as lateral transfers in this period included Jules Duchesneau

*As noted in chapters 4 and 5, there had been very few women and minorities at McCarthy & McCarthy in the 1950s and 1960s. The Toronto firm also began to change in this regard in the 1970s.

in 1965, Paul-Émile Bisaillon in 1971, Lawrence Poitras in 1970 and Pierre Lamontagne in 1972.

By the mid-1970s, francophone participation reached all levels in the firm. Even as lateral hiring placed francophone lawyers in senior positions, new hiring trends were providing an abundance of francophone associates and students at the entry levels. Tam Davis recalls that when he was hired in 1972, after a year at the Sorbonne and legal research with Frank Scott of McGill, he was the only anglophone among the five students accepted.[152]

Jean Archambault and Lawrence Poitras, two judges from the Montreal office.

Most of the early francophone leaders in the firm—Jacques Courtois, Jacques Tétrault, Charles Gonthier, Raymond Caron—had always worked at least as much in English with English-language clients as in French. By the late 1960s, however, they and their anglophone contemporaries Richard Weldon, Ross Clarkson, Benny Parsons, Derek Hanson and others had evidently made a commitment to strengthen the francophone component of their firm. One recently hired associate, assigned to an important client in the late 1960s, returned to ask Richard Weldon whether he was right for the task: a senior officer of the client firm seemed reluctant to work with a francophone lawyer. Weldon immediately informed the client that if it could not accept a francophone lawyer it would have to find another law firm.

Asked if Laing, Weldon deliberately made francophone recruitment a strategy for future growth, Jacques Tétrault said, "I think you are suggesting we had greater planning abilities than we had." Still, a once distinctively anglophone group of partners had dismantled a wall that had seemed almost insurmountable and, having done so, their firm's recruiting of francophone lawyers was vigorous. Their new hires no longer automatically came from McGill or even from Montreal; now they sometimes arrived with limited knowledge of English.

The new bilingualism they represented seems to have taken hold irreversibly at Laing, Weldon by the mid-1970s. As recently as 1971, the Quebec government's new laws requiring French to be the language of the workplace had provoked concern among some partners. By 1976 French had become almost standard in internal documents and partnership agreements at the law firm and was rapidly becoming the language of the workplace. By 1982 close to two-thirds (thirty-eight of sixty-one) of the firm's lawyers were francophones, a higher proportion of francophone lawyers than at any of Montreal's other old, formerly anglophone law firms.[153] At the same time, the firm had grown more rapidly than competing firms. In barely a decade, it had transformed itself.

Modernizing firm governance was part of the transformation. Authority had always devolved onto the lawyer with the most seniority, and Peter Laing, who had joined in 1944, inherited the senior partner's position in the early 1970s. Laing, however, left much of the management responsibility during this critical period to his partners, and in 1975, at the age of 60, he reduced his practice, resigned his partnership and became effectively a counsel to the firm. At that time the partners created a "policy board," soon to be renamed the executive committee. This was the first formal management structure the firm had, and it provided the first opportunity for senior lawyers to participate formally in the direction of their firm. However, it was a cautious reform: the name partners, determined by seniority, appointed the members of the new committee and remained the final authority.[154]

Barely six months later, Richard Weldon, founding chair of the policy board and still in his mid-fifties, was stricken with lung cancer and died shortly thereafter. Jacques Courtois succeeded him as senior partner, and in September 1976 the firm became Courtois, Clarkson, Parsons & Tétrault, usually known as Courtois, Clarkson. By the fortune of retirements and deaths, the firm had acquired a bilingual name and a prominent, influential francophone as senior partner—just months before the provincial election of November 1976 marked a fundamental change in Montreal, its business community and its lawyers.

COUNSEL TO "QUÉBEC INC."

THE NOVEMBER 15, 1976, election of the Parti Québécois on a separatist platform shocked English Montreal and the Montreal business community, including its law firms. Employees in the Montreal office of Courtois, Clarkson remember "tough times" and cutbacks as the firm prepared for whatever economic catastrophe the new government might provoke in Montreal. In the longer term, November 1976 did indeed mark a transition in Quebec's society, business and law.[155]

Between the Parti Québécois victory in 1976 and the first referendum on Quebec sovereignty in 1980, many of the largest Canadian corporations, long based in Montreal, moved their headquarters and sometimes their entire operations westward to Ontario. Perhaps the most prominent departure for Toronto was Sun Life, which had once been as influential in Montreal as Canada Life had been in Toronto but which now abandoned its landmark headquarters on Metcalfe Street. The offices of banks, trust companies, financial houses and industries also departed, not least among them the Lafleur firm's old client, CIL. Some of these changes would have happened anyway, as part of a long-term westward shift of the centre of gravity of Canadian and North American commerce, but November 1976 sharply accelerated the trend. With them went legal business that had supported the large commercial law firms of Montreal for generations.

Some Montreal lawyers and law firms followed their clients. At Courtois, Clarkson, some half-dozen anglophone lawyers chose between 1976 and 1980 to leave for careers—some very successful—in Toronto, Calgary and other centres. In general, however, the firm had committed itself to the great transition taking place in Montreal: the rise of francophone legal business. Even as old businesses departed, new francophone or bilingual enterprises and institutions were emerging as an important new client base for business law firms, if those firms were able to adapt to the new realities of Montreal.

Courtois, Clarkson, by planning or good fortune, had placed itself slightly ahead of this trend. Just at the moment when success in the new Montreal legal marketplace required francophone leadership, an ability to work in French and access to francophone business leaders, Courtois, Clarkson already had all three. None of its competitors was exclusively anglophone any longer, but in 1976 none had francophone participation to the degree Courtois, Clarkson did. As the corporations of English Montreal headed for Toronto, law firms that were already able to operate in French as well as English secured a crucial competitive advantage. Courtois, Clarkson had managed to adapt to the new francophone Quebec and the new corporate and legal world emerging in the province, before doing so began to look like merely chasing the trend.

Despite uncertainty in the Montreal business community and the long-term decline of Montreal's commercial dominance relative to Toronto (and Calgary), Courtois, Clarkson grew rapidly through the late 1970s and early 1980s. The average size of leading business law firms was rising rapidly everywhere in North America, in response to the growing complexity of corporate tax and business law, as well as the expansion of regulatory requirements, the growth of complex merger and acquisition deals, and other factors. Amid this general expansion, Courtois, Clarkson, once one of a dozen or more prominent Montreal practices, successfully situated itself within a first-tier group of four firms.* By the early 1990s, when it had merged into McCarthy Tétrault, it was the smallest of the four largest law firms in Montreal, but it had almost twice as many lawyers as the number 5 firm. By the end of the 1990s only Ogilvy Renault would be larger.[156]

Courtois, Clarkson continued to attract promising lawyers in the late 1970s. One was Gérald Tremblay, a rising litigator recruited from Stikeman Elliott in 1979, who quickly added great strength to the existing litigation department. Another was Yves Pratte. A Quebec City lawyer who had been dean of law at Université Laval and a key adviser to Quebec premiers Lesage and Johnson in the Quiet Revolution years of the 1960s, Pratte had served as CEO of Air Canada from 1968 to 1975. Prime Minister Trudeau named him to the Supreme Court of Canada in 1977, but Pratte found judicial office uncongenial. He left after barely a year and joined Courtois, Clarkson in Montreal. A very respected lawyer who set ruthlessly high standards and a relentless pace, Pratte could be a demanding taskmaster for young lawyers, but with his superb connections both in Ottawa and throughout the business and political worlds of Quebec, he played a crucial role in securing the firm's links to the emerging "Québec Inc." business community and helped make the practice a magnet for both legal talent and new clients.

*The others were Ogilvy Renault, Martineau Walker and Stikeman Elliott.

As the size of law firms grew rapidly in the late 1970s, interest in diversification, mergers and geographic outreach was high. Major American firms had been branching out within the United States and into Europe for years. Montreal's Stikeman Elliott had already expanded to London, England, and to Toronto, and McCarthy & McCarthy of Toronto was about to challenge Alberta's rules on interprovincial law firms. Courtois, Clarkson, as a leading Montreal practice eager to stay at the cutting edge of legal innovation, had to look into the opportunities.

The firm considered an office in London, England, but its first initiative was in Brussels. Canada was then looking to Europe as a way of reducing its dependence on the United States, and the partnership gambled that an office in Brussels, the headquarters of the European Community, could become a portal for the Canada-Europe legal opportunities that might develop. The office opened in 1975, staffed by lawyer Michael Peterson, but Canada's proposed "contractual link" with Europe came to nothing, and much the same fate met the Courtois, Clarkson office in Brussels, which was wound up in 1979.[157]

Yves Pratte, who left the Supreme Court of Canada to return to law and business with Clarkson Tétrault, made a huge contribution to the firm before his sudden death in 1988.

The firm continued to explore options for expansion. It had long been involved in provincial regulatory issues in Quebec City, and in 1979 it entered into merger discussions with a leader in that field, the established Quebec City law firm Langlois, Drouin. That firm, however, decided instead to open its own Montreal office, and Courtois, Clarkson's entry into Quebec City was postponed. It also started looking at opportunities to practise federal regulatory law in Ottawa. It took an interest in Calgary, as well, where the inflow of investment and the proliferation of head offices was attracting interest from law firms all over the country, but a 1977 agreement to cooperate with a Calgary firm was formally wound up in 1980, when the Law Society of Alberta began making known its hostility to interprovincial associations of lawyers.[158]

Courtois, Clarkson also explored the potential for an office or association in Hong Kong and China. Its principal discussions, however, focussed on Toronto, the other key centre of business law and the place where a lot of Montreal business was going. In 1980 the Montreal partnership agreed in principle to open an office in Toronto. As various options were canvassed, the most promising proposal came from Harry Macdonell, the McCarthy & McCarthy lawyer who had earlier been the Montreal-based chief executive officer of the Churchill Falls power project. The two firms began discussing how they might work together.

They quickly found many complementary interests. Both had long, proud traditions in litigation. Each, in fact, had a substantial medical malpractice specialty as regional counsel for the Canadian Medical Protective Association. They had few serious conflicts, there was work they could refer between Toronto and Montreal, and they shared interests in having their firms represented in Ottawa and overseas. No merger was proposed, but in 1980 McCarthy & McCarthy and Courtois, Clarkson began establishing an informal arrangement that came to be called, rather quaintly, a "best friends" agreement. Their memorandum of agreement, signed in March 1981, confirmed the two firms would try to give each other priority in referring work between the two cities. They would consult on legal issues and hold social events to build professional and personal relationships between them.[159]

By the beginning of the 1980s Courtois, Clarkson was growing and innovating and securing its position among the big four firms in Montreal. But it was not free of internal strife. Much of that focussed on Jacques Courtois, a senior partner.

In Montreal business circles, Courtois was a notable public figure with a high-flying personal style and many business interests beyond the law firm. Gregarious with his partners and associates, he was renowned for his practical jokes around the office and for his frequent distribution of Canadiens tickets to students and staff. But he was often away from the office on business, and some of his partners concluded that as senior partner he was too much the authoritative corporate CEO to be the kind of consultative, collegial leader they wanted. The rapidly growing practice had a substantial number of partners who wanted to share in the running of their own firm. By the early 1980s some began to complain that they felt like outsiders there.

Partnership meetings held to discuss these complaints led to promises of increased consultations, and the executive committee system was reorganized, but discontent simmered in 1980–81. During the summer and fall of that year, as many as sixteen partners gathered privately to discuss breaking away to form a new firm. At least one partner, however, was heard to say that instead of sixteen partners leaving it would be better to get rid of the one who was the problem. The threat of a breakup subsided only when the partners agreed to ask Jacques Tétrault to lead a task force that would investigate the "malaise" within the firm.

Jacques Tétrault's ad hoc committee (the other members were Tam Davis, Derek Hanson, Louis Lacoursière and Gérald Tremblay) conducted confidential interviews with all partners and delivered a report in early December 1981. The report proposed making the firm's executive committee elective (it was still appointed by the name partners) and electing the managing partner rather than determining authority strictly by seniority. The report also addressed communications issues, suggested a review of recruiting strategies and recommended the hiring of a full-time, qualified business manager. It noted concerns that some partners at Courtois, Clarkson were earning less than counterparts at comparable firms.[160]

Eventually, perhaps inevitably, the next annual review of allocations became the spark for further trouble. A debate ensued as to the proper allocation among senior partners. On January 27, 1982, the allocations decision was made by a formal vote of the executive committee, but Courtois remained dissatisfied with the allocations proposal.[161]

A lull followed through February. The executive committee, still led by Courtois, dealt with several matters that had been driven off the agenda by the allocations battle, including the possible venture in

Hong Kong and the hiring of accountant Richard Lapointe to fill the new senior administrative post the Tétrault report had recommended. On Friday evening, March 5, however, Jacques Courtois stopped by Ross Clarkson's office to say good-bye. Clarkson responded by wishing him a good weekend.

Courtois said, no, he was saying good-bye. He would not be back.

After a frantic weekend (during which Courtois agreed to delay his decision for a day) and a busy Monday, the executive committee convened at 5 PM on Tuesday, March 9. Courtois' resignation letter did not arrive until the meeting had ended, but their senior partner was gone. Worse, he had moved only a few blocks west along Dorchester Street and joined their rivals at Stikeman Elliott.

The executive partners took several quick decisions. By the time the offices opened the next morning, the partners had been apprised of the new situation, Courtois' name had been removed from the sign at the main entrance, and the receptionists had been instructed to answer the phones, "Clarkson Tétrault."[162]

CLARKSON TÉTRAULT

IN 1979 THE BARREAU DU QUÉBEC repealed the rule that since 1933 had required Quebec law firms to change their names every time their partnerships were reorganized. Law firms in Quebec soon began to exploit the business advantage of settling on short, permanent, preferably bilingual names. "Clarkson Tétrault," the new two-name appellation that the firm gave itself in March 1982, was the shortest formal name it had had since 1901. It promised to become a permanent brand in the Montreal legal marketplace, along with "Ogilvy Renault," "Stikeman Elliott" and others.

The stability lay in more than the name. After 1982, the practice became what it had seemed about to become in the mid-1970s: an ambitious, forward-thinking and *collegial* firm without a single dominating senior partner. It now had an elected executive committee, carefully balanced to include both older and younger partners. In Jacques Tétrault, who would remain managing partner until 1993, it also had a leader who did not wield the traditional authority of a senior partner but led by constant consultation and by the confidence the partnership came to repose in him. Tétrault's personal style was reserved and formal, but throughout the 1980s, as the firm continued to grow, he made a point of listening to his partners, making sure all had their views heard and their issues discussed.

Tétrault conveyed the same respect towards associates, and he sustained the commitment to diversity that had become characteristic of a firm where the accents of Westmount increasingly mingled not only with those of well-to-do francophone Outremont but also with those of young lawyers raised in Lac St-Jean or Abitibi. Hélène Leroux became the firm's first female partner in 1977; there were five by 1984. Lorna Telfer, later a leader in the partnership's securities group, recalls several occasions early in her career when Tétrault informed male clients, who clearly would have preferred a male lawyer, that he was giving their file to Telfer "because she was the right lawyer," as if daring them to complain. Telfer later became the first woman in the firm to have children while a partner. She acknowledges there were difficulties to overcome, but the gender tensions felt at McCarthy & McCarthy in Toronto during these years seem not to have had a counterpart in the Montreal firm.[163]

Courtois' departure had not affected the ambitious and outward-looking style the leaders sought to cultivate. To ensure continued growth, Yves Pratte and Gérald Tremblay led a review of recruitment practices and concluded that, in the increasingly competitive market, only middle-ranked students came around with applications. To secure the top students, they urged, Clarkson Tétrault needed much more assertive processes to identify and recruit the very best new lawyers each year. A wider review of the firm's situation in 1984, following two years of recession that had hit Montreal hard, urged that to be more profitable it needed to reverse its partner-associate ratio (then forty partners to only twenty-seven associates), needed more francophones in commercial practice (and more anglophones in litigation) and still needed to expand its francophone commercial clientele.[164]

Despite the recession of the early 1980s, the firm was still growing in numbers and profitability and expansion beyond Montreal remained on the agenda. The idea of opening an office in Hong Kong was abandoned after Courtois' departure, but an expansion into Ottawa was approved (22–15, in a divided vote). The Ottawa office opened in August 1982 with the recruitment of Dan Burtnick, an experienced Ontario lawyer with a practice in federal regulatory matters. The partners were assured Ottawa would be nothing like Brussels—there would be clients at once. The partners also wanted the Ottawa office to provide a window on federal politics, and they made an association with former politician and consultant Heward Grafftey. In the end, the political aspects of the office bore little fruit and the association with Grafftey was brief. Burtnick soon abandoned Ottawa and legal practice all together.[165]

Business considerations also limited the scale of the Ottawa office. Branch offices were still a new phenomenon in Canadian legal practice, looked on with suspicion by local practices that saw big city firms moving in on their turf. For Clarkson Tétrault, it was important not to compete in Ottawa with Gowling & Henderson, the large Ottawa firm that supervised the referral of Canadian Medical Protective Association litigation to lawyers across Canada. Clarkson Tétrault therefore made it clear that it was in Ottawa to represent its own clients in federal regulatory work and international trade business, not to compete with firms like Gowlings for the work of the local business community. With that limited mandate, the Ottawa office struggled for several years. The National Energy Board, one of the regulatory agencies, moved from Ottawa to Calgary soon after Clarkson Tétrault opened its office in Ottawa. In any case, the firm soon faced competition from other Montreal and Toronto firms that had also seized on the idea of expanding into the national capital. Gradually the potential for collaboration in maintaining the Ottawa office became one item where Clarkson Tétrault was eager to consider closer ties with McCarthy & McCarthy of Toronto.

The movement into Quebec City proved more immediately successful. In 1984, Yves Pratte and Jacques Tétrault renewed contact with the Quebec City firm of Drouin et Associés. The Drouin firm had been founded in 1872 by François-Xavier Drouin and maintained by his descendents down to his great-grandson, Richard Drouin. One of the oldest firms in the country, it had produced judges, *bâtonniers,* King's and Queen's Counsels, politicians and leading lawyers for many years. The Drouins were Conservatives, and members of the family had contested the constituency of Quebec East against two prime ministers, Wilfrid Laurier and Louis St. Laurent. (Marc Drouin later became Speaker of the Canadian Senate.) The Drouins' legal careers, particularly those of brothers Marc and Ross in the mid-twentieth century, were more successful. Initially prominent in criminal-defence litigation, they later represented Davie Shipbuilding and other leading Quebec City enterprises. By 1984 the firm had become a forty-lawyer Montreal/Quebec City partnership called Langlois, Drouin. A split in Langlois, Drouin that year produced Drouin et Associés, with just eleven Quebec City lawyers, but it still had

Richard Drouin, who led his century-old Quebec City firm into a merger with Clarkson Tétrault in 1985, became a senior partner in McCarthy Tétrault and a leader in its energy law practice in Canada and beyond.

The Hotel Windsor was one of Montreal's leading hotels until the 1950s. Only the hotel annex survived to become "Le Windsor," home to Clarkson Tétrault and McCarthy Tétrault, in 1987.

a strong labour law practice, particularly for Quebec public corporations, and it had very strong connections in business and government in the provincial capital: senior partner Richard Drouin would be chair and CEO of Hydro-Québec from 1988 to 1995.

The Drouin lawyers in Quebec City did not need convincing that to maintain a practice that was more than purely local they needed an alliance in Montreal. They were keen to merge with Clarkson Tétrault. Later several Quebec City partners would become strong supporters of further expansion and play significant roles in McCarthy Tétrault. In a 1984 memo to his partners, Jacques Tétrault suggested that the Drouin merger would enable Clarkson Tétrault to "better serve clients in the Quebec area" and "as in Ottawa, project an image of our firm as one which is close to the pulse of the political affairs of the state." The partners agreed, and Drouin et Associés merged into Clarkson Tétrault in June 1985.* [166]

In 1985 Clarkson Tétrault launched another kind of movement: to a new address in Montreal. Maison Royal-Trust (previously CIL House), the firm's home on Dorchester since 1963, was ceasing to fill its needs. The Webster family, long-time clients, drew its attention to the Windsor Hotel Annex on Peel Street just north of Dorchester, looking across Dorchester Square to the majestic old Sun Life building. The Windsor Hotel had once been among Montreal's most prestigious addresses, but it had declined after the closure of the old Windsor Station next door, and the main building had been demolished for construction of the CIBC Tower in the early 1960s. The small, elegant Windsor Annex just north of it was abandoned, nearly ruinous, and likely to be demolished.

Clarkson Tétrault decided that instead of moving to another high-rise office tower it would join the project to turn the Windsor Annex into a unique office complex. It even considered investing in the building itself, but as one of the partners said, "We concluded we should be lawyers, not real estate moguls." Clarkson Tétrault's agreement to become a key tenant (along with Cemp Investments and with Coopers & Lybrand, which was also a discontented tenant in Maison Royal-Trust) made viable the renovation of the old building into premium office space. The agreement was signed in 1985, and in 1987 Clarkson Tétrault announced to the world its new address: "Le Windsor." A piece of Montreal's architectural heritage had been saved, and Clarkson Tétrault had acquired office space that distinguished it from every other downtown law firm in Montreal. The celebration of the move coincided with a late commemoration of the centenary of the firm's founding.†

At about the time that it expanded into Quebec City, Clarkson Tétrault undertook a review of where it stood. The firm had nearly

*At the first McCarthy Tétrault partnership retreat, the handful of Quebec City partners happily claimed the national firm as their triumph. Had they not expanded first to Montreal, then absorbed Toronto and the west as well?

†The partners had long been under the impression that Eugène Lafleur launched his firm in 1887, not 1885.

tripled its numbers since 1972 (from twenty-five lawyers to sixty-nine) and was still growing rapidly (there would be 113 lawyers by 1990). Gross income in 1984 was thirteen times what it had been eight years earlier (five times, allowing for inflation). By the mid-1980s Clarkson Tétrault, like most corporate-law firms, was both expanding its numbers and embracing new levels of specialization and division of labour. It had long been strong in labour law, commercial real estate and general corporate work, and it had always had a highly regarded litigation department. In the 1980s further specializations and subspecializations developed. The financial and banking practice, greatly strengthened by Yves Pratte and eventually led by Michel Deschamps, expanded significantly. Hubert Lacroix, Jean-René Gauthier and Lorna Telfer developed a specialized securities practice. Telfer, who joined the firm in 1977, recalls that in her early years "we did everything," but in 1982 she spent nine months on loan to the Quebec Securities Commission. Newly expert in Quebec's new securities act, she thereafter joined in the general trend towards specialization.

Yves Bériault, who had joined the firm in 1973 (earlier he had clerked along with Gérald Tremblay at the Supreme Court of Canada, where they were among the first Supreme Court law clerks), developed an interest in competition law after working on litigation regarding competition in the sugar industry. He served as commission counsel to the Bryce Royal Commission on Corporate Concentration in the mid-1970s. Soon afterwards, new federal legislation generated substantial growth in the field of competition, monopolies and corporate concentration. "I had picked the right horse," recalled Bériault, "because now we had a really serious piece of legislation that applied to virtually everything a business does, and I was in the fortunate position of having been one of the few people involved in this area in Quebec." With Yves Comtois and Madeleine Renaud, Bériault built substantial expertise and a large client base for Clarkson Tétrault in competition law. The three partners eventually wrote a standard text in the field.

Computer and telecommunications law also was identified as a growth area. A report from Louise Martin (one of the firm's early female partners, who used a wheelchair) predicted that, as Ottawa began to permit competition in long distance telephone services, pay television, and eventually all forms of digital communications, new entrants and established companies would provide substantial work for law firms. She reported that Montreal competitors were already moving fast into this area and into intellectual-property law generally. Computer law soon became one area where the "best friends" arrangement with Toronto paid off: several Clarkson Tétrault lawyers worked closely with McCarthys' Daniel Cooper, then the recognized leader in the field, to develop a computer law practice in Montreal. The telecommunications practice expanded further with the recruitment in 1982 of Michel Racicot. Ann Bigué, formerly with the National Energy Board, helped build a practice in energy regulation issues after she joined the firm in 1980. As hydro-electric projects spread out into First Nations territories in northern Quebec, she also developed a related practice in aboriginal law.

Litigation remained a Clarkson Tétrault strength, with Gérald Tremblay, Graham Nesbitt, Louis Lacoursière, André Prévost, and their colleagues doing a growing volume of medical liability, product liability, labour, environmental and commercial cases.

In 1987 Clarkson Tétrault hosted a reception for the profession and the business community to celebrate the opening of its new offices at "Le Windsor." The firm was in good shape: cohesive and effectively managed, with a solid client base in both litigation and corporate practice and diversifying into several promising specialties. It was well established among the leading group of Montreal law firms, had successfully extended its reach to Quebec and to Ottawa, claimed to be the first Montreal firm to have moved decisively into word processing and computerized accounting, and had a strong corps of highly regarded practitioners and promising younger lawyers. The world of legal practice was continuing to change around it, however, and the firm was not going to rest on its laurels.

13 | LOOKING BEYOND MONTREAL

THROUGHOUT THE 1980S, Canadian law firms continued to grow, to merge, and to branch out across Canada and beyond. McCarthys' determination to practise in Alberta and British Columbia was the most controversial example, but other law firms were also beginning to follow their clients across provincial boundaries. Martineau Walker of Montreal developed an association with the Toronto firm Fasken Calvin in 1986, Stikeman Elliott already had an office in Toronto and several Canadian practices opened offices in London, U.K.

When a committee of Clarkson Tétrault partners undertook a review of their situation in 1984, they concluded that they were still mostly a large regional practice. The "best friends" arrangement with McCarthy & McCarthy continued, but it had not advanced very far. Integration between the Montreal and Toronto firms in the mid-1980s seemed to be settling in at the level of staff softball competitions, appearances at each other's firm dinners and the occasional exchange of legal advice or case referrals. While McCarthy & McCarthy was moving into Calgary and Vancouver and seeking to become a unified national partnership offering a full service to corporate clients in the major business cities of Canada, there remained some feeling at Clarkson Tétrault that the strongest potential for growth lay in the francophone business community of Quebec, and that perhaps the Ottawa office and the link to McCarthy & McCarthy should be re-examined.[167]

In May 1984 the Clarkson Tétrault partners, at a "think-in" at Montebello, Quebec, authorized a committee to investigate the potential for international associations. The committee languished for some time, and its preliminary report, delivered in August 1986, was far from a clarion call to action. Yves Bériault, its principal author, noted that interprovincial mergers were a trend that the firm might or might not follow, but which it needed to observe and study. He observed that although half Clarkson Tétrault's work had out-of-province aspects, the practice was doing well, growing in size and billings, and comfortably beyond the recession of the early 1980s, largely on the basis of its success in becoming a bilingual and Québécois law firm in the 1970s.

Members of the "Blue Macs" from McCarthy & McCarthy and the "Fleural" team from Clarkson Tétrault met several times for friendly softball matches in the 1980s.

On the assumption that interprovincial expansions were likely to continue, indeed were almost inevitable, Bériault's committee set out options for the firm to consider. Clarkson Tétrault could do nothing, simply maintaining the special relationship with McCarthy & McCarthy and letting the Toronto firm initiate changes if it wished. Alternatively, Clarkson Tétrault could abandon the McCarthy association to launch its own out-of-province offices, as Stikeman Elliott and Phillips & Vineberg were doing. Bériault's committee also noted the possibility of a full merger between Clarkson Tétrault and another firm, along the lines then being negotiated by McCarthy & McCarthy of Toronto and Shrum, Liddle & Hebenton in Vancouver. The report was unenthusiastic about such a prospect. "If such an association is made with a larger or stronger partner," it concluded, "we risk in the long or short term losing the ability to set our own course, becoming a 'branch plant.'"[168]

In its cautious attitude to interprovincial expansion and to the McCarthy alliance, Bériault's committee was expressing views that were widely held among the partners. In a May 1985 *tour d'horizon*, soon after he joined Clarkson Tétrault, Richard Drouin surveyed the potential for "un cabinet national," but his attention was almost entirely on opportunities within the Province of Quebec; he barely mentioned McCarthy & McCarthy. Also in 1985, Jacques Tétrault had told *Le Monde Juridique*, a Montreal legal magazine, that he thought "pan-Canadian" firms would emerge only in a more or less distant future. Acknowledging that "perhaps we have a special relationship with McCarthys—not exclusive but special," he declared that he personally was not yet convinced that expansion to Toronto was necessary to the firm's future.[169]

These were the statements of a partnership clearly not certain that it wanted to pursue interprovincial growth or to become a pan-Canadian, rather than a Quebec, law firm. Clarkson Tétrault was not a Péquiste firm by any stretch (the political ties of its leaders were mostly Liberal; several of its lawyers had been Quebec Liberal candidates or senior advisers to the party). Still, in its own way the firm had been at the leading edge of the transition in Quebec society, when control of the levers of economic power had been transferred with startling speed from the anglophone minority to the francophone majority. Clarkson Tétrault had become a French-majority, bilingual firm, open to Quebecers from all over the province. Its members were proud of that, proud to have been part of the emergence of new structures for Quebec business, politics and law. They were well aware of the benefits their firm had reaped by being part of the change, and they were determined to continue being part of that Quebec project.

In the 1980s McCarthy & McCarthy had more than twice as many lawyers as Clarkson Tétrault, and only Ogilvy Renault among the top-tier Montreal firms was competitive in size or overall revenues with the largest Toronto firms. Becoming a branch plant of a Toronto giant, if that was what interprovincial expansion meant, would not be good business for a Quebec law firm. McCarthy & McCarthy was already fully committed to its struggle to expand as a single unit into Calgary and Vancouver but, for many lawyers at Clarkson Tétrault, the vision of an interprovincial firm was no more appealing than it was to McCarthys' foes at the Alberta and British Columbia law societies.

Yves Pratte had been part of that consensus. He was very strongly committed to developing the practice's links to the new, French-speaking business community known as "Québec Inc." At one point he had considered opening his own Toronto practice to serve his clients' needs, but he was unlikely to support any interprovincial merger in which Clarkson Tétrault would became a minority partner in an English-dominated partnership.

Yves Pratte died suddenly in 1988, at just sixty-three. He had been very influential in nine years at Clarkson Tétrault and had contributed greatly to its legal strengths, and many of his partners continued to share his doubts about submerging their Quebec firm into a larger entity. Yet the partners of Clarkson Tétrault were running a substantial business in an increasingly competitive marketplace, very much subject to the will of the business community it served. They were aware they could not afford sentimentality: No firm was guaranteed a place at the leading edge where the big, intellectually challenging and remunerative files were found. The prosperity, even the survival, of large law firms depended not on sentiment or political preference but on reading accurately the changing needs of the business community. More and more, law firms' clients, even those that had grown up as francophone enterprises, were expanding beyond Quebec and looking to their lawyers to do the same. Size mattered, and it was not clear that a Montreal-based legal practice was going to be big enough. There was work to be done in Toronto for the clients of Montreal law firms. (Richard Drouin noted that he was going regularly to Toronto to do work for Abitibi Paper Company, on whose board he sat.) Having a "best friend" in Toronto was neither satisfying these clients' wishes for one-stop legal services nor putting money into the pockets of the Montreal partners. Even Pratte had begun to change his views and support some kind of larger relationship.[170]

McCarthy & McCarthy, for its part, was beginning to press Clarkson Tétrault to commit itself on the future of their association. In 1984, when Guy Fortin and Jocelyne Knoppers reported back on a visit to Toronto to discuss opportunities in computer law and intellectual property with Daniel Cooper and others at McCarthy & McCarthy, they described the reception they received. "They saw it almost as a joint venture for McCarthy and Clarkson Tétrault," wrote Knoppers and Fortin about the Toronto lawyers' attitude towards opportunities for intellectual property practice in Montreal. "They would like to do more and consolidate relations between our two offices. We sensed they were disappointed that our relationship had not been growing. They expressed the view of many of the lawyers in their office who were very keen for closer links and who had the impression that we were somewhat lukewarm."[171]

Montreal was reluctant to be drawn deeply into the mergers. "We were leery at the time in Quebec of having a full merger, because we felt that we would be eaten up by Toronto and that we wouldn't retain our culture," recalled Jacques Tétrault.[172] Clarkson Tétrault feared that if "Québec Inc.," the francophone client base that represented the future of business in Quebec, concluded the law firm was merely the local branch of one headquartered in Toronto, it would withdraw its confidence and eventually its business.

In 1985–86, at about the time Clarkson Tétrault's international affairs committee was reflecting on the firm's options, McCarthy & McCarthy and Shrum, Liddle & Hebenton, frustrated by the British

Columbia litigation that was preventing their merger, sought to preserve their momentum with a plan for a loose association. Both McCarthys and Shrum, Liddle & Hebenton favoured this plan only as an interim measure pending the outcome of the lawsuits, and this "partnership of partnerships" was not much more than a "best friends" declaration, since that was all that British Columbia law would then permit. Still Clarkson Tétrault chose not to participate.

By the late 1980s, however, the business and legal tide was encouraging the closer links that the McCarthy & McCarthy lawyers favoured over some uncertain "best friends" association. Since 1982's Freedman Report, the Federation of Law Societies had largely abandoned its opposition in principle to interprovincial mergers. By 1987 the Barreau du Québec was moving to reduce its restrictions against interprovincial links among lawyers. Above all, the lawsuits that still blocked mergers in British Columbia and Alberta were moving rapidly to a conclusion.

In the summer of 1988, with judgement expected in the British Columbia case *Martin v. Attorney General of British Columbia*, events began to come to a head. Should the verdict be favourable, McCarthy & McCarthy and Shrum, Liddle & Hebenton wanted to complete their merger as quickly as possible to become the first national partnership to open in British Columbia. And if the national firm was about to come together, Toronto and its western partners believed Montreal would want the opportunity to come in as a founding partner.

The British Columbia verdict was issued on September 6, 1988. The Alberta case was still awaiting a verdict from the Supreme Court of Canada, but in British Columbia McCarthys and Shrum, Liddle & Hebenton, suddenly free to merge, were determined to act at once, with Sholto Hebenton emphasising that, if they did not, other firms would step in ahead of them and win all the rewards of being first.[173]

The Montreal partners were reluctant to merge with firms outside Quebec, but they were also increasingly concerned with finding themselves caught in a "Quebec regional" trap. Faced with the possibility of a Toronto-Vancouver-Calgary merger that left them out, they came up with a counter-offer. During the summer of 1988, they revived the "partnership of partnerships" idea that the other firms had floated as a temporary expedient in 1986.

On September 8, 1988, just after the British Columbia court decision, the parties met in Montreal. Bériault, Tam Davis, Michael Dennis, Gérald Tremblay and Jacques Tétrault represented Clarkson Tétrault. Harry Macdonell, Tom Heintzman and Jim McCartney represented Toronto, with Richard Shaw and Sholto Hebenton representing the two western firms. At this meeting and subsequent ones in Ottawa and Toronto, the Clarkson Tétrault team presented a draft agreement for a partnership of partnerships. Clarkson Tétrault, McCarthy & McCarthy, and Shrum, Liddle & Hebenton would remain independent firms and continue to use their own names in their home provinces, but under this new association, to be called McCarthy Tétrault Shrum, they would open overseas offices as joint ventures and would share the Ottawa office that Clarkson Tétrault was already operating. Clarkson Tétrault argued that as separate firms they could even represent clients against clients of the others. If the partners in the various firms approved, they might be able to announce the new association as early as September 30, 1988.[174]

Jim McCartney of the Toronto office thought the proposal worth supporting. Toronto could still go ahead with its western mergers if the courts allowed them, he reported to his partners in August 1988. "However, it has been recognized for some years that this approach [that is, a loose association] was the only possibility with respect to Clarkson Tétrault.... If we do not move ahead with Clarkson Tétrault now, we run a risk of losing an opportunity which we have nurtured for several years."[175]

The leaders of Clarkson Tétrault felt they had moved a long way. "To make it more formal, to go ahead and do it, a huge amount of politicking [had to be done]," recalled one partner. In just two years, most of the Clarkson Tétrault partners had moved from resisting almost any further association to an agreement that would substantially link their firm's future with the future of the giant Vancouver-Calgary-Toronto partnership that McCarthy & McCarthy was developing. So it was a shock when the Montreal lawyers learned the results of the vote of the Toronto partnership on September 29, 1988.

In Toronto the partnership vote to seize the opportunity presented by the British Columbia verdict in *Martin v. Attorney General* by proceeding with a full merger with Shrum, Liddle & Hebenton was unanimous. So was support for a resolution to maintain "a strong relationship" with Clarkson Tétrault. But the Toronto partners voted down Montreal's proposal for a partnership of partnerships.

Toronto, having established a preference for full mergers over loose associations back in 1983, simply failed to see sufficient benefit in the partnership of partnerships that the Montreal firm was proposing. For the litigation lawyers in particular, the loose association "raised problems of conflicts and liability, without the potential for growth in revenues and profits of a fully merged firm." It seemed, in fact, not much different from the "best friends" association, except that, in the view of many Toronto partners, it exposed the firms to the risk of being conflicted out of work without providing in exchange the increased business that the partners in a full merger could hope to share. "The anxiety in the litigation department reached the point where they were not prepared to proceed," said Jim McCartney. "So we had to tell Clarkson Tétrault that the partnership of partnerships was off."

The McCarthy & McCarthy memorandum that reported the vote results went out of its way to stress that the Toronto partners respected Clarkson Tétrault's need for an independent identity in Quebec, and the Toronto partners expressed their unanimous support for preserving "a strong close relationship with Clarkson Tétrault."[176] But: "When they turned it down, the immediate reaction was: a slap in the face!" one Montreal partner remembered.

"After long discussion," the Clarkson Tétrault partners chose to have the minutes of their partnership meeting on October 4, 1988 merely express the firm's regret at the Toronto decision. Influenced by McCarthy & McCarthy's report on the vote, which emphasised Toronto's eagerness to preserve the relationship despite this impasse over the form it should take, the Montreal partners agreed to continue negotiations in search of a solution to the conflicts issue, where Montreal believed Toronto's view had been misguided. In late October, Jacques Tétrault and Michael Dennis reported to their partners that the Toronto vote meant that the partnership of partnerships had been "insufficiently explained ahead of time."[177]

Still, Toronto's rejection was taken hard in Montreal. Some Montreal partners believed they had moved as far as was possible, given the skepticism the Montreal marketplace would have about giving its legal business to a Toronto-dominated law firm. In return, they felt, they had been rejected. It seemed they might have to look elsewhere, "albeit reluctantly," as Tétrault and Dennis put it.[178]

With progress in Montreal stalled, McCarthy & McCarthy went ahead with its Vancouver merger. Shrum, Liddle & Hebenton became the British Columbia practice of McCarthy & McCarthy on February 1, 1989. At the end of April 1989, immediately after the Supreme Court of Canada judgement against the Law Society of Alberta's rules, Black & Company became McCarthy & McCarthy of Alberta. The need to move decisively in the west required McCarthy & McCarthy to take the risk that Clarkson Tétrault, having been left out of the founding of a nearly national firm, might never be willing to join it as a latecomer. "I didn't know what was going to happen," said Jim McCartney. "I didn't necessarily think we were going to lose the relationship completely, but. . . ."[179]

In the winter of 1988–89, a great deal of discussion continued in the Montreal firm. In October 1988 Jacques Tétrault and Michael Dennis had gone to London, England, to attend a seminar organized by McCarthy & McCarthy's London office. McCarthys had originally hoped that the Montrealers would be there as full partners, but even as a guest Tétrault found himself impressed by the way the international seminar demonstrated the scale and reach that the larger organization could offer. As conversations continued through the winter, Clarkson Tétrault began to move. In Jacques Tétrault's words, "we started thinking that really, if you're going to make any sense of a broader-based firm, you've got to have a merged entity." There was little doubt that McCarthy & McCarthy, now racing ahead with its own national firm, was far and away the best vehicle for that strategy.[180]

Jacques Tétrault and Michael Dennis with the documents that would merge Clarkson Tétrault and McCarthy & McCarthy to form the new firm of McCarthy Tétrault.

Perhaps a full partnership would be better than no partnership at all, Tétrault suggested, as he continued his consulting and listening work among his partners. The Montreal partners could see that the francophone business community of Quebec was itself operating far beyond the provincial boundaries; perhaps the concern that such clients would reject Clarkson Tétrault for doing the same thing was exaggerated. The confidence in Tétrault's judgement that had built up in the Montreal firm over many years, as well as cold analysis of where the practice stood, started to bring around some of the doubters. Tétrault: "I remember one partner of ours, he was quite strongly opposed to it, and I picked up the challenge, so to speak. I said, what are you scared of?... People started thinking about it and realizing that if we were going to have a prominent place in the legal profession we had to expand into the rest of the country, particularly Toronto, but also out west."[181]

On April 18, 1989, Jim McCartney in Toronto received a phone call from Jacques Tétrault and Michael Dennis in Montreal. To his astonishment, they said they had been talking, and perhaps they would like to hear a little more about how a merger might work. Nothing official, but....

"This was a very, very exciting moment," recalled McCartney more than a dozen years later. "They were downplaying it a bit at their end, but I certainly understood what was being said."* McCartney thought this too important to be conducted over the phone. He flew to Montreal the next day for an off-the-record chat. He, Dennis and Tétrault had lunch in a little restaurant near the Clarkson Tétrault offices and talked merger.

McCartney had brought with him some of the plans Toronto and Vancouver and Calgary had worked out for their own mergers. "Some elements in our national firm...were helpful to them," he recalled, "this kind of confederation approach, where we had two levels of management, with the day-to-day practice being managed in the local offices, and another layer of management at the national level, for policy."[182]

Back in Toronto the next day, April 20, McCartney sent Toronto's new managing partner, Arthur Scace, a memo on the situation emerging in Montreal.† "Tétrault and Dennis have come to the realization that a merger is the only approach that will provide the opportunities for growth that they, as well as we, are seeking." They were willing to take a merger proposal to their partners as a better alternative than the idea of a loose association that had collapsed the previous September. A merged partnership with a single name and partnership,

* "You could have knocked me over with a feather when Jacques phoned... and said the francophone members of the firm think we should be going for a full merger," was Harry Macdonell's recollection of his reaction.

† Arthur Scace, a tax law specialist and law society bencher who had also become a "relationship lawyer" for the firm with several of its major clients, had been part of McCarthys' management committee for several years. He succeeded Harry Macdonell as Toronto managing partner in February 1989. As part of the succession process, the management committee set up a task force, led by Scace, to review how the firm should govern itself.

but with regional administration for regional matters, had suddenly become possible.[183]

Clarkson Tétrault's partners approved further merger discussions in May 1989, and the deal McCartney, Tétrault and Dennis sketched out in the restaurant—a merged firm with strong regional elements—rapidly became the basis of discussions with Toronto. National management would be the task of a committee in which each region—British Columbia, Alberta, Ontario and Quebec—would have two representatives. Local matters would remain the purview of regional management teams, while the Ottawa office and other potential expansions would be addressed collectively. A great deal remained to be done in sorting out management details, integrating pension systems and negotiating an allocations regime. In the end, the pension system used at McCarthy & McCarthy prevailed; many of the younger Toronto partners would not have agreed to the more generous provisions of the Clarkson Tétrault pension system. Financial control systems were also to be based on McCarthy procedures. With the help of accounting consultants, an allocations regime was worked out in which each region within the firm would receive a proportion of total profits. How the Montrealers (and those in each of the other new regional components of McCarthy Tétrault) divided their money would be their business. Admitting associate lawyers into the partnership became, in theory at least, the responsibility of the national management, but in fact regional committees would do much of the serious picking and choosing.[184]

The deal breaker, if there was to be one, might be the name of the new firm. Montreal insisted from the start of the discussion that there had to be a francophone name in the merged entity. This was not vanity or a face-saving gesture, the Montrealers argued forcefully. Rather, it would express the understanding that for a national firm with a majority of English-speaking lawyers to have any chance of success in Quebec, indeed, for it to demonstrate that it truly was "national" in a bilingual country, it would have to make a public commitment to both languages and cultures. The commitment had to be there in the name.*

The Toronto partnership had long proceeded on the basis that whenever the national firm came into being, McCarthy & McCarthy would be its name. It was not just that the Toronto firm was the largest and oldest and wealthiest of those entering the merged partnership, nor that endless revisions to the firm's name as it grew would weaken its national "brand." Many Toronto partners had an almost tribal loyalty to the name that went back to D'Alton McCarthy Jr., that had been unchanged for seventy-five years and had endured even when Hayden, Matthews and others took over the partnership from the last member of the McCarthy family in the 1940s. The names of the Vancouver and Calgary firms had not been preserved in the Toronto-Calgary-Vancouver partnership completed in early 1989 (though in British Columbia the well-known Shrum, Liddle & Hebenton name continued to be used during a transitional period). Despite some criticism from other Vancouver lawyers, even a proud westerner like Hebenton had agreed—and persuaded his colleagues—that the brand value in "McCarthy & McCarthy" must outweigh local or personal pride. In any case, the McCarthy & McCarthy partnership agreement had since 1947 required unanimous consent of the partners for any change to the name. A single traditionalist, or a merger skeptic, or a francophobe partner could sink the change.

To push home its point about the need for a francophone name, Clarkson Tétrault did its homework. It retained a market research firm, Burson-Marseller, to survey the opinions of business leaders and opinion makers across Canada. The consultants returned with a strong recommendation: a leading law firm needed a simple, fixed brand with a maximum of two names and, for a "national" firm in Canada, one of

*In 1982 when Courtois, Clarkson, Parsons & Tétrault became Clarkson Tétrault, Benny Parsons had allowed his name to be dropped because of the importance of having a firm name that was both brief and bilingual.

the two names had to be French. (McCarthy & McCarthy, meanwhile, hired the Peat Marwick consultancy to do a similar study and received identical advice.) Gérald Tremblay and Yves Bériault, both well-respected practitioners with national reputations, met the Toronto partners in Toronto to impress on them the importance of this issue to the success of the national firm in Quebec.[185]

Jacques Tétrault with the merger documents that created McCarthy Tétrault.

"The name change was a very big issue," said Lorna Telfer, who had been drawn into the merger discussions in Montreal. "I have to say that my view was that you'd never get McCarthy & McCarthy to change anything. I was astonished."[186]

In fact, the name change had a lot of support in Toronto (and also in Vancouver, where Sholto Hebenton was an early advocate for "McCarthy Tétrault"). Many Toronto partners had grasped the advantage of a new name in signifying the birth of a new and truly national firm. And a bilingual name would be even more effective in conveying that message. No one seemed to note—at least, no one mentioned aloud—the irony of matching a French surname to that of D'Alton McCarthy, the champion of the English language who had destroyed his political career by his hostility to the role of the French language in Canadian public life.

Harry Macdonell, a lover of legal traditions, had the idea that it might be fine to call the merged firm "McCarthy Lafleur," in honour of the two great lawyers at the origins of the two practices. But in Montreal there was only one choice: "Tétrault" was the existing francophone part of the firm's name, and there was much loyalty to Jacques Tétrault for his decade of leadership and his marshalling of a consensus on the very contentious merger issue. It would be McCarthy Tétrault.

"I remember a number of partners," said Jim McCartney, "some of whom would have been the old-time, old-line McCarthy & McCarthy partners, standing up to voice the opinion that McCarthy Tétrault was a very good name because it symbolized all we wanted to symbolize: a new firm, a national firm, a firm strong right across Canada. I was anticipating a debate, but it resolved itself." Peter Beattie, a senior partner whose family had been associated with McCarthy & McCarthy since the 1920s, remembers being one of those who used his influence to support the name change. Even Beverley Matthews, still a force though long retired, gave instant support when Harry Macdonell called to consult him. What Montreal had assumed would be its most hotly resisted requirement turned out to be something the Toronto partners wanted almost as strongly. Toronto, Calgary and Vancouver approved "McCarthy Tétrault" without a dissenting voice.*

Litigation partner Gérald Tremblay and labour lawyer Richard Beaulieu hail the formation of McCarthy Tétrault.

*To acknowledge the loss of his name from the firm's name, the Montreal partners presented Ross Clarkson (then retired, but still a familiar presence) with the "Clarkson Tétrault" nameplate when it was removed from the entrance to "Le Windsor."

The partners of Clarkson Tétrault held a partnership vote on the national firm on January 15, 1990. The motion by Michael Dennis, seconded by Gérald Tremblay, "que l'étude se fusionne avec McCarthy," received unanimous support. McCarthy Tétrault, the merged partnership of a single law firm with offices in Vancouver, Calgary, Toronto, Ottawa and Montreal, would come into being on February 1, 1990.

THE NATIONAL LAW FIRM

AND STRATEGIC PLANNING

CANADA'S NATIONAL LAW FIRM | 14

"CANADIAN BUSINESS IS becoming increasingly unrestricted by time zones and geographic boundaries," Jacques Tétrault told a press conference in Montreal on the morning of January 31, 1990. Flanked by Arthur Scace, Richard Shaw and Sholto Hebenton from the Toronto, Calgary and Vancouver offices of McCarthy & McCarthy, the head of Clarkson Tétrault was announcing his partnership would merge with McCarthy & McCarthy the following day to establish a new law firm named McCarthy Tétrault. Tétrault declared, "We have now adapted our practices to better serve this rapidly changing business environment by becoming a truly national firm with an expanding international focus."[187]

The announcement in Montreal introduced a new powerhouse on the Canadian legal scene. McCarthy & McCarthy, Clarkson Tétrault, Shrum, Liddle & Hebenton and Black & Company had all been significant firms in their own cities, but their combination brought them to a new scale of operations. A decade earlier McCarthy & McCarthy, with just over 100 lawyers, had been the second-largest law firm in Canada, amid a cluster of Toronto and Montreal practices

Richard Beaulieu, Jacques Tétrault, Richard Shaw, Jim McCartney, William Atkinson, Arthur Scace, Gérald Tremblay and Sholto Hebenton celebrate the formation of the national firm, 1990.

of roughly equivalent size. All of Canada's leading law firms had grown rapidly during the busy years of corporate expansion in the 1980s, but this merger set McCarthy Tétrault far out in front. With over 450 lawyers, it suddenly had over 200 more than the next largest Canadian firm.[188]

It was the same with revenues. A decade earlier, McCarthy & McCarthy's gross revenues stood at about $15 million a year. Revenues of the four firms, had they been united then, would have been less than double that. McCarthy Tétrault would generate revenues approaching $150 million in its first year—a figure that no other Canadian firm could match. That would provide an unparalleled base upon which the new firm could undertake the technological innovations, marketing efforts, recruitment strategies, and expansion plans that were likely to determine success in the coming decades.[189]

Jim McCartney addresses his new partners in Montreal after announcement of the merger of Clarkson Tétrault with McCarthy & McCarthy in 1990.

The stature and reputation of the merged enterprise was just as impressive. What was being established was a single law firm that stood among the leading cluster of practices in each of Canada's major business centres. Everywhere it operated, McCarthy Tétrault's business law groups—corporate finance, mergers and acquisitions, general corporate, and tax—were very strong, with blue-chip clients and a significant share in the competitive, high-value, high-visibility "deal flow" associated with activity in the markets and headlines in the business press. Across several cities, McCarthy Tétrault brought together strong practices in banking, securities, commercial real estate and competition law. It stood at the leading edge in emerging fields such as telecommunications and information technology law (in 1990 the new acronym "IT" was still emerging from the vague label "computer law" and becoming a vital practice area in its own right). It had litigation departments serving all the civil litigation and regulatory needs of the firm's corporate clients, serving private clients in everything from criminal defence work to family law, building their strength in the emerging field of class action defence work, and continuing to do constitutional cases at the Supreme Court of Canada and substantial volumes of medical malpractice work in Ontario and Quebec. As well as these core strengths, the new firm had notable clusters of excellence in a whole range of specialties, from energy and mining practice to municipal and environmental law.

The merger had created both a new name and a new corporate brand. The bilingual name so carefully chosen suggested its determination to be a national rather than a local law firm, operating at the scale of the country rather than any particular city or region. To its new name McCarthy

THE WALL STREET JOURNAL

THURSDAY, FEBRUARY 1, 1990

LAW

McCarthy Tetrault Is Formed by Merger Of Canada Law Firms

By a WALL STREET JOURNAL *Staff Reporter*

MONTREAL–Two of Canada's blue-chip law firms merged, creating the first truly national legal practice north of the border.

McCarthy Tetrault has about 450 lawyers in seven offices across Canada. Overseas, the firm has a small London office and will open an outpost in Hong Kong this spring.

The new firm combines the practices of McCarthy & McCarthy, a 340-lawyer Toronto-based firm with strong representation in Western Canada, and Clarkson, Tetrault, a 110-lawyer Montreal-based firm. Both are more than 100 years old.

The merger "will be quite good for both of them," said Michael Crawford, executive editor of Canadian Lawyer, a trade publication. Mr. Crawford said the new firm is by far the largest in Canada and by virtue of its geographic reach is for now "the national law firm." He said there will be other mergers in Canada but 400-500 lawyers will be the upper size limit because of client conflicts. The pool of clients is too small in Canada to allow 1,000-lawyer firms to function effectively, he said. After McCarthy Tetrault the next-largest firm in Canada is Toronto-based Blake Cassels & Graydon, with about 300 lawyers, Mr. Crawford said.

The managing partners of McCarthy Tetrault said client conflicts aren't a problem. "One of the great delights was to discover how few conflicts there were," said Arthur Scace, managing partner of Ontario operations. Mr. Scace said that among the reasons for the merger was heightened competition. "There clearly is more marketing. The user of legal services is more knowledgeable," he said.

The Wall Street Journal *reports the McCarthy Tétrault merger.*

Tétrault joined a slogan: "A National Law Firm," which soon became "Canada's National Law Firm." Defining McCarthy Tétrault as "Canada's National Law Firm" quickly became the focus of its marketing strategy and a key part of its new public image.

The birth of McCarthy Tétrault was heralded by a campaign of advertising and press releases, and it elicited substantial media attention. It was covered as significant business news in *Maclean's,* the *Financial Post* and the *Wall Street Journal* and given coverage in general media in all the major Canadian cities. A top-flight corporate law firm able to operate across Canada was seen as a new and newsworthy phenomenon. The fact that a Charter of Rights victory at the country's highest court had made the firm possible added drama to the story, and the merger drew widespread and positive media attention.[190]

In the early 1990s, selling the concept of "Canada's National Law Firm" also helped establish ongoing and professional marketing as an important part of the new firm's activities. This brand emphasised McCarthy Tétrault's unique achievement in creating an interprovincial law firm strongly represented in all of Canada's leading business centres, and it would be central to McCarthy Tétrault's marketing for several years. Combined with now being the largest law firm in the country, the brand helped suggest the new operation was innovative, unique, and entitled to consideration by any potential client with national business interests. "If you're using a number of law firms across the land, you might consider the efficiencies of using one national law firm instead," read one early advertisement.

In fact, there was not yet a great deal of competition for the title of national law firm.

Through the 1970s and 1980s, law practices in all the major Canadian cities had been growing rapidly. The ever-expanding scale of the deals that corporate clients were bringing to the lawyers was obliging law firms to grow, as was the increasing complexity of the legislative and regulatory framework and the consequent need for specialized expertise among lawyers. Law firms were also driven to grow by the recognition that the five or so largest firms were most likely to be considered when profitable "megaprojects"—very large corporate mergers, financings, restructurings and other high-value business transactions—were in the works. In order to be "on the list," law firms sought to become big enough to have available, often on very short notice, substantial teams of skilled lawyers across the full range of business law specialties. Firms striving to enter or remain in the top tier in the leading Canadian cities had engineered several mergers of "downtown" legal firms, as well as undertaking recruitment at a pace rarely before seen.

Yet even as Canadian law firms expanded their numbers, few had matched McCarthy Tétrault's efforts to claim leadership in the building of a national practice. Stikeman Elliott of Montreal, long committed to national and international expansion, had built up a substantial presence in Toronto since the 1970s, had moved into London and Hong Kong, and had opened a Vancouver office on the heels of McCarthy & McCarthy. But within Canada it was a much smaller and more specialized practice than McCarthy Tétrault, which had effectively seized the "national firm" spotlight by its high-profile mergers, its years of litigation in defence of its right to expand and its vigorous promotion of itself as "Canada's National Law Firm."

Despite the concern within McCarthy & McCarthy in 1988 and 1989 that the Supreme Court decision might bring in a flood of competitors, there was no sudden rush of cross-Canada mergers. Most intercity expansions remained relatively small in scale, and the firms that tried them proved reluctant to go beyond loose associations of limited consequence and sometimes of limited duration. Fasken Campbell of Toronto and Martineau Walker of Montreal formed a "partnership of partnerships" affiliation in 1986 but did not move to a full merger for another decade. A cooperation agreement that was developed in the 1990s between Goodman & Goodman of Toronto and Phillips & Vineberg of Montreal proved to be short-lived, as was an agreement on shared overseas projects between Toronto's Osler Hoskin and Montreal's Ogilvy Renault.*

For most of a decade after the formation of McCarthy Tétrault, its leading competitors did little more than dip their toes into interprovincial waters. Osler Hoskin concluded in the late 1980s that "their major clients were already national in scope and quite satisfied in dealing with a Toronto legal office." Other practices similarly concluded that mergers were not yet necessary, or were too costly or too disruptive of existing firm cultures.[191] McCarthy Tétrault's substantial presence in all four of the principal Canadian business centres really did distinguish it from the other leading Canadian law firms.

McCarthy Tétrault in 1990 finally had achieved what its leaders had anticipated almost a decade earlier, when one of its National Law Firm Committee memoranda had argued that "If there are advantages to being national, then the first firm to become national will gain prominence while the others are trying to catch up." They now had a partnership with as much entitlement as anyone to be considered Canada's leading law firm, one that was both competitive across the country and oriented for the new kind of competition that was likely to emerge in the coming years. The test of this new McCarthy Tétrault was whether the contractual merger could become a true meshing of the strengths of four cities and 450 lawyers and, even more, whether a law firm of this size and scope could identify and maximize the advan-

*Mergers among Atlantic Canadian law firms soon after the Supreme Court of Canada decision in 1989 produced a pair of regional law firms in Atlantic Canada. In general, McCarthy Tétrault and other "national" Canadian firms have not competed directly against those regional firms.

tages that might flow from the ability to provide legal services on a national basis.

One challenge it had to face was an abruptly changing economy. Through much of the late 1980s, law firms in most Canadian cities had been rising with the tide of a prosperous economy and frenzied activity in financial circles. But by 1990 the boom was over. The new firm was launched on the market in a tougher and more competitive environment.

McCarthy Tétrault's other great challenge lay within. In 1990 it was a national law firm that was still also four regional operations, a merged firm but hardly a seamless one. The four practices had undergone significant changes in the late 1980s as they prepared for the merger, and local adaptations continued as they dealt with the consequences of the new structure.

FOUR REGIONS WITHIN A NATIONAL FIRM

THE TORONTO LAW OFFICE that was now the Ontario region of McCarthy Tétrault had grown rapidly during the decade of efforts to create a national law firm, and growth continued despite the economic slowdown at the end of the 1980s. Between 1979 and 1989 gross revenues at McCarthy & McCarthy, as it then was, had grown more than six times and the number of lawyers in the Toronto office had increased from barely 100 in 1979 to 205 just before the first western mergers of 1989. During the 1980s the firm had not only pursued mergers within Canada but had also taken the first steps into international operations with a small office in London, England, that opened in 1987. In 1988, when the small but respected Toronto firm of Tilley, Carson broke apart, McCarthy & McCarthy admitted to the partnership several of its lawyers, including the future McCarthy Tétrault chief executive officer W. Iain Scott.*

*A.S. "Pete" Kingsmill, Eric Spindler, W. Iain Scott and Henry Werczinski became partners, Jim Archer and Gordon Willcocks became counsel and Rob Robinson an associate.

The expansion from a few score to hundreds of lawyers and from one office to a national firm was not without growing pains. In October 1993 the Toronto office suffered McCarthy Tétrault's largest departure of a group of lawyers, when Alan Lenczner and four other litigation partners left to form a small firm that would specialize in litigation only. In 1985 Lenczner had won an unexpected victory in the Lac-Corona mining case begun by Douglas Laidlaw. By persuading the court to restore control of a huge new gold discovery in northern Ontario to Corona Corporation, a small exploration company, from the much larger Lac Minerals, which had been invited by Corona to help it develop the discovery, Lenczner had demonstrated in spectacular fashion that despite Laidlaw's death the McCarthy litigation department was as formidable as ever. Lenczner had, however, been among the litigators who sometimes contested what they saw as the corporate lawyers' viewpoint on national firm planning, allocations and other issues. In 1989, one of the few media items skeptical of McCarthy & McCarthy's national firm initiatives was a cover story in *Report on Business Magazine* that questioned whether the practice was as forward-thinking and entrepreneurial as it claimed to be. It included some stinging quotations from Lenczner.[192]

Arthur Scace of Toronto and Mitchell Gropper of Vancouver were featured in Report on Business Magazine's *cover story on the new national law firm.*

When Lenczner and his colleagues left, both sides assured the press that the parting was amicable, and McCarthy Tétrault did begin referring some work to the new partnership, which soon became one of the leading specialist litigation practices in Toronto. Personal ambitions and tensions aside, in fact, litigation boutiques were emerging throughout North America, almost in lockstep with the rise of very large corporate law firms. By the early 2000s it was estimated that half of Canada's leading litigators practised in specialist boutiques; it would have been surprising if none of McCarthy Tétrault's elite litigators had moved to boutiques, where they could attract and serve clients without the infrastructure of a large firm and the frustration of being "conflicted out" of significant retainers because some other part of the firm had represented an opposing party.

Despite the attractions of boutique practice, however, litigation departments continued to grow within the largest law firms and to attract and retain top practitioners. Since the 1970s, the courts' increasing emphasis on prior disclosure and examinations for discovery had been shifting the balance in litigation from oral presentation in the courtroom towards written factums and abundant documentation. As civil litigation became increasingly "paper-based," often it required the teams of lawyers, the specialized research abilities and the support services that large firms were uniquely equipped to provide.

At the same time, the growing importance of litigation (and regulation) in business affairs meant that corporate clients of practices such as McCarthy Tétrault generated an abundance of work that required close cooperation between litigators and corporate lawyers. In 1986, with John Robinette nearing the end of his very long career,* McCarthy & McCarthy had demonstrated it could still attract top-flight litigators when it recruited Ian Binnie from the federal Department of Justice. Binnie built up a stellar practice in constitutional,

*John Robinette continued to practise into the 1990s. He died in 1996 after some years of illness. The firm remembers him with the John J. Robinette Library in its Toronto office and in its knowledge management software system, named "RobiNETte."

aboriginal and international law matters as well as civil litigation, and he helped demonstrate that there was still a place in the largest law firms for top-rank courtroom lawyers. Twelve years later he was appointed directly from practice to the Supreme Court of Canada, where he sat with Charles Gonthier from the Montreal branch of the firm.

Toronto litigators Thomas Heintzman and Ian Binnie celebrate Binnie's appointment to the Supreme Court of Canada.

Less than a year after the formation of McCarthy Tétrault, the Toronto office was rocked by the discovery that one of the partners had been stealing from the firm. Daniel G. Cooper, who was among the first lawyers in North America to see the impact computers would have on business and the economy, had been instrumental in establishing McCarthy & McCarthy's early prominence in computer law. By the late 1980s he had built up a significant practice group in the Toronto office, and "computer law," rapidly being redefined as IT, or information technology, law, was growing into a leading-edge practice area. In November 1990, however, an internal review of disbursements revealed that Cooper had embezzled over $200,000 from the partnership by directing illegitimate payments to a numbered company under his control.

Confronted by Arthur Scace, newly installed as Toronto managing partner, Cooper immediately resigned. He was eventually disbarred, convicted and jailed. By applying the equity Cooper had held in the partnership, the firm largely recovered the stolen money. Despite the shock, the computer law practice continued to grow rapidly under new leaders in Toronto and the other offices across the country.[193]

In the early years of the national firm, the Montreal office faced neither the scandal of a disgraced partner nor the shock of a departure en bloc. Its most notable challenges were economic, for the downturn of the early 1990s hit Montreal's business community harder than Toronto's. The Montreal office strove to maintain its share of the highly competitive Montreal legal market, and through its own efforts and work generated through the national firm, it outgrew most of its rivals all through the 1990s. Leadership systems also preoccupied the Quebec region for several years. In 1993 Jacques Tétrault, who was just about to begin a term as national chair of McCarthy Tétrault, signalled to his partners that at age 65 he intended to step down as managing partner in Montreal. Tétrault's calm, quiet, authoritative leadership during more than a decade at the helm of the Montreal office had won him enormous respect among his partners. His impending departure led to a Quebec region partners' retreat and a wide-ranging review of the office's situation. What became known as the Rapport Burgogne (the "Burgundy Report," from the colour of its cover) aired concerns about the firm's competitive situation in the Montreal legal marketplace and about the need to improve planning and business development. It also suggested that no single individual could replace Tétrault. As a result, the partners established a four-person leadership team. The gregarious, high-profile litigator Gérald Tremblay became chairman and spokesperson for the region. (In one widely publicized triumph, Tremblay represented former prime minister Brian Mulroney in his successful action against the Government of Canada for impugning his reputation in the controversy surrounding Air Canada's purchase of Airbus passenger planes, but he also led many large, complex civil litigation cases and became recognized as one of the best counsel in Canada. He was honoured with the Order of Canada in 2003.) Yves Bériault, Hubert Lacroix and Tam Davis took on responsibility for professional, financial and administrative matters, respectively. This team leadership continued until 1997. By that time the pace of business had picked up, and

A black-tie dinner in June 1997 honoured Robert Black (seated, front centre), flanked here by Patrick Vernon and John Clarry, other Calgary partners and members of the National Management Committee from Montreal, Vancouver and Toronto.

the Montreal practice continued to diversify, particularly in corporate finance, banking, securities and other high-yield practice areas.

In 1997 the region reverted to a single regional managing partner, William Atkinson. Atkinson, who moved to Montreal from Quebec City to take up the role, had always been a supporter of the national firm and a believer in more streamlined, businesslike management of law partnerships. He vigorously supported the involvement of the Quebec region and its lawyers in McCarthy Tétrault's international ventures. Later he would advocate strongly for restructurings that would encourage lawyers in all offices to participate in "national" projects rather than pursue merely individual or local initiatives.

The Calgary office of McCarthy Tétrault, because of the boom/bust cycles of the Alberta energy industry, was perhaps the one hardest hit by the recession that coincided with the formation of the national firm. As Black & Company, the Calgary office had been able to draw on administrative and financial support from Toronto but, with the shift to the national entity, the Calgary office became a fully self-sufficient

Gordon Shrum in the Lawyers Lounge in his firm's new Pacific Centre offices in Vancouver in 1990. Shrum, a graphic designer before he turned to the law, influenced the design of the firm's premises.

region within McCarthy Tétrault. The transfer to Calgary of the headquarters of TransCanada PipeLines, a long-time client of the Toronto office, led to new work in Calgary and also helped confirm that in Alberta the firm would be seen as a utilities' law practice rather than an energy producers' firm. "Either you are with the producers or with the pipeline companies," explained Brian Malone, who in 1989 had succeeded Richard Shaw as the first "homegrown" managing partner of the Calgary office and had a large practice before the agencies that regulated pipeline developments. "Invariably your pipelines are going to conflict with your producers, so there's the line in the sand."

The firm was in the process of moving to larger premises in Calgary in 1989–90, but times of too much work and overcrowded offices could shift suddenly to times of surplus office space and too many underused associates. Richard Shaw, as managing partner in Calgary from 1987 to 1989, recalled a grim day in 1989 when five lawyers were laid off as the firm struggled to balance staff and client load. "The years 1990 to 1995 were tough years to be a managing partner," recalled Malone, "because we were bringing lateral people in, and those don't always work out. It was hard to get the Calgary mix of space, realization rate, lawyers, new hires and everything right."

In the late 1980s, even before the Supreme Court of Canada victory, Black & Company had undertaken merger discussions with some prominent Calgary firms. None came to fruition, partly because of the long-standing polarities between energy and utility companies in Alberta, but McCarthy Tétrault continued to be able to recruit well-regarded Alberta lawyers, including John Zaozirny, who had been minister of energy in the Alberta government in the 1980s. (Zaozirny also practised in the Vancouver office of McCarthy Tétrault.) In the 1990s the Calgary office grew by lateral recruitments of senior corporate and litigation lawyers from other Calgary firms who brought significant new clients with them. Already strong in corporate finance, tax and utilities work, the Calgary office continued to expand in commercial real estate and regulatory practice, and in the later 1990s the practice's innovations in royalty trusts and other financial instruments were widely recognized.

Calgary, like all the regional offices of McCarthy Tétrault, determined its own allocations rules, and one consequence of its vigorous recruitment of established senior practitioners from other Calgary firms was a growing emphasis on allocations based largely on billings. Calgary lawyers, it was said, favoured an "eat what you kill" philosophy—a situation attractive to highly productive senior lateral recruits who arrived at McCarthy Tétrault with their own clients, but one that risked shaping the Calgary office as a collection of competing sole practitioners rather than a single cohesive partnership. By the mid- to late 1990s, however, any lingering sense that McCarthy Tétrault's Calgary office was an outpost of eastern interlopers had largely faded. The fact that prominent Calgary firms were beginning to consider national associations of their own also helped assuage any lingering bitterness from the battles of the 1980s. By then the Calgary office had put the struggles of the early years behind it, and it rode the surging Alberta economy to rapid growth. "After 1995, boom! Away it went!" recalled Malone.

In Vancouver, McCarthy Tétrault could build on the reputation for high-quality legal work that Shrum, Liddle & Hebenton had developed before the merger. It maintained notable strengths in corporate real estate, labour and tax work. In 1988 it had also expanded its litigation department by absorbing the Vancouver litigation boutique Doust & Smith. Len Doust, who soon became counsel to the firm, maintained a wide-ranging and prominent litigation practice. Vancouver also retained a reputation for innovative thinking both in its legal practice and in its approaches to management. Its sabbatical policy, much the most developed of any of the constituent firms of McCarthy Tétrault, influenced firm-wide policy in the 1990s.

One innovation that rapidly spread from Vancouver to the entire enterprise emerged in the winter of 1994–95 when Mitch Gropper, having recently stepped down as managing partner in Vancouver, took a sabbatical and began looking casually into the new phenomenon called the World Wide Web. He quickly concluded that McCarthy Tétrault should have a Web site, and the first one, developed under his direction, went on-line in 1996. "We had one of the first Web sites of any law firm in the country," Gropper recalled. "At that time there were probably fifty law firms in the world that had one." It was the start from which the marketing department developed the much more elaborate McCarthy Tétrault Web sites of later years.[194]

It quickly became clear that digital networking offered great potential for a firm with many lawyers and widely separated offices. The practice's "intranet" soon allowed lawyers and staff in all its offices to share documents and information much more effectively. Digital technology and "knowledge management" systems would gradually become a vital element in the efforts to weld hundreds of lawyers in several widely separated regional offices into an effective, unified national law firm.

MANAGING THE NATIONAL FIRM

TO THE WORLD, the new partnership of McCarthy Tétrault presented itself as a single entity, Canada's national law firm. Since 1983 McCarthy & McCarthy had been committed to the view that its mergers should integrate all participating lawyers into a single partnership, rather than merely creating an association between largely separate firms. In 1990 McCarthy Tétrault's public announcements proclaimed the achievement of that concept.

Behind the shared name and the seamless unity evoked by the "national law firm" brand, however, the reality remained rather different. The western mergers of 1989 were based on a commitment to significant regional autonomy within the merged firm, and the entry of the Montreal partnership reinforced and extended these commitments. Clarkson Tétrault had long believed that the Quebec market would not support a law firm that did not (at the very least) retain its own name and identity within any pan-Canadian association. When the Quebec partners accepted a merger into a single unit with a shared brand, they still needed reassurance that local autonomy would be maintained.

The regional-autonomy principles that had grown up within the original McCarthy–Shrum, Liddle & Hebenton agreement provided this reassurance, and those principles were reinforced in the McCarthy–Clarkson Tétrault agreement of 1990. The changes in wording were slight from one merger to another, but they constituted a significant reinforcement of regional autonomy within the new firm. Regional profitability, defined as "a factor" in determining allocations in the McCarthy–Shrum, Liddle & Hebenton agreement, became "the principal factor" in the McCarthy–Clarkson Tétrault agreement. The views of regional partners were to be "of primary importance" in determining who should be admitted to partnership in each office. Distance, regional sensitivities, Quebec's requirement for significant autonomy and the differences in billing rates and compensation rates in each city had all worked against the instant integration of four law firms in four regions into one seamless whole.

The central governing institution of the merged McCarthy Tétrault was the National Management Committee. It had come into being with the 1989 Vancouver and Calgary mergers as a six-member committee: Toronto had three seats, Vancouver two and Calgary one. With Montreal's entry, the national committee grew to eight members: two from each of the four regions. Even though half the firm's lawyers and more than half its revenues were in Toronto, the merger agreement made full regional participation more important than representation by population or profitability in the composition of the expanded governing body.

Gérald Tremblay, Arthur Scace and Richard Shaw, members of the National Management Committee in the early 1990s.

The determination to avoid even the appearance of undue centralization was further underlined by the choice of its first national chairman. In November 1988 the Toronto firm had chosen Arthur Scace to succeed Harry Macdonell as managing partner of McCarthy & McCarthy.* But 1989 also saw the Toronto, Vancouver and Calgary mergers, under whose terms the new position of national chairman was to rotate among the three principal offices. Scace nominated Sholto Hebenton, one of Vancouver's two representatives on the newly formed National Management Committee, to be the first national chairman of McCarthy & McCarthy. Hebenton's selection recognized

*Scace was named to lead the Toronto firm by McCarthy & McCarthy's management committee, but with the understanding (for the first time) that if there were rival candidates the selection would be determined by a partnership vote.

the leadership he had shown in the Shrum, Liddle & Hebenton partnership and his tireless advocacy for the merger process, but choosing a non-Toronto partner as the founding chairman of the merged firm also underlined Toronto's commitment to making the merger work. Scace became Toronto's managing partner and a member of the National Management Committee. Hebenton served as national chairman for two years, through the merger with Clarkson Tétrault.

McCarthy Tétrault's federal concept affected two vital matters in the new firm: the allocation of profits and the admission of new partners. Both had originally been considered "national" matters to be handled by the leadership of the entire body. In the early planning for a national firm, the intention had been to move as rapidly as possible to a single profit pool, with all lawyers' allocations determined by a firm-wide ranking according to their contributions. But in each regional office, partners had grown accustomed to their own local approaches to allocations. Most of the constituent firms had adopted elaborate processes that authorized allocation committees to balance such factors as experience, billings, business development, client responsibilities and management duties when they granted each partner "points" that translated into shares of the profits. Many lawyers, however much they might contend with their local partners over points, resisted a merger in which authority for such judgements might vanish upwards to some remote and distant "national" committee.

Gradually, plans for a merged allocations process yielded to regional control of how each sector's profits would be distributed. "Points" were allocated to the regions in bulk according to their relative profitability, and partners in each region worked out their individual allocations much as they had done before the merger. Such a system put limits on the "one firm" model McCarthy & McCarthy had been striving for. So long as individual lawyers' incomes depended on their region's profitability, there was a disincentive to refer work to other regions. As Harry Macdonell described it, "Let's say, for example, we had corporate mining lawyers here doing a deal to purchase a mine in British Columbia. We'd want to keep every bit of work here. We'd only use the guys in B.C. to work out something that we couldn't possibly do or couldn't justify sending somebody out to do. That's not how a national law firm should work." But for the time being it was how McCarthy Tétrault had to work.*

Sholto Hebenton, long-time leader of the Vancouver practice and first chair of McCarthy & McCarthy's National Management Committee.

Partnership admissions saw the same evolution. The intention in the early 1980s had been to have a central committee select all new McCarthy Tétrault partners, but that aspiration gave way to agreement that local lawyers knew best their own associates and the needs of the local office. As a result, admission to the McCarthy Tétrault partnership became largely a regional responsibility. The Toronto litigation department, which retained a powerful esprit de corps based on its distinguished tradition, was perhaps most active in attempting to ensure that new litigators throughout the firm met its high standards. But the Torontonians' efforts to vet potential colleagues in other offices seem to have produced mostly resistance.

Regional responsibility for partnership admission proved relatively uncontroversial in the national firm's early years; regional distribution of profits was always more vexed. Initially, each region's share of

*Mitch Gropper of Vancouver recalled being provoked by the sight of Toronto partners of McCarthy Tétrault flying into Vancouver and making use of the boardrooms and facilities of the Vancouver office to work on deals that would generate revenue in Toronto, not Vancouver. "Charge 'em rent!" Gropper recalled growling.

the national profits was calculated on its share of production in the previous two years. During the recession of the early 1990s, however, Montreal, Calgary and Vancouver were harder hit than Toronto, and the production of the Toronto office rose more quickly than that of the other regions. Because distribution of profits was based on past performance, Toronto partners soon calculated that each year their allocations were increasing less rapidly than their share of production. The transfer of profits from Toronto to the other regions rapidly became a sore point. Difficult negotiations were required before a revised formula resulted in a more current application of regional profitability data to allocations among the regional offices. The whole process was another reminder of the centrifugal force that could affect professional partnerships in the absence of a full sharing of profits.

The inevitable inefficiencies related to regional profit centres were a reminder that McCarthy Tétrault had not yet overcome geography. Some partners felt that the confederation that constituted the "national firm" was in reality "four regional silos under a common brand." In 1990 McCarthy Tétrault had gone further than any other firm to enable lawyers in all Canada's principal business centres to begin building a single organization, but the obstacles in the way of combining four regional law practices into a single firm remained substantial.

One way to reinforce ties between the newly associated partners in different cities was referrals of work between the regions. At the time of the merger, some Montreal partners had feared McCarthy Tétrault might merely expedite the westward shift of business in Canada. Soon after the formation of the national firm, however, the Vancouver-based development firm IntraWest (then the Vancouver office's largest client) acquired the ski resort at Mont-Tremblant, north of Montreal, and commenced substantial redevelopment there. Tam Davis, a veteran corporate lawyer of the Montreal office, recalls how he was introduced to Trevor Bell of the Vancouver office and how a team of lawyers drawn from both offices, with Rosemarie Wertschek feeding tax advice from Vancouver, worked together for five months to launch IntraWest's big Quebec project. The project reassured Montreal lawyers that the national firm could send work in more than one direction, and it also helped demonstrate to clients the tangible benefits a national law practice could provide for their interprovincial activities. "We benefited very much from our association right from the get-go," recalled Davis. "The deal flow to Montreal was tremendous."[195]

Brian Malone, Calgary litigator and chair of the National Management Committee of McCarthy Tétrault 1995–97.

In the early talk of a national firm, expectations had been high that young lawyers, and even partners, would move among its offices, gaining experience and maintaining cohesion among the lawyers. Some lawyers did take temporary assignments in other offices, but a continuous uprooting from their home regions was never popular. As early as November 1989, the National Management Committee was anticipating how the new phenomenon called "electronic mail" might soon assist communication among lawyers in different offices.[196]

Another means of bringing the firm's lawyers together was partners' retreats. The first such retreat for the merged firm was held at Whistler, British Columbia, in April 1990. Many participants in that gathering recalled its impact on them and how they began to make both professional and personal discoveries about what the national firm offered them. Carol-Ann Laramée, at the time a new partner in the labour law department of the Montreal office, recalled that her immediate reaction was to declare that had she visited British Columbia earlier she would have abandoned Montreal for the west coast. A Vancouver partner who heard her suggested they could indeed use her if she was serious about moving. Laramée chose not to relocate, but many participants found themselves broadening personal connections and career aspirations as they met colleagues from the other regions.

Brian Malone, the Calgary litigator and managing partner, recalled the message of the guest speakers featured at the Whistler sessions. "These were lawyers from leading British and American firms, saying, 'Guys, why are you sweating this [national firm] stuff? This is the wave of the future!' We really began to feel then this was the way it was going to be.... That to me was one of the culminating events. Everybody felt good: litigators breaking off into sections and meeting with litigators, commercial with commercial, and so on."

Despite the disincentives to intercity cooperation that regional allocations had preserved, the strengthening of practice groups, in which specialists for each office could team up with their counterparts across the country, had been an aspiration for the national firm even before the mergers. Earl Phillips, who was a young labour lawyer at Shrum, Liddle & Hebenton in the early 1980s, recalled that soon after the first merger agreement was reached in 1984 "Gabe Somjen and I went out to Ontario and met with the labour group at McCarthy & McCarthy when they were having a weekend retreat. And we really started working closely with them from 1985."[197] Similarly, lawyers at McCarthy & McCarthy and Clarkson Tétrault had been sharing expertise and referring work during their "best friends" phase in the 1980s.

With such personal contacts and practice opportunities being reinforced at the retreats, firm-wide practice groups began appointing group leaders and arranging for seminars and information exchanges to link lawyers in the regional offices. At this stage, however, practice groups remained voluntary. They encouraged lawyers to consult and cooperate with their colleagues in the other offices, but lawyers remained under no obligation to link their practices to those of other offices.

One unofficial aspect of the Whistler retreat was a gathering of female partners. It was initiated by female partners in the Toronto office who had been active on women's issues there in the 1970s and 1980s. Their proposal for a pyjama party (or at least an informal, women-only gathering) to build solidarity among the women met some resistance. There had been gender tensions in the Toronto office, but some female partners from other offices regarded their firms as refuges from the general sexism of the local legal community more than sources of gender problems. The women's gathering at Whistler went ahead despite these cultural gaps and links among female partners were forged, but no formal women's network emerged within the national firm.

In the years after the mergers of 1989 and 1990, partners' retreats became a way to build cohesion among those from different offices.

WHAT A NATIONAL FIRM CAN DO

NATIONAL LAW FIRMS might be "the wave of the future," but McCarthy Tétrault's expansion across Canada had to mean more than simply more lawyers in more offices in more cities. The national "platform" had to demonstrate real advantages to clients and potential clients, and it had to provide lawyers with challenging work and prestige clients—and also with growing revenues and rising profits. After all the investments in interprovincial expansion in the 1980s, McCarthy Tétrault had to begin to demonstrate that the national firm was not merely bigger but could become more efficient, more successful and more profitable than it would have been had it remained several separate law firms.

At its first meeting, the National Management Committee of the newly merged McCarthy Tétrault formed a Strategic Planning Committee to pursue new business development opportunities. The committee canvassed a great many ideas and suggestions, but gradually it focussed on three objectives: first, to "cross-sell" its services to clients who already used one regional office or one practice group within the firm; second, to market McCarthy Tétrault to large Canadian and international enterprises doing business across Canada; and third, to pursue international opportunities.

Cross-selling based on its new geographic reach was an extension of the referral work the separate firms had been doing during their "best friends" stage before the mergers took place. But McCarthy Tétrault was also emphasising the range and quality of its legal services as well: an energy client would be encouraged to use the firm's banking and securities law expertise, while a tax client might be introduced to the labour law and real estate practitioners. Cross-promotion was the most obvious way to exploit the national scope, and it provided several quick successes. Since the National Management Committee's meetings rotated among all the offices and brought together several of the most senior partners, the firm began linking those meetings to client presentations, in which the leaders of the national body met the management of key clients in each region. In every region, the firm's leaders worked to educate significant clients on the breadth and depth of legal talent and geographic reach McCarthy Tétrault's new national platform could offer.

The second leg of McCarthy Tétrault's business development plan involved seeking more work from large Canadian and international corporations. Marketing to the country's leading corporations essentially meant exploiting the widely held perception that in law firms bigger really was better. In 1984 McCarthy & McCarthy's National Law Firm Committee had argued that as national law partnerships developed, a perception among clients that large and diversified firms had greater legal sophistication than those that remained local and small would help them to seize the market for large corporate retainers. After achieving its national-firm goal, McCarthy Tétrault, now by far the largest Canadian law firm and securely established in key cities across the country, was perfectly placed to exploit such perceptions. The advantage inherent in being the largest and most "national" of the Canadian firms became McCarthy Tétrault's most potent marketing strategy in the early and mid-1990s.

The success of such efforts depended on convincing clients that McCarthy Tétrault's national platform really could provide top-flight services on national transactions more cost-effectively than independent local firms in several cities. Making that proposition credible—and profitable—depended on achieving real efficiencies from the firm's rapid growth.[198]

Late in 1988, McCarthy & McCarthy in Toronto had hired its first chief operating officer. Hiring a non-lawyer executive had been one of the key recommendations of Arthur Scace's 1987 task force on reorganizing management of the Toronto firm, and Geoffrey G. Mackenzie took up the position on February 1, 1989, the very day the merger with Shrum, Liddle & Hebenton became effective. This experiment, however, did not work out well. Mackenzie, a chartered accountant who had held senior executive positions at Coopers & Lybrand, expected a degree of authority that would have been normal in many businesses, but the conviction that lawyers could be managed only by other lawyers remained strong in Canadian law firms in 1989. The partners proved not yet ready to delegate executive responsibilities to a non-lawyer, and

Mackenzie left within a year. He was not replaced, although his role was temporarily filled by William Goodlet, another accountant who had been involved in working out the financial details of the mergers. The new national firm continued with a "federal" administrative structure. From 1990 to 2001, less-senior executive directors headed largely separate administrations in each regional office.

New advertising initiatives were a key part of the launch of McCarthy Tétrault in 1990.

Several other large Canadian law firms also experimented with non-lawyer COOs at about the same time as McCarthy Tétrault. Few of them lasted long; partners remained reluctant to delegate substantial authority to professional managers. Marketing professionals also found law firms difficult employers in the early years of McCarthy Tétrault. Marketing staff who came from the corporate sector found marketing remained an alien concept to many lawyers, who tended to see marketing as "brochures and golf balls" rather than a more substantial process of business development. Gradually, marketing took on a more substantial role at McCarthy Tétrault. Particularly after 1997—when Lise Monette, a veteran of both corporate and law firm marketing departments, became director of marketing for McCarthy Tétrault—marketing became more than an occasional advertisement and began to produce comprehensive new-business proposals and national marketing campaigns.[199]

Student recruitment also grew steadily more complex, driven by law society regulation and the growing sophistication of law students as well as by internal factors. The top-ranked students in whom McCarthy Tétrault was most interested often found all the leading Canadian firms, and others in New York City, competing to hire them. McCarthy Tétrault was frequently successful in attracting its most sought-after candidates to its litigation practice, but in business law the competition from others was always intense.

In Toronto, the firm undertook a program to address gender and diversity issues. With the support of Daryl McLean, Linda Betts and Toronto's executive committee, the partnership began analysing its recruitment policies, and it became the first law firm to commission Catalyst, the women-in-business research organization, to help it develop new diversity policies. One of the things the Diversity Committee's research confirmed was that hiring women and minorities was less difficult than retaining them. By the mid-1990s women constituted a majority of law school graduates and visible-minority students were increasingly well represented among top graduates and among articling students hired at McCarthy Tétrault. But the pressure of large-firm legal practice always produced a measure of self-selection, and many bright, talented young lawyers decided they could have perfectly good careers elsewhere. With the pressures of family responsibilities still falling disproportionately on women, the attrition rate was particularly high among women, who were half or more of McCarthy Tétrault's new hires but a much smaller proportion of those remaining at the time of admission to the partnership.

This attrition among female lawyers, highlighted in the studies Catalyst did for the Toronto Diversity Committee, raised the "quality of life" issue in the mid-1990s. The diversity studies underlined how many talented associates were being recruited and trained at significant expense to the firm and then being lost on quality-of-life issues. It was not exclusively a women's issue, but it operated with particular force for women who felt pressure not to sacrifice family obligations and personal life so completely to their career demands. Unless and until law firms like McCarthy Tétrault could address these issues, they might never have significant numbers of female partners, and they would always be losing lawyers of great promise and potential.[200]

The Diversity Committee helped orient the firm towards part-time work where feasible, as well as leaves and sabbaticals, but the problem was deeply rooted in the nature of practice and in clients' expectations. As Daryl McLean, the Toronto business law partner and one of the first women to become a senior partner in McCarthys, put it, "It's difficult in the business section, because when a deal gets going, I can't say, sorry, I only work four days a week." The problem of lifestyle, affecting everyone but presented with particular force by the steady attrition among promising female associates, remained.

The national firm did begin to implement various administrative efficiencies and to exploit economies of scale. Its larger size quickly reduced its unit costs for insurance, staff benefits, software licences and other administrative costs. It slowly began to move towards firm-wide adoption of common software platforms and e-mail systems, and its intranet gradually increased links between offices and lawyers. Gary Wolff, an accountant who had joined McCarthy & McCarthy's administrative staff with Geoffrey Mackenzie and remained as executive director of the Ontario region (and secretary to the National Management Committee), argued in a 1991 memo that simply adopting the best practices of each region had already begun to improve administration in the national firm. "We have learned from the Vancouver office what 24 hour a day service means and what their expectations and standards of service are all about." Vancouver's accounting and reporting systems had spurred improvements in Toronto and nationally, he wrote. Wolff noted how Quebec's leaner economic climate had taught the Montreal office to focus on profitability and cost recovery more than Toronto had traditionally done. "We have become much tougher on financial issues because of the merger. Montreal is much more financially oriented than the Toronto office." As Wolff observed with some surprise, Montreal charged for receiving a fax from a client and Vancouver charged a fee to open a new client file. "Neither one really fits into [the Toronto office's] culture," he reported, but clearly they could.[201]

A larger issue, which Wolff began to emphasise in almost every monthly financial report he made to the National Management Committee, was work-in-progress, or WIP. WIP represented the value of legal work the firm had done but had not yet billed to the client. In 1990 McCarthy Tétrault's WIP amounted to more than two months' gross revenues (three months in some regions). Wolff demonstrated how dramatic improvements in cash position could be achieved by ensuring more prompt billing. Over the next couple of years, reforms to billing systems and attention to reducing WIP improved revenue collections significantly. Practical benefits such as these gradually began to overcome lingering doubts about the value of professional administration and reinforced the cost/benefit arguments for a more businesslike management of the practice.

More important, economies of scale really did seem to be achievable. In March 1994 Wolff reported that "growth is being achieved without significant cost increases." In March 1995 he reported on an excellent financial situation in which production had risen by 7.5 per cent while costs had been held level, resulting in an 11-per-cent growth in income over the previous year.

One clear proof that the national firm could deliver benefits through economies of scale was the shifting relationship between gross revenues and partnership profits. In the mid-1980s McCarthy & McCarthy's partnership income (after overheads were paid) had stood at barely 40 per cent of gross revenues, and the figure slipped below 40 per cent in the first years of the national firm. By 1996, however, partners' income had risen to 46 per cent of total revenues. It exceeded 50 per cent in 1996 and 1997. Profitability was actually increasing as the firm grew larger.[202]

The other proof of success lay in overall revenues. Revenues never grew by less than 5 per cent annually from the foundation of the national firm in 1990. McCarthy Tétrault was a $150-million-a-year operation in its first year. By 1998 revenues were reaching $250 million, and at the turn of the century they were closing in on $300 million.

Administrative innovations, cross-selling and marketing of the national brand could all help, though their impact remained quite limited in the mid-1990s relative to the potential of the national firm. Business development had been helped by the "national firm" brand, but it still depended heavily on the reputations of individual lawyers and their business-getting abilities. The national firm had not fundamentally changed the way individual lawyers went about their work, and a practice of several hundred lawyers was still operating in much the way it had when it was far smaller.

By the later years of the 1990s, a few lawyers within the firm began to raise questions about its structure and the inability to "unlock the value" in the partnership. There were quiet murmurings that even as part of a firm of hundreds of lawyers spread across four provinces, lawyers were still practising more as individuals than as part of one enterprise, feeling remote from the firm's decision-making processes, and finding it hard to leverage their skills and experience efficiently. The McCarthy Tétrault mergers had joined together first-rank firms in the four major business centres of Canada, but in the increasingly competitive and increasingly global marketplace for legal services it still had to be prepared to fight to maintain its place in every market it served. The national firm, successful as it was, was not yet providing the platform for McCarthy Tétrault to be the strong and effective competitor it could become.

DOMESTIC EXPANSION, INTERNATIONAL PRACTICE | 15

McCARTHY TÉTRAULT'S National Management Committee had concluded early that Canada was becoming a mature market for legal services. McCarthy Tétrault had only limited ambitions for further expansion within Canada, where domestic competition in the legal-services market was growing in Toronto, Montreal, Calgary and Vancouver despite the lure of the national firm and its cross-selling to established clients and marketing to new ones.

During the late 1980s, the Vancouver office opened a small branch office in suburban Surrey and in 1989 Toronto opened one in London, Ontario, but these were established to serve a few significant clients in those locations (principally IntraWest in Surrey and the Canadian Medical Protective Association in London) rather than to become substantial, independent regional offices. The London office grew steadily and by 2004 had more than twenty lawyers in both litigation and corporate practice, but the Surrey office was eventually closed. The vital requirement of McCarthy Tétrault's geographic expansion had been to become strong in the leading business centres of the country. In practice, Toronto, Montreal, Vancouver and Calgary were the only cities with the density of head offices and the volume of large commercial retainers to be vital to a firm of McCarthy Tétrault's scale. McCarthy Tétrault defined the "national" in "national law firm" commercially, more than geographically, and so further expansion within Canada was unlikely. It did not investigate mergers or "green field" opportunities in Winnipeg, Halifax or other cities across the country.

In Canada, the two remaining cities in which McCarthy Tétrault had interests were Ottawa and Quebec City. The Quebec City office that Clarkson Tétrault had acquired though its merger with Drouin et Associés eventually grew to more than thirty lawyers, and its regulatory work and related practices thrived as a branch of the Quebec region of McCarthy Tétrault. Late in the 1990s Quebec City partners led by Marc Dorion had great success in developing national and international project finance retainers and other sophisticated commercial-law opportunities. Clarkson Tétrault had also opened an office in Ottawa in 1982, and this small office was inherited by the national firm. After some early stumbles, Clarkson Tétrault's Ottawa office had built successful practices in trade law and in aboriginal claims work, both led by Michael Flavell, a Clarkson Tétrault lawyer who worked out of both Ottawa and Montreal. It was also developing a practice in regulatory matters, but Clarkson Tétrault had avoided competing for the legal work of Ottawa's local business community so as not to impede its relationship with Gowling & Henderson, the large Ottawa firm that dispensed medical malpractice litigation work on behalf of its client, the Ottawa-based Canadian Medical Protective Association. Without much local business, the Ottawa office had not grown large or become profitable.

McCarthy & McCarthy had considered an Ottawa presence of its own in the mid-1980s. The Toronto firm had come close to merging with a leading Ottawa practice, Herridge Tolmie, in 1984, but when it decided to defer the matter to focus on its merger with Shrum, Liddle & Hebenton in Vancouver, Herridge Tolmie chose to merge with Osler

Hoskin instead. A different Ottawa opportunity arose in 1987 when Thomas D'Aquino, CEO of the prominent lobby group Business Council on National Issues, proposed that McCarthy & McCarthy should launch a "public policy and strategic counsel" practice in Ottawa, with D'Aquino as its head.

Along with D'Aquino, the key asset of the public policy practice was to be the Honourable Donald S. Macdonald, the former federal finance minister who had begun his legal career at McCarthy & McCarthy before entering federal politics in 1962 and who had returned to the Toronto office when he left Prime Minister Trudeau's cabinet in 1977. Between 1982 and 1985 Macdonald had headed the Royal Commission on Canada's Economic Prospects, and his recommendations had launched free trade with the United States as a significant policy option for Canada. By 1987 Prime Minister Mulroney had made free trade the hottest item of national political and economic debate. Macdonald and D'Aquino (himself a prominent advocate for trade liberalization) made a very strong team around which the firm could build a public policy practice in Ottawa and Toronto, and preliminary steps were taken to launch a McCarthy presence in Ottawa around them.

In 1988, however, Macdonald returned to public service as Canadian high commissioner to the United Kingdom, and McCarthy & McCarthy allowed its public policy practice to languish. While it had long been customary for major American law firms to have Washington branches that did lobbying and public policy work, most formal lobbying in Canada continued to be done by non-lawyers. Only in the late 1990s did some large Canadian law firms begin developing public policy practices in Ottawa. Having tested the waters in the late 1980s, McCarthy Tétrault chose not to return.

In the meantime, the national merger had created problems for the lawyer who had built the largest practice in Clarkson Tétrault's Ottawa office, Michael Flavell. Flavell specialized in trade law, but many of his clients in trade disputes were American corporations, and after the McCarthy Tétrault merger many of the Canadian businesses on the other side were long-standing McCarthy clients. Flavell soon grew tired of being conflicted out of work. In 1993 he and two other lawyers from the Ottawa office left to form a specialist trade law boutique in Ottawa.

Their departure forced McCarthy Tétrault to consider either closing or redirecting its Ottawa office. The office could provide regulatory practice support for all of McCarthy Tétrault's offices, but that role left it too small to be very profitable. Some of the regions of the new national firm balked at supporting what seemed to be an unnecessary drain on their resources. By the 1990s, however, McCarthy Tétrault was shedding its reluctance about competing with local law firms in the Ottawa market, not least because Gowlings was building its own network of offices in Toronto and elsewhere. A substantial Ottawa presence by McCarthy Tétrault need no longer threaten the flow of CMPA work to its litigation departments in Montreal and Toronto. Within weeks of Flavell's 1993 departure, McCarthy Tétrault recruited Robert Chapman, a senior corporate lawyer, from another Ottawa firm. Chapman soon brought in significant Ottawa business clients, including several technology companies from Ottawa's "Silicon Valley North." Barbara McIsaac, a litigator from the Department of Justice, joined the office in 1994 and quickly built a substantial practice, particularly in regulatory law. She gained additional distinction as counsel to the judicial inquiry into abuses that occurred during the Canadian peacekeeping mission in Somalia. Tony Keenleyside, who had been in the Ottawa office since the Clarkson Tétrault years, maintained an expanding telecommunications and broadcasting practice.

By building up a local clientele to complement the expanding volume of federal regulatory work, the Ottawa office revived. In 1993 it operated on a stand-alone basis, though for administrative support and allocations it became part of the Ontario region, under the Toronto office. In 1995 the Ottawa team, already grown to eleven lawyers, presented the National Management Committee with a business plan for McCarthy Tétrault's "newest profit centre," proposing to emphasise regulatory and administrative work and technology law, along with a general Ottawa commercial practice. They estimated the office was now profitable and would remain so with a minimum of ten lawyers. In 1999 the national capital office became a fully self-supporting "region" of its own within McCarthy Tétrault, with its own ranking in regional allocations of profits. By the late 1990s it had almost twenty lawyers in "The Chambers," a modern office building with a heritage facade overlooking the National War Memorial in the heart of Ottawa.[203]

By then, international expansion had become an important target for future growth of the firm. McCarthy Tétrault's moves to complete its national mergers had taken place in the midst of the United States–Canada and North American free trade negotiations, Japan's and South Asia's emergence as economic superpowers and Europe's development as an economic union. The economic trends that became known as "globalization" were in full swing. Corporate clients of law firms like McCarthy Tétrault operated far beyond Canada's borders. One of the ambitions of the national firm was to enter effectively into the international market for legal services.

Both McCarthy & McCarthy and Clarkson Tétrault had made overseas ventures before completing their merger. Clarkson Tétrault had briefly had an office in Brussels, and McCarthy & McCarthy decided in 1986 to investigate a London office, at a time when European economic deregulation was promising to make London a capital of European business and finance. Most major Canadian law firms were just beginning to consider going into Europe, and there was a rush of Canadian law office openings in London in the mid-1980s. Clarkson Tétrault, still only "best friends" with McCarthys, chose not to participate in the London venture, but Peter Beattie of the Toronto office and Edward Kerwin, a securities lawyer who had moved from Toronto to Calgary to succeed Patrick Vernon as managing partner at Black & Company in 1984, undertook a study of the opportunities for Canadian law firms in London. They concluded, "If we are to remain as a top rank firm, we must have a presence in London." Kerwin moved from Calgary to London, along with tax practitioner Michael Quigley, to open the first McCarthy & McCarthy office there. In September 1987 Kerwin, flanked by sixteen lawyers from the Toronto office, together with representatives from Shrum, Liddle & Hebenton, Black & Company and Clarkson Tétrault, hosted a reception in the new London office to launch McCarthy & McCarthy's European venture.[204]

At the opening of McCarthy & McCarthy's office in London, England, Canadian high commissioner to the United Kingdom Roy McMurtry chats with McCarthy partner Donald Macdonald, who later succeeded McMurtry as high commissioner.

In its early years the London office, practising Canadian law exclusively, focussed on Eurodollar financings for Canadian clients who were raising money in Europe, on privatization work on behalf of North American investors interested in the large privatizations of the Margaret Thatcher government and on mergers and acquisitions work involving Canadian corporations. But steady growth remained elusive, the Canadian offices seemed far away and the London office remained small and costly. In 1991, after the mergers, McCarthy Tétrault committed itself to remaining in London for another three years, but to ease the high cost of office space in London it reached an agreement to share premises with an Irish law firm, Matheson, Ormsby. A year later the London office still employed only two lawyers and it was costing the partnership $250,000 a year. Success remained some years away for the London venture.[205]

Hong Kong was another prime target for McCarthy Tétrault's ambitions beyond Canada. Launching a Pacific Rim initiative had been part of McCarthy & McCarthy's merger agreement with Shrum, Liddle & Hebenton. Both firms were eager to use the enlarged base provided by the merged operation in order to make the costly but potentially valuable move into Asia. Within weeks of the McCarthy-Shrum merger, Vancouver partners Peter Fairey and Brent Kerr were investigating Asia-Pacific opportunities, and one of the first meetings of the National Management Committee confirmed the decision to open in Hong Kong before the end of 1989. Clarkson Tétrault, not yet part of the national firm, was also interested; it had looked at Hong Kong in 1982 and again in 1988, at which time Jacques Tétrault reported that the costs were "prohibitive." As Clarkson Tétrault partners debated joining the national partnership in 1988 and 1989, the potential to participate in international ventures became another argument in favour of the merger.[206]

Even with the resources of the national firm, opening an office in Hong Kong proved difficult and expensive. McCarthy Tétrault wanted to begin with a limited commitment to Hong Kong, but the Hong Kong Law Society required foreign firms to open substantial offices, with at least one partner present at all times. Simultaneously, the Law Society insisted that such offices could only advise on foreign business; they must not compete with the local bar. As a result, Law Society approval for the new office was withheld for months. McCarthy Tétrault's Hong Kong office finally opened in 1990. Brent Kerr of Vancouver and Clara Wong of Montreal, each of whom already had family connections and legal clients in Hong Kong, were among the pioneers of the new office.[207]

In the early years of the international offices, business development mostly relied on the same traditional means that law firms had used for decades to find and to build relationships with clients. Both in Hong Kong and in London, client development depended largely on the contacts resident lawyers and visiting senior partners could make in the local business community. In Hong Kong as in London, McCarthy Tétrault quickly learned that as a newcomer from overseas it did not have the reputation or connections that supported it so well in Canadian cities. "They were cutting it out of granite," recalled Brian Malone, Ed Kerwin's successor as Calgary managing partner, of the early struggles of the London-based lawyers to build a clientele, and it was not much different in Asia.

Brent Kerr of the short-lived Hong Kong office of McCarthy Tétrault, with Paul Sun, a client.

Despite the optimism about Pacific Rim opportunities, the partnership had agreed at the outset to limit its commitment in Hong Kong to just three years, during which Hong Kong had to become profitable or face closure. In 1992 the firm estimated that the Hong Kong connection had generated over $1 million in work, but costs were high and profits remained elusive. As prospects for Hong Kong's business community to survive the 1997 unification with China began to look brighter, the volume of business from Hong Kong Chinese investing in and immigrating to Canada fell below the targets the firm's Hong Kong business plan had set out. McCarthy Tétrault recruited no large "franchise client" among leading Hong Kong businesses doing business in Canada, and it had limited success in serving Canadian businesses going to Hong Kong to do business in Asia. By 1991 McCarthy Tétrault was looking for ways to reduce its costs in Hong Kong. In February 1993, after further requests from the Hong

Kong Law Society for a larger commitment to the Hong Kong office, McCarthy Tétrault decided to close the office when the lease expired in May 1993. In 1996 a National Management Committee review of overseas activities concluded it was "difficult for us to play a significant role in Asian transactions without a physical presence in the region," but the office did not reopen.[208]

By mid-1993, therefore, Canada's national law firm had only one small, expensive office in London to show for its international ventures. The overseas opportunities for a Canadian law firm, even one with the resources of McCarthy Tétrault, seemed small, the cost of entry dauntingly high. Within a year or two, however, McCarthy Tétrault began developing a new strategy for its international legal practice, one that soon made London a thriving office with an important role in the firm.

McCarthy Tétrault's new international ventures began not with free-standing offices attempting to drum up new business in distant cities but through the overseas extensions of practices in which McCarthy Tétrault already had domestic strengths. One of these was telecommunications law, and "telecom" became an early example of the new model of international business development in the national firm.

By the 1990s, less developed nations all over the world recognized that dependable telecommunication systems were essential preconditions for economic growth. To attract international capital, they needed reliable local and long distance telephone service that supported broadband networks and Internet traffic. Even countries that planned to compete in low-wage manufacturing recognized that in the emerging age of global marketing they had to have the telecommunications infrastructure that would keep their plants in touch with distant head offices, suppliers and markets.

Few national governments, however, were able to shoulder the investments required to build new telecommunications systems under public ownership. Even developed countries in Europe and elsewhere were privatizing telephone systems that had acquired a reputation for inefficiency or political manipulation while under public ownership. But as they looked to private-sector investment to build or take over telephone systems, national governments were often reluctant to see this infrastructure falling entirely under the control of foreign telecommunications giants and investment bankers.

For countries in this situation, Canada rapidly became a regulatory model. Canada had always had a mostly private telecommunications industry and was moving rapidly to more privatization and more competition throughout the sector. Yet the privately-owned businesses had for many years been under national regulation, supervised by a national agency, the Canadian Radio-television and Telecommunications Commission (CRTC). In the 1990s Canada's mix of private ownership and public regulation became a model for countries that wanted to attract private investment while maintaining national telecommunications policies.

McCarthy Tétrault was ideally placed to advise countries looking to emulate the Canadian telecom model. The firm's Toronto, Montreal and Ottawa offices already had a leading practice in Canadian regulatory work and in telecommunications generally. It had long represented many private-sector clients who had emerged to challenge the Bell monopoly (or, in some provinces, the public telephone system) as the CRTC expanded competition in Canadian telecommunications. McCarthy Tétrault's telecom practice groups worked in both English and French, and not only in the common law system but also in the civil law regime that applied not only in Quebec but also in continental Europe and in many former colonies of European powers.

In August 1995 two of the firm's Toronto lawyers, Henry "Hank" Intven and Jeremy Oliver, presented McCarthy Tétrault with a memorandum on international opportunities in telecommunications. Oliver was a corporate lawyer with mining and telecom experience who had practised in the two-lawyer London, U.K., office before returning to

Toronto; Intven had been executive director of telecommunications at the CRTC before being recruited to McCarthy & McCarthy in 1985, where one of his first projects was a federal government retainer to help draft Canada's new Telecommunications Act. Although the legislation's progress through Parliament took years, foreign governments quickly began seeking Intven's advice on the same subject. "In 1990, there were only twelve independent telecommunications regulators in the world; in 2000 there were almost a hundred," recalled Intven. McCarthy Tétrault's special expertise in telecom regulation was a commodity the world suddenly needed, and the market was huge.

Intven and Oliver proposed to McCarthy Tétrault "that the firm might make a commitment to developing international work in the telecommunications area." They wanted a "strategic, industry-focussed approach" for taking McCarthys' telecom experience overseas. From the start, they recognized that what they were proposing in telecommunications could have implications for the whole firm. McCarthys' leadership faced the challenge, they wrote, "of turning a large, highly successful but essentially inward-looking Canadian firm into a competitive player in international legal markets." Telecom law, they suggested, might be the place to start.[209]

In a supporting memorandum, Jeremy Oliver emphasised the significance of the move. "The firm must move to increase the amount of international work we do.... If we do not move more aggressively to capture international work, we risk losing out over time to those of our competitors who do so, in much the same way as some of our domestic competitors suffered, both in terms of clients and in terms of prestige, when we first moved to put the National Firm together...."

Oliver stressed that international work would require "a significant long term commitment" of time, money and energy, perhaps even "changes in the way the firm operates." He had experienced the frustration of relying on traditional business development techniques in London, where the McCarthy Tétrault brand meant much less than it did in Canada. Now he specifically advised *against* new overseas offices for general corporate practice. The logic of the international telecom project was that McCarthy Tétrault should market its legal services in specific overseas market niches where the firm had exportable expertise. His principal examples were telecom privatization and regulation and mining projects and their financing.[210]

These were both fields where McCarthy Tétrault's Canadian lawyers had proven domestic expertise that could translate to overseas markets, but Oliver still emphasised that international success would take a long time. "Starting from the back of the pack" would require a significant investment, he suggested. Cracking open international telecom markets would require planning and investment from the national firm. It would probably have to start with retainers underwritten by the World Bank and other international financial institutions, which could provide excellent business connections but expected competitive bidding on legal fees. For the international initiative to work, the national firm would have to support participating lawyers even as they put aside immediately billable work to develop business opportunities with long-term prospects.

The National Management Committee agreed to support the program, and the "sectoral initiative" in telecommunications blossomed more rapidly than Intven and Oliver had predicted. Intven recalled, "Our first really big project was in Indonesia," a country that had only about three telephones per 100 citizens in 1995. "We helped the Indonesian government to set up a structure, put out calls for applications, design a new regulatory framework, and then negotiate contracts with five consortia that ended up promising to put $6.2 billion into five different regions of Indonesia." Soon Oliver was in Jordan, advising on the creation of Jordan's telecom regulation agency and the privatization of the telephone system. Not long afterwards, he was reporting back on the hazards of riding "the Ougadougou choo-choo" as the firm acquired telecom and mining clients in West Africa. In 1997 the international telecom group was reporting on new developments going on simultaneously in the Middle East, Far East, Latin America and eastern Europe.[211]

International telecom projects generally relied on an eclectic mix of legal procedures, drawing on the local law of the country as well as the national laws of the financing parties and of the contracting telecom companies. McCarthy Tétrault's lawyers, with their Canadian telecom experience and general business law knowledge, were well placed to master this international mix, and they had the advantage that even high-end Canadian billing rates remained well below those of competing law firms from London or New York.

The Montreal office also had a strong telecommunications practice, one that had been cooperating with its Toronto counterpart before the firms actually merged. Montreal's expertise enabled McCarthy Tétrault to emphasise its ability to work overseas in both French and English and in civil and common law jurisdictions—a point soon demonstrated by (among others) Georges Racine from the Quebec City office, who plunged into the telecom practice after transferring to the London office in 1997. Knowledge of French and civil law proved particularly useful in opening up opportunities in francophone civil law jurisdictions in Africa.

Telecommunications was not the only international market for legal services in which McCarthy Tétrault began to find its feet. Lawyers from most offices in the firm had clients among the leading Canadian mining companies, and in the 1990s McCarthy Tétrault's mining lawyers increasingly went with the clients as they pursued development projects and acquisitions around the world.

A third significant field where McCarthy Tétrault began to find receptive international markets for expertise it had built up in Canada was electric-power generation. Here, too, many countries were seeking both to stimulate massive new developments and to privatize their existing electric utilities. Richard Drouin of the Quebec region, a former chair of Hydro-Québec, led the firm's forays in the international power development field, assisted by several lawyers from the Montreal and

Quebec offices as well as from other regions. Recalling one substantial energy project in Zimbabwe, William Atkinson (managing partner first in Quebec City, then in Montreal from 1997 to 2000) declared: "There were six McCarthy Tétrault lawyers on site for a month and a half—and four of them were from Quebec City."

The London office promoted its new premises in 2001, as international law projects spurred rapid growth.

These international projects, whether in mining, telecommunications, power or other fields entirely, required international financing, and the financing was frequently done in the United Kingdom. As a result the London office, already familiar with British privatization ventures, was drawn into a growing number of worldwide projects launched from the firm's Canadian offices. Thereafter McCarthy Tétrault's international ventures and its London office became symbiotic. The London office continued to do "inbound" Canadian work for British companies investing or doing business in Canada, but London-based financing for international projects in telecommunications, electricity and other industries quickly became a primary interest for the lawyers there.

London became less a local office seeking British clients interested in Canada and Canadian clients interested in Britain. Instead, it became the linchpin of McCarthy Tétrault's growing international practice, and as such it rapidly became successful and prosperous. The two McCarthy Tétrault lawyers in London in 1990 grew to more than ten within ten years, making McCarthy Tétrault the largest Canadian law firm remaining in London. By then the London office had the capacity to advise on English as well as Canadian (and international) law. Billings on London matters were rising rapidly, and though local revenues ($660,000 in 1997) did not yet match expenses, the London office's substantial contribution to the firm's international and sectoral revenues was now justifying the cost of the venture.* [212]

Indeed, the whole international practice based on sectoral initiatives in fields where McCarthy Tétrault had exportable expertise was proving successful. In the early 1990s the firm's International Practice Committee had been stressing that international ventures would require slow and costly development and would produce revenues only in the long term. By November 1996, however, international revenues were running well ahead of expenses. Early in 1997, indeed, concerns were raised in the National Management Committee that international initiatives might start to divert the firm's attention from its fundamental focus on domestic clients and Canadian legal practice. Still, in 1999 the partnership was proud to note that the magazine *Privatization International* ranked McCarthy Tétrault tenth overall (eleventh in power-generation projects and in telecom projects) among all global law firms advising on privatization and infrastructure work around the world. McCarthy Tétrault was the first and only law firm not based in London or New York to break into the global top ten.[213]

One area where McCarthy Tétrault's international business development did not immediately prosper was in North America, which really meant the United States and specifically New York City. In 1992 the firm's National Business Development Committee had argued that "first priority should be given to North America for international business development initiatives." But American competition for premium legal work was

*The London office's main boardroom is named for Jeremy Oliver, who died of cancer in 2001, aged thirty-nine.

fierce, and much of McCarthy Tétrault's cross-border work was done in association with leading New York firms, with whom it was reluctant to compete directly. In 1992 Gary Girvan, then a rising younger partner in the Toronto corporate finance/mergers and acquisitions practice, found his partners unenthusiastic about a more exclusive association with the Wall Street firm Cleary Gotlieb, where Girvan had worked on assignment from McCarthy & McCarthy in the 1980s.

With the ongoing integration of capital markets in North America in the 1990s, however, some of the firm's largest, most significant clients were telling them that McCarthy Tétrault should emphasise corporate finance, international tax issues, trade issues and mergers and acquisitions. In these fields, regulatory changes were making it increasingly easy for major Canadian corporations to go directly to New York capital markets for their financing and to Wall Street law firms for their cross-border legal advice. If McCarthy Tétrault had no New York capability, its most important corporate clients could bypass Toronto and go directly to American lawyers for their financing and mergers and acquisitions work, or even switch to the Toronto branch offices that some New York firms had already begun opening.*

McCarthy Tétrault, the corporate-finance lawyers concluded, needed either to "green field" a New York office of its own or to build "a joint venture arrangement with a brand name US firm which can provide a seamless cross-border capital markets and mergers and acquisitions service which we believe will be particularly attractive for Canadian corporations and financial institutions." Either step might threaten the flow of referral work from competing New York firms, but having better access to New York was a priority for the Toronto business lawyers. McCarthy Tétrault, but particularly the Toronto office, began discussions with a handful of leading New York firms, seeking to build the cross-border strategic alliance that would give its clients direct access to top-flight New York legal advice.[214]

*Wall Street firms with Toronto offices included Skadden Arps, Shearman & Sterling, Baker & McKenzie, and Dorsey & Whitney.

The firm hoped to have a deal struck by early 1997, but the search proved difficult. Some leading New York practices already had their own "Canada desks" and Canadian client lists and could not be drawn into an association. Others found the "branded" joint venture McCarthy Tétrault proposed too much like a merger for their taste. In the midst of McCarthy Tétrault's search, news came in 1999 that the Toronto firm Tory, Tory, Deslauriers & Binnington was stealing a march on its Toronto competitors by merging with the New York firm Haythe & Curley, creating a fully merged cross-border entity with 200 lawyers in Toronto and 75 in New York City.

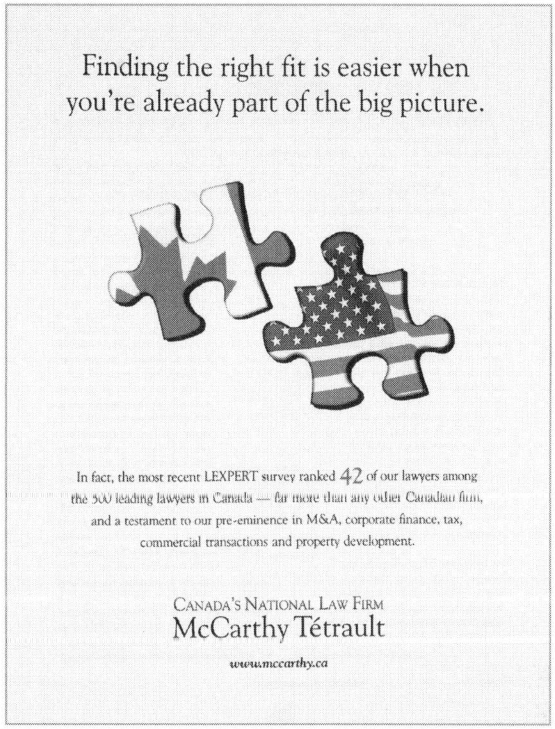

By the end of the twentieth century, success in cross-border legal practice was important to large Canadian law firms.

Within a few months, however, the business lawyers had what they needed: an alliance with the top-tier New York firm Fried, Frank, Harris, Shriver & Jacobson. Through the alliance, McCarthy Tétrault's Canadian clients would have privileged access to the expertise of a first-rate Wall Street practice without having to bypass their Canadian counsel. In exchange the New York firm, which had not previously done a large volume of Canadian work, acquired preferred access to the capital markets and M&A work of McCarthy Tétrault and its blue-ribbon Canadian client list. The "McCarthy/Fried Frank Alliance" became effective in June 2000. To facilitate liaison between the allied firms, McCarthy Tétrault opened its own small New York office.[215]

Meanwhile, the growing significance of cross-border and international ventures was putting new stress on fundamental aspects of McCarthy Tétrault's "federal" structure. McCarthy Tétrault was still a group of regional profit centres, in which the partnership within each region managed its own affairs and allocated the region's profits. Increasingly, international initiatives were "national firm" initiatives more than regional ones, driven by teams of lawyers drawn from all across the partnership. International work for a Canadian company was likely to involve lawyers from several Canadian offices and London as well, but if the head office of the client firm happened to be a client of one regional office, the regional profit centre model dictated that the revenues should be credited to the regional office, instead of being accounted as "international" revenue. In the early stages of the international successes, a formula was worked out to "tax" regional offices to provide a budget for the business development costs of overseas business, but regionalizing international costs and benefits was difficult, and there was no obvious regional beneficiary for the growing revenues that international work was delivering to the partnership.[216]

International success, in fact, was reinforcing the perception that the future of the firm lay in practice groups and industry-specific business development programs, not with regional offices. As Jeremy Oliver had suggested in his international-telecom memorandum in 1995, the international efforts of the firm were beginning to influence domestic business development strategies. A reappraisal of how McCarthy Tétrault should be managed and organized at home as well as abroad began to seem timely.

When McCarthy Tétrault completed its mergers in 1990, it was still innovative for a Canadian law firm to have offices in several Canadian cities. By the end of the 1990s, it was routine. The interprovincial firm (impermissible in the 1980s, still unappealing to many Canadian law firms in the early 1990s) suddenly became the norm, and McCarthy Tétrault lost its claim to be Canada's sole "national" law firm. At the same time, its attention was increasingly turning beyond the borders of

Canada. McCarthy Tétrault no longer sought an exclusively "national" image, and international developments in law firm management were much on the minds of the partnership's leaders.

These international issues were coming to the fore in January 1997 when Toronto partner Arthur Scace returned to the position of national chair. Since 1989 the chairmanship had circulated among representatives of the several offices: from Sholto Hebenton of Vancouver (1989–91) to Scace (1991–93) to Jacques Tétrault of Montreal (1993–95) and to Brian Malone of Calgary (1995–97). Scace's election to a second term reflected an innovation initiated by Malone, whose term had convinced him the job was too important to be rotated every two years among the offices. He argued the firm needed a full-time chair, and the partners agreed that in future the eight National Management Committee members (two per region) would choose a ninth person to be national chair. The chair would be based in Toronto but could come from anywhere in the practice and could be elected to consecutive two-year terms.

Scace reassumed the chair of the National Management Committee at a time when global trends in law firm management were becoming of consuming interest to the leaders of large practices, and the new definition of his role was a small step towards strengthening central management.

One sign of the new management trend might be called the *American Lawyer* phenomenon. The monthly magazine *American Lawyer*, founded by lawyer-entrepreneur Steven Brill at about the time McCarthy & McCarthy had begun planning its expansion into Calgary, had become one of the most successful legal publications in the United States, and its focus was always the business of law firms. A cornerstone of its influence was its annual "AmLaw 50" (from 2001, the AmLaw 100), a ranking of law firms by size and, more importantly, by profitability. The magazine was remarkably successful at acquiring traditionally confidential data about law firm revenues. Although its statistics were never entirely trusted, they were widely read and cited.

The magazine—and the consultancies and analysts who emerged at about the same time to advise on law firm management—expressed a new assumption about law firms. They observed that the fundamental criterion by which the success of a firm should be judged was not numbers of lawyers, offices or leading counsel, and certainly not some intangible like job satisfaction. The benchmark that really mattered for judging law firm success was now "PPP"—profit per partner.

The fundamental message legal consultants and legal journalists conveyed was that the most likely predictor of a leading firm's ability to remain competitive was its profitability, and its profitability depended increasingly on the ability to undertake and implement strategic planning. A successful law firm, they argued, had a simple partnership structure, a high ratio of associates to partners, centralized management, a carefully controlled cost structure, sophisticated client relationship processes and the ability to strategize and market itself in profitable market sectors, *as other businesses did*. This, they argued, was the kind of law firm that delivered high profits per partner, and only law firms that achieved that would have the revenues, as well as the leadership and businesslike organization, to succeed in the competition to recruit and retain the best lawyers and to attract the most profitable clients, whether in New York, London, Frankfurt, Hong Kong or Toronto.

In an increasingly competitive market for legal services, law firm analysts argued, only the strategically managed firm was likely to prosper. Its success, they suggested, would come at the expense of lawyers with traditional ideas of how law firms should be run. Its real competition might well come from other professions, notably accounting, already dominated by a handful of global partnerships with highly professional managements. These firms shared a commanding position in auditing and consulting and seemed poised to move into legal services as well.

By 1997, analyses on international law firm competitiveness were frequently being attached to briefing papers for meetings of the McCarthy Tétrault partnership and the National Management

Committee. Mostly, these confirmed that McCarthy Tétrault had good reason to judge itself by the emerging global standards for law firm performance. By the mid-1990s, international surveys of law firms consistently ranked McCarthy Tétrault among the thirty largest in the world. Its leading lawyers and practice groups were highly regarded in domestic and international surveys. As the only Canadian firm in the international top fifty it was well ahead of its domestic rivals, many of which were just beginning the expansion processes for which McCarthy & McCarthy and its partner firms had fought in the 1980s.

Tax specialist Arthur Scace led McCarthy & McCarthy into the national firm in 1990.

However, global comparisons also exposed McCarthy Tétrault's relative weaknesses. Divided as it was into regional profit centres, McCarthy Tétrault was not truly a single, centrally managed partnership. It was not well equipped to implement strategic business planning, and as a result a significant volume of its work continued to be in relatively low-value fields. Compensation for partners was still closely tied to the success of their regional office, rather than their contributions to the firm as a whole. The practice's partner-associate ratio was close to even, which meant it had more partners than many global firms with more lawyers and much greater revenues. For all these reasons, McCarthy Tétrault's place in global profitability rankings did not come close to its ranking by size. It was powerful in the Canadian marketplace, the comparisons suggested, but its domestic position might change rapidly if the emerging global competition among law firms came to Canada.

In response, McCarthy Tétrault began to develop two initiatives. One was directed by the national chair and the National Management Committee. The other started to work its way up from within the Toronto office.

Arthur Scace took to the road almost as soon as he became national chair of McCarthy Tétrault in 1997. Using his and the firm's extensive international connections to meet regularly with leaders of key law and accounting practices in New York and London, he began a close investigation of the evolving international trends for law firms. Between April 1997 and March 1998, Scace briefed the National Management Committee six times on his international consultations. Everything he heard from law firms, accountants and consultants in New York and London confirmed that law was becoming a highly competitive global business at a rapid rate.

There seemed to be two broad lines developing in the evolution of legal practice. On one hand, the leading British, European and American law firms, particularly the elite ones that specialized in corporate finance and mergers and acquisitions work, were rapidly evolving into transatlantic partnerships and extending their practices to all the major financial centres. Consolidation and extended geographic reach among law firms was now a global phenomenon. The day of the merely national law firm was already ending.

The competing alternative that loomed was the Multi-Disciplinary Partnership, or MDP. In theory, MDPs meant partnerships between accountants, management consultants and lawyers to build a single organization offering a whole range of professional services to businesses. In practice, it seemed inevitable that if this consolidation took place the MDPs would be led and dominated by accountants. Accounting and consulting firms like KPMG, Arthur Andersen and Ernst & Young already employed tens of thousands of professionals worldwide. They had built themselves into centrally managed, well-capitalized global enterprises on a scale far beyond even the largest of law firms. In any convergence between law, accounting and consulting, the giant accounting firms seemed certain to swallow the much smaller law firms.

Between 1997 and 2000, it seemed quite possible to Scace that McCarthy Tétrault might soon become a participant in one of the international mergers taking place, either by joining a global law firm or entering into an MDP with one of the accounting goliaths. In September 1997, when the merger of the global accounting companies Price Waterhouse and Coopers & Lybrand underlined the scope and speed of the integration process, the National Management Committee agreed that "a subcommittee of the managing partners and Scace would be established to act quickly if intercontinental mergers start to occur." In December 1998 Scace analysed how partnerships of British and European (particularly German) law firms were attempting to lock up the European legal-services market before the Americans took it over. In June 1999 he reported what looked like a watershed in law firm mergers: the merging of the top-ranked Clifford Chance of London with the powerful Rogers & Wells of New York.

Consolidation of legal services was shifting from national to international, Scace emphasised, but he remained confident that no firm matched McCarthy Tétrault's presence in the four major Canadian commercial centres and, as a result, "when attention is focussed on Canada, as predictably will ultimately be the case, our firm will register prominently." Meanwhile, the expansion of accounting firms into legal services also continued, most notably in Canada with the emergence and rapid growth of Donahue & Partners, a law firm associated with the international accounting and consulting business Ernst & Young.*

Law societies in several Canadian provinces and the Canadian Bar Association vigorously opposed multi-disciplinary partnerships, arguing

*Launched by Canadian lawyers employed by Ernst & Young, the firm was first called Donahue Ernst & Young. In 2001 it yielded to the Law Society of Upper Canada's rule against non-lawyers' names in law firm names, and became Donahue LLP. With Ernst & Young's support, it rapidly expanded to several Canadian cities.

that the inherent conflict between the confidentiality obligations of lawyers and the public disclosure obligations of auditors made such associations impossible. The governing bodies declared that it would be an ethical breach for lawyers to be partnered with non-lawyers, unless it was absolutely clear that the association was controlled by lawyers. (Governing bodies of accountants had made a similar analysis and concluded MDPs would be acceptable only if they were controlled by accountants.)

McCarthy Tétrault litigator Thomas Heintzman was president of the Canadian Bar Association as it argued the case against MDPs, but the firm's leadership was inclined to the view that if the market wanted MDPs, opposition by law societies and bar associations would probably be as quixotic as the campaign against interprovincial firms had proven in the 1980s.

In the end, however, the 1999 transatlantic merger of Clifford Chance and Rogers & Wells and the emergence in Canada of accountancy-linked law firms like Donahue & Partners marked the high point of professional convergence. The prospect that McCarthy Tétrault would soon become part of either a global law firm or a multi-disciplinary partnership faded very rapidly.

It became clear that the American, British and German law firms that were leading the international mergers were not particularly interested in maximum size or comprehensive geographic coverage. Their goal was to compete for a limited range of very high-value clients and work, mostly concentrated in corporate finance, mergers and acquisitions, tax, and related specialties. For that, transatlantic law firms needed a limited number of lawyers in a limited number of offices, located almost exclusively in the world's leading financial centres.

Absorbing a large law firm in Canada did not fit that model. Considering the limited amount of high-value work an international law firm might want to pursue in "smaller" countries like Canada, dominant practices like McCarthy Tétrault were already too large to be attractive merger partners. Measured by the standards of elite New York and London law firms, their revenues were too low and their clients and deals too small to add significant value to global leaders. As a result, international mergers among leading firms extended only to London, New York, Frankfurt and a handful of global business centres; for the most part they did not extend to Toronto, Sydney, Johannesburg or other secondary centres. McCarthy Tétrault did not want some competing Canadian firm to snatch away its leadership through an international merger, so it maintained a watching brief on international developments. But by the start of the new millennium the likelihood of leading Canadian law firms joining international networks had faded.*

The probability that the Big Five accounting firms would soon absorb the leading law firms through multi-disciplinary partnerships also ceased to be a threat (or lure), but this was the result of a specific event: the collapse of the Houston-based energy trading firm Enron Corporation in 2001. When Enron's financial manipulations were exposed, it plunged in a few months from US$100 billion a year in revenues to liquidation, and its collapse pulled down Arthur Andersen LLP. Arthur Andersen, accused of compromising its auditing standards in order to protect its consulting contracts with Enron, was abandoned by its clients and was effectively out of business by the summer of 2002.

*The Canadian situation was mirrored in Australia. There, too, a handful of national firms had come to dominate the corporate-law market. Even though these firms held extensive merger talks with the international giants, eventually none attracted a global merger partner.

The abrupt disintegration of one of accountancy's Big Five convinced the marketplace, much more decisively than law society jeremiads, that mingling separate professions in a single partnership really was problematic. The results of that shift in belief were felt around the world. The trend towards rapid integration of law firms with accounting/consulting companies evaporated, and the emerging global law practices were suddenly released from the threat that the Big Five accounting firms were about to swallow them or take away their businesses. In Canada, Donahue LLP and other "captive" law firms dissolved almost overnight. By 2001 McCarthy Tétrault was putting behind it the likelihood of imminent international mergers or a wholesale takeover by multidisciplinary partnerships.*

Nevertheless, both domestic and international considerations were pushing the law firm to re-examine the internal organization it had established at the end of the 1980s. The advantage, at least in branding, that McCarthy Tétrault had enjoyed since 1990 as "Canada's national law firm" was fading; by 2000 the partners were reconsidering the value of the brand. Competitors, either by merging with existing operations or "green fielding" new offices in Canadian business centres, suddenly produced a cluster of competing national firms.

In the 1980s, competitors that responded to McCarthy Tétrault's national initiative had done so mostly by building affiliations or associations with independent law firms in other cities. Most of these liaisons proved too fragile for the accelerating pace of competition. Associations that operated as independent units in each city offered too little to hold them together, and most either moved on to full mergers or dissolved their alliances. Ogilvy Renault of Montreal, Toronto's Osler Hoskin, and Vancouver's Ladner Downs had built one such network for overseas and interprovincial cooperation in 1989 and 1990, but it collapsed in 1996 (Ladner Downs had already withdrawn) as Ogilvy Renault launched its own Toronto operations. Goodman & Goodman of Toronto had begun an association with Phillips & Vineberg of Montreal, but when their merger talks broke down in 2000 the Montrealers withdrew.

Other loose "partnerships of partnerships" moved towards full mergers. Fasken Campbell of Toronto and Martineau Walker of Montreal, which had formed an association in 1986, moved in 1999 to a full merger and soon added the Russell & DuMoulin firm of Vancouver to become Canada's second-largest partnership, just slightly smaller than McCarthy Tétrault. In 2000, within days of splitting from Goodman & Goodman of Toronto, Montreal's Phillips

*McCarthy Tétrault's Calgary office recruited a group of Donahue "refugees" as that firm disintegrated.

& Vineberg merged with another Toronto firm, Davies Ward Beck. Meanwhile, Gowlings of Ottawa and Toronto undertook a series of mergers in Montreal, Toronto, Calgary and Vancouver in 2000 and 2001. Toronto's Borden & Elliott and Fraser & Beatty separately found merger partners in Montreal and western Canada, to produce the national firms Borden Ladner Gervais (in 2000) and Fraser Milner Casgrain (built between 1998 and 2002). Meanwhile, the powerful Toronto practices of Blake Cassels and Osler Hoskin also began developing national reach, mostly by "green fielding" new offices of their own, particularly in Montreal, rather than by mergers with established firms. Calgary's Bennett Jones, having retreated from merger talks with Tory, Tory, Deslauriers & Binnington of Toronto in 1999, began building up its own Toronto office.

By the start of the new century, Canada was experiencing the same phenomenon as other countries: the emergence of six or eight dominant law firms with offices in all the major business centres. In Britain the leading firms had long been called the "magic circle," in New York the "upper echelon," in Australia the "golden circle." Toronto had for decades spoken of the "Seven Sisters" of Bay Street. Now it was clear that a cluster of perhaps half a dozen national law firms was emerging in Canada, as leading Canadian corporate-law practices began operating as unified partnerships across several provinces.

The Canadian "top tier" still varied from city to city. Firms without national reach still dominated several markets, and further mergers or expansions by key enterprises could change the composition of the leading pool very rapidly. In 2003, however, an analysis by *Lexpert*, a Toronto business law magazine, identified seven partnerships that were emerging as the leading nationals: Davies Ward Phillips & Vineberg, Fasken Martineau, Fraser Milner, McCarthy Tétrault, Ogilvy Renault, Osler Hoskin and Stikeman Elliott.* [217]

* *Lexpert* had identified Toronto's Seven Sisters in 2002 as (in alphabetical order) Blake Cassels, Davies Ward, Goodmans, McCarthy Tétrault, Osler Hoskin, Stikeman Elliott and Torys. Of these, Torys and Goodmans remained largely Toronto-based (though Torys had a large New York office). Ogilvy Renault, Bennett Jones and Farris & Company continued to be leaders in Montreal, Calgary and Vancouver, respectively.

The rapid emergence of this national top tier was seen by outside observers as demonstrating the perspicacity of McCarthy & McCarthy and its merger partners in the 1980s, and confirming that the future lay with "the McCarthy model." That is, full mergers, rather than the largely discredited alternative of loose associations or partnerships of partnerships, were agreed to be the only practical option. Journalist Margot Gibb-Clark reported in 1999 that McCarthys' ten-year-old national-firm model give it "a clear head start over many competitors." A year later, Andrew Willis wrote in the *Globe and Mail:* "McCarthy Tétrault's model is the one that Canada's firms have adopted." *Lexpert* concluded in 2003 that "no firm can match McCarthy Tétrault in terms of its strong presence in all four major markets in Canada."[218]

By the later 1990s, however, the partnership's leadership in Canada had become a matter of degree, not the unique position it had previously enjoyed. Competition within the new cluster of dominant firms was fierce. The market for legal services had not expanded as fast as the largest law firms, and it was by no means certain that there would continue to be room in the top tier for all the contenders. International comparisons strongly suggested that in this kind of competition the advantages came not from being "national," or having the most lawyers, or from having effective media campaigns. The lesson from global leaders in the legal services marketplace was that the advantage went to those that proved themselves able to plan and manage strategically.

It was precisely here, beneath the satisfactions of being the largest law firm and the first to build a national platform, that concern was rising within McCarthy Tétrault. Long traditions of legal practice, reinforced by the loose management structure of McCarthy Tétrault's "federal" system of regional offices acting as independent profit centres, were hobbling its efforts at strategic management and systematic business development, just as those things were becoming critical to law firm success.

STRATEGIC PLANNING | 16

THE DESIRE TO MANAGE the firm's business differently was as old as McCarthy Tétrault. Soon after the 1990 merger, the National Management Committee had formed a National Business Development Committee to pursue the opportunities, such as "cross-selling" across the regions, provided by the national platform. The next year, when the National Management Committee was considering the likelihood of slow growth in Canadian legal markets and re-emphasising international operations, it formed a new International Business Development Committee, with key National Management Committee members included ex officio. Over the next year this committee canvassed a great many ideas, including alliances with New York and European firms, "regional business partners," and "country desks" within the firm.

Few of these proposals bore fruit, aside from the successful international sectoral initiatives in the mid-1990s. In 1998, however, a new planning initiative began to work its way up within the Toronto office of McCarthy Tétrault.

W. Niels Ortved, a litigator who had come to McCarthy & McCarthy in the 1980s from a small-firm, criminal defence counsel background, was elected as Toronto managing partner at the start of 1997 after having filled a number of other management roles, and he and his regional executive committee (Jim McCartney, Kirby Chown and Christopher Montague, along with administrator Gary Wolff*) immediately launched an examination of the Toronto office's competitive position. Its conclusion was that change was urgently required.

For Ortved, the crucial evolution in legal practice was being imposed from outside, from clients. Clients, he wrote in a 1997 brief to the Toronto partners, may once have been "loyal to firms providing legal work" and "typically passive" in assessing the services they received. They would "refer all their legal work to a single firm" and "rarely questioned the fees charged." Those days were over. Corporate clients and their legal departments had become "selective, demanding, and extremely cost conscious."[219]

*Montague left late in 1997 to join Toronto-Dominion Bank and was succeeded by litigator Malcolm Mercer, who also became the committee's informal statistician.

This change affected the litigation and business law sections of the firm equally. In the 1990s major banks, insurance companies and other financial institutions were broadening their options for legal services by dealing with more than one law firm. At the same time, the Canadian Medical Protective Association, which had been an exclusive litigation client of the Toronto firm (for Ontario) and the Montreal firm (for Quebec) for a century, also began spreading its work around, not from dissatisfaction with McCarthy Tétrault but in order to have more than one supplier of legal services. As well, the changing marketplace was breaking down the traditional separation between "solicitor's work" and "litigator's work." A great many takeover bids, restructurings and other large corporate transactions involved litigation or regulatory processes. "We've taken the position that your commercial practice is only as strong as your litigation support," said Ortved, "and we have demonstrated that is true in innumerable cases." In both Montreal and Toronto, McCarthy Tétrault had traditionally been rather unusual among front-rank business law firms in also having strong litigation departments, but in the 1990s the need to provide litigation expertise alongside business law services made litigation increasingly important to the national firms.

Ortved concluded that in response to the changing client environment and the heightened competition among law firms that had resulted, McCarthy Tétrault had to become very precise in matching its billings to the specific work done. Senior lawyers who made vital and decisive contributions were entitled to bill commensurately for their work, but it would have to be clear that the same rates were not routinely being charged for the lawyers who supported, facilitated and assisted. Such an approach was not entirely easy to apply. McCarthy Tétrault, like most leading Canadian law firms in the 1990s, had more partners than associates, and it was evident that partners were not restricting themselves to high-value, leading-edge cases, but were doing a good deal of routine work as well. "We had more supervisors than those supervised. I called it Upsidedowntown," recalled Ortved.* 220

Litigator Niels Ortved helped launch the strategic planning initiative after becoming the Toronto managing partner of McCarthy Tétrault in 1997.

*A mid-1998 study by the *Financial Post* showed that of Toronto's twenty largest law firms only one had more associates than partners.

Jim McCartney cited competition from other law firms as a second motivator for change. Comparative market analyses indicated that McCarthy Tétrault had performed quite well through the first half of the 1990s, but competition was intensifying, particularly in core business areas such as corporate finance, mergers and acquisitions and restructurings—all challenging, high-end and profitable fields. Some Toronto firms had limited themselves to capital markets work and were becoming very effective at pursuing promising opportunities, notably at this time in the technology and communications sectors. Some competitors were becoming more aggressive in recruiting highly regarded practitioners. McCarthy Tétrault, still in many ways a firm of individual lawyers across many diverse fields, was not yet fully organized to execute similar strategies. Leaders in the business law section were becoming concerned about the practice's competitive position in profitable, challenging new opportunities.

In October 1997 the Toronto executive committee sent the Toronto partners a blunt memo outlining the changing environment and the need to respond by encouraging leadership and identifying promising opportunities—and by reorganizing the firm to make these two goals achievable.[221] In January 1998 Ortved followed up by creating what became the Toronto Strategic Planning Committee, recruiting Tom Akin, Mary Beth Currie, Barry Ryan, Gordon Sato, René Sorell and Paul Steep to join McCartney and himself on the new committee. This was the formal beginning of an initiative that was to have large and lasting influence on the practice of law throughout McCarthy Tétrault. The October 1997 memo was barely three pages long but, as Ortved recalled in 2004, "we spent the next five years on it."[222]

Simply joining the committee was not, however, what Barry Ryan, a Toronto partner in the banking practice, would remember as the touchstone of his commitment to making change at McCarthy Tétrault. In the summer of 1998 Ryan took advantage of the firm's new sabbatical policy. He spent three months in Europe, away from the law and "reading the thirty-five novels that had been piling up," before returning to work refreshed and invigorated, but also with a renewed sense that the partnership was not all that it could be. He came back to the Toronto Strategic Planning Committee with a sense that McCarthy Tétrault's standing in the marketplace was under threat, and that partners of his generation (Ryan had joined McCarthy & McCarthy as a student in 1981) had to begin shouldering the leadership burden that earlier generations of partners had carried. "It was very clear by the early 1990s that our position was not as it had been. And I think there was this very strong group of young lawyers...this group of calls from the late seventies and early eighties who started to assume that role of leadership."

Gary Girvan, who was becoming recognized as one of the leading merger and acquisition lawyers in the country, recalled being galvanized when, late in 1997, he was part of a corporate finance team that had secured the promise of a very significant retainer from one of the firm's principal financial services clients, only to learn that another partner had put McCarthy Tétrault out of the running by accepting a much less substantial role on behalf of a rival institution. The incident confirmed Girvan's sense that the traditions of law firm practice, which entitled every partner to take on work much as a sole practitioner would, meant the partnership lacked any effective way of pursuing its larger interests and was wasting its strengths.

René Sorell, a highly regarded corporate finance and securities lawyer (called to the bar in 1978), recalled a more general frustration. He felt that under the loose, federalized partnership that had evolved, McCarthy Tétrault had become unable to reward its real leaders, give clear direction to associates, or deploy its strengths effectively. National management, saddled by the firm's structure with representative rather than executive duties, seemed to him unable to address the issues effectively. "The reason you had management in the 1990s," he said, "was to respond to crisis." Sorell felt the much celebrated feat of having built a national law firm meant little in the day-to-day business of effectively serving its clients. He feared McCarthy Tétrault was falling behind at that task and failing to address the problem. For him, that was the impetus that really built the Strategic Planning Committee into a vehicle for changing the way the firm did business.

The driving urgency for change, he believed, came from "a collection of lawyers who were worried. It was not just started by the top. We were concerned that we had had strengths in the past and we were not going to maintain them."[223]

The documentary record confirms that the Toronto Executive Committee instituted the process for strategic planning; it was Ortved who recruited Ryan, Sorell and the others to the Strategic Planning Committee. On the other hand, the firm had been talking of "strategic planning" for years without much visible impact on the way it did business. The mix of frustration and ambition building in some partners in the Toronto corporate and litigation departments did lend an edge to the project once it got started, as a younger generation of partners began to assert leadership. In Ryan's view, "The existing management recognized that it was time for that to occur and not only didn't get in the way of it, but actually supported it."

In the beginning, Toronto's ideas about strategy focussed on clients. The committee, however, rapidly shifted its attention inward, to the way the firm was run rather than to the clients it sought. It began to apply to McCarthy Tétrault ideas about law firm organization that were widespread in consultancies, in magazines like *American Lawyer* and *Lexpert* and in the best-managed professional practices, notably the global accounting and consulting partnerships.

Those who advocated these ideas of law firm management argued that group practice, rather than individual practice, had to be the basis of modern professional partnerships. Second, they looked for truly effective and measurable "leverage": procedures that systematized the delegation of work so that senior lawyers' time was used in the most productive manner. Third, they wanted "empowered" managers with genuine authority to direct the practice groups and the firm at large. Fourth, and perhaps most significant, they advocated permitting these managers to influence partners' allocations so as to reward contributions to the partnership's objectives. Client requirements were not forgotten, but transforming the firm's organization and its lawyers' work practices (rather than, say, simply reviewing business development strategies) had been identified as the fundamental requirement for success in the increasingly demanding legal-services marketplace.

Ever since authority in law firms had passed from strong owners or leaders (like Leighton McCarthy and Beverley Matthews at McCarthy & McCarthy in Toronto, or Gordon MacDougall and William Macklaier at the Lafleur firm in Montreal) to the collective rule of the whole partnership, Canadian firms had generally entrusted allocations decisions to committees largely separate from the elected administrators. Keeping allocations decisions away from management ensured that final authority—in allocations and in administration—remained with the partnership as a whole, but at a price. Management had been deprived of a standard management tool: financial reward. This the Toronto Strategic Planning Committee now proposed to change. In its plan, practice group leaders would acquire "significant input into the allocations process to influence groups and individuals."[224]

The law firm could continue to respect and reward individual achievement, but if it was going to stake its future on business plans made and implemented within practice groups, then contributions of partners to the success of their groups would have to become central to their allocations. "Non-billable" time, time not being spent directly on legal work for clients, would be recognized as a resource. Partners who devoted non-billable time to generating business, developing strategies or achieving leverage by directing work to other partners and associates would be rewarded in their allocations. More importantly, a partner's contribution to the success of the team's objectives would become more important than individual effort to his or her financial rewards. In Ortved's view, the older allocations regime had essentially become a seniority system rather than one that really rewarded leadership and accomplishment, and it was becoming untenable. "We really had to reorient the firm towards, 'What are you doing this year, and what's the value added to the firm?'"

To reinforce the process of change, the Toronto Executive Committee also began to push for a more rigorous partnership admissions process. To increase the ratio of associates to partners, the Toronto partnership ended the informal understanding that associates who remained for six years would be admitted more or less automatically into the partnership. To slow down the "partner track" and to allow more time for assessment of partner candidates, Toronto introduced the category of "income partner," an intermediate stage for those associates still being considered for admission. Partnership would become a greater reward for those who demonstrated their potential to lead once the new selection system was in place. Within a few years, the partner-associate ratio was being changed in the Toronto office. "It is absolutely one of those things that worked. And it has been adopted all over Canada," recalled Ortved.

Meanwhile, Toronto's Strategic Planning Committee prepared its report to the Toronto partnership. By then its proposals were growing into a campaign to change the culture of the firm, shifting it from a collection of largely autonomous partners to an organization whose members would work together systematically in pursuit of predetermined objectives. To persuade the partnership to buy their vision for McCarthy Tétrault, the advocates of change had developed a four-part strategy: identifying emerging weaknesses, offering a cure, suggesting potential rewards, and lobbying for support.

The Toronto Strategic Planning Committee report, delivered to the Ontario regional partners in May 1999, set out troubling weaknesses, but ones that many partners had already sensed. McCarthy Tétrault's market advantage as the original national law firm in Canada had been eroded by the recent mergers and expansions of its competitors. It now shared a "relatively saturated market" with increasingly sophisticated competitors, not only rival Canadian law firms but also international law firms and accounting firms. Its profitability, while satisfactory, was not keeping pace with the most successful competitors. Advantages presented by the creation of the national firm were not being seized.

Partners complained they could not use their time effectively, that too many key client relations depended on a handful of senior lawyers, and that too many partners and associates lacked a clear sense of what was expected of them. The desire for more business planning, more workload planning, and a less "reactive" management style was widespread, and the committee's proposals tapped into that frustration.[225]

Having laid out the weaknesses threatening McCarthy Tétrault's position, the committee offered a cure: strengthened practice groups with authority to plan and allocate work and to reward both leaders and members according to the group's successes. The report hinted broadly at the rewards that might flow. The grand ambition the committee proposed was "to make or maintain McCarthy Tétrault as the pre-eminent Canadian law firm in chosen specialty practice areas." It also offered a more individual reward: if the firm could successfully reorient itself, if it could reduce routine assignments and maximize the interesting, challenging and profitable legal projects that partners sought, then it could "provide a more fulfilling and rewarding professional life." If the new regime fulfilled its promises, partners might improve their situation, not by working more hours (as previously) but by concentrating their time on more interesting, more profitable work.

The Strategic Planning Committee presented its "Phase One Report"—two later phases were promised, one for working out the plan's details, the other for its implementation—to a general meeting of Toronto partners at the King Edward Hotel on June 10, 1999. It was a lively session. Some partners questioned why such changes were necessary when the firm's lawyers were already busy, often with more work than they could handle. The committee responded with data to show how individual lawyers, by accepting whatever retainers they were offered, were too often burying themselves in low-value, low-challenge tasks. The point of the strategic plan was not to have partners work more, they proposed, but to establish a regime that would let them work more productively, on the kinds of tasks they would prefer to be doing.

The planners denied they were seeking to streamline McCarthy Tétrault into a narrow business law and tax law specialty firm; the "strategically planned" partnership would retain a broadly based practice. They did acknowledge, however, that a strategically led McCarthys might well begin to reduce its activities in some areas, such as, for example, wrongful-dismissal work, which was likely to irritate potential corporate clients, and work for "vulture funds," which could alienate financial institutions and reduce the possibility of obtaining large restructuring projects from troubled companies. If accepting these kinds of retainers was keeping the firm from securing larger and longer-term objectives, the firm should move away from them.

The most resistance, obviously, might come from individual partners with strong client relationships, who might conclude that the whole shift to group practice undermined them. Enough of these partners, however, either accepted the threat/cure analysis of the Strategic Planning Committee report or felt confident they could thrive in the new environment. The King Edward Hotel meeting was long and lively, but the partnership ratified the Phase One report and authorized the committee to move ahead with more detailed planning and implementation.

THE PLAN GOES NATIONAL

TORONTO'S PHASE ONE report of June 1999 contained only a single sentence about all the McCarthy Tétrault lawyers and offices beyond Toronto. In a rather offhand way, it instructed the Executive Committee to "ensure coordination of Toronto initiatives with the National Management Committee." That a proposal for such fundamental changes could be planned in Toronto, virtually without reference to the rest of the firm, reflected the degree to which the regional offices had remained separate practices despite their common banner.

Many Toronto partners had been concerned about the delays that could arise if the planning report were submitted to the National Management Committee for its approval. Even in Toronto, a timetable originally set at six months had grown to eighteen, although Toronto lawyers could meet as frequently as they wished and generally knew each other well. The Toronto lawyers most eager for change feared that if the strategic plan went to the National Management Committee, it would inevitably be referred to each regional office for lengthy and uncoordinated discussions. They told themselves instead that the other offices, if they liked Toronto's innovations, could apply the changes nationally once they had been tested in Toronto. "They wanted to do this nationally," recalled René Sorell, "but we said, 'We are not a really national firm, and we can't wait to get a national firm in order to get this done.'"

Gérald Tremblay, eminent litigator and vice-chair of McCarthy Tétrault.

In fact, changes on the scale the Toronto office was now contemplating could *only* be done nationally. Niels Ortved recalled, "The more we did, the more it became obvious to us that to be successful, we had to distribute it to the other offices. We wanted to build up the practice groups to serve our clients better, and of course many of the clients had national issues for us to handle, and so we were going to have to bring in the other offices. If we were using allocations to reward change in Toronto, we would have to do the same elsewhere."

In any case, as soon as Toronto's Phase One report began circulating, the response from other offices was instantaneous, even explosive. The reaction made it clear that all regions were interested in this strategic planning initiative. More than that, the rest of the firm insisted that reform had to be much more than a Toronto project.

The Toronto plan came to the National Management Committee meeting in Vancouver in July 1999. Gérald Tremblay, one of the Quebec representatives on the National Management Committee, instantly said, "Wait! We cannot plan for one region alone. It's an opportunity for a national planning process." By 1999 lawyers from Montreal and Quebec City were already actively engaged in many of the firm's international activities. McCarthy Tétrault's large and profitable international energy projects, for instance, driven forward by Richard Drouin, had seen a great deal of involvement from influential Quebec partners. McCarthy Tétrault had helped create opportunities for them that would never have come to a local firm, and such experiences had convinced key members of the Quebec region that their future lay in using the national firm to achieve full access to Canadian and international work.[226]

William Atkinson, who had become managing partner of the Quebec region in 1997 (and vice-chair of the national firm in 1998), had immediately seen Toronto's strategic planning as a project that had to be larger than Toronto. Atkinson had been convinced by his years in the Quebec City office of Clarkson Tétrault in the 1980s that the sheer size of a central office always put the onus on smaller offices to avoid being left on the margin. "If we're not there for our Toronto partners—and our Vancouver or Calgary partners—things will happen without us. That's why I personally was so active in the business and the management," Atkinson said. "We said to Toronto, 'You can't build that by yourself. It has to be national, otherwise the pressure will grow and blow the firm apart. It does not make any sense for one part, even the biggest part, to do strategic planning without the whole body being involved.' Those were good discussions."[227]

Jim McCartney, who had been part of the Toronto Strategic Planning Committee and who succeeded Arthur Scace as chair of the National Management Committee at the beginning of 2000,* recalled, "A lot of the early energy to reform the firm came from Montreal. They said, 'We can make this firm work better if we get it properly integrated nationally, and we want to do that.' That shook Toronto out of its comfortable pew, and the Toronto partners embraced strategic planning on a national basis."

Quebec partners were not the only ones to seize on the reform ideas being debated in the Toronto office. Calgary partners had complained earlier that "the National Management Committee lacks the power to address our daily issues with the speed and pragmatism needed to run our business effectively. The regional inertia and prolonged consensus-building that has paralyzed decisions on most issues of importance in the past is a luxury we can no longer afford." One of Vancouver's frequent representatives on national committees, Trevor Bell, concluded it had been "an expensive mistake" to have continued managing on a regional basis for so long. Though he acknowledged "it took a while to get to know one another and to build that comfort level," he had become convinced by 1999 that "you can't run a business as big as ours on the old model of a consensual partnership. It just doesn't make any sense."[228] The concerns that had driven Toronto partners into the strategic planning initiative were hardly Toronto's alone.

In the fall of 1999 Toronto's strategic planning project was reconstituted as a national endeavour, and in the process several aspects of the Toronto office's reform proposal were modified. The new awareness that dissatisfaction with the status quo affected all regions enabled the national team to be more hard-hitting in its presentations to the partnership. "Partners want a different culture," one presentation declared. McCarthy Tétrault, the team's report said, was involved in more major

*At the December 1999 National Management Committee meeting, Scace's last as chair, it was noted that he had attended every single one of the 102 committee meetings since the McCarthy Tétrault merger of 1990.

transactions and more high-value litigation than any other Canadian firm. It had significant penetration among Report on Business 1000 and Fortune 500 companies, and it was "viewed as first tier" by major business enterprises. These were precious advantages, yet the report was blunt about the partnership's structural weaknesses and the need for change. "The sole practitioner style is damaging the firm. There is overwhelming partner support for unlocking the firm's value."[229]

The national project applied greater resources to its task than had Toronto. Soon after the planning process "went national," the firm engaged C. Randy Lewis from the Hildebrandt consulting company to assist the reform project. Lewis had strong views about how law firms should be governed. They needed "strong leadership and less democracy," he told the planning committee. "The governing body of well-managed firms is small and led by a dynamic individual or small group."[230] Lewis also convinced McCarthy Tétrault that its strategic planning team had to be small: there should be no more than seven members, all influential, respected partners but not managing partners. The National Management Committee recruited André Prévost and Tam Davis from the Quebec region, Barry Ryan and René Sorell from Ontario, William Smith from Alberta and Rosemarie Wertschek from British Columbia, plus national chair Jim McCartney.

"What I remember," recalled André Prévost, "is it was the first time we shared across regions what our future could be and how we could make the whole firm the dominant one. What struck me was not only the respect but the real interest of each region's members for the others, for the strengths, weaknesses, and what the whole firm needed. It was the first time we began to learn those things about all the other offices."*

The Hildebrandt researchers also helped quantify a great deal of data about the firm and its business, and they conducted hundreds of interviews and client

*As the team's duties expanded it added four members, and a symbolic breakthrough was achieved when the Quebec region proposed the abandonment of regional balance in selecting them. "Pick the right people. We don't have to be pro rata. That's the whole point," Bill Atkinson recalled saying. The additional members were Atkinson, Doug Ewens, Malcolm Mercer and Earl Phillips (one from each region, in fact).

surveys about McCarthy Tétrault's market position. As a result, the National Strategic Planning Committee backed up its case for change with extensive statistics on the way the firm actually operated. Perhaps the most memorable chart the national strategic planning team presented to the partnership became known as the "Viking Ship." This was a bar chart that presented both the volume and the value of business done by the firm, and like a Viking long ship it displayed a spectacular peak at both ends. On the left side, one tall bar showed the nearly 60 per cent of McCarthy Tétrault client matters that generated fees of less than $25,000 each and less than 10 per cent of revenues in total. On the right side, another tall bar showed the 60 per cent of revenues that came from the tenth of all client matters that were worth more than $250,000 each.

The "Viking Ship" was vivid proof that, while McCarthy Tétrault had moved beyond routine family wills and house transfers, it still did too many of their corporate equivalents. Its lawyers, including partners, were spending far too much time on small matters that kept them busy but were neither very challenging nor notably profitable. It was not hard to see the benefits that would flow if the firm could shift its activities from the mass of low-value matters on the chart's left side towards the high-value cases on the right.

Some of the proposals for change at the national level built directly on ones sketched out in Toronto: essentially, that the firm should move to a group practice system in which group leaders and group members would be responsible for establishing objectives for each practice group and rewarded for results in achieving them. The National Strategic Planning Committee, however, was more direct than the Toronto proposals had been in describing what it called "The McCarthy Tétrault Lifestyle Predicament" ("Time demands... have become significant and unrelenting. Virtually every professional questions his or her ability to sustain the pace.... Partners and associates would be a lot happier if they could see a time in the future when they were working less desperately.") and in suggesting that implementing a strategic plan could actually address that issue. "The current lifestyle predicament of partners is the product of individual practitioners indiscriminately taking on matters many of which are small, create conflicts, and produce only modest amounts of short term revenue," the national committee declared. A firm-wide shift to group practice systems, in other words, would not only improve business efficiency within the firm; it might even improve the lives of the lawyers, by enabling them to manage their time and their responsibilities more effectively than they could do as individuals.[231]

The National Strategic Planning Committee was at pains to emphasise that strategic planning did not mean turning McCarthy Tétrault into a specialist law firm that focussed on a few practice lines and abandoned all others. McCarthy Tétrault, the team declared, was not seeking to throw away its diversified strengths to become a "narrowly focussed specialty firm" or a larger version of a specialized business law boutique. It would retain its ability to do complex trial litigation. It would continue to serve emerging businesses and new-economy initiatives. It would continue to provide full-service legal advice to its clients. The principal difference the committee was proposing was that in future the firm would apply its new strategic planning abilities, less to take it out of particular fields of practice than to maximize in all practice areas the high-value, high-interest, cutting-edge work to which its aspirations had long been directed. The new Strategic Plan promised to raise everyone's boat, not to throw anyone overboard.

The national plan went significantly beyond Toronto's in its suggestions for the firm's governance. The new model of practice group operations made little sense unless the groups operated on a completely national basis, integrating lawyers from every office. If the change was successful, the partners' professional relationships would come to depend more on their firm-wide practice group than on their local office and regional management. Even their allocations would depend on the judgement of their national practice group, not their local partners.

Clearly the old, autonomous regional office structure and allocations regime could not coexist with the system being proposed. Instead, the National Strategic Planning Committee began to sketch out a fully integrated partnership with a single profit pool and a single allocations system. It would be supervised by "integrated national management at the firm level" and led by managers "who have the authority to manage and supervise the implementation of firm priorities, who are accountable for results, and whose responsibilities are well understood by the firm."*

In taking up these themes, the national process was addressing governance issues that the local process in Toronto had not been able to confront directly. Strategic planning, in fact, had twin goals. The practice group project addressed how lawyers worked, but it was now becoming clear that the practice groups had to be directed by one integrated, centralized national firm management. "Really there were two strategic plans," said Jim McCartney. "One was planning the business. The other was planning the governance to make the first one feasible."

The Strategic Plan was to be presented to the partnership for approval in principle in November 2000. As the deadline approached, members of the committee grew concerned over the response they would receive. The broad objectives of the Strategic Plan were rousingly ambitious. The supporting documents were packed with illustrations of McCarthy Tétrault's great advantages and with praise for the firm and its lawyers, drawn from Hildebrandt's client surveys. Strategic planning would enable the partnership "to represent the most economically significant players in key business markets," "to be the firm of choice for all major legal matters," "to attract and retain the best and brightest lawyers" and, above all, constantly repeated in Strategic Plan communications, "to be the dominant law firm in Canada."[232]

*While centralized management followed logically from the practice group orientation McCarthy Tétrault was moving towards, it was also a standard part of Hildebrandt recommendations on law firm management, already implemented by some Hildebrandt clients in the United States, though less so in Canada. The proposals for McCarthy Tétrault, in other words, were not unique to the firm—a fact some partners found reassuring.

Nevertheless, the Strategic Plan proposed an unprecedented change in the way partners worked and were paid. It also proposed a significant delegation of the partners' authority over work and pay to a new management regime. Members of the strategic planning team were vividly aware that they were proposing not only to fundamentally reorganize the way partners worked and were rewarded, but also to move beyond the regional compromises upon which the national firm had been built in 1990. They had no certainty about the reactions of the partners.

The national Strategic Plan was presented in November 2000 at a partners' retreat in Scottsdale, Arizona. Earlier retreats at Whistler, Quebec City, Banff and Niagara-on-the-Lake had reflected the firm's geographic regions; Scottsdale became the first held outside Canada. McCarthy Tétrault took over a resort hotel and convention centre on the edge of the desert, and the partners from all the regional offices gathered for the three-day conference. Discussion of the Strategic Plan, followed by a partnership vote to ratify or reject it, was the vital element on the program. "The task force went down a day early, and as we were talking, we thought it might be a disaster," recalled André Prévost from Montreal. " 'I hope it's not going to be a zoo!' we were saying!"

The strategic planning team was asking for approval of a set of principles for the reorganization of practice. The partners were invited to approve of: ongoing planning to determine the business priorities of the firm, a new commitment to group rather than individual practice, leadership by newly empowered executives "who have the authority to manage" (both at the practice group level and in the firm as a whole), an integrated allocations system directed by management and, finally, the development of a governance structure and compensation system to make the other principles feasible. René Sorell of Toronto, who with Tam Davis of Montreal made the main presentation that preceded the vote on the Strategic Plan, recalled being optimistic. "My expectation was that it would be voted for, because we were all there in a collegial atmosphere and going along was the expected thing. And there wasn't an alternative on offer." Despite those advantages, Sorell and Davis's presentation encountered what Sorell described as "a lot more discussion than we expected, a real discussion in a room full of hundreds of partners, people who had a real talent for being critical."

André Prévost, managing partner in Montreal from 2000 to 2004.

As the discussion continued, support for a decisive break with the status quo grew stronger, and eagerness to act translated into support for the committee and its proposals. Partners who had not been part of the project, partners esteemed as practitioners and business-builders, and partners who would continue to thrive without a practice group model began standing up to declare that this was what the firm needed and had been awaiting. Enthusiasm for the mission proposed by the strategic planning team—"to confirm McCarthy Tétrault as the country's dominant law firm"—seized the room. National chair Jim McCartney, who chaired the meeting, felt the wave of support and asked if the partners were ready to vote. They were, and the vote by show of hands was virtually unanimous.

Suddenly the room was erupting as partners stood up to applaud and cheer. "It turned into an ovation," recalled René Sorell. "That really shook me. It was a surprising and momentous outpouring." For André Prévost, "there was a mood of acceptance that this was going forward: if not now, never. There was a real sense of commitment, of opening up. It really was one of the highlights of my whole career." For Jim McCartney, "it felt like a new beginning for the firm when the whole room approved. It was a great upbeat feeling."

The Scottsdale commitment, like the Phase One ratification in Toronto in 1999, was only an approval in principle, although success there gave momentum to the steps that followed. The partnership had agreed to go forward with a process of reorganization, but all the specific details remained to be developed, discussed and voted on. There was yet another stage to complete in the process: implementation.

"I never travelled so much in my life," recalled André Prévost about the year that followed the Scottsdale meeting. The committee that had presented the plan at Scottsdale was reorganized as a larger National Strategic Planning Task Force to work out the details in consultation with partners across the firm.* It was clear that, as well as working out a detailed implementation plan, they had to engage the partnership, to a degree never before attempted, in a firm-wide discussion of objectives. If they succeeded, partners would not only be well informed of the details and implications of the change when they voted but would also have defined a common set of goals across all the widely separated offices.

Scottsdale mandated the Task Force to draft a formal Strategic Plan to be presented in March 2001, voted on by June and fully implemented by November. The Task Force reported in March, on schedule, but there was no immediate move to a ratification vote. The March report gave the partnership its first detailed statement of the specific changes that implementation of the Scottsdale principles would entail, and the proposals provoked vigorous debate that led to significant modifications and much more extensive discussions than had been contemplated in the original schedule. The March document eventually produced two supplementary documents, one in July 2001, the

*Task Force members after Scottsdale were Bill Atkinson, Paul Boniferro, Tam Davis, Doug Ewens, Jim McCartney, Malcolm Mercer, Niels Ortved, Murray Paton, Earl Phillips, André Prévost, Barry Ryan, Richard Shaw, Godyne Sibay, Bill Smith, René Sorell, Paul Steep and Rosemarie Wertschek.

second in October 2001. All three reports were attended with what Prévost called the "road show," an extended series of regional meetings, small group discussions and individual interviews to refine details of the proposal and to address partners' concerns about the whole process.

The most hotly discussed aspects of the Task Force recommendations concerned the governance of the firm. The March report unveiled for the first time the specific management plan emerging from the strategic planning process. The new governance system dispensed almost entirely with decision making by mass partnership meetings, and it put an end to autonomous regions and weak administrative-only managers. If the partners approved, McCarthy Tétrault would henceforth have a corporate style of governance with a single, firm-wide leadership headed by a chief executive officer, assisted by three other full-time leaders, under the stewardship of a board composed of the CEO and ten elected directors. "Significant authority is conferred on the senior management team," read the first page of the Task Force recommendations, "including significant influence over compensation.... We are recommending a governance and allocations model which is designed to give managers the authority to manage, to do so on an integrated national basis, and to do so supported by partners sharing a single national profit pool." The CEO and the management team he or she chose would have substantial day-to-day managing authority, subject only to the general policy-making supervision of the board at quarterly meetings. For the first time, one strong, central leadership team would begin to wield executive authority within McCarthy Tétrault.[233]

The March 2001 plan proposed that the chief executive officer, like the rest of the board, would be directly elected. "It is of utmost importance that the CEO derives his or her authority directly from the partners and not from the board," read the Task Force's report. To many partners, however, the implication was that partners might find themselves merely ratifying candidates presented by a nominating committee that was itself heavily influenced by the firm's leadership. During the discussions, a consensus emerged that the partners should elect the ten board directors from a slate of at least twenty nominees. Additional candidates could be nominated by just 5 per cent of the partnership (or fewer than twenty partners).* The board would in turn appoint the CEO, subject to the approval of the partners, providing a clear delegation of authority from partners to the board and to the CEO.

The discussions and questions that went on during 2001 addressed the governance system exhaustively and produced several revisions to the March proposals. The matters most extensively discussed, however, were not necessarily the decisive factors weighing upon the partners. The heart of any professional partnership is its allocations regime, and everyone knew the success or failure of the Strategic Plan might well be determined by individual partners' calculations of what would happen to their personal incomes under an allocations regime designed to emphasise and reward group achievement rather than individual accomplishment.

Under the new system, all partners would develop personal practice plans with their groups. Management would review and propose changes to plans that were not consistent with group objectives, and non-fulfilment of personal plans could adversely affect a partner's allocation. As the report declared, "The emphasis on group achievement constitutes a departure from the separate (and in some cases quite different) allocations systems currently found in the four regions." It was inevitable that many partners would find themselves speculating about how the new regime might affect their work habits and cause their own personal allocations to rise—or fall.

The changes proposed by the Task Force reports during 2001 meant not just a new direction of practice for individual lawyers but virtually a

*For at least five years there would be guaranteed minimums for regional representation on the board. A standard three-year term would be phased in to provide for rotation of a third of the board each year.

new constitution for McCarthy Tétrault. As a result, the approval required for the changes was the kind of supermajority that constitutional changes usually require. The road shows were not simply concerned with explaining and modifying the Strategic Plan. They were also a campaign to secure its approval, to try to carry the mood of Scottsdale through a year of working out intricate details of firm management.

For André Prévost, managing partner in the Quebec region from 2000 to 2004 and a member of the Strategic Planning Committee before and the Task Force after the Scottsdale meetings, one surprising discovery of the Task Force consultations was just how diverse his law firm really was. Prévost had expected the greatest resistance to come from his own colleagues in the Quebec region. "I foresaw difficulty in Quebec—for historic reasons, for reasons that had been developing for 130 years, you might say!" But he found many Quebec partners believed the safeguards established in 1990 were no longer necessary or helpful to them. After a decade of strong support for regional autonomy, they were now more intent on fully joining and benefiting from the national firm than on protecting their position in it.

"My take on all this," Prévost continued, "had been that it was easier in Toronto to bring partners around to that kind of structure.... And I imagined Calgary, as an offshoot of Toronto, would have the same outlook about things." In fact, Calgary had long since become as distinctly autonomous as any regional office within McCarthy Tétrault, and it was the region whose practices were least in harmony with the culture that the Strategic Plan was recommending. During the 1990s the Calgary office had protected itself against the fluctuations of the Alberta economy by recruiting senior lawyers who brought significant clients with them. In the fluid, flexible Calgary business culture, personal relationships remained fundamental, and these lateral recruits naturally protected their personal relationships with "their" clients and the revenues from them. As a result, the Calgary partnership had gradually shifted to the most "arithmetic" allocations formula within McCarthy Tétrault. That is, Calgary allocations were closely aligned to an individual lawyer's client billings, whereas in the other offices allocations committees generally made greater allowances for mentoring, for professional leadership and generally for non-billable, firm-building contributions. McCarthy Tétrault's Calgary office had grown and prospered through the later 1990s, but it was developing a reputation, even in Calgary, as a home for strong sole practitioners rather than a unified practice.

The Strategic Plan, with its orientation towards group practice and movement away from rewarding partners solely or largely by their billable hours, challenged Calgary's style of practice perhaps more than that of any other regional office. Much of the "road show" discussion in Calgary was intended to reassure partners there that they too stood to benefit from "unlocking the full value of McCarthy Tétrault's national platform." Calgary partners were not alone in their concerns; there were partners in every office with qualms about the impact a group practice system could have on their own careers. However, as the time came for the partnership to vote on the revised proposals, some members of the Task Force, in Alberta and elsewhere, saw winning enough support among Calgary partners as probably the greatest challenge to the success of the whole initiative.

The partnership had agreed that the changes proposed in the strategic planning proposals would require a 75-per-cent approval rating (by partners and by allocation points) in each region. The decision would be made by an unprecedented secret-ballot vote of the entire partnership, to take place in each office on Monday, October 29, 2001. In the end, every single one of the firm's 368 partners voted on that day.* It was a simple yes-no vote. In each office, the regional managing partner tallied the ballots.

*Jim McCartney recalled that Toronto banking law expert Bradley Crawford, who was on holiday in Britain and close to retirement in any case, had decided not to vote, despite his sympathy for the proposals. McCartney secured a proxy from him and voted on his behalf.

The partners were voting on the Task Force's final recommendations, including the "Core Principles of the Strategic Plan." If these were approved, the objective of McCarthy Tétrault would be "to be Canada's dominant provider of legal services to major enterprises." The core principles called for McCarthy Tétrault "to be the Canadian law firm of choice for major enterprises, to be the market leader in legal services valued by major enterprises, to create a superior professional atmosphere based on group activity and commitment, to enhance existing strengths, and to accept and carry out work which is profitable and consistent with the Strategic Plan."[234]

McCarthy Tétrault's strategic planning initiatives had largely been conducted in secret and were generally not noted in the legal press, and the specific proposals being voted upon remained unknown outside the partnership. But for its advocates the Strategic Plan had come to seem as crucial to the firm as the steps in the 1980s that built McCarthy Tétrault into a national firm. Going national had not been determined by a single yes-no decision; it had required a sequence of steps involving many people over several years. Still, the goal then had been to secure business advantages for the firm in a legal-services marketplace that even in the 1980s was becoming more challenging, more competitive and more business-oriented than the traditional professional partnership of earlier times.

The building of the national firm had made McCarthy Tétrault the Canadian trend-setter in the great law firm expansions of the 1980s and 1990s, as well the country's largest. The Strategic Plan promised to be no less significant. The national firm had provided a platform but, in the heightened competitive environment of the twenty-first century, central management, sophisticated business planning and coordinated practice had emerged as the new requirements for a law firm that sought to remain near the forefront, let alone to position itself as Canada's dominant law firm. This time, the choice depended directly upon the ballots of the partners: yes or no to the recommendations of the Strategic Planning Final Report.

A few days after the partnership vote, the National Strategic Planning Task Force circulated a memo to everyone at the firm.

> On Monday, October 29, 2001, the partners of McCarthy Tétrault voted on a proposal to create an innovative new governance structure to more fully integrate our firm's offices into a single operating unit, organized by national practice groups and headed by a CEO and a ten-member board of directors.
>
> The results of the vote were overwhelmingly in favour of the proposal.[235]

In every region, the partnership had given the strategic planning proposal the required supermajority of votes and allocations points. At the end of 2001, McCarthy Tétrault prepared to become a new kind of national law firm.

17 TO UNLOCK THE VALUE

IN THE SPRING OF 2004 W. Iain Scott, chief executive officer of McCarthy Tétrault, reflected on the rapid changes his firm had undertaken since the partners' ratification of the Strategic Plan in the fall of 2001. "We sometimes describe the way the firm used to be as 350 partners flying in loose formation." Since the spring of 2002 it had been Scott's mandate as CEO to change that situation. "In this environment, it's important that we know what we're doing and who we're doing it for. And not only that I know it, but that every partner knows it."

McCarthy Tétrault's National Management Committee had moved immediately after the Strategic Plan's ratification in October 2001 to set in place the new governance structures. The first step was the election of the new board of directors. Twenty-four candidates, including some of the firm's most influential partners, were nominated for the ten positions, providing a broad range of regional backgrounds, ages and practice specialties. Their candidate statements provided individual views on the firm's needs and the role the board should play, but all the candidates declared their support for the Strategic Plan and the changes it proposed.

The election results, announced on January 15, 2002, produced a board of strategic planning veterans and regional leaders. Trevor Bell of Vancouver, Richard Shaw of Calgary, Murray Paton and René Sorell of Toronto, and Tam Davis of Montreal had served on the national Task Force, and both Bell and Shaw had been regional managing partners. Gérald Tremblay of Montreal had been vice-chair of the firm and a long-time member of the National Management Committee, and Gary Girvan of Toronto had been on the Toronto management committee. The others elected were veteran Montreal commercial lawyer Warren Goodman and two Torontonians, M&A practitioner Eric Spindler and tax lawyer Judith Woods. Soon after the election, national chair Jim McCartney wound up the last meeting of the National Management Committee and handed authority over to the new directors. (McCartney, who had helped launch the national-firm initiatives in the late 1970s and had been involved in the strategic planning process since its origins in Toronto, was approaching retirement and did not seek election to the board.)

The board, with the help of an executive-recruiting consultant, set about seeking a chief executive officer, who would also chair the board as its eleventh member. This was the crucial position in the new structure. Once in office, the CEO would wield broad authority over the direction of the firm, subject only to supervision by the board at quarterly meetings.

The board considered both internal and external candidates but its attention gradually focussed on Iain Scott, a business lawyer in the Toronto office who had not previously held any senior role in firm management. Scott, a 1979 call to the bar who had joined McCarthy & McCarthy in 1988, was highly regarded by his colleagues for his legal skills, business sense and open mind. Scott was appointed by the new board and ratified by the partnership early in 2002. In April he relinquished his practice to become the first full-time chief executive officer.

Since McCarthy Tétrault's recent innovations had been widely noted by other firms and by the legal and business press, Scott could expect constant scrutiny. On November 7, 2001, Andrew Willis of the *Globe and Mail* had written, "The first Canadian firm to establish a truly national practice in the 1980s, McCarthy Tétrault is now planning to overturn tradition again by adopting a modern corporate structure.... If it works, watch others imitate the experiment." Within weeks of Scott's appointment *Chambers Global*, an influential worldwide directory of leading lawyers, included McCarthy Tétrault, "one of the country's most respected legal brands," among its "Top Ten Firms in North America," noting the partnership's particular strengths in finance, mergers and acquisitions, competition, litigation, communications, real estate, tax and energy law. It was the first time a Canadian law firm had cracked *Chambers Global*'s North American top ten.[236]

"The firm is clearly breaking new ground," reported Lexpert, *the business law magazine, when it made McCarthy Tétrault's new governance structure its July 2002 cover story.*

Scott appointed his management team. A key choice was Kenneth Morell, a management consultant with operational experience at one of the accountancy Big Five, who became chief operating officer. The other positions were internal appointments from among the partners: Gérald Tremblay became vice-chair, and Scott appointed Trevor Bell of Vancouver national professional resources leader and Owen Johnson of Toronto national practice group leader. The principal regions continued to have a regional managing partner (initially Earl Phillips in British Columbia, Clifford Johnson in Alberta, Kirby Chown in Ontario, and André Prévost in Quebec). Each continued to be the local spokesperson for McCarthy Tétrault, but authority over the firm's business affairs and the implementation of the Strategic Plan, as well as partnership admissions, allocations and other crucial matters, was shifting from the regional leaders to the new national ones.

While most of those appointed to the leadership positions were firm members familiar to the partners and had been selected for their professional leadership as well as their management interests, McCarthy Tétrault now had a management hierarchy of a kind common in corporations but still unusual in law firms. The new firm-wide management was the CEO's team and reported to Scott. "I would not have wanted the job if I was going to be handed a slate of people," he said.

It was Scott's assignment to oversee implementation of the new vision of large-firm legal practice proposed by the Strategic Plan. The firm believed it had the lawyers and the clients to become "Canada's dominant provider of legal services." The crucial task was unlocking the value already present within McCarthy Tétrault, and the first step to doing so was to empower the practice groups. In August 2002 Scott announced leadership appointments for seven national practice groups: Corporate Finance, Mergers & Acquisitions was headed by David Tennant and Gordon Thompson; Financial Services by Barry Ryan; Labour & Employment by Earl Phillips; Litigation by Louis Lacoursière and Malcolm Mercer; Real Property by Abraham Costin; Tax by Doug Ewens, and Technology, Communications & Intellectual Property by George Takach. As well, there were specialty practice groups in Bankruptcy and Restructuring and in Municipal, Environmental, and Competition Law and industry-specific practice groups for the Health, Mining, Hospitality and Energy industries and for the firm's international practice. Every lawyer had a home in one core practice group and could be attached to other groups and subgroups.[237]

The practice groups had existed previously, but now they acquired new authority for business development and supervision of practice, and significant input into decisions about allocations. Practice groups would establish which teams of lawyers would act for the clients of the group, and so they would be deeply involved in the management of individual lawyers' practices. Through consultation with the group and its leaders, each lawyer in a practice group would develop a personal practice plan that defined his or her role within the group. Ultimately, partners' allocations of profits would depend on the success of their group and the achievement of their personal objectives within the group.

The task of the practice groups was to focus the firm's strengths on the most promising, challenging and profitable lines of work, and the new management team was deeply involved in defining who and what those clients and business lines should be. Soon after taking charge as CEO, Scott introduced a "key client" strategy in which McCarthy Tétrault would identify the select group (initially thirty, later growing to forty-five) of the largest and most promising clients across every practice sector and every part of the country, so that the firm could begin developing strategies to serve them more effectively. In Scott's words, "That allowed us to focus a lot of people on a very small group of clients. It helped us deal with conflicts issues. And it also let people know what they should be doing when they get up in the morning. If we can be the biggest service providers to the best clients in this country, we will be where we should be!"

Gradually, Scott and the practice group leadership added similar programs to identify a second tier of "significant clients" (generally involving billings over $250,000 a year) and a third tier of smaller but still promising clients. "When the whole firm knows who these clients are and everybody is working on these teams, it will, I believe, allow us to focus resources that still are dispersed."

Fundamental to the "key client" and "significant client" initiative was an effort to ensure that McCarthy Tétrault provided a broad range of legal services to the identified clients. The firm intended its practice groups not to pursue markets and clients independently but to coordinate their work as elements of a single firm, combining their specialized skills to provide all the strengths of McCarthy Tétrault to the clients. In effect, these key client initiatives were intended to deliver on the older cross-selling plans and to focus the firm's energies on the desirable end of the "Viking Ship" graph, that relatively small number of clients who produced most of the revenues as well as much of the work that was most challenging and satisfying to the partners.

Scott acknowledged that achieving such a focus on the firm's most promising opportunities could mean choosing not to pursue some business opportunities. "We were asked last year to bid on a significant piece of work for one of the banks," recalled Scott. "It could have been over $10 million worth of work. In times past, everybody would have said, 'Well, $10 million, we should go for it.' But it was what we would call mid-level commodity work, and when we talked to our practitioners about what they wanted to do with their practices, there wasn't a lot of enthusiasm. We chose not to go after it. In times past, that wouldn't have been the case. There would have been people saying, 'Oh, it'll keep me busy.'"

In the new structure, the CEO had unprecedented authority in recruiting lawyers. Scott was authorized to recommend to the board the immediate admission of lateral recruits to the partnership (hitherto a power reserved to the whole partnership, or at least each regional partnership), and where he saw opportunities or gaps to fill Scott began using this authority to undertake swift and confidential recruitment moves. When the Ernst & Young–tied law firm Donahue & Partners began to crumble early in 2002, Scott's new authority enabled McCarthy Tétrault to recruit twenty-two of its Calgary lawyers as a group. Despite some subsequent departures, the move confirmed the value of having a single executive empowered to seize such recruitment opportunities.

Growth in lawyer numbers was not, however, a priority of the new management. "In terms of overall size, I would be surprised if we grew significantly in the near term, at least in the absence of a notable strategic opportunity. I don't think we need to grow," said Scott. Adding lawyers was less important than being strongly placed in the right legal markets and serving them efficiently.

To that end, McCarthy Tétrault began applying across the whole firm the new partnership admission practices that the Toronto office had been implementing since its own strategic planning process in 1997–99. The firm continued to recruit associates, but it also began to apply more rigorous partnership admission criteria, designed to ensure that any associate admitted was already a proven leader who could deliver enough work to keep his or her associates suitably employed. Toronto's category of "income partner," an intermediate status between associate status and full partner, was introduced across the firm.

As a result of these innovations, the number of associates at McCarthy Tétrault became larger than the number of partners for the first time in decades. In early 2004 Scott expected the associate-to-partner ratio to continue to grow until the firm had a smaller core of partners directing the practice of a larger pool of associates who delivered the work and honed their own abilities to become future leaders. While McCarthy Tétrault did not expect that the Canadian legal scene would soon see "leverage ratios" matching those of New York City and London, England, where leading law firms had long had four to six associates per partner, an eventual ratio of at least two associates per partner seemed plausible to Scott. "Historically, partners here and in many other firms were admitted if they were good lawyers and good people, and the business side of it was number 3 on the list. Now we want all three."

Not surprisingly, the change in governance and practice proved stressful. Partners' allocations for 2003, announced late in 2002, were the first ones determined by the partners' new personal practice plans and by the achievements of their practice groups. With allocations reflecting group performance, some practice groups, still hard hit by the economic downturn that had started in 2001, saw allocations reduced for more than half of their partners. "I had partners coming to see me, I mean five or six times," recalled André Prévost, who was concluding his term as Quebec regional managing partner in 2003. "They were insecure. That was the year we discovered all the things we did not know about the implementation. I had to say, 'Give it a chance, help us reach our goals, and you will see it will be possible.'"

CEO Iain Scott salutes Daniel Johnson, former premier of Quebec and counsel to McCarthy Tétrault in Montreal since 1998, at a reception in Johnson's honour in 2004.

During these upheavals, the Quebec region lost a couple of partners to rival national firms that were rapidly building up their Montreal offices. The situation was more critical in Calgary, where the sole practitioner style now came up against the firm's new group practice ethos at a time when business in Calgary was booming and many Calgary lawyers were busier than their colleagues elsewhere. In the end, the Calgary office lost several partners who concluded their individual careers would be better served outside McCarthy Tétrault's new practice group system.

Fortunately, benefits of the new practice model and governance regime also became evident during 2003. The firm's increased leverage, its more focussed business lines, and its new emphasis on getting maximum value from its lawyers' time all were aimed at increasing profitability across the firm. Before the end of 2003 it was clear that these efforts were succeeding. Profitability was already rising significantly, and the allocations for 2004 were reassuring. "I think we've had enough water under the bridge now to see that it is the right way," said Scott in 2004. "Financially, we're doing significantly better over the last three years. We were always doing very well, but we've had three great years and another good year this year, even though we've gone through a pretty rocky economic cycle." André Prévost in Montreal had the same sense: "In 2003, it was difficult being the managing partner. The allocation for 2004 helped a lot."

John Manley, a former deputy prime minister of Canada who joined McCarthy Tétrault in 2004 as counsel in its Ottawa office, celebrates with CEO *Iain Scott at an Ottawa firm reception.*

Meanwhile, McCarthy Tétrault was also pursuing distinctly different ways to enable the integrated national partnership to unlock the value within the firm. One was "knowledge management," or KM, an effort to build new ways for lawyers to share their expertise. When law firms had only a handful of partners and associates, they could consult across their desks about the best way to handle a transaction, about the implications of recent judgements, or how best to handle a thorny client issue. A large firm had much more expertise to share—but its sheer scale seemed to preclude the informal sharing.

In the corporate-finance practice, "there was a thing that was hot a few years ago called 'high-yield financing,'" said Toronto M&A lawyer Gary Girvan, trying to explain what KM could do, "and we had done more than anyone in the country, twenty-five of them. But there was not one lawyer here who had done two of them, so we were all beginners." What the firm needed was a way for those "beginners," who might be in Calgary or Montreal, routinely to share experiences and reinforce each other's expertise. As Girvan sketched out the appeal of a network that would allow McCarthy Tétrault lawyers to pool that kind of knowledge, rather than repeating the research and drafting processes that other partners might recently have undertaken for other clients, a competitive gleam came into his eye. "If we could do that as a law firm, we would *kill* the competition!"

In 2000 the National Management Committee approved development of a KM project that came to be called RobiNETte in honour of John Robinette's uncanny ability to put his finger upon the crucial point within masses of legal information. RobiNETte was not merely to be an archive of documents (readily available on-line through an information retrieval system run by the firm's librarians). It was intended to enable the lawyers to provide ongoing summaries of and commentaries on their experiences with transactions and cases for the benefit of other firm lawyers working on similar issues.

The new group practice structure encouraged the integration of RobiNETte into McCarthy Tétrault's practice culture because RobiNETte would enable distant group members to tap into each other's experiences. By 2002 specialized knowledge managers had been attached to each of the firm's seven practice groups, and KM practices had been integrated into performance benchmarks for each group.

RobiNETte would cost millions of dollars in software development and ongoing operating costs; it was a project only a large and profitable law firm could contemplate and a way for McCarthy Tétrault to make size an advantage, not an obstacle. As Girvan put it, "It's not what we know; it's what the firm knows. When you hire me, you are hiring McCarthy Tétrault, hiring the promise that I can deliver the whole McCarthy Tétrault team and all its expertise. I can't do that if I don't know what everyone else has done."

In 2004 Iain Scott believed McCarthy Tétrault's innovations were paying off and that the firm was on the way to fulfilling the aspirations expressed in its Strategic Plan. In the short term, the firm could show a notable rise in profitability despite challenging economic conditions and vigorous competition. But the changes in practice culture, business development and organization seemed to Scott to be of greatest significance in unlocking the value of the firm for the longer term.

In 2003, Lexpert *magazine headlined McCarthy Tétrault's Information Technology practice and its leaders—George Takach of Toronto, Cheryl Slusarchuk of Vancouver, Michel Racicot of Montreal, and Barry Sookman of Toronto.*

At the start of the twenty-first century, "unlocking value" within a large law firm had two aspects. One was to offer services in the principal places where its most important clients were, whether that was Montreal, London, Calgary or New York City; by the year 2000 McCarthy Tétrault had largely done that. The initiatives of the 1980s had given it a national platform unmatched by any of its rivals, even at the end of the 1990s. In an upbeat message to his partners in mid-2003, Iain Scott noted that recent statistics showed McCarthy Tétrault acted for eight of the ten largest companies in Canada, as well as for most of the top ten banks, real estate companies, utilities and pipelines, forestry companies, eleven of the top twenty-six life insurers and no less than one-third of the top 500 companies in Canada.[238] Economic studies undertaken for the National Strategic Planning Committee had confirmed that many of these clients regularly used lawyers from more than one of McCarthy Tétrault's offices. That ability to deliver first-class legal service to the most desirable clients in all of Canada's leading business centres had been crucial to McCarthy Tétrault's ability to position itself as "Canada's National Law Firm" in the 1990s.

The second requirement for unlocking the full potential within McCarthy Tétrault was to make the law firm work efficiently and to ensure that size, specialization and geographical dispersal were advantages rather than burdens. The late 1990s, with increasing sophistication among clients driving increasing competition among law firms, had seen the culmination of a thirty-year evolution in which lawyers who had once seen themselves as learned professionals pursuing something like a vocation had gradually redefined themselves as being in the legal-services business. This message was driven home at a McCarthy Tétrault partnership retreat held at Whistler, British Columbia, in September 2002, just after the new practice group structure had become fully operational. At Whistler, Scott and his leadership team made the case that competition among elite law firms had grown so intense that the ultimate determinant for success and survival was "PPP"—profit per partner. Over the long term only law firms whose profitability matched or exceeded that of its competitors would continue to be able to hire the best students, invest in the best technologies and support systems, and retain the best lawyers. These were the elements a law firm required: to provide superior service to its clients, but also to generate the challenging and satisfying work that the most effective partners would continue to value and to seek.

Much had changed in twenty-five years. In 1977 McCarthy & McCarthy's Long Range Planning Committee had declared as one of its two principal recommendations that "it is essential that the working atmosphere be preserved even at the cost of increased profitability or money incomes." Even in 2002, some partners did not find the "profits per partner" message entirely congenial. There were losses to mourn in the transition of law firms toward more businesslike practice—and in the ongoing pressure on partners that it implied. But efficiency, in the end, was better than losing the race. It was plain that only firms that became efficient and competitive in the provision of legal services were likely to remain among the leaders of their industry.

The 1970s and 1980s had seen law firms like those that united to form McCarthy Tétrault transformed from handfuls of partners in single-city offices into organizations with hundreds of lawyers and many offices. In those years, geographical expansion and numerical growth had changed Canadian law firms, perhaps more than anything had since the emergence of the long-lived corporate law firm in the late nineteenth century. Yet the transition from the forty-lawyer firm to the 700-lawyer firm had not automatically transformed the organizational culture of the newly enlarged law firms. Typically, even the largest had remained under-managed associations of autonomous partners, at least compared with the corporate entities they advised and other professional service organizations. What McCarthy Tétrault was undertaking through its strategic planning process was the second stage of the transformation of law firms: the application of modern managerial theory, under the pressure of competition. The consequences of that shift will be a trend for the twenty-first century to observe.

The aspirations expressed at the end of McCarthy Tétrault's strategic planning process in 2001 had been to establish the firm as "Canada's dominant provider of legal services to major enterprises" and to provide "a superior professional environment" for the firm's lawyers. Since their appointment in 2002, Scott and his leadership team had worked to refine these goals. Early in 2004 they set out in detail for the board of directors how McCarthy Tétrault should define its goal of dominance and the benchmarks by which the partners should judge their success in achieving it.

Scott and his team made the case that McCarthy Tétrault should aspire to be a "wholly integrated" law firm. They demonstrated how, after all the expansions and consolidations among large law firms in recent years, some of McCarthy Tétrault's national competitors continued to operate as loosely affiliated networks of individual practices. Others had narrowed their focus to an exclusive emphasis on business law: essentially corporate finance, mergers and acquisitions, and tax. McCarthys' competitive advantage, argued Scott and his team, lay in being neither of these. McCarthy Tétrault had and should retain top-ranked practices in litigation, in technology law, in real property and in other areas. The leadership believed the emerging Canadian business environment did not consider these practices merely as adjuncts to narrowly defined business law; instead, key clients saw them as essential aspects of the services they expected from law firms. It followed that McCarthy Tétrault should not limit itself to an exclusive business law practice. When all the firm's national practice groups were fully integrated with equally strong groups in corporate finance/mergers and acquisitions and in tax, then McCarthy Tétrault would be uniquely placed to meet all the high-end needs of the very best clients. McCarthy Tétrault would stand out in the legal-services marketplace not only for the quality of its lawyers but also for being better integrated than its broadly based competitors and more broadly based than its narrowly focussed competitors.

(above and opposite page) Marketing, forbidden to law firms a couple of decades earlier, became a vital part of business development during the 1990s.

The board of directors endorsed these goals, and the leadership team laid out the emerging plan for the firm in meetings with all the practice groups. At a partners' retreat in Montreal in September 2004, the partnership endorsed an ambitious set of objectives. McCarthy Tétrault should rank first or second in each of its principal lines of practice in each of the regions where it was located; it should secure the largest share of the high-end work of its key clients, including their litigation work, and it should be recognized for superior client service and for having more leading practitioners in every key practice and in each region. By reaching these objectives and by making effective use of the revenues that would flow as a result, the firm could provide all the resources to sustain the superior practice environment in which the very best lawyers would choose to work.

At the Montreal retreat, Iain Scott argued that it would take just three to five years to confirm the achievement of these benchmarks. That became the timetable that would establish that McCarthy Tétrault truly had secured the position of dominance to which it aspired.

"We talk about dominance, but really we mean survival," René Sorell reflected in 2004. At first glance, it seemed implausible that survival should be an issue at a law firm whose constituent parts have been among the elite of the Canadian legal profession for 150 years, and that had solid grounds for declaring itself "Canada's premier law firm." Yet for decades consolidation and competition had been inexorably reducing the number of "downtown" law firms in leading Canadian and American cities. Large and prominent practices had vanished abruptly from the scene in both Canada and the United States. Notable law firms that went out of business in 2003 alone included the long-established Vancouver firm Campney Murphy and, in the United States, the 900-lawyer San Francisco-based giant Brobeck Phleger Harrison. Before them, the abrupt fall of Arthur Andersen and of accountancy-tied law firms like Donahue & Partners in Canada had demonstrated the vulnerability of professional service firms if they made the wrong choices and their clients suddenly found compelling reasons to go elsewhere. Firms that failed to compete effectively did not necessarily die, but many Canadian firms that were indisputably top-rank in their own cities a generation ago have slipped to second-tier or third-tier status over the years.

Despite the endurance of some famous names, staying at the top had never been a privilege law firms could take for granted. Montreal law firms had spent the last decades of the twentieth century adjusting to the shift of corporate power towards Toronto, and the ranks of leading firms there had changed significantly in those years. Clarkson Tétrault had prospered under that challenge, but other venerable Montreal firms had faded from the front rank. In Calgary and Vancouver some of the long-established leaders remained very strong, but the emergence of national firms had shaken up rankings almost as much as the opponents of national law firms had feared in the 1980s. In Toronto, partnerships had been quietly concerned for years about a whole series of economic trends that might one day reduce the need for high-end corporate-law practices there. These included the potential impact of bank mergers, the "hollowing out" of head offices in Toronto as Canadian firms were absorbed into larger entities, and the potential for Canadian business to go directly to Wall Street instead of through domestic institutions for their financing requirements. There, too, some once prominent partnerships had faded from the front rank. In 2002 Iain Scott told his partners he expected that the "Seven Sisters" of elite law firms might soon subdivide into three or four acknowledged leaders and a second grouping.

As its aspiration to "dominance" suggested, McCarthy Tétrault was in no danger of vanishing or even of losing its place at the cutting edge of legal practice. But its history demonstrates that ever since its constituent firms began to emerge in the nineteenth century their leaders had been making key decisions that had placed or kept their practices among the front-runners. D'Alton McCarthy Jr.'s decision to move to Toronto in the 1870s enabled him to use his success in law and public life as the basis for a leading corporate-law practice. Gordon MacDougall's business-law successes in the early twentieth century gave his Montreal firm a corporate practice to stand alongside the litigation strength Eugène Lafleur had established since the 1880s. In the 1950s Beverley Matthews' skillful manoeuvres and John Robinette's brilliance transformed McCarthy & McCarthy from the "house law firm of Canada Life" into a strong, broadly based corporate and litigation law practice.* In the 1960s and 1970s leaders at Clarkson Tétrault made a series of choices that sustained their firm through the business and social upheavals those years brought to Montreal. Similarly, the decisions of Robert G. Black in Calgary in 1980 and of the founders of Shrum, Liddle & Hebenton in Vancouver in the 1960s brought new law firms into being and eventually to prominence. The national firm decisions that built McCarthy Tétrault in the 1980s had similar impact, and time is likely to show that the strategic planning initiatives at the start of the new century were just as crucial.

In 2005 McCarthy Tétrault could celebrate 150 years of legal practice at or near the first rank among Canadian law firms. Throughout that time, it has grown and changed along with the legal needs of the country. Its lawyers have responded to, and influenced, the legal and constitutional evolution of Canada, from the Privy Council decisions on federal and provincial rights in the 1880s, through the Persons case of 1929 to the interpretation of the Charter of Rights and Freedoms since 1982. The firm's leading clients, including at different times resource

*In 2003, in one of the largest corporate mergers of the year, Canada Life, a client since at least 1876, was absorbed by GreatWest Life Assurance Company of Winnipeg, and McCarthy Tétrault, which had supplied board members and legal advice to the company for over a century, ceded that retainer to GreatWest's lawyers. By 2003, however, the loss was far from being the body blow it would have been to McCarthy & McCarthy fifty years earlier.

companies, financial institutions, utilities, professional organizations, national and international enterprises and technology firms, have themselves tracked the evolution of the Canadian economy and society from the mid-nineteenth to the twenty-first century.

In 1900 or 1950 or even 1975, no one would have predicted the emergence of 2005's McCarthy Tétrault from the small and local law firms that existed in those years. Given the pace of change among law firms and their clients, it is equally impossible to predict what McCarthy Tétrault might evolve into as the twenty-first century progresses. The history of the firm suggests only a single constant, other than the unceasing need to find and nurture legal skill and deliver it to the satisfaction of the clients. That constant is leadership.

Sophisticated and empowered management is a very recent phenomenon among Canadian law firms. For most of their history even the largest and most influential law firms have been relatively casually organized; they were run by lawyers who retained a good deal of freedom to organize their practices and their partnerships as they chose. Yet in the firms that have endured and succeeded the lack of formal organization has rarely meant a dearth of leadership. At every stage of the growth of the law firms that became McCarthy Tétrault, this history suggests there have been leaders who made crucial choices, secured new clients or determined new directions. The success of those choices, whether in the 1880s or in the 1980s or at various moments in between, enabled the firms to remain at the front, with the ability to consider new choices as the legal environment shifted again.

Building the national law firm in the 1980s and then building the new governance system to match the new scale of practice at the start of the twenty-first century have been the most recent strategic choices in a long line that goes back to D'Alton McCarthy's decision to launch a Toronto law firm in 1877. That responsibility for building McCarthy Tétrault is the challenge that continues to engage the firm.

APPENDIX A

THE JUDGES OF McCARTHY TÉTRAULT

NOT EVERY LAWYER seeks an appointment to the bench. Eugène Lafleur of Montreal and John J. Robinette of Toronto, two of the most distinguished litigators of the firms that became McCarthy Tétrault, declined repeated offers of judicial appointments, including, in Lafleur's case, appointment as chief justice of Canada. Over the years, however, more than fifty members of the firms, most but not all of whom have come from the litigation departments, have served as judges or have joined (or returned to) the firm as counsel after leaving the bench.

Jean Archambault: Practised in the Montreal office 1972–92, appointed to the Quebec Superior Court 1992.

Gregor Barclay: Practised in the Montreal office 1910–34, appointed to the Quebec Court of Appeal 1934.

Jean Beetz: Appointed to the Quebec Court of Appeal 1973, appointed to the Supreme Court of Canada 1974. Joined the Montreal office as counsel 1989–91, upon his retirement from the bench.

W. Ian C. Binnie: Practised in the Toronto office 1986–98, appointed to the Supreme Court of Canada 1998.

Claude Bisson: Appointed to the Quebec Superior Court 1969, promoted to the Court of Appeal 1980, appointed chief judge of the Court of Appeal 1996, joined McCarthy Tétrault as counsel 1996 upon his retirement from the court.

John W. Brooke: Practised in the Toronto office 1955–63, appointed to the Ontario High Court of Justice 1963 and to the Court of Appeal 1969.

Catherine Bruce: Practised in the Vancouver office 1977–78, appointed to the Provincial Court of British Columbia.

Alan W. Bryant: Practised in the Toronto office 1989–2004, appointed to the Ontario Superior Court of Justice 2004.

Colin L. Campbell: Practised in the Toronto office 1967–98, appointed to the Ontario Superior Court of Justice 1998.

Michel Côté: Practised in the Montreal office 1975–88, appointed to the Quebec Superior Court 1988.

Louis Crête: Practised in the Montreal office 1984–94, appointed to the Quebec Superior Court 1994.

Michael J.P. Cuddihy: Practised in the Montreal office 1972–75, appointed to the Quebec Expropriation Tribunal (from 1988, the Expropriation Division of the Court of Quebec) 1975.

Pierre J. Dalphond: Practised in the Montreal office 1984–95, appointed to the Superior Court of Quebec 1995.

Barry M. Davies: Practised in the Vancouver office 1979–80, appointed to the Supreme Court of British Columbia 1996.

David H. Doherty: Practised in the Toronto office 1985–88, appointed to the Ontario High Court of Justice 1988 and to the Court of Appeal 1991.

François-Xavier Drouin: Practised in Quebec City 1872–1914, appointed to the Superior Court of Quebec 1914.

William F. Ehrcke: Practised in the Vancouver office 1980–81, appointed to the Supreme Court of British Columbia 2003.

Willard Zebedee "Bud" Estey: Appointed to the Supreme Court of Canada 1977. Joined the Toronto office as counsel 1989, upon his retirement from the court.

James M. Farley: Practised in the Toronto office 1989, appointed to the Ontario High Court of Justice 1989 and to the Ontario Court of Justice, General Division (now the Superior Court of Justice), 1990.

Jane E. Ferguson: Practised in the London, Ontario, office 1990–2004, appointed to the Ontario Superior Court of Justice 2004.

George D. Finlayson: Practised in the Toronto office 1953–84, appointed to the Ontario Court of Appeal 1984.

Paul-Arthur Gendreau: Practised in the Quebec City office 1982–86, appointed to the Quebec Court of Appeal 1986.

Eileen E. Gillese: Practised in the London, Ontario, office 1989–91, appointed to the Ontario Superior Court of Justice 1999 and to the Court of Appeal 2002.

Charles Gonthier: Practised in the Montreal office 1957–74, appointed to the Quebec Superior Court 1974, promoted to the Quebec Court of Appeal 1988 and to the Supreme Court of Canada 1989. Returned to the Montreal office as counsel 2004 upon his retirement from the Supreme Court in 2003.

Susan E. Greer: Practised in the Toronto office 1973–91, appointed to the Ontario Court of Justice, General Division (later the Superior Court of Justice), 1991.

Allan R. Hilton: Practised in the Montreal office 1975–98, appointed to the Quebec Superior Court 1998 and promoted to the Court of Appeal 2003.

Heather Holmes: Practised in the Vancouver office 1981–82, appointed to the Supreme Court of British Columbia 2001.

Frances E. Howard: Practised in the Vancouver office, appointed to the Provincial Court of British Columbia.

Ralph Hudson: Practised in the Vancouver office to 1982, appointed to the Supreme Court of Yukon Territory.

James Knatchbull Hugessen: Practised in the Montreal office 1958–72, appointed to the Quebec Superior Court 1972, became associate chief judge 1973, appointed to the Federal Court of Canada, Appellate Division, 1983.

George Miller Hyde: Practised in the Montreal office 1929–50, appointed to the Quebec Court of Appeal 1950.

Pamela Kirkpatrick: Practised in the Vancouver office 1978–89, appointed to the Supreme Court of British Columbia 1992.

M. Marvyn Koenigsburg: Practised in the Toronto office 1977–82, appointed to the Supreme Court of British Columbia 1992.

Louis Lacoursière: Practised in the Montreal office 1975–2003, appointed to the Quebec Superior Court 2003.

Robert Everett Laidlaw: Practised in the Toronto office 1919–23, appointed to the Supreme Court of Ontario, Appellate Division, 1943.

Julien Lanctôt: Practised in the Montreal office 1980–98, appointed to the Quebec Superior Court 1998.

Brian Malone: Practised in the Calgary office 1983–99, appointed to the Federal Court of Canada, Appellate Division, 2000.

Thomas Melnick: Practised in the Vancouver office 1985–86, appointed to the County Court of British Columbia 1987 and to the Supreme Court of British Columbia 1990.

Wallace Nesbitt: Practised in the Toronto office 1883–92, appointed to the Supreme Court of Canada 1903, resigned 1905. Counsel to the Toronto office 1905–16.

Lawrence A. Poitras: Practised in the Montreal office 1970–75, appointed to the Quebec Superior Court 1975, named associate chief judge 1983, chief judge 1992.

Yves Pratte: Appointed to the Supreme Court of Canada 1977, resigned 1979. Counsel to the Montreal office from 1979 to his death in 1988.

André Prévost: Practised in the Montreal office 1975–2004, appointed to the Quebec Superior Court 2004.

Georgina M. Quijano: Practised in the Vancouver office 1977–92, appointed to the Supreme Court of British Columbia 1995.

Barbara Romaine: Practised in the Calgary office 1982–97, appointed to the Court of Queen's Bench of Alberta 1997.

William B. Scott: Practised in the Montreal office 1913–52, appointed associate chief justice of the Quebec Superior Court 1952.

Karen Sharlow: Practised in the Vancouver office 1982–90, appointed to the Federal Court of Canada, Trial and Appellate Divisions, 1999.

Kenneth Smith: Practised in the Vancouver office 1988–93, appointed to the Supreme Court of British Columbia 1993 and to the British Columbia Court of Appeal 2001.

Lynn Smith: Practised in the Vancouver office 1974–83, appointed to the Supreme Court of British Columbia 1998.

Ronald E. Sobier: Practised in the Toronto office 1963–89, appointed to the Tax Court of Canada 1990.

Elizabeth M. Stewart: Practised in the Toronto office 1978–2003, appointed to the Ontario Superior Court of Justice 2003.

Barry Stuart: Practised in the Vancouver office, appointed to the Territorial Court of Yukon 1985, later chief justice of Yukon.

James Williams: Practised in the Vancouver office, appointed to the Supreme Court of British Columbia 2002.

Judith M. Woods: Practised in the Toronto office 1978–2003, appointed to the Tax Court of Canada 2003.

APPENDIX B

SOURCES AND ACKNOWLEDGEMENTS

McCARTHY TÉTRAULT has an efficient management system for its client records, which are protected by rules of client confidentiality and solicitor-client privilege—and which I neither saw nor sought to see. What I did see for the writing of this history were the records of how the law firm has administered itself. McCarthy Tétrault gave me extensive access to these. At times I was studying handwritten nineteenth-century ledger books, at other times, the minutes of firm policy discussions just months after they occurred.

For most of the last century and a half, lawyers rarely ran their own law firms with the kind of sophisticated management systems that they advised corporations, businesses and public institutions to adopt. As this history suggests, it is only in recent decades that law firms have begun to apply formal, systematically documented management processes to their own operations. Only for the last twenty-five or thirty years has there been an administrative structure generating systematic files: committee minutes, correspondence files, annual financial reports and so on. As a result, most of the early history of the firms that became McCarthy Tétrault has been drawn together from scattered and incomplete sources, even though the firms' librarians, particularly those in Toronto and Montreal, have for some years been collecting memorabilia that survives from those early years and have preserved some excellent materials.

I supplemented the written records by talking with lawyers and staff who recalled their predecessors and who have themselves experienced first-hand the startling changes that legal practice in general and this law firm in particular have seen in recent decades. I conducted more than a hundred interviews with individual lawyers and staff members in the firm and with interested parties beyond it, and I only regret not having had the opportunity to do hundreds more. In time, the transcripts of these interviews will themselves become part of the historical record of McCarthy Tétrault.

Because I depended so much on the memories of firm members, my principal acknowledgement must be to all the partners, lawyers and staff of McCarthy Tétrault. In every city and office, lawyers were wonderfully accommodating about making time in their busy schedules to talk with me. They consistently proved to be frank, perceptive, illuminating and articulate in their consideration of any and all aspects of their firm's history. It was the same with staff, who not only took up my administrative or organizational challenges with alacrity but always had a great deal of firm lore to share.

I am grateful to them all, individually and collectively. In addition I am indebted to the following firm members, former members and interested outsiders for specific acts of assistance or simply for contributions to my knowledge of the subject:

In Montreal, Yves Bériault, André Prévost, Madeleine Renaud, Murielle Bush, Danielle Miller, Daniel Murphy and Ronald Renault, and from outside the firm retired chief justice Alan B. Gold (counsel to Davies Ward Phillips & Vineberg), Mr. Justice Lawrence Poitras (counsel, Borden Ladner Gervais), Richard Pound (partner, Stikeman Elliott) and Senator Maurice Riel (counsel, Stikeman Elliott).

In Toronto, Mary Percival of McCarthy Tétrault's John J. Robinette Law Library has dedicated herself to the firm's history and its archives for many years. Her support and that of all her staff was invaluable. Also Kirby Chown, Peter Grant, Lee Krone, Lise Monette, Pat Tellis and Gary Wolff, and from outside the firm Brian Bucknell and librarian Sandra Petrosic for access to records held by Osler Hoskin LLP, Mr. Justice Colin Campbell, legal historian Curtis Cole, Professor Martin Friedland, Mr. Justice George Ferguson, Susan Lewthwaite and her colleagues at the Archives of the Law Society of Upper Canada, the Osgoode Society for Canadian Legal History, Professor and Mrs. E.J. Revell, and Jim Tory (counsel, Torys).

In Calgary, librarians Phyllis Thornton and Lee Sudrich, and from outside the firm the staff of the Legal Archives Society of Alberta, and Professor Louis A. Knafla of the University of Calgary.

In Vancouver, former British Columbia attorney general Brian Smith, Mitchell Gropper (now at Farris & Company), Alec Robertson of Davis & Company, Mr. Justice Frank Maczko, Madame Justice M. Marvyn Koenigsberg, Keith Liddle, the late David Roberts of Campney Murphy, and Professor John McLaren of the University of Victoria.

For help with the photographs, I am particularly grateful to Daniel Murphy in Montreal, Lee Sudrich and Kim Pryhitko in Calgary and Michael Luk in Vancouver.

For the publication process, I am grateful to designer Ingrid Paulson and to Susan Rana and her staff at Douglas & McIntyre, and above all to Ramsay Derry, McCarthy Tétrault's publishing consultant and also the editor of the work, with whom it was a pleasure to work so closely over more than two years. And finally my family: Louise Brophy and our daughters Elizabeth and Kate, who may know more than they ever expected to about lawyers and their histories.

NOTES

ABBREVIATIONS:

AO	Archives of Ontario
DCB	*Dictionary of Canadian Biography*
LAC	Library and Archives of Canada, formerly National Archives of Canada
LSUCA	Law Society of Upper Canada Archives
MTA	McCarthy Tétrault Archives
OHA	Osler Hoskin Archives
Law Lists	Canadian legal directories published under a variety of titles by different publishers since 1860.

McCARTHY & McCARTHY: A TORONTO LAW FIRM

1. Details of the McCarthys' Irish legal careers are found in Edward P. Keane, Beryl Phair and Thomas U. Sadlier, eds., *King's Inn Admission Papers 1607–1867* (Dublin: Stationary Office for the Irish Manuscripts Commission, 1982). Marriage and family details are drawn from McCarthy family tree data preserved in MTA (Toronto), File D'Alton McCarthy, Family History.
2. On the role of Catholics in the Irish legal profession, see Colum Kenny, "The Exclusion of Catholics from the Legal Profession in Ireland, 1537–1829," *Irish Historical Studies* 25 (November 1987), p. 337. Incomplete lists of lawyers who converted are published in Eileen O'Byrne, *The Convert Rolls* (Dublin: Irish Manuscripts Commission, 1981). They include no McCarthys who can be linked to what became the "Canadian" family.
3. MTA (Toronto), File D'Alton McCarthy, Family History.
4. One child, John G. McCarthy, was sent back to Britain for schooling, and the comment about McCarthy Sr.'s failure at farming was part of an application to have the boy accepted

as a charity student at Christ's Hospital, London. MTA, File D'Alton McCarthy Jr., Family History. McCarthy Sr.'s admittance as a solicitor is in LSUCA, Solicitors' Rolls, June 7, 1855.

5. LSUCA, Roll of Barristers and Solicitors' Rolls, 1859–61. The *Law Lists* report the dates and places where they practised.
6. *DCB*, vol. X, "D'Arcy Boulton," by Hereward Senior.
7. On Barrie, see Andrew F. Hunter, *The History of Simcoe County*. Barrie: Simcoe County Historical Society, 2 vols., 1909, reprinted 1948, 1982.
8. Firm details from *Law Lists*. D. Lally McCarthy comment from the unpublished draft memoirs of D. Lally McCarthy, held in LSUCA, William Howland Fonds.
9. Boultbee was quoted in 1898 when McCarthy died. Clippings in MTA (Toronto), File D'Alton McCarthy Jr., Death.
10. Comment of T.W. Torrance, a Barrie lawyer, included in clippings in MTA (Toronto), File D'Alton McCarthy Jr., Death. John McCarthy, undated letter to D'Alton McCarthy (c. 1896), AO, J.L.G. McCarthy Papers.
11. For a summary of D'Alton McCarthy Jr.'s public life, see *DCB*, vol. XII, "D'Alton McCarthy" by Larry L. Kulisek.
12. On the economic history of the Ontario timber trade, see Ian M. Drummond, *Progress Without Planning: The Economic History of Ontario from Confederation to the Second World War* (Toronto: University of Toronto Press, 1987). The statement about McCarthy's $200,000 debt is from his friend A. Boultbee, quoted above. McCarthy's statement to Macdonald is noted below.
13. OHA, Toronto, Partnership Agreements.
14. On Osler generally, see Curtis Cole, *Osler, Hoskin & Harcourt: Portrait of a Partnership* (Toronto: McGraw Hill, 1995). Lally McCarthy's comment is from his unpublished draft memoir.
15. OHA, Toronto, Firm Ledgers, vol. 1.
16. Case statistics compiled from Quicklaw searches by Mary Percival of the John J. Robinette Law Library at McCarthy Tétrault in Toronto.
17. See Paul Romney, *Mr. Attorney General* (Toronto: University of Toronto Press, 1986), particularly chap. 6, and John Saywell, *The Lawmakers* (Toronto: University of Toronto Press, 2002), for differing interpretations of the constitutional issue and the case law.
18. Mowat quotation from A. Margaret Evans, *Sir Oliver Mowat* (Toronto: University of Toronto Press, 1992), p. 155.
19. On McCarthy's political views, see J.R. Miller's articles, "As a Politician He is a Great Enigma: The Social and Political Ideas of D'Alton McCarthy," *Canadian Historical Review* 58 #4 (December 1977), pp. 399–421, and "D'Alton McCarthy, Equal Rights, and the Origins of the Manitoba School Question," *Canadian Historical Review* 53 #4 (December 1973), pp. 369–92.
20. Macdonald's judicial offer, LAC MG 27 I E7 D'Alton McCarthy Papers, November 7, 1878. McCarthy declines cabinet post, LAC, John A. Macdonald Papers, McCarthy to Macdonald, June 25, 1884.
21. On Honoré Mercier, see the biography by Pierre Dufour and Jean Hamelin in *DCB*, vol. XII. On the politics of this period, Peter Waite, *Arduous Destiny: Canada 1873–1896* (Toronto: McClelland & Stewart, 1971) remains useful. McCarthy's alarm at Mercier's politics comes through in his parliamentary speech of 1890, cited below.

22. J.R. Miller, *Equal Rights: The Jesuit Estates Act Controversy* (Montreal: McGill–Queen's University Press, 1979).
23. J.R. Miller, "Equal Rights for All," *Ontario History* 65 #4 (December 1973), pp. 189–210.
24. Canada, House of Commons, *Debates*, 1890, McCarthy speech, January 22 and following days.
25. Macdonald comment from Kulisek, "D'Alton McCarthy." All other quotations from *Debates*, 1890.
26. OHA, McCarthy, Osler Firm Accounts, passim.
27. OHA, McCarthy, Osler Ledgers, passim. On Cox, Mackenzie and their milieu, see Michael Bliss, *Northern Enterprise: Five Centuries of Canadian Business* (Toronto: McClelland & Stewart, 1987), chap. 12 and 13.
28. OHA, Firm Ledgers, passim.
29. OHA, Firm Accounts, passim. Street addresses are reported in the *Law Lists* and confirmed by surviving examples of firm letterhead, etc.
30. Comments from obituary notices gathered in MTA, File D'Alton McCarthy Jr., Death, and from Lally McCarthy's draft memoir, LSUCA, Howland Fonds, D. Lally McCarthy Files.
31. MTA (Toronto), File D'Alton McCarthy Jr., Death.
32. Cole, *Osler, Hoskin & Harcourt.*
33. Cole, *Osler, Hoskin & Harcourt.*
34. Nesbitt Agreement, MTA (Toronto), Partnership Agreements File #2. Firm income figures from OHA, Firm Accounts. Lally McCarthy's story of "Deadman" Stewart is in his draft memoir at LSUCA.
35. The Beatty, Blackstock and Blake firms are discussed by Ian Kyer and T.R. Regehr, respectively, in Carol Wilton, ed., *Inside the Law: Canadian Law Firms in Historical Perspective* (Toronto: Osgoode Society, 1997).
36. Leighton's early feelings about his uncle are expressed in family letters preserved at AO, J.L.G. McCarthy Papers. Details on his Simcoe campaign are in MTA (Toronto), File Leighton McCarthy.
37. W.R.R. Riddell quotation from "The Lawyer, An Address to the Ontario Bar Association," *Canadian Law Times* (December 1907). Zebulon Lash quotation from Michael Bliss, *A Canadian Millionaire: The Life and Business Times of Sir Joseph Flavelle* (Toronto: Macmillan, 1978), p. 58.
38. *DCB*, vol. XIII, "George Albertus Cox" by Michael Bliss.
39. On Cox's insurance interests, see Ian Drummond, "Canadian Life Insurance Companies and the Capital Market 1890–1914," *Canadian Journal of Economics and Political Science* 28 #2 (May 1962), pp. 204–24.
40. Bliss, *A Canadian Millionaire*, p. 197.
41. Janice Tyrwhitt, *Small Things Grow Great: The First 150 Years of the Canada Life Assurance Company* (Toronto: Canada Life, 1996). MTA (Toronto), File Leighton McCarthy, "Toronto Club Speech February 13, 1945."
42. Cole, *Osler, Hoskin & Harcourt*, pp. 62–64.
43. Comments of W.C. Terry and Beverley Matthews in *McCarthy & McCarthy: A History* (Toronto: privately published, 1978), and of client Elizabeth Bethune Campbell, *Where Angels Fear to Tread* (Boston: privately published, 1935).

44. MTA (Toronto), Edith Sheppard File. The quotation is from a personal letter, part of a collection lent to the firm by Edith Sheppard's family.
45. Cole, *Osler, Hoskin & Harcourt*, p. 89 and app. II.
46. Kenneth Lipartito and Joseph Pratt, *Baker and Botts in the Development of Modern Houston* (Austin, Texas: University of Texas Press, 1991). Robert T. Swaine, *The Cravath Firm and Its Predecessors* (New York: 3 vols., privately published, 1946–48), particularly vol. II, pp. 3–15.
47. Constance Backhouse, "Gretta Wong Grant: Canada's First Chinese-Canadian Female Lawyer," *Windsor Yearbook of Access to Justice* 15 (1996), pp. 3–46. In 1990, the Osgoode Society for Canadian Legal History recorded an Oral History Interview with Gretta Wong Grant.
48. MTA (Toronto), Arthur Scace, Oral History Interview. John Clarry, in his oral history, confirms Scace's memory of the transfer.
49. MTA (Toronto), Oral History Interview with Peter Beattie, 2003.
50. MTA (Toronto), Minutes of Management Committee, February 12, 1979.
51. *McCarthy & McCarthy: A History.* In an era when advertising by lawyers was considered inappropriate, the law firm produced this history of itself as a confidential, internal document. No author is credited, but Toronto management committee minutes show that partner Ross Butters supervised the project and Gweneth McGregor, a consultant working with the firm's tax department, did a good deal of the writing.
52. Minutes of the management committee exist from 1973, but a note in 1977 indicates that it had then existed for six years. MTA, Management Committee Minutes.

BLACK & COMPANY: LAW AND BUSINESS IN CALGARY

53. Hardy's *Canadian Law List* 1909–11 (Toronto: Hardy's, 1911).
54. James H. Gray, *Talk to My Lawyer: Great Stories of Southern Alberta's Bench and Bar* (Edmonton: Hurtig, 1987), quoted in chap. 8.
55. On Bennett, see P.B. Waite, *The Loner: Three Sketches of the Personal Life and Ideas of R.B. Bennett* (Toronto: University of Toronto Press, 1982), p. 31. The Bennett Lougheed firm and feud is described in Jack Batten, *A History of Bennett Jones Verchere* (Calgary: Bennett Jones, 1997). On early Calgary lawyers and judges, Louis Knafla, "Goodall and Cairns: Commercial, Corporate, and Energy Law in Alberta, 1920–42," in Carol Wilton, ed., *Inside the Law: Canadian Law Firms in Historical Perspective* (Toronto: Osgoode Society, 1996), pp. 320–56. The files of the Alberta Legal History Archives Society of Alberta in Calgary were also very useful on Alberta law firm history.
56. Fred H. Diehl, *A Gentleman from a Fading Era: Eric Lafferty Harvie* (Calgary: Devonian Foundation, 1989).
57. Estimates on lawyer mobility from Federation of Law Societies of Canada, Report of Special Committee on Inter-Provincial Law Firms ("The Freedman Report"), June 1982. Copy in MTA (Toronto), J.C. McCartney Files, Merger Documents, Box 2. Also Gillian Stewart, "Law of the West," *Calgary* (September 1981), pp. 40–43, 109–12.
58. MTA (Toronto), J.C. McCartney Files, Calgary Committee, McCartney to Management Committee, October 9, 1979.

59. MTA (Toronto), McCartney Files, Calgary Committee, Calgary Committee to Management Committee, January 11, 1980. The Calgary Committee comprised Peter Beattie, Basil Cheeseman, Colin Coolican, Ewens, McCartney and Patrick Vernon.
60. MTA (Toronto), J.C. McCartney Files, Calgary Committee, "Report of the Committee on Business Opportunities in Calgary" to Management Committee January 11, 1980.
61. Cheeseman's notes on the phone conversation are in MTA (Toronto), J.C. McCartney Files, Calgary Committee. Robert Black reported the Law Society of Alberta's version of the conversation in a memo of March 16, 1981, in *Black & Company: A History* (Toronto: McCarthy & McCarthy, privately printed, 1989) at tab 2. This volume is a compilation of key documents about Black & Company, bound for presentation to members of the firm upon its merger with McCarthy & McCarthy in 1989. A copy is held in MTA (Toronto).
62. MTA, John Clarry Management Memos, Management Committee decision re special partners meetings for January 15 and April 13, 1981. Clarry's memo to the Law Society, February 18, 1981, *Black & Company: A History,* tab 1.
63. Jon R. Bauman, *Pioneering a Global Vision: The Story of Baker and McKenzie* (Chicago: Baker & McKenzie, 1999).
64. Joan M. Travostino, "Regulating Multistate Law Firms," 32 *Stanford Law Review* (1980), p. 1211.
65. Richard Pound, *Stikeman Elliott: The First Fifty Years* (Montreal: McGill–Queen's University Press, 2002).
66. W. Wesley Pue, "Becoming Ethical: Lawyers' Professional Ethics in Early Twentieth Century Canada," in Dale Gibson and Wesley Pue, eds., *Glimpses of Canadian Legal History* (Winnipeg: Legal Research Institute, 1991), pp. 237–77.
67. MTA (Toronto), Clarry Management Memoranda Files, J. Clarry memo re Calgary, December 2, 1980.
68. Richard Pound, *Stikeman Elliott: The First Fifty Years,* pp. 83–85.
69. MTA (Toronto), J.C. McCartney Files, Calgary Committee, G.P.H. Vernon, "Reflections on Contesting Legality of Rule 154," April 9, 1982, and comments from Ewens and Shaw in the same file.
70. *Black & Company: A History,* tab 6, "Submission to the Benchers Re Rule 154 by J.W. Beames, QC" April 24, 1982, with a transcript of the discussion that followed.
71. *Alberta Report,* June 13, 1983, "The Outsiders Fight Back."
72. Federation of Law Societies of Canada, Report of Special Committee on Inter-Provincial Law Firms ("The Freedman Report"), June 1982. Copy in MTA (Toronto), J.C. McCartney Files, Merger Documents, Box 2.
73. MTA, John Clarry Management Memos, Committee decisions November 17, 1982: J.C. McCartney to National Management Committee, October 14, 1982.
74. *Black & Company: A History,* tab 7, Black & Company statement of claim, Court of Queen's Bench of Alberta, Judicial District of Edmonton, December 16, 1982.
75. Advice from the Milner, Steer firm and views of McCarthy partners on the litigation are included in MTA (Toronto), J.C. McCartney Files, Calgary Committee. Black's memo of November 29, 1982, in *Black & Company: A History,* tab 6.

76. Shaw's annotation is on the copy of Black's November 29, 1982, memo included in *Black & Company: A History*, tab 6. Shaw identified his handwriting.
77. MTA (Toronto), Black & Company Financial Statements 1982–89. Scace's comment from Osgoode Society Oral History Interview with Scace, Beverley Matthews and John Clarry, September 1989 (copy in MTA).
78. MTA (Toronto), J.C. McCartney Files, Long Range Planning File, Draft Memo re National Firm, May 9, 1984.
79. *Alberta Law Reports*, Second Series, Court of Queen's Bench, Dea J., "Black et al. v. Law Society of Alberta," Reason for Judgment, August 20, 1984.
80. *Alberta Law Reports*, Second Series, Court of Appeal, Lieberman, Kerans, and Stevenson JJA, Black et al. v. Law Society of Alberta, Reasons for Judgment, March 4, 1986.
81. *Black & Company: A History*, tab 1.
82. MTA, John Clarry Management Memos, National Law Firm Committee Memo, October 31, 1983.
83. MTA, John Clarry Management Memos, Partners Meeting, November 16, 1983.

SHRUM, LIDDLE & HEBENTON: WEST COAST INNOVATIONS

84. This summary history of the B.C. bar draws on Alfred Watts, *History of the Legal Profession in British Columbia 1869–1984* (Victoria: Law Society of British Columbia, 1984), Carol Wilton, ed., *Inside the Law: Canadian Law Firms in Historical Perspective* (Toronto: University of Toronto Press, 1996), and DCB.
85. Christine Mullins and Arthur E. Harvey, *Russell & DuMoulin: The First Hundred Years* (Vancouver: privately published, 1989).
86. *Canadian Law Journal*, 1910, quoted on the Davis & Company Web site, www.davis.ca.
87. Reginald H. Roy, "Law on the Pacific Coast: Bull, Housser and Tupper, 1945–90," in Wilton, ed., *Inside the Law*, pp. 498–529. Farris history from the firm's Web site, www.farris.com.
88. MTA, Oral History Interview with Gordon Shrum.
89. Planning Committee Report, April 1981, copy in Sholto Hebenton's personal file on firm history.
90. Statistics based on *Canadian Law Lists* for British Columbia.
91. Clarkson Gordon Management Review, February 9, 1984, copy in Sholto Hebenton's personal file on firm history.
92. The McCarthy Tétrault law library in Vancouver preserves a file of the *Shrumbleton News*.
93. J.C. McCartney Files, National Law Firm Correspondence, National Law Firm Committee to Management Committee on Vancouver contacts, January 25, 1984.
94. Doug Ewens described Black's contribution in MTA (Toronto), Clarry Management Memos, November 16, 1984, Ewens to Clarry, May 8, 1984.
95. J.C. McCartney Files, Merger Documents, Box 2, Vancouver, Merger agreement November 1, 1984.

96. MTA (Toronto), J.C. McCartney Files, National Law Firm Committee Memoranda, July 6, 1984.
97. J.C. McCartney Files, Merger Documents, Box 2, Shrum, Liddle & Hebenton submission to Law Society of British Columbia, November 4, 1984.
98. Attorney General Smith's letter was also published in *The Advocate,* the publication of the Vancouver Bar Association, in vol. 43 #1 (January 1985), p. 25, along with Byran Gibson, "Inter-Provincial Law Firms and the Merger of Shrum, Liddle & Hebenton and McCarthy & McCarthy," pp. 15–24.
99. Giles's statement is from his letter to the treasurer of the Law Society of B.C., April 25, 1985. Copy in MTA (Toronto), J.C. McCartney Files, "Re: Merger, #1."
100. Quotations are drawn from coverage of the B.C. benchers' debate in *Canadian Lawyer* (June 1985), p. 8, "Attention Swings to Alberta after McCarthy-Shrum Ruling."
101. Oral History Interview with Brian Smith, Victoria, June 2002.
102. MTA (Toronto), J.C. McCartney Files, Merger Files, Box 2, Hebenton to McCartney, June 5, 1985.
103. MTA (Toronto), J.C. McCartney Files, Merger Files, Box 1, Hebenton to Clarry, September 30, 1986.
104. MTA (Toronto), John Clarry Management Memos, partners meeting November 16, 1983, enclosing a letter of September 22, 1983.
105. MTA (Toronto), John Clarry Management Memos, re partners meeting November 19, 1984, enclosing memo from Michael Royce to Clarry, August 7, 1984.
106. Royce to Clarry, August 7, 1984.
107. MTA (Toronto), J.C. McCartney Files, National Law Firm Correspondence, Ron Slaght to National Law Firm Committee, July 20, 1984, and Douglas Laidlaw to National Law Firm Committee, August 14, 1984.
108. MTA (Toronto), Douglas Laidlaw Files, obituaries and news clippings.
109. MTA (Toronto), Clarry Management Memos, re partners meeting October 1, 1984.
110. MTA (Toronto), J.C. McCartney Files, Merger Documents, Box 2, Vancouver, Merger Agreement November 1, 1984.
111. MTA (Toronto), J.C. McCartney Files, Merger Documents, Box 1, Vancouver, Hebenton to McCartney, June 28, 1988, includes copies of the letters solicited by the attorney general's counsel, Jack Giles, from the seven lawyers, six of whom were litigation specialists.
112. Supreme Court of British Columbia, *Martin v. Attorney General of British Columbia,* Reasons for Judgment of Callaghan J., September 6, 1988, p. 32. Hebenton's comment: J.C. McCartney Files, Merger Documents, Box 2, Vancouver, Hebenton to McCartney, June 28, 1988.
113. Fraser Elliott's and Heward Stikeman's lobbying of the British Columbia government regarding interprovincial law firms is noted in Richard Pound, *Stikeman Elliott: The First Fifty Years* (Montreal: McGill–Queen's University Press, 2002). Attorney General Brian Smith (personal interview) also recalled their influence.
114. Law Society of British Columbia, *Benchers' Bulletin,* October 1988.
115. MTA (Toronto), J.C. McCartney Files, National Law Firm Correspondence #1, Hebenton to McCartney, July 15, 1988.
116. Sholto Hebenton, Memorandum to all partners, Interim Report on Partnership of Partnerships, September 9, 1988, in Sholto Hebenton's personal file on firm history.

117. MTA (Toronto), J.C. McCartney Files, Merger Documents, Box 1, Vancouver, Merger Agreement and allied documents for McCarthy & McCarthy and the Vancouver partners, February 1, 1989.
118. Supreme Court of Canada, Reasons for Judgment in *Law Society of Alberta v. Black & Company*, April 20, 1989, in *Black & Company: A History*, tab 9. Scace's comment from Osgoode Society Oral History Interview with Scace, Beverley Matthews and John Clarry, September 1989 (copy in MTA).
119. MTA (Toronto), National Management Committee Minutes, February 10, 1997, has a report of the Law Society of Alberta proceedings.

CLARKSON TÉTRAULT: THE LEGACY OF EUGÈNE LAFLEUR

120. www.genealogie.umontreal.ca, entries for Coussi *dit* Lafleur. David R. Williams, "Eugène Lafleur," *DCB*, vol. XIV (forthcoming). The most detailed study of Eugène Lafleur's life and career is a chapter in David Ricardo Williams, *Just Lawyers* (Toronto: University of Toronto Press, 1995). In 1980 Tom Shaughnessy was commissioned by Courtois, Clarkson to write a history of the firm entitled "Fleural—A Tradition of Advocacy." It was never completed, but there are copies of the draft in the Montreal office of McCarthy Tétrault and MTA (Toronto).
121. Douglas Mitchell and Judy Slinn, *The History of McMaster Meighen* (Montreal: McMaster Meighen, 1989), p. 11.
122. This account relies heavily on Brian Young, *The Politics of Codification: The Lower Canadian Civil Code of 1866* (Montreal: McGill–Queen's University Press, 1994).
123. G-Edouard Rinfret, *Histoire du Barreau de Montreal* (Cowansville, Quebec: Editions Yvon Blais, 1989).
124. The following draws particularly on Blaine Baker, "Ordering the Urban Canadian Law Office and its Entrepreneurial Hinterland," 48 *University of Toronto Law Journal* (1998), pp. 175–251.
125. "William Badgley" in *DCB*, vol. XI, and "John Abbott" in vol. XII. Mitchell and Slinn, *The History of McMaster Meighen*, chap. 1 and 2. Douglas H. Tees, *Chronicles of Ogilvy Renault 1879–1979* (Montreal: Ogilvy Montgomery Renault, 1979).
126. Rinfret, *Histoire du Barreau*. On Cartier's law practice, Brian Young, "Dimensions of a Law Practice: Brokerage and Ideology," in Wilton, ed., *Beyond the Law: Canadian Law Firms in Historical Perspective* (Toronto: University of Toronto Press, 1990).
127. Mitchell and Slinn, *History of McMaster Meighen*. Tees, *Chronicles of Ogilvy Renault 1879–1979*.
128. *Lovell's Montreal Directory* first lists Lafleur & Rielle in its 1886–87 edition.
129. Tom Shaughnessy, *Fleural*, compiles many tributes to Lafleur at the time of his death. The quotation here is from Walter Johnson, KC.
130. Williams, "Eugène Lafleur" in *Just Lawyers*.
131. Ibid.
132. Ibid.

133. Gilles Gallichan, *Les Québécoises et le barreau* (Quebec City: Septentrion, 1999). Williams, "Eugène Lafleur."
134. The 1918 controversy over Lafleur's religion is discussed by Williams, "Eugène Lafleur," pp. 46–47.
135. The library of McCarthy Tétrault in Montreal preserves a complete set of Lafleur's opinions in 30 volumes, as well as his "Notes of Cases" and his indexed collection of commentaries and case citations related, item by item, to the Quebec Civil Code and Code of Procedure.
136. Based largely on Williams, "Eugène Lafleur."
137. Williams, "Eugène Lafleur."
138. John Dales, *Hydroelectricity and Industrial Development: Québec 1898–1940* (Cambridge: Harvard University Press, 1957).
139. Dales, *Hydroelectricity.* Details on MacDougall in *Canadian Who's Who,* various years.
140. Dales, *Hydroelectricity.*
141. H.H. Lank and E.L. Williams, *The DuPont Canada History* (Montreal: DuPont Canada, 1982).
142. Shaughnessy, *Fleural* (ca. 1982), copy on file MTA (Montreal).
143. Memories of the Aldred Building were provided by Margaret Donovan and other staff members whom I interviewed at McCarthy Tétrault in Montreal in 2001.
144. Details based on Shaughnessy, *Fleural,* on notes of Ronald Renault, a former office manager, on file MTA (Montreal), and on oral interviews with long-service staff.
145. *Canadian Who's Who,* various years, for biographies of MacDougall and Macfarlane. MacDougall obituary, Montreal *Gazette,* July 28, 1947.
146. Jacques Tétrault, Oral History Interview.
147. Ibid.
148. On Ogilvy Renault see Tees, *Chronicles of Ogilvy Renault.* The "factory" nickname for the firm was in use by the 1930s.
149. Jacques Tétrault, Oral History Interview.
150. MTA (Montreal), Partnership Agreements Files.
151. Michael Levinson, Oral History Interview.
152. Tam Davis, Oral History Interview.
153. The comparison is based on a count of francophone names (clearly only an approximate indicator) at Clarkson Tétrault and several other leading Montreal firms in *Canadian Law List, 1982.* Francophones were about 38 of Clarkson Tétrault's 61 lawyers listed that year.
154. MTA (Montreal), Executive Committee Minutes, Notes for December 9, 1975 and March 31, 1976, provide some detail on the evolution of the policy board.
155. Staff Oral History Interviews.
156. Statistical comparisons based on *Canadian Law Lists* for various years.
157. MTA (Montreal), Agreements and Contracts File, Declaration December 9, 1975, on efforts in Brussels since January 1975.
158. MTA (Montreal), Executive Committee Minutes, June 15, 1979 (re Langlois Drouin discussions), and Agreements and Contracts File, Agreement with Ballem McDill, December 1, 1977. The agreement of January 25, 1980 (in the same file) to terminate the Ballem McDill association notes the original plan was never acted upon.

159. MTA (Montreal), Agreements and Contracts File, Tétrault to Harry Macdonell, March 26, 1981, "The McCarthy Connection," summarizing Macdonell's memo of February 18, 1981.
160. MTA (Montreal), Rapport du Comité Tétrault, December 1981.
161. MTA (Montreal), Executive Committee Minutes, January 20 and 27, 1982.
162. MTA (Montreal), Executive Committee Minutes, March 9, 1982.
163. Lorna Telfer, Oral History Interview.
164. MTA (Montreal), Executive Committee Minutes, report on recruitment, April 18, 1982. Partnership Minutes, Report of a committee of partners on the state of the firm, April 14, 1984.
165. McCarthy Tétrault Executive Committee Minutes, May 13, 1982. Partnership Committee Minutes May 21, 1982. Agreements and Contracts File, Tétrault to Burtnick, June 3, 1982. Agreement with Grafftey Management Co., July 16, 1982.
166. MTA (Montreal), Executive Committee Minutes, July 18, 1994.
167. MTA (Montreal), Partnership Minutes: Memo to Partners Meeting on Future of the Firm, April 14, 1984.
168. MTA (Montreal), Executive Committee Minutes, August 1986.
169. *Le Monde Juridique,* November 1985, conversation with Jacques Tétrault.
170. MTA (Montreal), Clarkson Tétrault Executive Committee Minutes, Drouin to Tétrault, January 1988.
171. MTA (Montreal), Executive Committee Minutes, December 1984.
172. Jacques Tétrault, Oral History Interview.
173. MTA (Toronto), J.C. McCartney files, National Law Firm Correspondence #1, Hebenton to McCartney, July 15, 1988.
174. MTA (Toronto), J.C. McCartney Papers, Misc. Administrative Files, September 16 and 19, 1988. Notes on meetings with Clarkson Tétrault in September 1988 regarding an affiliation.
175. MTA (Toronto), J.C. McCartney Papers, Misc. Administrative Files, Memorandum September 20, 1988.
176. J.C. McCartney, Oral History Interview.
177. MTA (Montreal), Jacques Tétrault Files, Tétrault and Dennis, October 28, 1989.
178. MTA (Montreal), Clarkson Tétrault Partnership Minutes, October 4, 1998. Tétrault and Dennis, Memorandum to partners, October 20, 1989.
179. J.C. McCartney, Oral History Interview.
180. Jacques Tétrault, Oral History Interview.
181. Jacques Tétrault, Oral History Interview.
182. J.C. McCartney, Oral History Interview. Harry Macdonell, Oral History Interview.
183. MTA (Toronto), J.C. McCartney Papers, Misc. Administrative Files, April 20, 1989, McCartney to National Management Committee.
184. MTA (Montreal), Partnership Agreements File, Memo of Clarkson Tétrault merger committee to all partners, November 21, 1989.
185. MTA (Montreal), Partnership Agreements File, Memo of Clarkson Tétrault merger committee to all partners, Supplementary Notes November 21, 1989.
186. Lorna Telfer, Oral History Interview.

THE NATIONAL LAW FIRM AND STRATEGIC PLANNING

187. MTA, J.C. McCartney Files, Clarkson Tétrault #3, McCarthy Tétrault Press Release, January 31, 1990.
188. Cole, *Osler, Hoskin & Harcourt*, app. II.
189. MTA (Toronto), Financial Statements.
190. MTA (Toronto), File Clarkson Tétrault, Merger 1990.
191. Cole, *Osler, Hoskin & Harcourt*, p. 225.
192. Robert Collins, "The National Dream of McCarthy & McCarthy," *Report on Business Magazine* 5 #10 (April 1989), pp. 42–51.
193. MTA (Toronto), Cooper File, includes Arthur Scace's memo to staff, November 12, 1990, and selected news clippings.
194. Mitch Gropper, Oral History Interview. MTA, Minutes of National Management Committee, April 24, 1995.
195. Tam Davis, Oral History Interview, January 23, 2002.
196. MTA, Minutes of National Management Committee, November 20, 1989.
197. Earl Phillips, Oral History Interview.
198. MTA, National Management Committee Minutes, Report of National Business Development Committee on Long Range Strategy, August 22, 1994.
199. MTA, Minutes of National Management Committee, March 19, 1990. Oral History Interviews with Gary Wolff and Lise Monette.
200. Oral History Interviews with Elizabeth Stewart and Sheena MacAskill, November 15, 2001.
201. MTA, J.C. McCartney Files, Long Range Planning Committee File, Wolff to McCartney, October 30, 1991.
202. MTA, McCarthy Tétrault Financial Statements 1985–99.
203. MTA, Minutes of National Management Committee, December 17, 1991, January 25, 1993, February 2, 1993, March 8, 1993 and September 19, 1995. Oral History Interviews with Robert Chapman and Anthony Keenleyside.
204. MTA, McCarthy & McCarthy Management Committee Minutes, November 17, 1986 and September 21, 1987.
205. MTA, Minutes of National Management Committee, October 22, 1991.
206. MTA (Montreal), Clarkson Tétrault Executive Committee Minutes, May 1988, with Tétrault report on Hong Kong and Singapore, April 28, 1988.
207. MTA, Minutes of National Management Committee, August 20, 1990.
208. MTA, Minutes of National Management Committee, May 27, 1991, December 17, 1991 and February 2, 1993.
209. MTA, Minutes of National Management Committee, August 21, 1995, Intven and Oliver Memorandum.
210. MTA, Minutes of National Management Committee, August 21, 1995, with Oliver Memorandum of April 23, 1995.
211. MTA, Minutes of National Management Committee, December 15, 1997, International Telecom Business Plan. Hank Intven, Oral History Interview.

212. MTA, National Management Committee Minutes, October 17, 1997.
213. MTA (Toronto), Toronto Executive Committee Minutes, attachment. "McCarthy Tétrault ranked in top 10 Worldwide."
214. MTA, Minutes of National Management Committee, December 16, 1996. Gary Girvan, Oral History Interviews.
215. MTA, Toronto Executive Committee Minutes, August 26, 1999. National Management Committee Minutes, March 27, 2000.
216. MTA, Minutes of National Management Committee, April 9, 1999. Richard Miner to National Management Committee.
217. John Alexander Black, "The Seven Sisters," *Lexpert* 4 #3 (January 2003).
218. Margot Gibb-Clark, "McCarthy's Reinvents the Practice," *Globe and Mail*, p. B10, December 6, 1999, and Andrew Willis, "Canadian Law Firms Struggle to Build Common Culture," *Globe and Mail*, p. B18, November 23, 2000.
219. MTA, Toronto Executive Committee Minutes, Executive Committee to all Partners, October 27, 1997.
220. Financial Post 500, 1998, cited in MTA, Toronto Executive Committee Minutes, July 18, 1998. W. Niels Ortved and Jim McCartney, Oral History Interviews.
221. MTA, Toronto Executive Committee Files, Executive Committee to All Partners, Re Long Range Planning, October 28, 1997.
222. MTA, Toronto Executive Committee, October 28, 1997, January 12, 1998. Niels Ortved, Oral History Interview.
223. Oral History Interviews with Barry Ryan and René Sorell, May 2004.
224. MTA, Phase One Report of Toronto Strategic Planning Committee, June 10, 1999, p. 13.
225. MTA, Phase One Report of Toronto Strategic Planning Committee, June 10, 1999, p. 16.
226. MTA, National Management Committee Minutes, July 25, 1999.
227. William Atkinson, Oral History Interview, October 2, 2002.
228. Calgary partners to National Management Committee, MTA National Management Committe Minutes, April 9, 1999. Trevor Bell, Oral History Interview, November 26, 2001.
229. MTA, McCarthy Tétrault National Strategic Planning Presentation, Scottsdale, November 24, 2000, tab 1, Task Force Report.
230. C. Randy Lewis to National Strategic Planning Task Force, quoted in MTA, National Management Committee Minutes, January 28, 2001.
231. MTA, McCarthy Tétrault National Strategic Planning Presentation, Scottsdale, November 24, 2000, tab 2, Tam Davis and René Sorell, "Remarks Concerning Recommendations," p. 5.
232. J.C. McCartney Files, National Strategic Planning: Hildebrandt International Findings and Observations Report, October 30, 2000. MTA, McCarthy Tétrault National Strategic Planning Presentation, Scottsdale Presentation, November 24, 2000, tab 1, Task Force Report.
233. MTA, Recommendations of the National Strategic Planning Task Force, March 30, 2001.
234. MTA, Final Recommendations of the National Strategic Planning Task Force, October 15, 2001, tab 3.

235. MTA, National Management Committee, Memo to Staff, November 2, 2001.
236. Andrew Willis, "Pioneering Law Firm," *Globe and Mail Report on Business*, November 7, 2001. *Chambers Global: The World's Leading Lawyers 2002–2003*.
237. W. Iain Scott, Memo to the firm, August 2, 2002, "New Leadership Team."
238. McCarthy Tétrault Report (July–August 2003), Message from the CEO. Scott was applying recent statistics from the *Financial Post* FP 500 and the *Report on Business Magazine* Top 1000 listings.

ILLUSTRATION CREDITS

All illustrations come from the McCarthy Tétrault Archives or the collections of individual lawyers and staff of McCarthy Tétrault, except the following, which are used with the permission of these organizations:

page 3: photograph by David Batten of digitalfreedom.ca
page 21: Law Society of Upper Canada Archives
pages 29, 119, 121, 123: Glenbow Archives
page 79: Toronto *Star* Archives
page 121: Legal Archives Society of Alberta
page 278: *Report on Business* magazine and Edward Gajdel Photography
pages 357, 365: *Lexpert* magazine

INDEX

Page references to captions are in italic type.
Page references to sidenotes are marked "n."